ULPIAN

ULPIAN

Tony Honoré

CLARENDON PRESS · OXFORD

1982

Oxford University Press, Walton Street, Oxford OX2 6DP

London Glasgow New York Toronto
Delhi Bombay Calcutta Madras Karachi
Kuala Lumpur Singapore HongKong Tokyo
Nairobi Dar es Salaam Cape Town
Melbourne Auckland

and associate companies in
Beirut Berlin Ibadan Mexico City

Published in the United States
by Oxford University Press, New York

British Library Cataloguing in Publication Data

Honoré, Tony
Ulpian.
1. Ulpian   2. Law – History and criticism
I. Title
340'.109   K437.U/
ISBN 0–19–825358–3

Library of Congress Cataloging in Publication Data
Honoré, Tony, 1921–
Ulpian.
Bibliography: P.
Includes index.
1. Ulpian.   2. Roman law—History.   I. Title. Law
340.5'4 81–21230   AACR2
ISBN 0–19–825358–3

Typeset by Macmillan India Ltd, Bangalore.

Printed in Great Britain
at the University Press, Oxford
by Eric Buckley
Printer to the University

Sed neque ex multitudine auctorum quod
melius et aequius est iudicatote, cum possit
unius forsitan et deterioris sententia et multos
et maiores in aliqua parte superare

Preface

This is the fourth book in a series of studies of Roman lawyers and Roman legal sources based on an analysis of style and working methods. In *Gaius* (1962) the key idea was first put forward that each writer makes his own dictionary and is the criterion of his own authenticity. My use of these principles to reconstruct the life and outlook of Gaius was widely thought to be speculative. By the time of *Tribonian* (1978) and *Emperors and Lawyers* (1981) more exact techniques of investigation had been worked out, and tried on material which was amenable to them. These techniques have also been used in the present study, which has affinities in particular with *Tribonian*.

Ulpian's writings, as presented mainly in Justinian's *Digest*, surpass in volume those of any other Roman jurist and, indeed, amount to 40 or 41 per cent of that work. Composing mainly under Caracalla (AD 211–17), he collected, condensed, and systematized the Roman legal tradition as it had been transmitted to him. In this he was a forerunner of Tribonian, who undertook a similar task on behalf of Justinian three centuries later. His *opus* foreshadows the later codification. Scholars like Ulpian and Tribonian tend to write in a consistent style and to follow a regular pattern of work. Given these habits and the bulk of their surviving work, certain methods of analysis prove profitable. I have made use of two.

The first is based on work method and particularly on the idea of a work stint. In investigating the methods of Justinian's compilers I adopted the idea, suggested by the number of books to be read and the approximate dates of excepting, that Tribonian's committees had a reading stint of a book (corresponding to what would now be called a chapter) per committee per day.[1] In regard to Ulpian I suggest in Chapter 6 a writing stint of a book a week.[2] Both suggestions are hypothetical, of course. But in each case we know that a great volume of work was accomplished in a short time and can even say roughly how much was done and how long was taken to do it. In the context of an administrative culture which was nothing if not methodical, my hypotheses are by no means far-fetched. Once adopted, they provide a framework of dates and motivations which, when they can be tested, fit the other historical data very well. It is true that

---

[1] Honoré (1978) 170–3 (originally *LQR* 88 (1972) 530).
[2] Below ch. 6 p. 160.

in neither case was the planned stint rigidly adhered to. But the divergences were minor.

The resistance to such suggestions is coloured by romanticism. The Roman jurists could not, it is supposed, have been so mechanical in their work, so indifferent to subject-matter. But Roman lawyers were expected to master the whole law, not to be specialists in this or that branch of legal learning. That they could turn their mind readily to the labour of the day made them no more mechanical than does the regular work pattern of a Max Kaser in our own age.

The other method consists, as before, of the analysis of the style of texts with a view to determining their authorship. Such studies presuppose, in the first place, proper concordances. Fortunately it has been possible in investigating texts attributed to Ulpian to use not merely *VIR* and Levy's *Ergänzungsindex* but the *Corcordance to the Digest Jurists* (*CDJ*) prepared by Josef Menner and myself. Once the proportion of the total material which is, on the face of it, Ulpianic has been determined by line or work count, one can compare the occurrence of words or expressions in Ulpian with their occurrence in other jurists and in the non-Ulpianic legal material as a whole.

In doing this I have tried to avoid two snares. One is the Scylla of supposing that numerical data can supplant the more traditional forms of historical investigation or that they are a substitute for a trained sense of literary style. They cannot be. In the end the appeal is always to the verdict of a competent scholar who has read the texts and who is sensitive to nuances of thought and expression. Unhappily few scholars have so far read the texts author by author or period by period, and until they do only a handful will be in a position to form a judgement about the merits of these studies.

The Charybdis of impressionism is equally dangerous, and has in the past been even more harmful to the study of Roman law. Impressionism, on which the study of interpolations was until recently based, entails that the author's impression prevails over the probabilities suggested by counting the texts in which a certain word occurs and seeing how these are distributed between different authors and different historical periods. As a counter to this danger, in chapter 2 of this book, on Ulpian's style, the technique has been adopted of taking the *Digest* as the pool of legal writing to be studied and then contrasting the words and expressions to be found in the 40 per cent attributed to Ulpian with those to be found in the 60 per cent attributed to other authors. Once this has been done, and once norms of Ulpianic style have been fixed, it becomes possible to revise some traditional attributions of texts. Thus, in chapter 4 it is argued that a number of works attributed in the *Digest* to Ulpian are spurious. The same technique is in principle applicable to the determination of glosses and interpolations in Ulpian's texts, though this task is not within the scope of the present book.

The criteria by which expressions are listed as Ulpianic are explained in chapter 2. These criteria are not statistical in character, though some of them could be reformulated in terms of word frequencies. Hence, for example, hapax legomena, which may provide a clue to general features of a writer's style, are listed, in addition to expressions which occur with greater frequency. Experience shows that, with a little practice, Ulpian's style becomes reasonably easy to recognize. The reader who is prepared to take trouble will be able to progress beyond the limits of this book and to disentangle glosses and interpolations from genuine parts of the text.

The book itself, however, has quite limited, though ambitious, objectives. It seeks to give an account of Ulpian's career, to formulate criteria of his style, to distinguish genuine from spurious works, to establish which rescripts he composed on the emperor's behalf, and to fix the dates of his works and their rhythm of composition. It also deals with his use of sources. Obviously this is only a beginning. Ulpian's contributions to the development of the substantive law remain untouched. So does his place in the history of Latin scholarship, particularly in the eastern provinces. I prefer to offer explicit solutions to a limited range of conundrums rather than to attempt too much.

Whether these solutions are on the right lines remains to be decided by the tribunal of scholarly opinion. It now has enough examples on which to form a judgement. In reaching this judgement scholars may wish to put to themselves two questions. First, if the conclusions to which these relatively new methods lead are consistently in accordance with what we know from other historical sources, why is this the case? Secondly, if my colleagues are inclined to scepticism, ought they not to try the experiment of reading some part of the texts in the way I suggest?

I have to thank John Stannard and Jane Hornblower for their help with the laborious work of checking text references.

TONY HONORÉ

Contents

CHAPTER I

Background and Career

I. THE SEVERAN AGE

Marcus Aurelius Antoninus (AD 161–80) departed from the recent practice that a Roman emperor should, during his lifetime, adopt an experienced and able man as his successor. Instead, he made his son Commodus, then a lazy and frivolous youngster of sixteen, joint ruler (177) and thereby ensured that Commodus would succeed him. The sole reign of Commodus (180–93) ended in misgovernment, discontent, and assassination. Of the various contenders who emerged in 193, the victor was Septimius Severus (193–211).[1] But it took him two civil wars and nearly four years (193–7) to make himself sole master of the Roman empire, and the effort left its mark both on him and on his subjects.

One of Severus' aims was to revive, or seem to revive, the policies of Marcus and the Antonine age, since Marcus was considered, then and later, a model ruler. So, in 195, when the issue of the civil war was still not finally resolved, Severus arranged to be adopted by Marcus. The adoption was retrospective and fictitious. Marcus had been dead fifteen years. Nevertheless, it was carried through in detail. Severus' elder son, Bassianus, later known as Caracalla,[2] was then aged seven. He was given the dynastic name Antoninus, then and later his official designation. Severus tried to steer a course between repeating Marcus' mistake over Commodus and disinheriting his own son. He gave Caracalla a good education, saw to it that he had ample military experience, made him consul three times during the next sixteen years, and introduced him to the complexities of civil business. Caracalla was able, though not in a literary or academic sense, quick-witted, though impatient, a good judge of character. He was a man of plebeian tastes, liked soldiering, was not averse to menial tasks. With the military he passed as one of them.

At times it was possible to think of him as a future emperor who would

---

[1] Hasebroek (1921) has a good account with chronology 190 f. See also Platnauer (1918, reprint 1965), Jardé (1925), Hammond (1940), Murphy (1945), Hannestad (1944), Barnes (1967), Alföldy (1968), Mihailov (1963), A. Birley (1971) with bibliography 361 f. and prosopography of family 293 f.

[2] RE 2.2434 Aurelius no. 46; Dio 77 – 8.1 – 10 (hostile); Herodian 4.7.4 – 7; Th. Schulz (1909). As a judge see Nörr (1972) 25; Kunkel (1953) 255. On young emperors see Hartke (1951).

enjoy success and justify the usurped name Antoninus. At others he was clearly unhinged. Then his violent temper and bitter feuding with Geta,[3] his younger brother, left no room for illusion. Geta, a year younger, was palpably incompetent. While Caracalla was promoted Augustus in 198, the younger son was kept in the subordinate position of Caesar for more than ten years thereafter. Ultimately Severus, whether in the indulgence of old age, in disillusion with Caracalla, or simply for administrative reasons, made Geta too an Augustus during the campaign in Britain of 209. Even more than the similar act of Marcus in 177, this was to court disaster. Once again, dynastic motives clashed with the demands of good government and prevailed.

Septimius was more than an ambitious ruler. He was deeply concerned for the security and welfare of the empire, and spared no effort in its service. Not specially gifted as a general, he repeatedly won victories in both civil and external wars. He was lucky and self-confident, and had an acute sense of political realities. He saw a great deal to do, and was impatient to do it. He moved fast. In 197, when the civil war was over, he invaded Parthia and pushed the frontier of the empire eastwards. At the end of his reign, in 209 – 11, he was trying to push the British frontier northwards, perhaps to occupy the whole island. Events by and large justified his boldness.

Nevertheless he had debts to pay. It was the troops of Pannonia that had brought him to power, and his campaigns depended on a loyal army. Hence the balance between civil and military power was not the same as it had been under Marcus. It swung the way of the soldiers. They obtained concessions: higher pay,[4] permission to live with their wives,[5] other privileges. The events of 193 – 7 taught them again the lesson of AD 68, that the sword makes and unmakes rulers. Severus, who had helped teach the lesson, tried to obliterate it. In 193 he tricked the praetorians, who had killed Pertinax, and disarmed them.[6] But this *tour de force* was an expedient, not a long-term solution to the problem of military indiscipline.

Severus was also well equipped to manage civil and legal affairs. Though not as well educated, says Dio, as he would have liked to be, he had a critical and inquiring mind, and was trained in what was called 'philosophy'. He was a man of many ideas and few words.[7] His interests were wide and practical. Whether he had received a legal education is obscure, but he was

[3] *RE* 2.4.1565 Septimius no. 32 (Fluss); Dio 76.7.1, 77.1–2; Herodian 3.10.3–4, 4.3.2–4.4.3; Alföldy (1972) 19.

[4] Herodian 3.8.4–5 also mentions the right to wear gold rings (the mark of equestrian rank, in practice confined to centurions etc.). See also Domaszewski (1900) 218; Sander (1958) 102; Whittaker (1969) 308–9.

[5] Herodian 3.8.5. Whether soldiers' marriages were previously void in certain cases is debatable: Volterra (1951) 645[1]; Kaser (1971) 1.317.

[6] Herodian 3.13.2–12.

[7] Dio 76.16.1–2; Eutropius 8.19.1 cf. *HA* Severus 18.5–6. He composed an autobiography-Dio 75.7.3; Herodian 2.9.4; Victor 20.22.

certainly assiduous as a judge[8] and appointed lawyers to important posts. He was keen to improve the working of the legal system. The permanent criminal commissions (*quaestiones perpetuae*), which from the republic had exercised criminal jurisdiction in Rome, now ceased their cumbrous operation.[8a] The urban prefect was given unlimited jurisdiction at first instance over crimes committed in the city or within a hundred miles of it. The praetorian prefect[9] had similar jurisdiction in Italy beyond the hundred-mile limit.[10] In addition, the praetorian prefect had an unlimited appellate jurisdiction in civil and criminal cases.[11] In this he acted, theoretically, as the emperor's delegate.[12]

Delegation was inevitable, especially with an emperor as ambitious as Severus. The office of praetorian prefect, generally held by two prefects at a time, had grown by a process of piecemeal delegation into the most important, next to that of the emperor himself, in the whole range of appointments. Mainly a military post,[13] its duties spread from the command of the praetorian guard, stationed in Rome, to the superintendance of the armies in the provinces. Its civil business, especially legal appeals, now increased to the point at which one of the two prefects was sometimes a lawyer. It was thus that Papinian, Macrinus, and Ulpian, men of legal rather than military careers, came to hold this, the highest equestrian office.

Another aspect of the administration of justice was the rescript system.[14] The emperor provided a free legal advice service, for which the office *a libellis* was responsible. From the Severan age far more rescripts survive than from previous reigns, and there is little doubt that the number of rescripts really increased. In this domain, too, the emperor took his duties seriously.

It was the impulse provided by government that made the age a great one for law and lawyers. The Severan jurists, Papinian, Paul, Tryphoninus, Messius, Menander, Ulpian, Modestinus, all knights, had a sense of common purpose. They were to see that justice was freely available and that the law prevailed.[15] This common aim gave direction to their professional activities. Whether they were advising the emperor as members of his council, composing rescripts for him in the office *a libellis*, or writing treatises for the use of governors, judges, officials and private citizens, they worked to the same end. It is a mistake to think of advice

---

[8] Dio 76.17.1–2; *HA* Severus 8.4.

[8a] Garnsey (1967).

[9] Howe (1942) 42; Strachan-Davidson (1912) I. 158.

[10] *Collatio* 14.3.2 (Ulp. 9 *off. proc.*, referring to the *lex Fabia*), Passerini (1939) 236.

[11] Mommsen (1887) II 1113 f.; *RE* 22.2391 (Ensslin); Kaser (1966) 365; Howe (1942) 29 f.

[12] Howe (1942) 40.

[13] Howe (1942) 7 f.; Palanque (1933); Passerini (1939); Durry (1938).

[14] Honoré (1981) Ch. 2.

[15] Howe (1942) 43; Schiller (1953) 60.

given to the emperor as 'bureaucratic', private writing or practice as 'free'. Both rested on professional discipline, and history records nothing to suggest that lawyers were under pressure to give opinions in a sense convenient to the government.

Severus was the only emperor to come from Africa. That does not make him an 'African emperor',[16] but it explains the relatively cosmopolitan outlook of his régime. He came from an area where Punic was spoken,[17] and Punic is the language that Ulpian mentions, after Latin and Greek, as an example of one that the parties to certain legal transactions may choose.[18] The age was aware of cultures other than Latin and Greek. Severus' second wife, Julia Domna, came from a part of Syria where, though Punic had not been spoken for two centuries or more, the vernacular was Aramaic. Ulpian mentions this language ('Assyrian') also as one of the languages that is permissible for certain legal purposes.[19]

It was an unexpected act on Caracalla's part to make all the free inhabitants of the empire, with obscure but unimportant exceptions, Roman citizens, but it was not contrary to the spirit of the dynasty and the age. By the *constitutio Antoniniana*[20] the different provinces, east, west, and south, were put on a level. Other distinctions too were blunted. With their new privileges,[21] soldiers had a status closer to that of civilians. Women were more prominent than before, both as property owners and in politics. In the imperial circle the Syrian princesses Julia Domna, her sister Maesa, and Maesa's two daughters Soaemias and Mamaea had influence behind the scenes. But they also figured prominently, with official titles, on coins,[22] and, on one famous occasion, in the senate.[23] Rank and class still depend on wealth,[24] but other boundaries, social and conceptual, are blurred.

The levelling that occurred was the product of strains and tensions. The wars of Marcus brought to a close the easy-going days when the resources of government were ample to meet civil and military requirements. Even without civil war, the end of the second century would not have been comfortable. Civil war set the emperor and the senate at variance. At the behest of Didius Julianus, the senate in 193 declared Severus a public

---

[16] Subtitle of Birley (1971).

[17] Birley (1971) 43, 106, 124 (Septimius and Domna will have had three languages in common: Greek, Latin, and Aramaic) cf. Millar (1968).

[18] *D.* 32.11 pr. (Ulp. 2 *fid.*), 45.1.1.6 (48 *Sab.*).

[19] *D.* 45.1.1.6 (48 *Sab.*).

[20] Literature in Gianelli—Mazzarino (1956) II 397; *RE* 2.2446; Millar (1962); Gilliam (1965); Seston (1966); Herrmann (1972).

[21] Above, nn. 4—5.

[22] *RE* 11.916, 926, 948; Mattingley v² (1975) 156—70, 430—6, 531, 536—42, 576—8; VI¹ (1962) 119—20, 128—9, 132—3, 135—6, 144, 147—52, 156, 160—1, 165—7, 168—9, 174, 179—81, 184—8, 190, 192—4, 196—7, 203—4, 209, 221; Robertson (1977) 98—102, 127—33, 163—8.

[23] Dio 79.17.2.

[24] Garnsey (1970) 221 f.

enemy. It then changed sides.[25] When in 196—7 Severus quarrelled with Clodius Albinus, a strong minority of senators sided with Albinus, a relatively mild man, who prided himself on his clemency.[26] Severus had had a fright, and having crushed Albinus, had some of the dissentients executed on his own authority. This was to violate the model of a good ruler, and mistrust festered.[27]

For this reason, and because he had great ambitions, Severus came to rely to an increasing extent on his own family and associates. Inevitably he delegated much. He trusted a friend of his youth, Fulvius Plautianus, to whom he was bound by emotional ties, and treated him almost as a partner.[28] A man of great ability and, like Severus, from Africa, in the end Plautianus became sole praetorian prefect and accumulated enormous power. Had it not been for Severus' two sons, the situation would have been manageable. Severus would have made his friend a Caesar or junior Augustus, and the latter would have proved himself a good emperor. But Caracalla had been made Antoninus in 195 and Augustus in 198, so that this course was ruled out. The clash was resolved in another way. In 205 Caracalla and his mother, by an ingenious plot, had Plautianus killed.[29] The strains were temporarily reduced, but once again effective rule had been sacrificed to dynastic interests. The remaining thirty years of the Severan age were spent, in a context of dynastic ambition, wrestling with the resulting problems. Severus tried to improve his sons' ways by moving them from Rome to the Italian countryside (205—7)[30] and, later, taking them to Britain on his last military expedition (208—11).[31] When he died Julia Domna sought to keep the peace between them.[32] She was unsuccessful but, after Geta's murder at the end of 211,[33] still tried to make up for his murderer's unbalance. Maesa tried to restrain Elagabal (218—22)[34] with no more success. So intractable were the problems of an empire conducted by, or in the name of, young men spoiled by premature adulation and power that some, among both governors and governed, were disillusioned with the tradition which saw in public service the true end of human endeavour.

[25] Dio 73.16—7.
[26] Herodian 3.5.2; Dio 75.7—8.
[27] Dio 75.8.4; Herodian 3.8.1—3.
[28] *RE* 7.1.270 Fulvius no. 101 (Stein); *PIR*[2] F 554; Howe (1942) 69 no. 17; Birley (1971) 294—6; Grosso (1968a) 7. Their quarrels and reconciliations and Severus' remorse after Plautianus' death point to the truth of Herodian 3.10.6, cf. Dio 76.5.1—2.
[29] Dio 76.2.3—4; Herodian 3.11.1—3, 3.12.12 gives an official version; Hohl (1956) 33; Birley (1971) 231—5.
[30] Herodian 3.13.1.
[31] Herodian 3.14—5; Dio 76.11.
[32] Herodian 4.3.8—9.
[33] Dio 77.18.2—3.
[34] Herodian 5.5.5—6, 5.7.1—3. On Elagabal see Hay (1911), Pflaum (1978).

In this age of strain and frustration the minds of many turned inwards. There were powerful Christians. The ex-slave Callistus took the see of Rome (*c.* 217−23),[35] against the challenge of his opponent and critic Hippolytus. Julia Mamaea,[36] the mother of Alexander Severus, was inquiring enough to arrange a meeting with the Christian intellectual Origen (*c.*185−254). Other religions, hovering on or near the borders of monotheism, attracted devotees. The cult of Elagabal, the god of Emesa, whence Julia Domna and her family came, was one. The last Antoninus, nicknamed from the god to whom he was so devoted, saw the deity as a jealous sun-god. His demands, hardly less exclusive than those of Jahweh or Christ, led his emperor-priest into a troublesome challenge to the traditional Roman state religion.[37] Elagabal wanted to invert the relations of politics and religion. Far from being the handmaid of state policy, as hitherto, religion was to become the prime concern of the emperor and people. Elagabal's reign warns us that, in sacred affairs also, the easy-going days are over. It foreshadows the Christian revolution that is to come a century later.

Ulpian[38] was not one to take refuge in introspection or religion. A great lawyer and briefly, like Plautianus, sole praetorian prefect, his immense energy and deep concern for the welfare of the state leaves its mark on every page of his writing. His vision has survived in the mythology of the reign of Alexander (222−35). In this idealized picture,[39] a pliable young ruler defers to the wisdom of his seniors, especially his chief minister. He inaugurates a golden age of just but firm rule according to law. The reality was different.

II. ULPIAN: SOURCES

The main source of information about Ulpian is naturally his own writings. These tell us, either directly or by inference, a good deal. They were composed mainly under the sole rule of Antoninus Caracalla (211−17), as the frequent references to joint constitutions of him (*imperator noster, imperator Antoninus*) and his dead father (*divus pater, divus Severus*) make clear.[40]

---

[35] Gianelli−Mazzarino (1956) II 291 f.

[36] Eusebius *Hist. eccl.* 6. 21.

[37] Herodian 5.5.3−10, 5.6.3−10.

[38] Bibliography *RE* 5.1435, 1506 (Jörs); Berger (1953) 750; *NDI* (1957) 19.1106 (Orestano); Santalucia (1971) 196[1] Crifò (1976) 708. The most important items are Pernice (1885, reprint 1962); *RE* 5 (1905) 1435 (Jörs); *PIR*[2] D 169; Kunkel (1967) 245; Pflaum (1960) no. 294; *RE* 9A 1 (1961) 567 (Mayer-Maly); Modrzejewski−Zawadski(1967); Frezza (1968); Syme (1970); Orestano (1973); Nörr (1973); Crifò (1976); Honoré (1962, 1981).

[39] *HA* Severus Alexander, especially 3−12, 15−24, 39−51.

[40] Ch. 6 p. 132 f.

Apart from this, two rescripts of Alexander Severus [41] inform us of the prefectures which Ulpian held in AD 222 under that emperor. A papyrus from Egypt[42] makes it plain that he was killed some time before May/June 224. Of the historians Dio,[43] as summarized by Xiphilinus, mentions his prominent role early in the reign of Alexander, about which Herodian[44] is silent. Aurelius Victor (*c*.360)[45] mentions him briefly, as do the epitomes of Festus (363–70)[46] and Eutropius (364–78).[47] There is an important passage in Zosimus (c.500)[48] and briefer ones in Zonaras (1118–43)[49] and Syncellus.[50] The 'mythistorical' *Historia Augusta* gives him a prominent role. He is mentioned in the life of Pescennius Niger,[51] in that of Elagabal,[52] and most notably in Severus Alexander,[53] where he guides the young emperor's footsteps along the paths of justice and good government.

My earlier account of Ulpian,[54] published in 1962, though admittedly only part of a 'preliminary survey', left a good deal to be desired. I proposed a threefold division of the jurist's career. First, there was a period during which he was secretary *a libellis* to Severus and Caracalla, which I thought might run from 200 to 212. At this time he was composing rescripts on points of law on the emperor's behalf. This could be inferred from a comparison of the style of the rescripts with that of Ulpian's other writings. Secondly, under the sole rule of Caracalla (211–17) and then Macrinus (217–8), Ulpian devoted himself to writing legal treatises. This period of literary activity stretched into the early part of Elagabal (218–22), say into 219 or 220. Thirdly, there was the period of Ulpian's prefectures, which might have begun under Elagabal and continued, under Alexander, until 228, when he was murdered.

The present account retains the three periods but alters their limits. All three turn out to be shorter than I formerly thought. A thorough comparison of Ulpian's private writings with the rescripts of the early third century shows that the period proposed for his tenure of the office *a libellis* was too long. Instead of a period running from 200 to 212 the present work

---

[41] *CJ* 8.37.4 (31 March 222), 4.65.4.1 (1 Dec. 222).

[42] P. Oxy. 2565, Barns–Parsons–Rea–Turner (1966) 102.

[43] Dio 80.2.2–4, 80.3.2

[44] Herodian 6.1.4 says in general terms that legal and civil business was entrusted under Alexander to men of eloquence and legal experience.

[45] *De Caesaribus* 24.

[46] *Breviarium rerum gestarum populi Romani* 22.

[47] *Breviarium ab urbe condita* 8.23

[48] *Historia Nova* 1.11.2. Also Lydus (490–c.560) *de mag.* 1.48.

[49] *Annales* 12.15.

[50] *Chronographia* 1.673.

[51] *HA* Niger 7.2

[52] *HA* Ant. Heliogabalus 16.1.

[53] *HA* Sev. Alexander 15.6, 26.5, 27.2, 31.1, 34.6, 51.4, 67.2, 68.1.

[54] Honoré (1962) 207–12.

proposes a stretch from March 202 to May, or possibly a little later, 209. The argument for these limits is set out in chapter 9. The middle period of writing is now reduced to the years 213 to 217 and nothing is assigned to the reign of Elagabal. The reasons for this somewhat compressed chronological scheme are explained in chapters 5 to 7. The third phase of Ulpian's career is even more drastically reduced. P. Oxy. 2565 showed that Ulpian's death must be placed not in 228 but substantially before the middle of 224.[55] His praetorian prefecture lasted only about a year. The effect of closer investigation has therefore been to retain the broad picture of three periods but to open up gaps between the first and second (209–12) and the second and third (218–22). I have also become convinced that it is impossible to rely on the *Historia Augusta* to fill in the gaps.

   How to use this work undoubtedly presents a problem. It can neither be trusted nor wholly discounted. The best approach is probably to fix the course of events in the first instance without regard to what it says. Whether *HA* can add to the picture so obtained depends on assumptions about its sources and aims. Following Straub,[56] I have assumed that, at least in certain instances, the author had access to legal sources or to reliable information about the law and lawyers. In dealing with such matters his method is often the deliberate distortion of the truth rather than pure invention. At times it would seem that the distortions have a serious purpose. This may be connected with the date of composition, which many would place in the last decade of the fourth century. This was a time when, at least in the quaestor's office, interest in the classical jurists revived. The only citation of a classical jurist to survive in the imperial constitutions between 327 and 426 comes in 396.[57]

III. ULPIAN: NAME AND ORIGIN

Ulpian's fellow lawyers usually call him Ulpianus, or, in Greek, Οὐλπιανος[58]. But a few texts,[59] including two rescripts of Alexander, speak of Domitius Ulpianus. So does a text of Ulpian's contemporary, Paul, in which he reproduces a letter from a friend or client which refers to an opinion of Ulpian. Lactantius simply calls him Domitius.[60] The gentile

---

[55] Barns–Parsons–Rea–Turner (1966) 102–4.

[56] Straub (1972), (1978); cf. Dirksen (1842), Dessav (1889), and recently Syme (1968), (1972a); Chastagnol (1964), (1967), (1970).

[57] *CTh.* 4.4.3.3 (21 March 396 *auctor prudentissimus iuris consultorum Scaevola*), cf. 1.2.10 (20 March 396 *definitione iuris consultorum*).

[58] *D.* 26.6.2 (Mod. 1 *excus.*: Οὐλπιανὸς ὁ κράτιστος) 27.1.2.9 (2 *excus.*), 27.1.4 (2 *excus.*: Οὐλπιανὸς ὁ κράτιστος), 27.1.8.9 (3 *excus.*), 27.1.10.8 (3 *excus.*), 27.1.13.2 (4 *excus.*: Δομίτιος Οὐλπιανὸς); Dio 80.1.1, 2.2, 2.3; Syncellus *Chron.* 1.673; Zonaras XII 15.

[59] *CJ* 8.37.4 (31 March 222), 4.65.4.1 (1 Dec. 222); *D.* 19.1.43 (Paul 5 *qu.*), 27.1.13.2 (Mod. 4 *excus.*: Δομίτιος Οὐλπιανὸς); *HA* Alexander 68.1; Dio 80.1.1 (Δομιτίῳ τινὶ Οὐλπιανῷ).

[60] *Div. inst.* 5.11.19.

name Domitius is thus firmly established. There are no other Domitii Ulpiani, unless we can make something of an inscription on a water pipe found some seven miles from Centumcellae (Civitavecchia).[61] Here, near Santa Marinella, on the coast north-west of Rome, a pipe belonging to a large building was found with the following inscription:

CNDOMITIAN . NIULPIANI

Bormann[62] and others have taken this to refer to the jurist, and Kunkel follows suit.[63] If the inscription is read continuously, the reading 'Domitiani' is not possible, in view of the double N, and hence it becomes plausible to read it as:

CN DOMITI ANNI ULPIANI

though the dot between the two Ns, which may not really exist, is awkward. If this reconstruction is correct, the owner of the large country house on the coast near Rome was Gnaeus Domitius Annius Ulpianus. Is he the same as the jurist Ulpian? There are two points of connection. First, no other Domitius Ulpianus is known. Secondly, the villa clearly belonged to a wealthy man. Though this would not in itself serve to identify the owner as our Ulpian, a statue of Meleager has been found in the area of the villa. Meleager,[64] poet and Cynic philosopher of the first century BC, came from Gadara but lived in Tyre. Ulpian, we shall see, was also connected with Tyre. The statue therefore seems appropriate to the residence of a wealthy scholar from Tyre. There is a good case for concluding that the house was owned by a Domitius Ulpianus from Tyre. He might be the jurist or some other member of a family of scholars.

Pride in Tyrian achievement was certainly a feature of the jurist's personality. In his first book *de censibus*, written in the reign of Caracalla, and datable, if the arguments adduced in chapter 7 are right, to 213 or 214[65] Ulpian describes Tyre as his town of origin, splendid, famed for its various quarters, possessing an ancient history, strong in arms, and faithful to its treaty with the Romans.[66]

> est in Syria Phoenice splendidissima Tyriorum colonia, unde mihi origo est, nobilis regionibus, serie saeculorum antiquissima, armipotens, foederis quod cum Romanis percussit tenacissima

[61] *CIL* XI. 3587; Kunkel (1967) 252; Crifò (1976) 738.
[62] Above, n. 61; *RE* 5.1346 (A. Stein); *PIR* 2¹ 19, 25; 3² 39; Passerini (1939) 324.
[63] Kunkel (1967) 252.
[64] *RE* 15.1.481 Meleagros no. 7 (Geffiken); K. Radinger (1895); A. Wifstrand (1926).
[65] Below, pp. 164–7.
[66] *D.* 50.15.1 pr. (Ulp. 1 *cens.*). On Tyre see Krall (1888), Fleming (1915), on municipal administration Liebenam (1900), Vittinghoff (1951), Nörr (1969).

He describes Tyre as the place of his *origo*. This notion has been carefully analysed by Nörr.[67] *Origo* is the ground on which a person acquires a local citizenship at birth, and by metonomy, therefore, citizenship of origin. As Ulpian himself points out,[68] the status of citizen of a municipality is acquired either by birth (*nativitas*), manumission, or adoption. To this a constitution of Diocletian and Maximian[69] adds adlection, i.e. co-option. In the latter constitution *origo* appears in the place of *nativitas*. Hence *origo* refers to a local citizenship acquired by birth. This depended, in the case of birth in lawful marriage, on the father's status as citizen, not on the place of birth as such. Hence we may infer that Ulpian's father was a citizen of Tyre. Tyre was therefore (assuming he did not change it) Ulpian's local community or home town, his *patria*, as distinct from Rome, the common fatherland of all Roman citizens, *communis patria*.[70]

No other jurist speaks of his home town in similar terms, but then no other jurist, except perhaps Celsus and Iavolenus a century before, is as extrovert as Ulpian. Nor do any of them refer, as does the Levantine jurist, to 'my fellow-citizen' (*popularis meus*).[71] Tyre, like the other cities of Syria— Laodicea, Berytus, Sidon, Caesarea, Emesa, and above all Antioch— aroused strong loyalties. These cities constantly jostled for position and honour. Tyre's reputation for valour was justified in part by its resistance to Alexander the Great in 332 BC. From 64 BC onwards the Romans recognized and maintained its autonomy, though that of course meant less from the second century AD than it had before. Claudius allowed the town to call itself Claudianopolis. In AD 66 it took part in the war against the Jews. Its antipathy to them was pronounced. An ally of Rome, *civitas foederata*, from early times, from the end of the first century AD Tyre provided auxiliary cohorts for the Roman army. Hadrian, who admired Paul of Tyre, the orator, and who was drawn into a bitter war with the Jews, gave it the title of metropolis. With its weaving, metal-working, and glass manufacture, above all its purple dyes, it prospered in the peaceful days of the empire.[72] It maintained trading stations at Puteoli[73] and Rome.

Tyre played a part in the civil war which brought Septimius Severus to power. After Pertinax was murdered on 28 March 193, Septimius and Pescennius Niger were proclaimed emperors by their troops at Carnuntum on the Danube and Antioch in Syria respectively.[74] While Severus

[67] Nörr (1963) 525 = RE Supp. X (1965) 433.
[68] D. 50.1.1. pr. (Ulp. 2 ed.).
[69] CJ 10.40.7 pr. (Dio. et Max. AA et CC).
[70] RE Supp. X (1965) 454, Brewer (1868) 82, and Jörs RE 5.1436 argue that Tyre was Ulpian's birthplace.
[71] D. 45.1.70 (Ulp. 11 ed.).
[72] RE 2.7.1876 (Eissfeldt); Kunkel (1967) 249517; Crifò (1976) 739; Rey-Coquais (1978) 44, 54 f.
[73] CIL X 1601, CIG V 853.
[74] Hasebroek (1921) 190 f; Downey (1961).

marched on Rome the east rallied to Niger. Septimius occupied Rome and then, on 9 July, left for the east. It was not until the last months of the year that he was able to win an important victory over Niger at Cyzicus. In 194 Niger's support began to dwindle, as Egypt and Arabia went over to Septimius. Severus won another victory between Cius and Nicaea, perhaps in January 194, and his army, overrunning Bithynia and Galatia, marched into Cappadocia. While this happening, says Herodian, there was an outbreak of local rivalries in Syria[75]. Laodicea, the enemy of Antioch, and Tyre, hating Berytus, declared for Severus. When on his retreat Niger reached Antioch, he heard the news of their opposition and dispatched Moroccan spearmen and archers, who looted and set fire to the two rebel cities. At Tyre 'they set fire to the whole city, with much looting and killing'.[76] Herodian puts these dissensions down to the traditional feuding of Greek cities. There may have been another reason for Tyre's support of Septimius. Tyre and Sidon were the founding cities of Carthage, and Septimius, apart from his fellow Caesar, Clodius Albinus, was the first, indeed the only, emperor from Africa.

To prevent a repetition of the sort of revolt that Niger had been able to muster in the east, the victorious emperor divided Syria in two. He deprived Antioch of its status as capital of the much-truncated Syria Coele, and made Tyre capital of the newly formed Syria Phoenice. Phoenice extended to the north to include Emesa and Palmyra. It became the seat of the *koinon* of Syria and of the phoenikarch.[77] Some years later, perhaps after 198, Severus made Tyre a Roman colony and settled in it veterans of the *legio III Gallica*.[78] It was now called *colonia Septimia Severa metropolis*. Ulpian mentions,[79] after the lyrical passage quoted, that Severus and Caracalla gave Tyre the Italian right (*ius Italicum*) for its 'signal and outstanding loyalty to the state and the Roman empire'. Since Caracalla became an Augustus in January 198, this grant cannot have occurred before that year. It may have been made on the same occasion as the grant of colonial status, or later. *Ius Italicum*[80] carried with it notable privileges, including exemption from capitation and land tax (*tributum capitis, tributum soli*).

It has been said that Elagabal reduced Tyre in rank because of a military revolt, and that Alexander restored it to the position it had held under Severus and Caracalla.[81] Ziegler, in a careful study,[82] examines the

[75] Herodian 3.2.7–3.3.5; Felletti–Maj (1950) 22.
[76] Herodian 3.3.5.
[77] *RE* 2.7.1900
[78] *RE* 2.7.1900
[79] *D.* 50.15.1 pr. (Ulp. 1 *cens.*); Ziegler (1978) 498.
[80] *RE* 10.1238 (see Premerstein); Luzzatto (1951) 79; Vittinghoff (1951) 465; Berger (1953) 530; Ziegler (1978) 499.
[81] *RE* 2.7.1900–1.   [82] Ziegler (1978) 493.

evidence. In the civil war between Macrinus and Elagabal, Sidon, Tyre's twin town, took the side of Elagabal. While it is not proved that Tyre sided with Macrinus, it evidently lost some privileges, and is not called a *colonia* or metropolis on coins of the reign of Elagabal, except the early ones. It seems, then, that Tyre fell into disgrace, but not immediately after the defeat of Macrinus. Whether the disgrace was connected with the revolt of the *legio III Gallica*, which, having raised Elagabal to the throne, later rebelled, is doubtful, since the legion was stationed not in Tyre itself, but in nearby Raphaneae. At any rate, Alexander restored Tyre's privileges.

In view of Ulpian's intense local patriotism the history of Tyre in the Severan period must be borne in mind in interpreting his career. In it the reign of Elagabal (218–22) forms an awkward gap.

Ulpian's connection with Tyre elicits speculation on another point. Is he identical with the Oulpianos who presides as toast-master at the dinner of the *Deipnosophistae* of Athenaeus? Speculation about this may in the end not turn out to be very profitable, but the relation between them has been a prominent theme of writings about Ulpian and his career.[83]

The *Deipnosophistae*, 'philosophers of the dinner-table' is a work in fifteen books in the form, common in ancient literature, of a symposium, or discussion at dinner. The discussion, unbelievably boring, is almost entirely about the meaning and derivation of words, the passages in which they feature in Greek literature, and their use or misuse. Oulpianos, the toast-master, refuses to eat any dish until satisfied as to the etymology of the word or words used to name or describe it.[84] He goes through the menu, indeed, in a spirit of pernickety linguistic cavillation. It is this trait that enables the dinner party, with some adjournments, to last for fifteen books. The Deiphosophist Oulpianos is depicted as a learned but bad-tempered pedant, one of whose main concerns is to preserve the purity of the Greek language against Roman infiltration.[85] He professes not to understand Latin words or words derived from Latin. He behaves like an exceptionally pedantic Frenchman inveighing against the incursions of *franglais*.

None of this would point to a connection with Ulpian the jurist were it not that Athenaeus wrote about the end of the second century and Oulpianos is described as coming from Tyre.[86] The date of the tedious compilation cannot be fixed exactly, but it must be later than the death of Commodus in 193. Book 12 refers to Commodus in a disrespectful way. Commodus is the emperor who 'in our own times' sat in his chariot, with

[83] Kaibel (1887) intro; Dittenberger (1903) 1–28; Krüger (1912) 239[143]; Kunkel (1967) 249–51; Crifò (1976) 715–34. The references in the text to Oulpianos are collected in Kaibel (1887) III 564; cf. *RE* 5.1435 (Wissowa). Background in Bowersock (1969).

[84] Athenaeus 9.401. Editions by Kaibel (1887), Gulich (1969), Cf. Mengis (1920).

[85] Athenaeus 3.98c, 3.12f, 8.361.

[86] Athenaeus 1.1d (Τύριος), cf. 8.346c (Σύρων), 9.368c (Συραττικέ).

the club of Hercules beside him and a lion skin spread out below,[87] 'trying unsuccessfully to imitate the god'. But there are signs that the date of composition is not much after 193. Of the participants, some at least are drawn from real life. The host Larensis, a Roman knight, giving the dinner party in Rome, seems to be identical with P. Livius Larensis, *pontifex minor*, known from a touching but undated inscription on a tombstone dedicated to him by his wife.[88] Galen the doctor, one of the guests, can hardly be other than the famous anatomist and physiologist, who, like the dinner guest, came from Pergamum.[89] The real Galen is thought to have died about 199,[90] so that, if Athenaeus means us to think of him as alive, the dramatic date cannot be later than the end of the second century. That we are to think of him as alive is an inference *e contrario* from the fact that, at end of the work, Oulpianos dies. In the closing stages of the banquet he gives an elaborate explanation of the different sorts of wreath, and concludes 'So I will make my exit, as in a play, after my speech'.[91] Not many days later, adds Athenaeus, as if Oulpianos foresaw the fate that was to be his, 'he died in hope, with no time for illness, but a grief to us his companions'.[92]

It is virtually impossible to record, even in a work of fiction, the death of someone who is actually alive, or, if he is dead, to place his death in the wrong period. It looks, therefore, as if, supposing there was a real Oulpianos who served Athenaeus as a model, he died about the last decade of the second century. This chronology has led some scholars to postulate that Oulpianos was the jurist's father.[93] Others, beginning with Kaibel who edited the *Deipnosophists* in 1887, have preferred to identify Oulpianos and Ulpian.[94] This is also the opinion of Crifò, who has discussed the evidence most recently.[95] Kunkel rejects both identifications.[96] Although it is not certain that all the guests depicted at the banquet are based on real people, it seems likely that so prominent a member of the company as Oulpianos will have been. So perhaps Oulpianos really existed. But he and Ulpian differ radically. Oulpianos is a partisan of Greek culture, an Atticist in matters of language. He is called a thinker and word-fancier, ($\phi\rho\text{o}\nu\tau\iota\sigma\tau\dot{\alpha}$ $\kappa\alpha\grave{\iota}$ $\lambda\text{o}\gamma\iota\sigma\tau\dot{\alpha}$)[97] hyper-critical ($\phi\iota\lambda\epsilon\pi\iota\tau\iota\mu\eta\tau\dot{\eta}\varsigma$),[98] and nicknamed $\kappa\epsilon\iota\tau\text{o}\acute{\upsilon}\kappa\epsilon\iota\tau\text{o}\varsigma$ "Mr Is-the-term-found-

[87] Athenaeus 12.537; Wenger (1953) 232[112].
[88] *CIL* VI 2126.
[89] *RE* 7.1.578 Galenos no. 2 (Mewaldt); *PIR*[2] G 24
[90] *RE* 7.1.581 (born 129 and according to Suda s. v. and attained 70).
[91] Athenaeus 15.686c.   [92] Ibid.
[93] Dittenberger (1903) 1, 19 f.
[94] Kaibel (1887) 1 6 f.; Mengis (1920) 23 f.
[95] Crifò (1976) 721–2, 734; *contra* Wenger (1933) 232[14].
[96] Kunkel (1967) 251
[97] Athenaeus 9.401b.   [98] Athenaeus 14.613c.

or–not?"[99] There is nothing to suggest that he is a jurist, or has even a nodding acquaintance with the law. The last thing to which Oulpianos would devote himself is the study of Roman law. Galen at least is given the right profession, though nothing he says at the feast shows that Athenaeus had read any Galen. Masurius the lawyer, another guest,[100] if he is meant to be the jurist Masurius Sabinus of the reign of Tiberius, is also in the right discipline, though he has outlived his time by 150 years. Athenaeus had clearly not read him either. The guests are indeed rather loosely attached to their presumptive historical models. Hence it can be argued that a jurist might be turned into a philologist, an admirer of things Roman into a passionate defender of the Greek language. Crifò sees in Ulpian's discussions of the terms used in legacies a parallel to his Greek counterpart's discussions of etymology.[101] But the gulf between them is deep. The jurist is a man of affairs, concerned to adapt the law to the exigencies of society and government. In the interpretation of legacies his guide is the intention of the testator, as evinced by his verbal and social habits, not Attic or antiquarian purism.[102] To identify Ulpian with Oulpianos we should have to suppose a satirical purpose on the author's part, a wish to caricature. It would be pleasing to attribute so much wit to the flat-footed pedant Athenaeus. A Greek intellectual of a certain type might indeed take pleasure in depicting a Roman jurist as a logic-chopping boor. The obstacle is that the meticulous scholarship of 'the wise Oulpianos',[103] is meant to be admired. If satire was intended, it was not carried through consistently.

In the end the common points consist in the attachment of Oulpianos to Tyre and Syria: he is a 'Syratticist',[104] just as Ulpian is a proud citizen of Tyre. That is hardly enough. Ulpian's violent death comes twenty-five or thirty years later than the likely date of composition of the *Deipnosophists*: 223 against some date between 193 and 199. In other points they diverge too far for plausibility, even if we allow for a turn of mockery which Athenaeus does not otherwise display. Oulpianos can hardly be Ulpian. Nevertheless, it would be something of a coincidence if there were no connection between two scholars, each proud of his connection with the city of Tyre, possessing the same cognomen and living within a generation of one another. Oulpianos need not be Ulpian's father, but he might be a member of a family of Tyrian scholars from which the jurist also sprang. And if Ulpian's path led him to the highest post in the Roman state, next to

[99] Athenaeus 1.1e.
[100] Athenaeus 1.1c; 5.186, 196, 221; 6.271; 14.623, (an interpreter of laws second to none) 633, 634, 639, 15.687.
[101] Crifò (1976) 724 f.
[102] D. 34.2.19.8 (Ulp. 20 *Sab.*)
[103] Dittenberger (1903) 1, 19; *PIR*[1] D145; Syme (1971) 155[5]. For Greek views of Romans see Fuchs (1938), Palm (1959). Forte (1972).
[104] Athenaeus 9.368c.

the emperor, he never ceased to be, indeed he rose to high office partly by virtue of being a careful scholar.

Ulpian came from Tyre, then, and perhaps belonged to a family of scholars. Kunkel suggests that his evident pride both in Tyre and in Rome can best be explained if his family was descended from Roman or Italian merchants who had been established for some generations in Tyre.[105] He also points out that the gentile name Domitius is found far less in the eastern than the western provinces, and may go back to the first century AD, when the senatorial families with this *gentilicium* such as the Ahenobarbi, Calvini, and Corbulones had not yet disappeared.[106] The combination Gnaeus Domitius was also commoner along the senatorial families of the first centuries than later, and hence, if Ulpian is to be identified with the owner of the house near Centumcellae, or is a member of the same family, the hypothesis of his descent from a forebear who acquired Roman citizenship in the first century is strengthened. It may be significant that Cn. Domitius Corbulo was governor of Syria in AD 60−3. He is the only Domitius known to have held that province before the time of Ulpian. He had as legate a stepson Annius Vinicianus, so that this second *gentilicium*, also found on the pipe near Centumcellae, may be traceable to the same period.[107] Ulpian's family had therefore probably been established in Tyre as Roman citizens for several generations. The jurist certainly knew Greek as well as Latin, and may have known Aramaic. But attempts to show that his writing betrays a strong Semitic or Greek influence have come to nothing.[108] His Latin, though in some ways colloquial, is notably pure and correct. It is more like the Latin of the first than of the third century.

IV (A). ULPIAN'S CAREER: THE REIGN OF SEVERUS 193−211

We have virtually no evidence about Ulpian's early career. It has been asserted that he began as assessor to a praetor, or to the praetorian prefect Papinian, or with a procuratorship in Gaul. None of these assertions withstands scrutiny.

The notion that Ulpian was assessor to a praetor stems from a text in book 11 of his edictal commentary,[109] which belongs to the reign of Caracalla, and, if the argument in chapter 5 is accepted, to 213. The passage concerns the legal effect of coercion. Does it simply afford a defence, or is it a ground for demanding the restoration (*restitutio*) of the state of affairs

---

[105] Kunkel (1967) 248.

[106] Kunkel (1967) 253.

[107] Kunkel (1967) 254.

[108] Heineccius, *Opera* II 249; Kunkel (1967) 251; Kalb (1888) 127; Volterra *St. Dec.* 3. 158 f.; Wenger (1953) 519[311]; Volterra *SDHI* 3 (1937) 158.

[109] *D.* 4.2.9.3 (Ulp. 11 *ed.*); Wenger (1953) 519[311]; *NDI* (1964) 355; *contra* Kunkel (1967) 331[697], (1974) 415.

which existed before the guilty party resorted to it? Ulpian says that he knows from personal experience (*ex facto scio*) that when the Campanians terrorized someone (presumably a rich man) into promising them something in writing (no doubt to construct or repair a public work), 'our emperor' (Caracalla) gave a rescript that the promissor could approach the praetor to obtain restitution (i.e. to be freed from his promise). Ulpian was sitting with the praetor (*me adsidente*) and, impliedly on his advice, the praetor ruled that the man in question could either sue the Campanians or wait to be sued and raise a good defence.

The rescript must belong to the early part of Caracalla's sole rule, 211 or 212, and Ulpian's personal experience either to those years or to 213. As Jörs[110] first pointed out, Ulpian cannot have held the junior post of paid legal assessor as late as the reign of Caracalla. Even if we disregard the evidence that he was secretary *a libellis* to Severus and Caracalla between 202 and 209,[111] he was by then a lawyer of such authority that he could write in a lofty way of a certain view being 'rightly expressed' by Caracalla[112] and compliment the emperor Marcus for giving a rescript 'in accordance with our opinion'.[113]

The verb *adsidere* does not mean 'to act as an assessor' but 'to sit with (a judge) in order to give advice on the law'.[114] In the context therefore *me adsidente* means 'when I was sitting with and advising the praetor'. Naturally it is implied that the praetor took Ulpian's advice. Otherwise he would not mention the point. To be an assessor in the sense of holding a paid post, normally a junior one, is only one form of *adsidere*. A person can 'sit with' a judge as a member of his *consilium*, or individual expert. Here the praetor was faced with a technical problem: how to give practical effect to Caracalla's rescript. What was more natural than that he should ask one of the two leading experts on the praetor's edict (Paul was the other) to sit with him?

It is in any case doubtful if praetors had paid assessors. Behrends has made a thorough investigation of the position of legal assessors in the Roman empire.[115] It is commonly thought that the office originated in the provinces and in the second century spread to the Roman prefectures, but was never available to the ordinary republican magistrates such as the praetor.[116] Behrends disagrees. In his dialogue on *Peace of Mind* (*de*

---

[110] *RE* 5.1438.

[111] Below, ch. 8; Honoré (1981) 59–64.

[112] *D.* 50.15.3.1 (Ulp. 2 *cens.*), 17.1.6.7 (29 *ed.*), 48.19.8.12 (9 *off. proc.*), cf. 50.2.3.1 (3 *off. proc*), 28.6.2.4 (6 *Sab.*).

[113] *D.* 29.1.3 (2 *Sab.*).

[114] *D.* 1.22.6 (Pap. 1 *resp.*; citizen not enjoying public salary can *adsidere* in *consilium* of *curator reipublicae*), 1.22.5 (Paul 1 *sent.*; *consiliarius*).

[115] Behrends (1969) 192, 216. Earlier view Hitzig (1893).

[116] *RE* 1 (1894) 423 (Seeck); Kaser (1966) 367; Kunkel (1967) 331.

tranquillitate animi) Seneca cites a passage from Athenodorus, who asks rhetorically whether the work of the urban or peregrine praetor, who reads out to petitioners the form of words supplied by his assessor (*qui adsessoris verba pronuntiat*) is really more valuable than the contemplations of a philosopher concerned with the nature of justice, piety, contempt for death, or other such lofty topics.[117] This is strong evidence that in the middle of the first century AD these praetors had legal advisers. But it is not shown that the advisers were paid officials. The office does not feature in anybody's recorded career, then or later. To assist a praetor in this way may well have remained an unpaid service to be performed, as a matter of public duty, by senior lawyers such as Ulpian. Indeed, this way of putting the matter may suggest the wrong perspective. From the government's point of view the presence of senior imperial concillors in the ordinary courts may have been regarded as a way of supervising the administration of justice, in the manner of Tiberius[118] or Hadrian.[119]

The incident of the extortionate Campanians, then, shows Ulpian advising a praetor not as a paid assessor early in his career but as a senior jurist and legal scholar in middle life. Though no other text is as explicit as this, there is more than one which likewise suggests that Ulpian was advising a praetor. Thus, in his book on trusts (*fideicommissa*), Ulpian discusses a gift of water to a freedman by way of trust.[120] He was consulted about the trust (*consulebar*) and replied (*dicebam*) that such a trust was valid in areas such as Africa or Egypt where there was a water shortage. The use of the imperfect shows that this was not a written *responsum*, but neither is it an ordinary disputation. A disputation would be introduced by 'it is asked' (*quaeritur*), 'it was asked' (*quaerebatur*), or the like. Here Ulpian is consulted, perhaps by the *praetor fideicommissarius*, in any case orally. In another passage[121] Ulpian mentions a trust by which a legatee is asked to emancipate his children. Ulpian remembers saying (*retineo me dixisse*) that the children could not sue on the trust, since the *praetor fideicommissarius* does not protect children subject to a trust as he does slaves. This, too, could be a personal reminiscence of advice given to the praetor with jurisdiction over trusts.

The same seems to hold for the praetor in charge of guardianship (*praetor tutelaris*). An incomplete text from *Vatican Fragments*,[122] drawn from Ulpian's monograph on the office of that praetor, mentions a case in which on Ulpian's advice, *me suad (ente)*, the praetor decided to compel a freedman

---

[117] Behrends (1969) 193, citing Seneca *de tranq. animi* 3.4
[118] Suetonius *Tiberius* 31.2.
[119] *HA* Hadrian 21.1.
[120] *D.* 34.1.14.3 (Ulp. 2. *fid.*).
[121] *D.* 35.1.92 (5 *fid.*).
[122] *FV* 220 (1 *off. pr. tut.*); Pernice (1885) 355.

to act as curator of the son of the woman who had freed him. Again, this is drawn from Ulpian's own recollection (*memini*).

Two or three other texts, based on cases which Ulpian remembers, look as if they might record advice given by him to one of the praetors having jurisdiction in Rome.[123] As we shall see, there are at several periods in his career (202, 205–7, 211–12, 222–3) at which Ulpian is likely to have been resident in or near Rome, and in the first three of these his preoccupations would not have been incompatible with his spending time in court advising one or more praetors.

As a knight, Ulpian was junior in rank to the praetors, who were senators. In authority, however, he was senior, as a text from book 5 *ad edictum* shows.[124] The jurist says that when he was in a country-house with the praetor (*ego cum in villa cum praetore fuissem*), he allowed (*passus sum*) a manumission to take place before the magistrate despite the absence of the lictor. The expression *passus sum* is noteworthy. In an earlier generation Salvius Julianus says of a similar problem (whether a magistrate could manumit his own slaves or whether there was conflict of duty and interest in such a case) that he persuaded (*suasi*) some praetors who consulted him that it was proper for them to manumit their own slaves, *vindicta*, with the rod of office.[125] Here, in an analogous situation, Ulpian 'allows' it. The text belongs to a period before 213, perhaps 211, and the incident in the country villa cannot be later than 208, if it is accepted that Ulpian accompanied Severus to Britain in that year. More than any other text, this demonstrates the absurdity of supposing that Ulpian held an assessorship in the reign of Caracalla. Nor can Dorotheus' version of the text, preserved in the *Basilica*,[126] that Ulpian was staying in the country with a praetor with whom he was sitting (ὧτινι συνήδρευσα), be prayed in aid to support Ulpian's alleged assessorship. Dorotheus no doubt knew the Campanian text in which Ulpian speaks of the praetor deciding *me adsidente*, and mistakenly drew an inference about the capacity in which he found himself with the praetor in the country. If Ulpian had a large villa near Centumcellae, perhaps the praetor was visiting him there.

Two passages of the *Historia Augusta* say that Ulpian and Paul were legal advisers to Papinian. In the life of Niger[127] they are both said to have been members of his *consilium* (*qui Papiniano in consilio fuerunt*) and in that of Alexander[128] they are both said to have been assessors of Papinian (*qui tamem ambo assessores Papiniani fuisse dicuntur*). If the interpretation

[123] *D.* 36.1.18.5 (4 *fid.*); *FV* 242 (1 *off. pr. tut.*); *D.* 26.1.18 pr. (2 *fid.*), 4.3.2 (11 *ed.*).
[124] *D.* 40.2.8 (5 *ed.*).
[125] *D.* 40.2.5 (Iul. 42 *Dig.*), cf. 22.1.3.3 (Pap. 20 *qu.*).
[126] *Bas.* 48.6.2 (Heimbach 4.624), ad *D.* 40.2.6.
[127] *HA* Niger 7.3–4. On Papinian see Costa (1894–9); Kunkel (1967) 224; *Pal* I 803–946; Mommsen (1890) 30 = (1905) II 64.
[128] *HA* Alexander 26.5.

suggested by *Niger* is given to '*assessor*'—an unpaid legal adviser— there is no objection to this, though it cannot be taken as true simply on the authority of the *HA*. The second passage is objectionable only if the assessorship is taken to be a paid, and relatively junior, post. By the time that Papinian became praetorian prefect in 205, after the fall of Plautianus, Ulpian had, if the argument of chapter 8 is accepted, been secretary *a libellis* for nearly three years. Paul was then a legal member of the *consilium* of Severus and, to judge from his reports of cases before the emperor (*decreta*, *sententiae imperiales*), secretary *a cognitionibus*.[129] Neither could have been a paid assessor to Papinian as praetorian prefect. It is true that the praetorian prefect's assessors seem to have been chosen by the emperor personally.[130] This was reasonable, given the importance of the praetorian prefect's jurisdiction and the fact that in legal theory he sat as the emperor's delegate. One would therefore expect the post of assessor to the praetorian prefect to be more senior and better paid than that of assessor to a provincial governor.

But the head of a central office, a *scrinium*, is too senior to hold such a post. Nevertheless, some rather close relationship between Ulpian and Papinian seems likely. It is not merely that, if the argument in chapter 9 is accepted, Ulpian succeeded the senior jurist in the office *a libellis* in 202, or that Papinian is the only contemporary jurist whom Ulpian cites by name more than once.[131] In book 6 *ad Sabinum*, which probably belongs to 214, the Tyrian jurist says that Papinian argued that the speech to the senate (*oratio*) of Severus on gifts between husband and wife applied only to donations of tangible objects, not to donatory stipulations.[132] Ulpian here uses the imperfect (*Papinianis recte putabat . . . non putabat*), and this is his only such use in relation to a contemporary. Though the precise context is lost, the imperfect implies that Papinian expressed his opinion orally: 'argued', 'denied'. The reminiscence might come from a disputation, in which case Ulpian must have been a pupil or follower of the senior jurist. Alternatively, the debate in which Papinian expressed his opinion might have taken place in the imperial council. Ulpian had some connection with Papinian, then, but was not his paid assessor.

A third suggestion about Ulpian's early career is that he had an equestrian post, for example a procuratorship, in Gaul. Bremer[133] argued for a close connection between Ulpian and Gaul. There are certain passages in which the jurist makes use of Gaul or things Gallic by way of example. A trust can be left in a tongue other than Latin or Greek, for instance Punic or

---

[129] *D.* 4.4.38 (1 *decr.*), 29.2.97 (3 *decr.*), 36.1.76.1 (2 *decr.*), 49.14.50 (3 *decr.*).

[130] *CIL* XI. 6337; Ti. Claudius Zeno Ulpianus *ex sacra iussione adhibitus in consilium praef. praet. item urbi*; Pflaum (1960) no. 294; Howe (1942) 37.

[131] Ulpian mentions him 116 times: Honoré–Menner *CJD* (1980) 66.

[132] *D.* 24.1.23 (Ulp. 6 *Sab.*).

[133] Bremer (1883) 84; *contra* Crifò (1976) 738.

Gallic.[134] 'My Italian estate' includes slaves who are normally employed in Italy, though I may send them on a mission to a province, 'for example Gaul', to collect debts or buy supplies.[135] *Provinciae continentes* are those provinces which adjoint Italy 'for example Gaul'.[136] A text in book 5 *ad Sabinum* speaks of a legacy imposed on 'the heir to my Gallic property'.[137] Marble quarries are said to renew themselves 'as in Gaul and also in Asia'.[138]

What do these passages imply? Not that Ulpian held a junior post in Gaul. If he travelled with Severus in 208 through that province on his way to Britain, and back with Caracalla and Geta in 211, he could hardly fail to notice that Gaul adjoined Italy, and to learn at least something of the conditions of life obtaining there. There is indeed an argument against his having had a close connection with Gaul. In Ulpian's list of towns with Italian right (*ius Italicum*)[139] he does not mention anywhere in Gaul or the west, whereas Paul does.[140] Ulpian's reference to the Gallic language in *de fideicommissis*[141] (probably 213 or 214) is interesting. In book 48 *ad Sabinum* (about 216) the examples of languages other than Greek and Latin are now Punic and 'Assyrian' viz. Aramaic.[142] This may be an indication that Ulpian moved east between these dates. If he was in attendance on Caracalla or Julia Domna, he must have done so. And while in book 5 *Sab.* (perhaps 214) a testator speaks of his Gallic estate (*res Gallicanae*)[143] in 38 *Sab.* (about 216) a tutor is appointed to the ward's 'African or Syrian estate'.[144] This points to a similar direction of movement.

Ulpian says that a wife's personal effects, not part of the dowry, are called παράφερνα by the Greeks and *peculium* by the Gauls (*Galli*).[145] As Calder showed,[146] this usage is found in Galatia as well as Gaul, and it may be from there that Ulpian derived his information. But even if he came upon it in reading or while travelling through Gaul, this does not imply that he held a junior post there. The positive evidence is flimsy. Nevertheless, it is interesting that the examples which Ulpian selects, of languages and of areas in which a person might have a separate person to administer his property, are Syria,[147] Gaul,[148] and Africa;[149] the first his home province,

[134] *D.* 32.11 pr. (2 *fid.*).
[135] *D.* 28.5.35.3 (4 *disp.*).
[136] *D.* 50.16.99.1 (Ulp. 1 *off. cons.*).   [137] *D.* 30.4.1 (Ulp. 5 *Sab.*).
[138] *D.* 24.3.7.13 (36 *Sab.*).
[139] *D.* 50.15.1 (Ulp. 1 *cens.*).
[140] *D.* 50.13.8 (Paul 2 *cens.*).
[141] *D.* 32.11 pr. (Ulp. 2 *fid.*).
[142] *D.* 45.1.1.6 (48 *Sab.*).   [143] *D.* 30.4.1 (5 *Sab.*).
[144] *D.* 26.2.15 (Ulp. 38 *Sab.*).
[145] *D.* 23.3.9.3 (Ulp. 31 *Sab.*).   [146] Calder (1923) 8.
[147] *D.* 45.1.1.6 (48 *Sab.*), 26.2.15 (Ulp. 38 *Sab.*), cf. 48.22.7.6, 14 (10 *off. proc.*).
[148] Above, nn. 134–8.
[149] *D.* 32.11 pr. (2 *fid.*), 45.1.1.6 (48 *Sab.*). According to Dio 77.6.1a Caracalla combined the vices of all three.

the third that of Severus, the second that of Caracalla's birth, and the campaign against Albinus.

We can only guess how Ulpian began his career. I have the impression, for what it is worth, that he was attached to the court of Severus from an early date. This was certainly true of Papinian, who was secretary *a libellis* not later than September 194.[150] Ulpian's point of view about provincial government is that of the central administration. His haughty way of referring to high officials, his 'permission' to the praetor to manumit without a lictor,[151] reflects the attitude of a man has spent little or no time in relatively humble provincial posts. The references which we find in Ulpian to the special conditions of Arabia, Egypt, Asia, or Africa[152] can be accounted for without supposing that he held posts in these provinces. Familiarity with petitions and appeals from these areas, and travel with Severus in Africa in 203 – 4, through Gaul to Britain in 208 and back again in 211, will have provided a stock of instances. My guess is that Ulpian was Papinian's assistant in the office *a libellis*. If so, he was with Severus and Papinian on two eastern campaigns in 194 – 6 and 197 – 9, against Albinus in Gaul in 197, in Egypt in 199 – 200, and in Syria in 201. Indeed, he was with the emperor for virtually the whole of his reign. This cannot be proved, and it may be doubted, since the existence of a post of assistant in the office *a libellis* is not attested. Given the volume of legal work, however, that Septimius took on the shoulders of his government, assistance of this sort by an able lawyer cannot be ruled out. If Ulpian, as I think, did not hold the equestrian posts (*advocatus fisci*, provincial procuratorships) normally associated with a legal career at this period, but pursued a substantially unbroken career in the central government, one could understand better both his mastery of the problems of administration in the central offices and his relative lack of private practice.

This last point has not received the attention it deserves. The other leading lawyers of the Severan age, Papinian, Paul, and Modestinus, all had a large private practice. The *responsa* of Papinian and Modestinus both run to nineteen books, Paul's to twenty three. In comparison with them, the two books of *responsa* attributed to Ulpian, even if they were genuine, form a meagre output. Whereas the others all keep a balance between scholarship, private practice, and public service, Ulpian, a better scholar than the others, omits the middle element almost entirely. It is true that, apart from the questionable books of *responsa*, three *responsa* of Ulpian are mentioned in the sources.[153] It cannot be said that had no practice, but its

150 Below, ch. 8 p. 195 f. *CJ* 2.23.1 (26 Sept. 194).
151 *D.* 40.2.8 (Ulp. 5 *ed.*), cf. Talamanca (1976) 95.
152 *D.* 47.11.9 (Ulp. 9 *off. proc.* Arabia), 47.11.10 (Ulp. 9 *off. proc.* Egypt), 32.55.5 (25 *Sab.* Egypt), cf. Bonneau (1969), *D.* 1.16.4.5 (1 *off. proc.* Asia), 34.1.14.3 (2 *fid.* Africa); *contra* Bremer (1868 reprint 1968).
153 Below, ch. 4 p. 115 f. and nn. 123 – 5.

extent was minimal in comparison with that of his leading contemporaries.

The first firm point in Ulpian's career, if the argument in chapter 8 is accepted, is March 202, when he succeeded to the post of secretary *a libellis*, held by Papinian from 194 until then, and began to compose imperial rescripts.[154] He continued in that office until the summer or perhaps the autumn of 209.[155] This date, which is deduced from the style of the rescripts of that period, presents a problem in regard to a passage in the *HA* life of Niger.[156] The pretender Niger, it is alleged, was concerned to prevent rapid changes of administration in the provinces. He therefore advised Marcus and Commodus to change provincial governors only after a full five-year period. In regard to civil administration he suggested that assessors should continue in the provinces (departments) in which they had been assessors: *ut adsessores in quibus provinciis adsedissent, in his administrarent*. This policy was followed by Severus and many later emperors as is shown, *HA* continues, by the prefectures of Paul and Ulpian. They were members of Papinian's *consilum* and later, after Paul had been secretary *a memoria* and Ulpian *a libellis*, were at once both made prefects.

The life of Pescennius Niger is one of the least satisfactory subsidiary lives in the *HA*. Indeed, on a view which goes back to Hasebroek,[157] it is a falsification through and through. There is no reason to credit Niger with the sober counsels about administrative continuity attributed to him. These are more probably opinions which the author of the *HA*, writing in the late fourth century, thought to advocate by proxy, putting them in the mouth of one of his historical *personae*. As Straub has argued, this was a favoured *HA* technique in regard to legal and administrative matters, about which the author had views, perhaps derived from experience in the central offices of government. Thus, in the late empire rescripts were attacked on the ground that they were often elicited contrary to the general law.[158] To support this view, the author of *HA* attributes to Macrinus a policy of refusing to issue rescripts.[159] The equestrian emperor is made to put this on the ground that it would be a crime to give the force of law to the whims of Commodus, Caracalla, and other untrained rulers. Trajan, says *HA*, seldom answered *libelli*, in case favours granted to particular individuals might be extended to other cases.

The reason why no rescripts of Macrinus are known is, of course, that his short reign was treated as that of a usurper, and his acts were annulled. The statement about Trajan is untrue, but not implausible. The *Codex*

---

[154] Below, pp. 198–9; *CJ* 2.3.3 (25 March 202); *RE* 5.1436 (Jörs).

[155] Below, pp. 199–200; Honoré (1981) 63–4.

[156] *HA* Niger 7.2–4.

[157] Hasebroek (1916), (1921) vi.

[158] *CTh.* 1.2.2 (29 Aug. 315), 1.2.3 (3 Dec. 317/8), 1.2.9 (28 Sept. 385), 1.2.11 (6 Dec. 398); Straub (1978).

[159] *HA* Macrinus 13.1.

Gregorianus contained no rescripts earlier than Hadrian, and the references to Trajan's rescripts in legal writing are fewer by far than for Hadrian and his successors. Indeed the *HA* passage on Macrinus, though an invention, presupposes a knowledge of the legal sources sufficient to distort them without falling into evident absurdity. Another such instance occurs in the life of Tacitus, who is represented, by virtue of his historian homonym, as pro-senatorial. The emperor Tacitus, says *HA*, set free all his urban slaves of both sexes, but was careful not to exceed 100, so as not to appear to infringe the Caninian law (*lex Fufia Caninia*).[160] The story is absurd. If Tacitus had more than 100 urban slaves, he did not free them all. If he had fewer, he ran no risk of transgressing the letter or spirit of the *lex*. The *lex* did indeed forbid an owner with 500 slaves or more to manumit by will more than 100. As Gaius points out,[161] he could nevertheless manumit as many as he liked *inter vivos*, either before the magistrate (*vindicta*) or informally. The author of *HA* knows this. His point is that Tacitus, supposedly a model emperor, is so anxious to observe the spirit of the law that he treats himself a debarred from manumitting more than 100 even *inter vivos*. The attribution of this attitude to Tacitus is not to be taken seriously. It is a mere device by which the author, who favours strict limits on manumission, puts forward a conservative point of view. The limits were removed by Justinian in 528.[162]

It may be then, that, in relation to Ulpian's career also, the author of *HA* had access to a good source which he adapted for his own ends. This source perhaps said the Ulpian was Papinian's assistant. If this is taken to refer to the *libelli*, it may be true. The source may have said, again truly, that after a long tenure of office by Papinian, Ulpian succeeded him, also for a long term. The passage in *Niger* may therefore have had a sound substratum. As it stands, it contains a falsehood. After holding the *libelli* Ulpian 'was at once made prefect'. If this means praetorian prefect it is wrong. Ulpian left the *libelli* in 209 but was not made prefect until 222. Nor did he attain the prefecture immediately after Papinian, who left office in 211. Even if we suppose that the author means to refer to a lesser prefecture, such as the prefecture of supply (*praefectura annonae*), which Ulpian held early in 222, he can hardly have been appointed to it until after 217. As to what the passage says of Paul, his career is so obscure that, on any interpretation, its truth remains in doubt.

The first surviving rescript which appears to be by Ulpian is dated 25 March 202,[163] and this to my mind implies a date of birth in 172 or earlier.[164] On 1 January 202 Severus and Caracalla entered on a joint

---

[160] *HA* Tacitus 10.7.
[161] Gaius *Inst.* 1.44.
[162] *CJ* 7.3.1 (1 June 528).   [163] *CJ* 2.3.3.
[164] Honoré (1962) 207 where, on the basis of appointment *a libellis* in 200, I suggested a date of birth in 163–70; *contra* Crifò (1976) 739[203].

consulship in Antioch.[165] They then journeyed through Asia Minor to the west, passing through Tyana, Nicaea, Byzantium, and Perinthus. They perhaps visited the legionaries of Moesia and Pannonia.[166] In April there were festivities in Rome for the emperor's return and his victories. Caracalla married Plautilla and Geta assumed the *toga virilis*.[167] The change in the office *a libellis* is to be associated, therefore, with the return of Severus from the east. Once back in Rome the emperor was an assiduous judge and occupied himself with problems of civil administration.[168] Ulpian was to remain at the *libelli* for the next seven years,[169] and, as such, may be assumed to have accompanied Severus and Caracalla to Africa in 203 to 204, returning for the assassination of Plautianus in January 205[170] and the subsequent appointment of Laetus and Papinian to a joint praetorian prefecture.[171] He will have gone with the emperor, his two sons, Julia Domna, and Papinian across Gaul to Britain in the spring of 208, a year from which we have eight surviving rescripts.[172] In 209 there are only four.[173] Only the first two of these, dated 13 January and 1 May, are clearly by Ulpian.[174] The third, of 13 July,[175] is probably, the fourth of 31 December[176] certainly, by another hand. In this year Severus and Caracalla went north from their base in York to campaign against the Caledonians, while Julia Domna and Geta remained behind.[177] Geta was put in charge of the Roman province and of the civil business of the empire,[178] which included the issuing of rescripts. During the course of the year, though it is uncertain exactly when, Geta was made an Augustus,[179] a fact which was known in Athens in October or November 209. The change from Ulpian to his successor at the *libelli* is to be seen in this context. Probably, like Papinian, he went north, and a new secretary was left with Geta to see to the issue of rescripts. The last rescript composed by this new secretary is dated 28 December 211,[180] which is near to the date of Geta's murder. The new secretary presumably was loyal to Geta and paid the penalty.

[165] Hasebroek (1921) 125–30, 190f.; *HA Severus* 16.8.
[166] Hasebroek (1921) 125; Herodian 3.10.1; Dio 75.15.3–4; Mihailov (1963) 113; but there is no evidence that Severus was in Sirmium on 18 March as stated by Hasebroek: Whittaker (1969) 1.325.
[167] Hasebroek (1921) 126 (13–19 April).
[168] Herodian 3.10.2.
[169] Below, ch. 8 pp. 196–200.
[170] Hasebroek (1921) 136–8; Birley (1971) 232–5.
[171] Herodian 3.13.1; Pflaum (1960) nos. 219–20; Howe (1942) nos. 21, 22; *PIR*[1] M 43; *PIR*[2] A 388.
[172] *Corp. Iur. Civ.* 11 ed. Krueger 490.
[173] Ibid.
[174] *CJ* 7.62.1, 7.74.1; below, p. 199.
[175] *CJ* 8.18.1; below, pp. 199–200.
[176] *CJ* 7.8.3; below, p. 200.
[177] Hasebroek (1921) 142–3, 148–9; Dio 76.13; Gilliam–Mann (1976).
[178] Herodian 3.14.9.
[179] Below, ch. 8 pp. 200–1.
[180] *CJ* 6.44.1 (28 Dec. 211); Honoré (1981) pp. 64–5.

Not Ulpian. He must have gone on with Severus and Caracalla in 209. In 210 Severus, ill with gout, remained in York while Caracalla campaigned. At the beginning of 211 preparations were made for a third campaign, but the death of Severus at York on 4 February brought them to a halt.[181] It is possibly at this period, in the first five weeks of 211, that we should place the first five books of Ulpian's comment..ry *ad edictum*. There is a noticeable change of style between the fifth and sixth books.[182] The sixth book, if the argument of chapter 5 is right, belongs to the beginning of 213. The first five should therefore have been composed some time before this. Their style is subdued, and they fit a period of tension. The period from 1 January to 4 February amounts to five weeks, and if, as I argue in chapter 6,[183] Ulpian's normal rate of composition between 213 and 217 was a book a week, it may have been the same at this earlier period. It is possible, therefore, that the first five books were composed at this period when the court was waiting for Severus to die. This presupposes that Ulpian had taken his law books and notes to Britain. That the court travelled, even on campaign, with all the documents necessary for carrying on the civil administration, including trials and the issue of rescripts, seems certain in view of the fact that rescripts continued to be issued.

IV (B). ULPIAN'S CAREER: THE REIGNS OF CARACALLA AND MACRINUS (211−18)

After the death of Septimius, Caracalla decided to make peace and return to Rome.[184] He was already, as Dio makes clear, acting as if he were sole emperor,[185] making appointments on his own initiative, and plotting his brother's murder.[186] The *libelli*, however, remained in the same hands until the end of 211.[187] That Caracalla gave Ulpian some office on Severus' death is not evidenced but not impossible. Since Ulpian survived the massacre of Geta's supporters, he was either neutral, which was difficult, or sided with Caracalla. We tend to think of the struggle between the brothers in the light of Caracalla's brutal and treacherous fratricide. In 211, however, there were arguments in favour of Caracalla's point of view. It is true that respect for Severus' ultimate wishes pointed to joint rule. In his last years he had decided on a joint succession, and his last words were said to have enjoined harmony on his children.[188] The Roman law of intestate

---

[181] Dio 76.15; Hasebroek (1921) 145−7.
[182] Ch. 5 pp. 146−8.
[183] Below, p. 160.
[184] Dio 77.1.1.
[185] Dio ibid.
[186] Dio 77.1.3 f. Herodian 4.3.1 f. plausibly mentions mutual plots.
[187] Honoré (1981) 64−5.
[188] Dio 76.15.2.

succession, if taken as an analogy, made surviving children joint heirs.[189] Perhaps these arguments, and the friendship of Severus, weighed with Papinian. On the other hand, Severus had allowed over ten years to pass before raising Geta to the same status as his brother, though the latter was only a year his senior. Everything that Severus had done until 209 pointed to contempt for Geta's abilities and respect for those of Caracalla. Even the promotion of 209 could be seen as a matter of necessity, not choice. It was enjoined by the need to ensure the continuity of civil business. Caracalla, thirteen years an Augustus, was suited by experience, if not by temperament, to be a ruler. Geta was not, though some who were hostile to Caracalla, such as Herodian, attribute to him in his later years[190] signs of moderation and of intellectual interests. Unless one Augustus was clearly senior, the other auxiliary, as with Marcus and Lucius Verus, the auguries for joint rule were bad. Indeed, continued joint rule would surely have been worse that Caracalla's monarchy.

There is no reason, then, to reject the possibility that a lawyer with Ulpian's keen appreciation of the practical needs of government sided with Caracalla or sat on the fence. The issue was decided at the end of 211, when the elder brother lured the younger to a meeting, supposedly of reconciliation, with their mother Julia Domna and had hidden centurions strike him down. Despite her no doubt genuine distress, she continued to work closely with her elder son and he to rely on her.[191]

If the arguments of chapter 5 are accepted,[192] Ulpian's five-year programme of legal writing began in 213. Up to then he had written little: only five books of edictal commentary, perhaps in early 211, and, before 211, a monograph on excuses from guardianship (*de excusationibus*).[193] What was the relation of his ambitious synopsis to the policies of Caracalla's government? One view is that, disliking the tyranny of Caracalla, he withdrew from public life to devote himself to scholarship. This possibility cannot be entirely dismissed. Julia Domna seems at various periods to have consoled herself with 'philosophy', i.e. intellectual pursuits.[194] This did not prevent her from performing her public duties and helping Caracalla to run the empire.[195] So in the case of Ulpian. A period of freedom from office may have been welcome on personal grounds: we cannot tell. But the literary enterprise on which he embarked is one which fits well the policy of Caracalla's regime and, in particular, the *constitutio Antoniniana*.[196] Once

---

[189] Kaser[2] (1971) 695. The principle went back at least to the XII Tables.

[190] Herodian 4.3.2−3, cf. Alföldy (1972).

[191] Dio 77.2.3−6, 77.18.1−3; Schönbauer (1965) 105.   [192] Below, p. 153.

[193] Lenel *Pal.* 2.899−903, especially *FV* 125, 147, 149; below, ch. 7 p. 173.

[194] Dio 75.15.7, 77.18.3.   [195] Dio 77.18.2.

[196] Literature in Gianelli−Mazzarino II (1956) 397; *RE* 2.2446; Crifò (1976) 633−4; Sasse (1958), (1965) 329; de Visscher (1961); Millar (1962) 124; Gilliam (1965) 81; Herrmann (1972) 519; Gaudemet (1967) 528; Gundel (1966); Jones (1968); Saumagne (1966); Segrè (1966); Seston (1966); Talamanca (1971); Wieling (1974).

that edict had extended citizenship to the free citizens of the empire, with certain exceptions not of the first importance, it became a duty of government to provide for its citizens, new and old, a lucid exposition of Roman law. Who better qualified to provide this than the learned lawyer from Tyre? On this view, Ulpian was not sulking during the reign of Caracalla, but, on the contrary, playing a leading role in giving substance to the new dispensation.

Whether this view is tenable depends on many factors, one of which is the date of the *constitutio Antoniniana*. This has traditionally been put in 212, but that dating can be, and has been, challenged.[197] The matter can be approached from two points of view. In book 22 *ad edictum* Ulpian says[198] that all those who are in the Roman world have been made Roman citizens by the constitution of the emperor Antoninus (Caracalla). On the arguments presented in chapters 5 to 7, which are independent of the dating of the constitution, this text belongs to about the middle of 213. Hence, if those arguments are sound, the *constitutio Antoniniana* must be earlier than that.

Alternatively one can try to date the constitution independently of Ulpian's text, and then relate Ulpian's enterprise to the date so fixed. One argument for 212, the traditional date, is that Dio deals with the edict,[199] which he says was directed to increasing the revenue, in conjunction with other events which occurred immediately after Geta's murder at the end of 211. Secondly, that murder is often taken to be the occasion for the thanks which, according to P. Giessen 40,[200] along with the extension of citizenship, Caracalla offers the gods for his escape from danger. For the elder brother represented the killing as an act of self-defence against the younger who had plotted to assassinate him.[201] In the Giessen papyrus, also, the edict which follows that relating to the *constitutio Antoniniana* is subscribed 11 June 212 and was posted in Alexandria on 10 February 213. The third edict on the papyrus belongs to 215 or 216. Hence if the texts are in chronological order the first should be earlier than 11 June 212, or at least than 10 February 213. Lastly, arguments as to the date have been based on the effect of the constitution in causing newly enfranchised citizens to adopt the name Aurelius in recognition of their emancipation by Caracalla.

None of these arguments is conclusive. Dio is no annalist; Geta's alleged plot was not the only danger that Caracalla evaded during his reign[202]; the papyrus need not have recorded the edicts in chronological order. Nevertheless, the struggle with Geta and the guilt of having killed him,

[197] Millar (1962) 124; Crifò (1976) 627.
[198] *D.* 1.5.17 (Ulp. 22 *ed.*).
[199] Dio 77.9.4—5.
[200] On which see Sherwin—White (1973) 279 f.
[201] Dio 77.3.1; Herodian 4.4.3—4.
[202] *HA* Caracalla 5.8; Seston (1966) 877 (Caracalla's illness during German campaign of 213).

whether to forestall attack or not, was for Caracalla psychologically more traumatic than any incident that occurred later, and so more suited to be the occasion of a grand gesture.

Perhaps the most relevant evidence is that drawn from the adoption of the name Aurelius by newly enfranchised citizens. This is not always easy to interpret, both because it would take some time for all but the politically alert to understand the new state of the law, and because the use of the name Aurelius may have explanations other than recent enfranchisement. Gilliam[203] adduces a gravestone from Saittai in Lydia which records the death of a lady on 3 March 213. Though she is not described as an Aurelia her husband and sons are given the imperial name. This would seem to show that news of the constitution reached that area in or soon after March 213. An inscription of 13 January 213[204] records as M. Aurelius Claudius Pompeianus a man who on the same day eight years later is simply Claudius Pompeianus. The Aurelius of the first inscription could be interpreted as giving effect to the *constitutio Antoniniana*, something later regretted. While the evidence is inconclusive, nothing positive can be said to point to a date later than the traditional 212. Until such evidence is found, the interpretation of the edict which sees it as intended to erase the memory of, or at least propangandize the victor's version of, Geta's murder is the more persuasive.

Cosmopolitian ideas, in the spirit of Alexander of Macedon, were in tune with Caracalla's outlook. The same can be said of Ulpian. His version of the law of nature extends, indeed, beyond the human species to animals.[205] He contemplates the use of languages such as Punic, Gallic, and Assyrian (Aramaic).[206] By the date of the text which mentions Assyrian (216) Caracalla was planning to marry the daughter of the king of Parthia and to realize Alexander's dream of a united empire.[207]

It seems, then, that Ulpian is attuned to the ideology of Caracalla's reign. Can one go further? If the *constitutio Antoniniana* belongs to 212, and Ulpian's gradiose plan was executed from 213 onwards, was it part of Caracalla's, or Julia Domna's vision that he should reduce the Roman law of nearly a thousand years to manageable order for the sake, among others, of the new citizens? Readers of the jurist's edictal commentary will notice what pains he takes to show that the praetor's edict is not merely a set of provisions adapted to the ways of Romans, but reasonable, useful, sensible, and appropriate to all.[208] On that view, which I believe to be the one

---

[203] Gilliam (1965) 74; Herrmann (1972) 519, 526; earlier evidence Bell (1947).
[204] *CIL* XIII 7338; Schleiermacher (1961) 166–8; *Ann. épig.* (1962) 228.
[205] *D.* 1.1.1.3 (1 *inst.*).
[206] *D.* 32.11 pr. (2 *fid.*), 45.1.1.6 (48 *Sab*).
[207] Dio 78.1.1; Herodian 4.10.11; Gianelli–Mazarrino (1956) 284–5; Walser (1975) 628, 645. Doubts by Timpe (1967) 470, *contra* Vogt (1969) 279.
[208] e.g. *D.* 2.2.1 pr. (3 *ed.*), 2.13.1 pr. (4 *ed.*), 2.14.1 pr. (4 *ed.*), 2.7.1 pr (5 *ed.*), 3.1.1 pr. (6 *ed.*), 3.5.1

[*See opposite page for n. 208 cont.*]

justified by an attentive reading of the texts, Ulpian was not simply producing a commentary to rival or surpass that of Paul. He was attempting something new, in the light of a political development which, after a slow evolution over two centuries, had now reached its maturity.

The motives behind the *constitutio Antoniniana* resolve into three. Least important, perhaps, is the desire to increase revenue, though Dio, to discredit Caracalla, makes it the principal consideration.[209] The amount raised by extending inheritance tax to the new citizens could not be very great, given that the richest were citizens already. Capitation and land taxes were paid even by non-citizens. Of greater psychological significance was the emperor's design to appease the gods (nominally to thank them) by increasing the circle of their worshippers. P. Giessen 40 emphasizes this motive.[210] In the long term the third strand, universalism, was more important. The dynasty drew strength from areas what were not wholly Roman or Greek: Africa for instance, and Syria. In the latter, at least, universalist religions were widespread: sun-worship and various sorts of monotheism. Though no intellectual, Caracalla was quick-witted. He was aware of the prevailing currents of opinion, some of them associated with his mother and her circle. A lawyer from Syria, exposed to the same winds and alive to the simplification that common citizenship would bring, might well support or even suggest the change. It was the sort of grand but simple idea to appeal to Caracalla, an intelligent man bent on greatness but impatient of niceties. Besides, it possessed an anti-establishment flavour which may have been to his taste. Caracalla liked to mix with soldiers, live austerely, and take his share of menial tasks. He would not have been displeased by the irritation which his measure caused to those, already citizens, the value of whose status was diluted by the extension of citizen rights.

Crifo attaches importance to the circle of Julia Domna as an element in Ulpian's intellectual life.[211] It is Philostratus of Lemnos who speaks of her 'circle' and calls her a φιλόσοφος.[212] Dio also speaks of her as 'giving

(10 *ed.*), 4.1.1 (11 *ed.*), 4.3.1 pr. (11 *ed.*), 4.4.1 pr. (11 *ed.*), 27.6.1 pr. (12 *ed.*), 4.6.1 (12 *ed.*), 4.9.1.1 (14 *ed.*), 11.1.2 (22 *ed.*), 9.3.1.1 (23 *ed.*), 11.6.1 pr. (24 *ed.*), 10.4.1 (24 *ed.*), 11.7.12.3 (25 *ed.*), 13.5.1 pr. (27 *ed.*), 14.1.1 pr. (28 *ed.*), 14.3.1 (28 *ed.*), 14.4.1 pr. (29 *ed.*), 16.3.1.2, 4 (30 *ed.*), 25.5.1 pr. (34 *ed.*), 26.10.1 pr. (35 *ed.*), 27.4.1 pr. (36 *ed.*), 47.6.1 pr. (38 *ed.*), 39.4.12 pr. (38 *ed.*), 47.4.1.1 (38 *ed*), 38.1.2 pr. (38 *ed.*), 47.6.1 pr. (38 *ed.*), 37.4.8 pr. (40 *ed.*), 37.5.1 pr. (40 *ed.*), 37.6.1 pr. (40 *ed.*), 37.8.1.1 (40 *ed.*), 37.11.2 pr. (41 *ed.*), 38.2.1 pr. (42 *ed.*), 37.12.1 pr. (45 *ed.*), 38.6.1.5 (46 *ed.*), 29.4.1 pr. (50 *ed.*), 40.12.14 pr. (55 *ed.*), 47.8.2.1 (56 *ed.*), 47.9.1.1 (56 *ed.*), 28.8.7.1 (60 *ed.*), 43.3.1.1 (62 *ed.*), 43.4.1.1 (62 *ed.*), 42.8.1.1 (66 *ed.*), 43.3.1.2 (67 *ed.*), 43.8.2.1 (68 *ed.*), 43.8.2.10 (68 *ed.*), 43.9.1.1 (68 *ed.*), 43.15.1.1 (68 *ed.*), 43.16.1.1 (69 *ed.*), 43.18.1.1 (70 *ed.*), 43.19.3.12 (70 *ed.*), 43.20.1.39 (70 *ed.*), 43.21.1.1 (70 *ed.*), 43.22.1.7 (70 *ed.*), 43.24.1.1 (71 *ed.*), 43.26.2.2 (71 *ed.*), 21.1.1.2 (1 *ed. cur.*).

[209] Dio 77.9.5.   [210] P. Giess. 40.11.

[211] Crifò (1976) 734–6; Nörr (1972) 20, literature at 21[58]; *RE* XI 926, 923; Benario (1958*b*); Gilmore Williams (1902); Mundle (1961).

[212] *Vit. soph.* 2.30.1.

herself to philosophy' (φιλοσοφεῖν).[213] The terms are to be taken loosely.
A φιλόσοφος is a person with theoretical interests, and to philosophize is
to have such interests.[214] What Julia's were can perhaps be inferred in part
from the fact that she persuaded Philostratus to write the biography of
Apollonius of Tyana.[215] He was a miracle-worker and saint, or on another
view a charlatan, of the time of Domitian, before whom he is said to have
been strikingly outspoken in his own defence. On one interpretation, his
life as written by Philostratus is meant as a pagan counterpart to the
Christian gospels. Some Christians certainly took it in that sense.[216]
Though Ulpian must have known Julia Domna well, it is questionable to
what extent he sympathized with the values which the life of Apollonius
seeks to propagate. When dealing with claims for medical fees before the
provincial governor, he denies any claim to those 'who make use of
incantations or imprecations or, if I may resort to the vulgar term adopted
by impostors, of exorcism'.[217] This is strong language, and rules out any
close sympathy with miracle-workers, pagan or Christian. 'Those are not
forms of medicine', he goes on 'although some people say in their favour
that they have done them good'. In the same passage, which probably
belongs to 215, Ulpian rules out claims for fees by philosophers, although
philosophy is a sacred calling, *res religiosa*.[218] It should be the first principle
of philosophy not to work for money. For the same reason professors of
civil law cannot claim fees.[219] Their profession, which in a famous passage
of the *institutiones* Ulpian calls 'the true philosophy'[220] in contrast with that
which is simulated, is highly sacred, *res sanctissima*, and should neither be
valued nor devalued by assessment in monetary terms.

Why does Ulpian assert that law is the true philosophy? Nörr has offered
a plausible explanation.[221] Thinking people were no longer content with
the traditional way of life, serving the state, and conforming with the
received laws and customs. They were looking for something more
satisfying. Some found it in new religions, Christianity or sun-worship.
Others turned to philosophy. Intellectuals were expected to have some
articulate set of values other than mere conservatism. At a time when
Tertullian had abandoned law for religion[222] and Gregory Thaumaturgus

[213] Dio 76.15.6−7.

[214] Nörr (1973) 568.

[215] Philostratus *Vit. Apoll.* 1.3; Nörr (1972) 21; MacMullen (1967).

[216] Eusebius *Contra vitam Apoll.*; Lactantius *div. inst.* 5.3. There are parallels in *Vit. Apoll.* 8.30−1.

[217] D. 50.13.1.3 (Ulp. 8 *omn. trib.*).

[218] D. 50.13.1.4 (Ulp. 8 *omn. trib.*).

[219] D. 50.13.1.5 (Ulp. 8 *omn. trib.*).

[220] D. 1.1.1.1 (Ulp. 1 *inst.*).

[221] Nörr (1973) 555; Frezza (1968) 368.

[222] Q. Septimius Tertullianus (*c.*160−240) expressed hostility to the Roman empire after his
conversion to Christianity (*c.*195) and especially to Montanism (*c.*207). Whether he is the same as the
contemporary jurist Tertullianus (Pal. 2.34−23) is an open question: *RE* 5.1.822; Kunkel (1967) 236;
Barnes (1971) 22−9.

was soon to do the same,[223] a lawyer who was alive to the new currents needed to defend his calling by showing that it was based on reason and served the ideal of justice for all. This is why Ulpian, no theorist and, in the strict sense, no philosopher, advances the claim that law is the true philosophy.

The study of law is the highest form of 'philosophy' because law gives to notions of right and wrong[224] a concrete, practical form, and because its intellectual demands are exacting.[225] Philosophy in a narrow sense, though not on a level with law, is to be respected. Superstition, for example Judaism,[226] or imposture, for instance that practised by exorcists,[227] is condemned. If we bear these moral rankings in mind, it is not difficult to see how Ulpian stood in relation to Julia Domna and the intellectuals whom she patronized. He sympathized with their cosmopolitan outlook. Outspoken and self-confident himself, he will have liked the freedom of speech, παρρησία, which Philostratus attributes to Apollonius of Tyana.[228] Whether we can go further, and attach him to any particular school of philosophy, in the narrow sense, or to any particular religion, is doubtful. Lawyers who are interested in philosophy tend to treat it eclectically, as a source of ideas rather than of systems.

Frezza[229] argues that Ulpian's outlook is Neoplatonic rather than Stoic. The jurist reflects one current of ideas in the Syria of his age. Thus Porphyrius, who was born at Tyre about 234,[230] was a Neoplatonic philosopher who affirmed, in a manner antipathetic to the Stoics, the rational character of animals.[231] It looks as if the famous passage of Ulpian on the law of nature, in which he asserts that animals are thought to know about marriage, the procreation of children and their education by experience[232] (*peritia*), and hence not merely by instinct, is to be taken as Neoplatonic. In regard to the *actio de pauperie*, too, he makes the liability of the animal owner depend on whether the animal acts *contra naturam*. His examples show that, here too, he is attributing rational behaviour to animals.[233] The stoics, on the other hand, and the Christians, if Origen is taken as representative, thought of man as the sole rational creature. Lower animals were governed wholly by instinct.[234]

---

[223] *In Originem* 1.7 (*Patr. Gr.* 10.1052−3).

[224] *D.* 1.1.1.1 (Ulp. 1 *inst*: *iustitiam namque colimus et boni et aequi notitiam profitemur, aequum ab iniquo separantes, licitum ab illicito discernentes, bonos non solum metu poenarum verum etiam praemiorum quoque exhortatione efficere cupientes*. Note the practical emphasis).

[225] Gregory Thaumaturgus, *in Orig.* 1.7, above, n. 223.

[226] *D.* 50.2.3.3 (Ulp. 3 *off. proc*.).

[227] *D.* 50.13.1.3 (8 *omn. trib.*).

[228] *Vit. Apoll* 1.28−32, 4.44, 5.28, 6.32, 6.42, 7.11, 7.32−3, 8.5.

[229] Frezza (1968) 363.

[230] *RE* 22.1 275, 276 (Beutler)

[231] Porphyrius *de abstinentia* 3.10; Dierauer (1977) 262−3.

[232] *D.* 1.1.1.3 (Ulp. 1 *inst*.).

[233] *D.* 9.1.1.7 (Ulp. 18 *ed*.).   [234] Origen *Contra Celsum* 4.86f.

It would be a mistake to attribute to the jurist a system of philosophy rather than a set of values. One of Ulpians's values was certainly that of participation in public life. Quintilian seems to have had a deep influence on Ulpian's prose style, and his attitude to public affairs, rather than that of Seneca, shaped Ulpian's.[235] That the jurist was sensitive to religious feeling is clear from the terms in which he describes the profession and study of the law. It is hardly possible to be more precise. Book 7 *de officio proconsulis* contained a catalogue of imperial rescripts against Christians.[236] This does not itself demonstrate hostility to Christianity. But Ulpian was surely hostile to any system of thought which led its devotees to prefer private salvation to public responsibility. His 'philosophy' is that which Howe attributes to the jurists of the age collectively,[237] a determination to see that justice was done to all. The extra element which he brought to this professional philosophy was the conception of the lawyer as priest, called by the gods to see that right prevails. Which particular god or gods we cannot know.

In a broad sense, Ulpian certainly belonged to the circle of the imperial family. In *de censibus*, to be dated to 213 or 214, he tells us that he knows that Caracalla allowed his cousin Julia Mamaea to retain the consular dignity acquired through her first marriage though she later married a second husband not of consular rank.[238] Her second husband was, in fact, Gessius Marcianus,[239] father of Alexianus, the future emperor Alexander. He mentions, too, that indulgence was granted to Arrius Meander, legal counsellor to the emperor, so that he was, by way of exception, excused from a guardianship already assumed.[240] It is indeed rewarding to analyse the texts in which Ulpian claims to know something or relate something from personal experience, often using terms such as *scio, retineo, memini*, or the like. Most of these are reminiscences of cases, such as those in which he advised a praetor,[241] or of his reading from books.[242] Others concern practice and procedure, for example that of provincial governors, as regards sentencing, relegation, or torture.[243] One or two shed light on other interests or experiences. Thus, Ulpian knows that some ships do not take cargo but only passengers. These may be restricted by their owners to particular routes, for instance the crossing from Cassiopa or Dyrrachium to Brundisium.[244] Perhaps he had made this crossing himself on the route

235 Quintilian *Inst. or.* 11.1.35, cf. 12.2.17.
236 Lactantius *div. inst.* 5.11; Barnes (1968).
237 Howe (1942) 43.
238 D. 1.9.12 pr. (2 *cens.*).
239 *RE* 7.1.1328 (Stein); *PIR²* 9 171; Birley (1971) 297.
240 D. 4.4.11.2 (Ulp. 11 *ed.*).
241 D. 4.2.9.3 (11 *ed.*), 4.3.2 (11 *ed.*), 28.5.35.1 (4 *disp.*).
242 D. 49.2.1.4 (1 *appell.*).
243 D. 48.18.3 (14 *Sab.*), 48.13.7 (7 *off. proc.*), 48.22.7.9 (10 *off. proc.*), cf. *FV* 242 (1 *off. pr. tut.*).
244 D. 14.1.1.12 (Ulp. 28 *ed.*).

between Rome and Tyre. Again, the interdict against changing the course of a public river should be construed so as to permit the defence of public or private interest. Ulpian knows, he says, that in practice landowners do dam rivers and alter river banks for their own purposes.[245] Provided they do no harm to their neighbours, this should be allowed. These are the words of a landowner.

What were Ulpian's relations with Caracalla, Julia Domna, and the imperial court during the time when he was writing his treatises? Definite conclusions are not possible, but there is some suggestive evidence. If the dating proposed in chapters 5 to 7 is correct, there was some evolution in Ulpian's attitude. From about the spring of 213 he begins to give Caracalla priority over Severus:[246] *imperator Antoninus cum divo patre* rather than *divus Severus et imperator noster*. Texts which draw on personal experience, with *scio* and the like, are found in 213 and 214 but not thereafter until well into 217.[247] Again, passages which adopt a condescending tone towards Caracalla and other emperors belong to 213 or 214.[248] Texts which refer to Caracalla with more elaboration than is necessary in a legal text (*imperator Antoninus Augustus*), continue as far as 52 *ed.*[249] and 37 *sab.*[250] late 215 and spring of 216 respectively. A text of early 217 points out that, contrary to Cicero's view, a defendant may fail to appear for a good reason, for example fear of a tyrant's cruelty, enemy attack, or domestic sedition. This seems to be the only reference to tyranny in the juristic texts.[251] In the reign of Macrinus, Ulpian speaks of Caracalla simply as Antoninus, and restores Severus to his proper seniority.[252] Ulpian therefore adapted himself to the political climate. The facts set out suggest that initial warmth and exuberance cooled or subsided in the later stages of Caracalla's reign. That would not be surprising. Whether Ulpian remained at court or withdrew to his estates to write, or began at court and later withdrew, is an open question. He continues to cite constitutions of Caracalla throughout the reign,[253] but it is impossible to tell whether these are recent.

IV (C). ULPIAN'S CAREER: THE REIGNS OF ELAGABAL AND ALEXANDER (218–23)

If the argument of chapters 5 to 7 is accepted, Ulpian finished his five-year plan of composition at the end of 217, under Macrinus. There is no evidence that he wrote anything further. In 1962 I supposed that a second

---

[245] *D.* 43.13.1.7 (Ulp. 68 *ed.*).   [246] Ch. 5 pp. 133–8, 153.

[247] Ch. 7 p. 166. There is a gap in *scio* texts between 21 *Sab* (second half of 214) and 68 *ed.* (not before spring 217).

[248] Ch. 7 p. 165.

[249] *D.* 36.4.5.16; ch. 5 p. 135.   [250] *D.* 26.1.3.1; ch. 6 p. 150.

[251] *D.* 42.4.7.4 (59 *ed.*).   [252] Ch. 5 p. 141.

[253] Up to *D.* 47.10.7.6 (57 *ed.*), early 217.

edition of *de censibus* was prepared under Elagabal.[254] The reason was that
Paul apparently attributes to Elagabal the grant of *ius Italicum* to Emesa,[255]
while Ulpian attributes it to an *imperator noster*,[256] who by reference to other
such grants, e.g. to Tyre, appears to be Caracalla. The two texts could be
reconciled if it was accepted that Ulpian revised his *de censibus* in the reign
of a new *imperator noster*, viz. Elagabal. But this rather forced hypothesis is
probably wrong. Paul has made a mistake,[257] and the grant to Emesa goes
back to Caracalla, as one would expect from the fact that his mother's
family came from there. Again, Lenel thought[258] that the five books *de
adulteriis* were written after the death of Caracalla. But Mommsen is
probably right[259] in arguing that the *divi Severus et Antoninus* of book 1 of
that work is a retrospective alteration. In truth we lack reliable clues to
Ulpian's career under Elagabal. On the one hand it is possible that he shared
in the disfavour which seems to have befallen Tyre fairly early in Elagabal's
reign. Since in the reign of Alexander Ulpian emerges as a close
collaborator with the emperor's mother and almost a guardian of the
young emperor,[260] it is reasonable to suppose that in the conflict between
Elagabal and Soaemias on the one side and Alexander, Mamaea, and Maesa
on the other, in late 221 and 222, Ulpian sided with Alexander. Yet that
does not exclude the possibility that Ulpian held office under Elagabal. The
scandals surrounding the emperor-priest, his neglect of official business, his
attempt to revolutionize the state religion, his overt homosexuality and
transvestism, did not prevent respectable people from holding office under
him.

Only the *HA* and Aurelius Victor have something to say about Ulpian's
fate under Elagabal. The author of *HA*, in his life of that emperor, records
that early in 222, when he was trying to secure Alexander's removal from
office or death, he told the senate to leave the city.[261] Sabinus, a man of
consular rank 'to whom Ulpian had written books' remained, and escaped
death because the centurion to whom Elagabal gave the order was hard of
hearing. 'He also removed [viz. from Rome] Ulpian the jurist, as he was a
good man, and Silvinus the orator, whom he had appointed teacher of the
Caesar [viz. Alexander]. Silvinus was killed but Ulpian saved.'

The author is mischievously pretending that the (Masurius) Sabinus on
whose *ius civile* Ulpian wrote a commentary in fifty-one books was a man
of consular rank, a *vir consularis*, of the time of Elagabal. This is a frivolous

[254] Honoré (1962) 212.
[255] *D.* 50.15.8.6 (Paul 2 *cens.*).
[256] *D.* 50.15.1.4 (Ulp. 1 *cens.*).
[257] Gualandi (1963) II 200–1; d'Ors (1942–3) 42–3, *contra* Mommsen (1908) II 155, Karlowa
(1901) II 748, Fitting (1908) 97, Krueger (1912) 238[123].
[258] *Pal.* 2.931[2].
[259] Mommsen (1905) II 169.
[260] Zonaras 12.15; Zosimus 1.11.2.
[261] *HA* Elagabal 16.1–4.

invention. The *HA* life of Elagabal up to this point (chapter 17) is, however, not without value; much of it seems to be drawn from Dio and Herodian.[262] Herodian himself says that, regretting the adoption of Alexander and the influence of his teachers over him, Elagabal removed them from the court, executed the most distinguished, and drove others away.[263] Ulpian would have been an obvious choice to instruct Alexander in legal and administrative matters. Hence the *HA* statement that he was expelled towards the end of Elagabal's reign is not to be rejected out of hand.

Victor has a different account.[264] Speaking of Alexander, he says that he retained Ulpian in the praetorian prefecture, to which Elagabal had appointed him. Paul was, at the beginning of Alexander's reign, restored to his country, and by his treatment of these lawyers Alexander showed his zeal for equity and his attitude towards the best people. In this account, then, Paul, not Ulpian, has by inference been banished by Elagabal. That emperor made Ulpian praetorian prefect and Alexander retained him in the post. This last statement cannot be true, since Elagabal's two praetorian prefects, who remained loyal to him, were killed at the same time as their master.[265] Although not totally impossible, a praetorian prefecture for Ulpian under Elagabal would have to belong to an earlier part of his reign, and it is strange that it should not be mentioned in any other source. Even the *HA* seems to have doubted Victor's report, since, according to its life of *Alexander*, 'some say that Paul and Ulpian were made prefects by Elagabal, others by Alexander'. Perhaps Victor took the statement from the elusive imperial chronicle, the *Kaisergeschichte*,[266] but in that case it seems that the chronicle was mistaken.

What, then, was Ulpian doing during the reign of Elagabal? Given his personality, he cannot have been inactive. He was not writing. He may have taught Alexander, at least in the years 221–2. He may have held one of the lesser prefectures, such as the prefecture of supply (*praefectura annonae*), in which office he appears early in Alexander's reign.[267] There was some continuity between the officials of Elagabal and Alexander. Valerius Comazon, praetorian prefect under the former, later out of office, returns as urban prefect in Alexander's reign.[268] Rescripts of 3 February[269] and 19 February 222,[270] in the last month of Elagabal's rule,

262 Pflaum (1978) 157. Barnes (1972) 53 says the source is Marius Maximus. On Elagabal generally see *RE* 2.15.391, *PIR*[1] v 184.
263 Herodian 5.7.6.
264 Victor *Caes.* 24.   265 Dio 79.21.1.
266 First postulated by Enmann, *Philologus Supp.* IV (1884) 337–501. See Howe (1942) 105.
267 *CJ* 8.37.4 (31 March 222).
268 *RE* 2.6.2412 Valerius no. 134; *PIR*[1] v 42; Pflaum (1960) no. 290; Howe (1942) 74 no. 30.
269 *CJ* 9.1.3 (3 Feb. 222 *non aliter . . . nisi prius* cf. Honoré (1981) 72).
270 *CJ* 4.44.1 (19 Feb. 222 *per vim coactus*, cf. Honoré (1981) 72–3, *male fide enim emptio irrita est*, cf. *CJ* 2.3.8, 12.Sept. 222).

look to be by the same hand as those of the first months of Alexander. Indeed a text of 30 December 218,[271] preserved in the epitome of the Gregorian code, is apparently in the same style. So Alexander's first secretary *a libellis* held office in Elagabal's reign and was retained by Alexander. Indeed, he may have held that office for several years. It is not impossible that Ulpian, too, was retained in or restored to an office to which Elagabal had appointed him.

Elagabal's behaviour, though hardly surprising in a boy who, brought up as a priest and surrounded by women, became emperor at the age of thirteen or fourteen, undermined his position. Attempts were made to restore it by marrying him to Annia Faustina, a descendant of Marcus, in 221,[272] and persuading him to appoint his cousin Alexianus, now called Alexander, Caesar, probably on 26 June 221.[273] These failed, and many of Elagabal's supporters deserted him. On 13 March 222 he, his mother and his two praetorian prefects were murdered.[274] Alexander succeeded him on 13 or 14 March,[275] and on 31 March refers in a rescript to Ulpian as prefect of supply, jurist, and friend (*secundum responsum Domitii Ulpiani praefecti annonae iuris consulti amici mei*).[276] The term *amicus* is added here, as in other rescripts, to emphasize that the office holder enjoys the emperor's confidence. Its technical meaning is that of a person admitted (or who would be admitted) to greet the emperor at his morning salutation.[277]

A further rescript of 1 December 222 instructs the owner of a warehouse, a victim of breaking and entering, to approach the provincial governor who, if he thinks a heavy punishment is called for, will send the culprit to 'Ulpian, praetorian prefect and my parent' (*ad Domitium Ulpianum praefectum praetorio et parentem meum*).[278]

The order of Ulpian's offices is in itself nothing unusual.[279] Praetorian prefects, especially on the civil side, were mainly recruited from prefects of Egypt, prefects of supply (*praefecti annonae*) and prefects of police (*praefecti vigilum*). An able lawyer who had held the *libelli* might hope, apart from a further secretaryship in the central offices (for example the Latin letters, *epistulae Latinae*), to proceed to a prefecture, and, in exceptional cases, the praetorian prefecture. Papinian is known to have had the *libelli* and, after an interval of three years, the praetorian office.[280] He may have occupied one

[271] *Epit. Cod. Greg. Herm. Vis.* 14.1 (30 Dec. 218).

[272] *PIR*² A 710; Dio 79.5.3−5, 79.9.4.

[273] Herodian 5.7.1−6; Whittaker (1970) II 58¹; Dusanic (1964).

[274] Dio 79.21.1; Herodian 5.8.8; *HA* Elagabal 17.4−7.

[275] Whittaker (1970) II 74¹.   [276] *CJ* 8.37.4 (31 March 222).

[277] *RE* 1.1831 (Oehler); Crook (1950) 163¹³⁶, Grosso (1968) 207f.; *D.* 49.1.1.3.

[278] *CJ* 4.65.4−1 (1 Dec. 222). On the praetorians see Durry (1938) Passerini (1939); on the office see Palanque (1933), Ensslin (1954).

[279] Howe (1942) 16f.; Modrzejewski−Zawadski (1967) 565, 610−11; Ensslin *RE* 22.2 (1954) 2391−2502; Reinmuth (1935), (1967).

[280] *RE* 1.572; *PIR*² A 388; Pflaum (1960) no. 220; Kunkel (1967) 224; Honoré (1979) 57−8, (1981) 56−9.

of the lower prefectures in this intermediate period. Modestinus held the
libelli and, later, the prefecture of police.[281] He is not known to have gone
to the praetorian command. The structure of Ulpian's career therefore
conforms broadly to the pattern of the period.

Ulpian's promotion to the praetorian prefecture was procured, it seems,
by Julia Mamaea.[282] There were two stages in it. In the first he was placed
over the two existing praetorian prefects, Flavius and Geminius Chrestus,
who had been appointed by Alexander at the beginning of his reign,[283] in a
supervisory role. Later, but perhaps before the rescript of 1 December,
Ulpian had Flavianus and Chrestus put to death and became sole prefect.[284]
He had then secured the sort of pre-eminence enjoyed by Plautianus.
Though, unlike the latter, he was not actually related by marriage, so far as
we know, to the emperor, his position as Mamaea's man of confidence
justified his being described as a sort of father to Alexander, *parens meus*.[285]

The exact details of the events by which Ulpian attained a sole prefecture
and a dominant position in the state, in far less time that it took Sejanus or
Plautianus to do the same, are obscure. Dio, as summarized by Xiphilinus,
speaks of Ulpian with some disdain.[286] As soon as he became emperor,
Alexander entrusted to 'one Domitius Ulpianus' the command of the
praetorians and the other affairs of the empire. After excusing himself for
not being able to give a full account of the events of the reign because of his
absence from Rome, Dio returns to Ulpian. He corrected, says the
historian, many abuses introduced by Elagabal, but put Flavianus and
Chrestus to death in order to succeed them. Not long afterwards he was
attacked by the praetorians at night and killed, though he ran to the palace
and took refuge with the emperor and his mother.

Zosimus has a different account.[287] The young Alexander's good
disposition aroused hopes for his reign. He appointed Flavianus and
Chrestus prefects. They were not without experience in military matters
and highly capable in civil affairs. But Mamaea, the emperor's mother,
placed Ulpian over them as a supervisor and virtually a joint emperor.
Ulpian was an outstanding law-maker and able both to handle current
affairs and to foresee future needs with accuracy. In disgust at Ulpian's
promotion the soldiers secretly plotted to do away with him. Mamaea
heard of this, and, as soon as she detected the plot, made away with the
plotters. Ulpian was then made sole master of the prefectorial authority.
However, he became suspect to the troops, for reasons which Zosimus

[281] *RE* 8.1.668; *PIR²* H 112; Kunkel (1967) 259; Honoré (1981) 78–81.
[282] Zosimus 1.11.2.
[283] Zosimus *ibid.*; Zonaras 12.15.
[284] Dio 80.2.2; Zosimus 1.11.3; Zonaras 12.15.
[285] *CJ* 4.65.4.1 (1 Dec. 222).
[286] Dio 80.2.2–4.
[287] Zosimus 1.11.2–3; followed by Jörs *RE* 5.1437, cf. Syncellus *Chron.* 1 673.

cannot accurately explain, since historians differ about the matter. A revolt occurred and he was killed. Even the emperor was unable to come to his assistance.

Whatever its source, the account in Zosimus is plausible and not really inconsistent with Xiphilinus' epitome of Dio. There were three periods. In the first Flavianus and Chrestus were Alexander's prefects. Then Ulpian was put over them as a super-prefect. This aroused resentment, and, getting in the first blow, Ulpian and Mamaea forestalled a possible (or perhaps known) plot by having Flavianus and Chrestus put to death. Like Caracalla, Ulpian believed that, when conflict is inevitable, a pre-emptive strike is best.

The details are obscure. Dio, as epitomized, does not mention Mamaea's part in securing Ulpian's promotion, but it must be remembered that when Dio wrote, though Ulpian was dead, Mamaea was still living. Zosimus is therefore probably right in attributing Ulpian's ascendancy to Mamaea. The HA reports that Alexander regarded Ulpian as his guardian, first against his mother's opposition, then with her gratitude (Ulpianum pro tutore habuit, primum repugnante matre deinde gratias agente).[288] The first part is roughly correct, since it corresponds to the rescript of 1 December 222 in which Ulpian is the emperor's 'parent'.[289] The second may be a mere embroidery, or reflect a change of policy on the part of the imperial ladies Maesa and Mamaea. Perhaps they first favoured Flavianus and Chrestus, then switched to Ulpian. The same theme returns, impliedly, in a later passage of the HA life.[290] After a list of (largely imaginary) councillors of Alexander, all men of great wisdom, we are told that, in the first days of his reign, they were brushed aside by a band of evil men (et hos quidem malorum cohors depulerat, quae circumvenerat Alexandrum primis diebus). Afterwards these evil councillors were killed or expelled and the good ones took their place. Perhaps this is meant to reflect the replacement of Flavianus, Chrestus, and their supporters by Ulpian and his, though an attack on the advisers of Arcadius or Honorius may also be intended.

At any rate Mamaea and Ulpian (and Maesa if she too was on the same side) seem to have been guilty of undue haste in disposing of Flavianus and Chrestus. They intended, no doubt, to undo the abuses of Elagabal's administration and to reduce the troops, praetorian and legionary, to discipline. Their aims were admirable, but the methods chosen were calculated to maximize resentment. Ulpian's sole prefecture recalled the overmighty Plautianus. And whereas Plautianus was a successful general, Ulpian had nothing to commend him to the troops.

The revolt which ended in Ulpian's death will occupy our attention

[288] HA Alexander 51.4.
[289] CJ 4.65.4.1 (1 Dec. 222).
[290] HA Alexander 68.1.

later. The present task is to fix, if possible, the chronology of the events of 222. This has been carefully investigated by Modrzejewski and Zawadski.[291] They think that Flavianus and Chrestus were eliminated early in the summer of 222. Ulpian then remained sole prefect until the spring of 223 when new colleagues were appointed.

The rescript of 1 December 222 which speaks of Ulpian as praetorian prefect[292] need not imply that he was then sole prefect. Nevertheless, he probably was. Dio writes as if Ulpian's ascendancy came right at the beginning of Alexander's reign.[293] On the other hand, some time must be allowed after Ulpian's appointment as super-prefect for the praetorians to hatch a plot against him, and for Mamaea to discover it. Some significance may attach to the fact that the number of rescripts greatly increases from September 222 onwards,[294] and that a new secretary *a libellis* is composing them from not later than 15 October of that year.[295] Ulpian would certainly have pressed Alexander to pay close attention to that branch of the administration. The evidence drawn from rescripts suggests that he was fully in control by September or October, but perhaps not as early as the summer. The elimination of Flavianus and Chrestus may not have taken place before August.

Though Zosimus says plainly that Ulpian was sole prefect after the death of his two subordinates, he apparently did not long remain so. The album of Canusium,[296] which is dated to October 223, mentions among its senatorial patrons, in this order, T. Lorenius Celsus, M. Aedinius Iulianus, L. Didius Marinus, and L. Domitius Honoratus. Of these Domitius Honoratus was prefect of Egypt, an equestrian post, towards the beginning of 222,[297] and Aedinius Iulianus held the same post towards the end of 222 and the beginning of 223.[298] Hence they must have acquired the rank of senators shortly before the album was inscribed. At this period of Alexander's reign there was a short-lived practice by which a praetorian prefect was automatically given senatorial status. On Modrzejewski's interpretation the Canusians were recording two pairs of praetorian prefects of the year 223. Lorenius Celsus and Aedinius Iulianus were, he thinks, the prefects in office in October 223 when the album was set up, Didius Marinus and Domitius Honoratus had held office earlier the same year. Ulpian is not mentioned, and must already have been dead.

---

[291] Modrzejewski–Zawadski (1967) 565, cf. Jardé (1925) 37; Howe (1942) 100.
[292] *CJ* 4.65.4.1 (1 Dec. 222).
[293] Dio 80.1.1.
[294] *CJ* has 15 rescripts from February to August, 36 for the last 4 months of the year.
[295] Honoré (1981) 71–2.
[296] *CIL* IX 338; Pflaum (1948) 37f.
[297] *PIR*² D 151; Howe (1942) 76 no. 37; Pflaum (1948) 40. On the prefects of Egypt see A. Stein (1950).
[298] *PIR*² A 113; Pflaum (1960) no. 297; Howe (1942) 76 no. 38; Pflaum (1948) 39.

Modrzejewski[299] holds therefore, that the pairs of praetorian prefects are listed in the *album* in reverse order of seniority, the Canusians feeling it necessary to mention the existing office-holders first. Since the whole argument rests on the assumption that the album records the patrons according to precedence, this is a bold view. But even if, with Grosso,[300] we retain the listed order of seniority, it nevertheless seems clear that in 223 Ulpian was obliged to accept junior colleagues in the prefecture.

Why was Ulpian's pre-eminence so soon undermined? The *Chronicon Paschale*[301] records incidents lasting all night (διανυκτέρευσις) for three successive days during 223. According to Dio-Xiphilinus,[302] even during Ulpian's lifetime there was a popular uprising against the praetorians, the cause of which was trivial. The fight lasted for three days and there were many killed on either side. The soldiers were defeated and turned to arson. The people, afraid that the whole city would burn, reluctantly came to terms with them. This uprising may be the disturbance assigned by the *Chronicon Paschale* to 223. If so, Ulpian's failure to control the praetorians perhaps undermined his prestige and led to the appointment of additional prefects. It was already becoming clear that a civilian, though capable of acting as joint prefect, like Papinian, was at sea when left on his own. The government, which should have learned the lesson of the reign of Macrinus, that an equestrian lawyer could not by himself control the army, had failed to do so.

Once Ulpian's reputation had been undermined he fell as quickly as Macrinus or Elagabal. He was attacked by the praetorians at night. He made for the palace and the protection of Alexander and Mamaea, but the soldiers followed. The emperor could not save him.[303] In the aftermath, says the epitome of Dio, Epagathus, who was largely responsible for the death of Ulpian, was sent to Egypt as governor. This was in order to prevent a possible disturbance in Rome if he should be punished there. He was taken thence to Crete and executed.[304] There were many rebellions by different people, and some of them caused serious alarm, but they were suppressed.

The death of Ulpian was a serious blow to the government. Like Macrinus, Mamaea had unsuccessfully tried to restore discipline and reduce the power of the troops. The regime survived, but only just, by virtue of dynastic prestige. Epagathus, a powerful figure of freedman stock, could not safely be arrested in Rome. To remove him, he was promoted to the prefecture of Egypt. The publication in 1966 of P. Oxy. 2565, recording

[299] Modrzejewski-Zawadski (1967) 593 f.
[300] Grosso (1968) 205; Chastagnol (1970) 45.
[301] *Chron. Pasch.* ann. 223; Modrzejewski–Zawadski (1967) 584–5.
[302] Dio 80.2.3; Jardé (1925) 63.
[303] Dio 80.2.2; Zosimus 1.11.3; Zonaras 12.15.
[304] Dio 80.2.3.

declarations of births in Egypt, showed that he was prefect in May/June 224 but ceased to be so immediately thereafter.[305]

This made it clear that Ulpian must have died before the middle of 224, not, as most scholars previously supposed, in 228. I shared this mistaken assumption, for which there were seemingly good grounds in Xiphilinus' summary of Dio. In excusing himself for his thin account of the early years of Alexander, Dio[306] explains that, after an illness, he went to his province of Africa, then, on returning to Italy, was sent as governor first to Dalmatia, then to upper Pannonia. The praetorians complained of Dio to Ulpian, since he ruled the Pannonian troops with a firm hand and they (the praetorians) feared that they would be compelled to submit to similar discipline. But Alexander paid no attention to their complaints and appointed Dio to a second consulship, as his colleague. This consulship can be dated to 229.[307]

Dio's account, highly compressed, suggested that his second consulship followed closely on the complaints to Ulpian. In any case these could not have been made until Dio had held this third provincial governorship, in Pannonia. Even if, contrary to the logic of Dio's narrative, his African command is put in the reign of Elagabal rather than Alexander, it is not easy to see how complaints about Dio's conduct in Pannonia could have been made to Ulpian before the summer of 223—the time when, on Modrzejewski's estimate, Ulpian was assassinated.

Perhaps the solution to the difficulty is that Epagathus need not have had very long in Egypt before he was taken to Crete and done to death. Suppose that Ulpian was killed in August 223. Epagathus became prefect of Egypt at the beginning of the following year and left in May or June. Dio was in Dalmatia in 222, in Pannonia in 223. News of his harshness there reached the capital and gave rise to complaints during the summer of 223, when Ulpian was nearing the end of his career as prefect. It is perhaps worth nothing that another reshuffle at the *libelli* took place in the second half of 223, not later than 28 October and perhaps as early as 30 August.[308] The incoming secretary, Herennius Modestinus,[309] was a pupil of Ulpian. The change was not therefore directed towards undoing Ulpian's work. Yet it may have been occasioned by his death, which presumably had its repercussions on other office holders. All things considered, a date in August 223[310] seems, on the evidence available, a reasonable estimate of the moment when his brief ascendancy ended.

Its very brevity presents a problem. If Ulpian held the reins of power for

---

[305] Barns–Parsons–Rea–Turner (1966) 102; Grosso (1968 b).
[306] Dio 80.1.2.
[307] Constitutions in *Corp. Iur. Civ.* II (ed. Krugger) 492.
[308] Honoré (1981) 73–4.
[309] Honoré (1981) 76–81.
[310] Chastagnol (1970) 45 argues for spring 223.

no more than a year or so, why do the sources, Dio as well as Victor, Zosimus, and the *HA*, make so much of his role? Dio says that he put right much that had gone wrong under Elagabal. No doubt an energetic and determined man could achieve much in a year. It is difficult to be specific. The *HA* contains detail, but it is of little value except as showing how its author thought a virtuous young ruler should behave. Its general plan is to contrast the evil Elagabal with the good Alexander.[311] If the author is indeed writing in or about AD 395, he presumably has in mind the emperors Arcadius and Honorius, then aged twelve and eleven respectively, and perhaps also Stilicho, who effectively ruled the west from 395 to 408. His history is addressed not to its ostensible patrons Dioletian and Constantine, but to them. Now the author of *HA*, like Ammianus Marcellinus,[312] is a partisan of the rule of law. It was natural for him to emphasize Alexander's strict adherence to legality and the leading role played by lawyers in his reign. Thus 'Ulpian is said to have been councillor of Alexander and the master of an office'[313] (*nam et consiliarius Alexandri et magister scrinii Ulpianus fuisse perhibetur*). No doubt the jurist was a member of Alexander's judicial council. He cannot have been the head of an office. His seniority was too great, and the three weeks between Alexander's succession and 31 March, when Ulpian is prefect of supply, is not long enough for another office to be held. 'He ordered that lawsuits and other business should be examined and analysed by the heads of the offices and by lawyers who were learned and loyal, before being submitted to himself.'[314] This sounds like historical wish-fulfilment by someone who has worked in one of the central offices.

Two passages concern Alexander's private audiences with Ulpian. 'After dispatching letters he admitted all his friends at once, and talked to them all together. He never received anyone alone except his prefect i.e. Ulpian who in view of his exceptional sense of justice, always advised him as a judge. Whenever he sent for someone, he called in Ulpian too'.[315] This, had it been the case, would have given Ulpian complete control over access to the emperor, and hence a dominant influence over him. Another passage asserts the 'notable fact that Alexander never granted an private audience in the palace except to the prefect and Ulpian'.[316] No doubt we should read 'except to the prefect Ulpian'. Herodian, who does not mention Ulpian, also speaks of the way in which Alexander was isolated from possibly corrupting influences and encouraged to spend much of his time on legal business.[317] As the author of *HA* sees the matter, the constant presence of a

---

[311] Pflaum (1978) 157.
[312] Ammianus 21.16.11, 22.9.9, 22.10.2, 30.4.11 f.
[313] *HA* Alexander 26.5 echoing Eutropius 8.23 or his source, cf. Festus 22.
[314] *HA* Alexander 15.6.
[315] *HA* Alexander 31.1−3.
[316] *HA* Alexander 67.2.   [317] Herodian 6.1.5−6.

just and experienced lawyer will prevent a young emperor from listening to calumny and being misled into injustice. It may all the same be true that Ulpian for a time controlled access to Alexander and so prevented others acquiring a rival influence over him.

The remaining *HA* references to Ulpian concern his stimulating conversation, which led Alexander to invite him to dinner frequently,[318] and Alexander's alleged project to make different classes wear different dress. Ulpian and Paul, it is said, opposed this on the ground that easy recognition would multiply insults and lead to brawls.[319]

In sum, the *HA* pictures Alexander as a good emperor because he treated Ulpian as his mentor and governed mainly according to his advice.[320] Clearly the author's account of the relations between them reflects his view of the way in which government should operate when the emperor is young and has an adviser of outstanding capacity. On one particular point he has attracted defenders. Both in the life of Niger and in that of Alexander, Paul[321] is said to have held a prefecture. As regards the proposal for distinctive dress, both are said to disapproved. Hence some have argued that they were joint praetorian prefects, though no text actually says this. Balog devoted a long article to defending the joint prefecture.[322]

A joint praetorian prefecture is really not possible. In the year that Ulpian was in that office we know the names of six actual or probable prefects under him.[323] Paul is not one of them. Besides, he was senior to Ulpian, and should have had precedence over him, had they held the office jointly. The case for a joint prefecture rests simply on an extensive interpretation of the *HA* passages mentioned.

Was Paul a praetorian prefect after Ulpian? Certainly he was alive and writing in the reign of Alexander.[324] There is no independent evidence that he was a prefect. We are not so well informed about the holders of the office in the reign of Alexander that we can rule out the possibility, but on balance I think he was not. The author of *HA* has rather, to embroider his story, exploited the knowledge, perhaps obtained from legal sources, that Paul was alive and active in Alexander's reign. Two famous lawyers are better than one. Writing in a period in which there was a revival of interest in classical law—the only reference in imperial constitutions to a classical jurist between 327 and 426 comes in 396.[325]—he wishes to recommend

---

[318] *HA* Alexander 34.6.
[319] *HA* Alexander 27.2.   [320] *HA* Alexander 51.4.
[321] *HA* Niger 7.3; Alexander 26.5 and cf. 27.2.
[322] Balog (1913) 339−421; Wenger (1953); Salmon (1971) 664 still argues for Paul's prefecture, denied by Jardé (1925) 38. Modrzejewski−Zawadski (1967) 607 are undecided. See also Howe (1942) 105.
[323] Flavianus, Geminius Chrestus, Didius Marinus, Domitius Honoratus, Lorenius Celsus, Aedinius Iulianus; Modrzejewski−Zawadski (1967) 593.
[324] *D.* 31.87.3, 4 (Paul 14 *resp.*), 49.1.25 (20 *resp.*).
[325] *CTh* 4.4.3.3 (21 March 396 *prudentissimus iuris consultorum Scaevola*) cf. *HA* Caracalla 8.3.

that emperors should follow the advice of eminent lawyers, and sees in the prominence he gives to Paul a way of reinforcing the impression created on the reader's mind by his praise of Ulpian. Though nothing actually rules out a praetorian prefecture for Paul, I think a lesser prefecture (supply or police) is more likely.

In the end we have little idea of Ulpian's policies and achievements during his brief period of power. At the beginning of Alexander's reign praetorian prefects were for a short time automatically adlected as senators.[326] This may have been one of Ulpian's ideas. In a passage written under Caracalla or Macrinus he gives men of prefectorial status higher rank than the wives of senators.[327] According to Herodian, the senate under Alexander elected sixteen councillors as advisers to the emperor, men of mature wisdom and seemly behaviour.[328] Alexander did nothing without their approval. With a weak and pliable young emperor, indeed, the senate was able to secure that the imperial council was composed in the way it wanted. The author of *HA*, who is pro-senatorial, embroiders this theme. So far as Ulpian is concerned, there is no warrant for attributing to him a specially favourable attitude to the senate. He did indeed favour constitutional government, but the adlection of praetorian prefects to the senate was a step in downgrading the senate, not raising its status. If, as *HA* says, it[329] was justified on the ground that senators should not be judged by non-senators, this only made it worse, since it implied that it was essential for praetorian prefects to be members of the body which judged senators.

Herodian records that those who had been unjustifiably promoted by Elagabal were removed from their offices. Civil and military business was entrusted to competent persons.[330] Such steps are straightforward and, indeed, obvious in the circumstances. It can be assumed that they are included in the matters which, Dio says,[331] Ulpian put straight.

More important, I believe, is Ulpian's contribution to the ideal of constitutional government, of which the mythology of Alexander's reign is an expression. That reign claimed to be one in which law and custom were respected. No one was executed without trial,[332] prosecutions for treason were rare,[333] appointments were made according to precedent and on the advice of those best qualified to judge,[334] decency prevailed.[335]

---

[326] *HA* Alexander 21.3–5; Howe (1942) 104; A. Stein (1963) 246 f. Not for long: *CAH* (1939) 61 (Miller).

[327] *D.* 1.9.1 pr. (Ulp. 62 *ed.*).

[328] Herodian 6.1.2. Jardé (1925) 21 makes this body a council of regency, un-Roman.

[329] *HA* Alexander 21.5.

[330] Herodian 6.1.4.

[331] Dio 80.2.2.

[332] Herodian 6.1.7.

[333] *CJ* 9.8.1 (11 April 223 *etiam ex aliis causis maiestatis crimina cessant meo saeculo*).

[334] Herodian 6.1.3–4.

[335] *CJ* 9.9.9 (26 Jan. 224 *castitas temporum meorum*).

Herodian, who substantially accepts the propaganda of the regime,[336] does not associate these themes with Ulpian. Yet they correspond closely to what we can deduce of the jurist's outlook from his writings. To him the law, since it incorporates those moral and philosophical notions which can be given effect in practice, is the key to good government. It is Ulpian, composing a rescript on behalf of Severus and Caracalla, who formulates the principle that, though the emperor is not bound by law, nothing so becomes him as to abide by it.[337] It is he, among the jurists, who depicts the lawyer as a priest, and sees law as providing a guide to right and wrong and an incentive to choose the former.[338] The ideal for which he stood excited support from persons as diverse as Herodian, Ammianus, and the author of *HA*, all members of what would now be called the middle class, who cannot depend for their protection on personal influence.

Ulpian was, however, ill equipped to rule the empire as a sort of imperial consort.[339] He soon made enemies among the praetorians. The examples of Papinian, Macrinus (an ex-praetorian prefect), and himself show that the troops, praetorian and legionary, needed little provocation to turn against a lawyer-prefect who lacked military skill and success.[340] Ulpian was outspoken and self-confident: a difficult, critical man. He strikes the reader as exceptionally self-centred.[341] Such a man is easily led into confrontation. He may fail to realize how his own conduct has undermined his credibility. Ulpian, the upholder of the rule of law, had engineered, for reasons good or bad, the killing of Flavianus and Chrestus.

It may be helpful to summarize what has been deduced about Ulpian's career. Born before 172, and a citizen of Tyre by birth, he probably came of a family of scholars which had long possessed Roman citizenship. His early career is obscure, but may have been closely connected with the imperial family and Papinian. From March 202 to about May 209 he held the office of secretary *a libellis*, and was consequently attached to the court of Severus. In 209–10 he probably accompanied Severus, Caracalla, and Papinian on their campaign in northern Britain. The first five books of his *ad edictum* may have been composed in early 211. His main works, prompted by the *constitutio Antoniniana*, were written in 213–17 under Caracalla and Macrinus. His career under Elagabal is obscure but he may have held a lesser prefecture (e.g. supply) and been expelled as a teacher or supporter of Alexander towards the end of his reign. Under Alexander in 222 he was prefect of supply at the end of March, and was then, at

---

[336] Herodian 6.2 (though critical of Mamaea), cf. perhaps Calpurnius Piso 1.71 (Champlin (1978) 95) but against Champlin's dating G. B. Townend *JRS* 70 (1980) 166–74, R. Mayer ibid. 175–6.

[337] Just. *Inst.* 2.17.8; Honoré (1981) 100[622], 137[381].

[338] *D.* 1.1.1.1 (Ulp. 1 *inst.*).

[339] Or *corrector status reipublicae* (Modrzejewski–Zawadski, 1967, 594; Pflaum, 1948, 42).

[340] Syme (1972 *b*).

[341] Ch. 2 pp. 60–5.

Mamaea's prompting, placed in a supervisory position over the praetorian prefects Flavianus and Chrestus, as a sort of *corrector reipublicae*. Perhaps in August he had them killed and succeded as sole prefect. In 223 two further pairs of praetorian prefects were successively appointed to work under him: one consisted of Lorenius Celsus and Aedinius Iulianus, the other of Didius Marinus and Domitius Honoratus. These appointments may have been occasioned by the rioting between praetorians and citizens of Rome which lasted three days and nights in 223. About August 223 he was attacked by the praetorians and killed, at the instigation of Epagathus, the efforts of Alexander and Mamaea to protect him being of no avail.

CHAPTER 2

Ulpian's Style

The study of Ulpian's style[1] is the basis of this book. Only by depicting it accurately can we distinguish the spurious from the genuine among the works and texts attributed to him. Only from data concerning style is it possible to reconstruct his working methods, fit dates to his compositions, and set him in his true historical and political context.

The method followed will be the same as that adopted in my other studies of the Roman legal sources and their authors.[2] The style is depicted by listing distinguishing marks of varying degrees of distinctness. The list is composed according to a rule-of-thumb method, which is intended to reflect a disciplined sense of style, and which rests on a foundation of theory. The method, as applied to Ulpian, is the following.

The material to be considered in the first instance consists of the texts attributed to Ulpian in Justinian's *Digest*. Those amount to 40 or 41 per cent of the whole *Digest*, according to whether we count lines or words.[3] In order to qualify for inclusion in the list of marks of style a word or expression must occur in these *Digest* excerpts three times more frequently than in all other jurists. In other words, the Ulpianic instances must form 75 per cent of the whole. The word or expression listed must, in addition, not be too contextual. It must not be the sort of word that is used primarily because of the subject-matter of the discourse, in the way in which we may expect *fideiussor* to appear in a passage dealing with suretyship.

That is only the first step in compiling a style-list. The list must next be scrutinized in order to eliminate those expressions which occur in Ulpian with a frequency no greater than or not much greater than they do in one or more of his contemporaries. If the list is to be of use for the purpose of identifying the author of disputed texts, this step is essential. The rule of thumb adopted is that, in principle, expressions must occur in Ulpian with four times as great a frequency as in the works of any of his contemporaries. Thus, given that Paul's excerpts amount to about 17 per cent of the *Digest*,[4]

---

[1] Pernice (1885); Volterra (1937).
[2] Honoré (1978), (1981).
[3] Lines 40.73 per cent (Honoré (1972) 291); words 41.56 per cent (*CDJ* intro. §4).
[4] Counting words 16.74 per cent (*CDJ* intro. §4).

so that we have about $2\frac{1}{2}$ times as much from Ulpian as we have from Paul, an expression must occur with ten times greater frequency in Ulpian than in Paul in order to qualify for the list of Ulpianic marks of style. This rule is, however, modified to the following extent. Provided that Ulpian's texts yield three-quarters of the whole, an expression can be listed as a mark of his style even if there is a single text containing it from another contemporary jurist. Thus if there are five texts in all, four from Ulpian and one from, say, Callistratus, the expression can be listed. This is so although the frequency of the expression in Ulpian is not in that case four times greater than it is in Callistratus, since the volume of excerpts from Ulpian in the *Digest* is thirty-seven times that of excerpts from Callistratus.[5] On the other hand, if there are two such texts from a contemporary jurist, the four-times-frequency rule is strictly applied. The reason for the exception is that an expression may be distinctive of the work of a given author despite a stray mention in another author's work. Two such mentions, on the other hand, cast doubt on its distinctiveness.

The procedures followed rest on a theory, but it is not a statistical theory.[6] In particular, the rules set out are not intended to provide estimates of the frequency of use of certain words or expressions by Ulpian and other jurists in their writing as a whole. They are intended rather to show that these expressions, irrespective of their actual frequencies in Ulpian and other authors, are relatively distinctive. This distinctiveness is indicated, positively, by the fact that a high proportion of all surviving instances of the expressions occur in Ulpian's work, and, negatively, by the fact that a low proportion of instances occurs in the work of any other jurist. The strength of the indication varies, of course, according to the total number of instances, but, even in the case of a hapax legomenon, it is better than nothing. This is one of the reasons why, in addition to frequently occurring words and expressions, hapax legomena are also listed.

But there is another reason. The delineation of style does not rest on distinctiveness alone. If it did, the cataloguing of marks of style would be a purely mechanical phenomenon. The style of an author is constituted by those marks of his writing which not merely distinguish him from others but also pervade his work and cohere with one another. For a feature may be distinctive of an author and yet confined to a particular work or period of work. In that case it does not mark the author's style so much as his style when writing this or that work, or at this or that period of time. This may indeed have its importance. When we come to elucidate Ulpian's working method and order of composition in chapters 6 and 7, we shall be looking for the sort of feature which is relatively evanescent. For the moment our main concern is with over-all traits.

[5] Ulpian (41.56) divided by Callistratus (1.12) equals 37.11.
[6] Honoré (1976) 109–11, (1978) xv–xvi, 71–6, (1981) x–xiii.

Hapax legomena and expressions which occur only a few times look at first sight as if they could be relevent only for a given work or period, but that is not the case. For there may be groups and classes of hapax legomena and like features. Nothing particular turns on the fact that *suasor* is hapax in Ulpian.[7] But when we discover that *suasus* is also hapax,[8] we begin to suspect a fondness for this root. Hence we may suspect, when we come across a text with *suasio*, another hapax in the legal literature,[9] that Ulpian is the author of the text. Little significance attaches in itself to the fact that *ceteroquin*[10] is found twice in Ulpian and in no other *Digest* author. But when we notice that this is only one of a large range of conjunctions and linking phrases which are confined, or virtually confined, to him,[11] we are entitled to see in his effort to link each sentence and clause to its predecessor one of the distinguishing points of his work.

This leads to the third feature which is to be looked for in listing marks of style, viz. that they should cohere. They should add something to what in the end will amount to an identikit of the author, not simply increase the extent of a catalogue. Some words and expressions clearly satisfy all three features: they are distinctive, pervasive, and cohere with other listed expressions. An example, for Ulpian, is *proinde*, 'accordingly', used as a conjunction. This occurs 203 times in the *Digest* in Ulpian's work and at most four times (perhaps only once) in that of other jurists.[12] It is highly distinctive. It occurs in twelve different works attributed to Ulpian, and in fifty different books of his edictal commentary, which runs to eighty-one books. So it is also pervasive. It provides a striking example of Ulpian's use of introductory conjunctions to link a sentence with what has preceded. It is therefore coherent with other features. But, in its contribution to building up a picture of our author's pen, *proinde*, though it occurs 203 times, differs only in degree from *suasor* which occurs once. For that, too, fits the image of a man who has a general preference for the shorter word— *suadere* for *persuadere* and its derivatives. Indeed the most apparently isolated hapax legomenon must be allowed to figure in the list of marks of style, if only because the present author may have failed to see its bearing on the wider landscape.

The use made of the listed marks of style is threefold. The presence of a mark in a text is some evidence of the genuineness of the text. The absence from a text of marks of Ulpian's style is some evidence of its spuriousness. The concentration of such marks in a particular work or part of a work is a sign that these were composed at about the same time. But the weight to be

[7] *D.* 4.4.13 pr. (11 *ed.*).
[8] *D.* 9.2.9.1 (18 *ed.*).
[9] *CJ* 5.62.1 (1 May 204).
[10] *D.* 28.5.35.3 (4 *disp.*), 49.14.29 pr. (8 *disp.*).
[11] Below, nn. 13–126.
[12] Below, nn. 74–80.

put on these inferences is variable, and must be left to be assessed by the informed reader. The absence from a work like the *opinions*, excerpts from which run to several thousand words, of a very distinctive and pervasive feature of Ulpian's style (for example *proinde*) is a strong argument against the genuineness of the work. Its presence in *de officio curatoris reipublicae* strongly favours the genuineness of the latter. The absence of *suasus* and *suasor* from these works, on the other hand, affords a very slight argument either way. The effort made in this chapter to compile a long, though of course still incomplete, list of plausible marks of Ulpian's style is meant to assist, not to foreclose critical judgement.

For purposes of this study the *Digest* texts attributed to Ulpian are initially treated as genuine, though references to Citati in the footnotes draw attention to phrases which have attracted suspicion. This is because we must not prejudge whether particular works or texts or parts of texts are spurious, but consider that question only after an attempt has been made to delineate a coherent style on the assumption of genuineness. In chapter 4 I argue that five works attributed to Ulpian by *Digest* inscriptions are spurious, and clearly some other texts have been altered in the post-classical period or by Justinian's compilers. The study of these alterations lies outside the scope of this book, although a few hints are given at the end of this chapter as to how such a study might be approached. For the present I disregard such alterations, partly to avoid prejudging disputed issues, and partly because any pervasive and coherent feature of Ulpian's work as it has come down to us in the pages of *Digest* is unlikely to be anything but genuine. No post-classical copyist or editor and no member of Justinian's commission could introduce more than occasional variations in the work of a classical author. They could not rewrite it.

What, then, are the broad characteristics of the writer from Tyre who has left such a mark on the law of Europe and of countries of European colonization? His style is exceptionally clear, uniform, and of a piece. He writes rather as if speaking. Short words are preferred to long ones, short clauses to elaborate structures. Sentences and phrases are linked together by connecting words to ensure the flow of the discourse, even when this means, as it often does, beginning a sentence with *et*. The prose is forceful, direct, and forward-looking. As in the praetor's edict, future tenses are often preferred to the present: 'the contract will be valid' rather than 'the contract is valid'.

Clusters of verbs, particularly those derived from different clauses, such as tend to occur in authors who place the Latin verb at the end of a clause or sentence, he takes pains to avoid. Hence the direct object often comes after the verb, or the participle after the auxiliary. Lucidity is Ulpian's prime aim and achievement. The reader seldom doubts his meaning. Consequently, elegance and variety are sacrificed. His is a prime example of plain Latin prose, comparable with that of Caesar in an earlier age, in which familiar phrases are constantly repeated. He rarely strains to achieve a rhetorical effect, and by the use of longer words to point an antithesis. His tone is on the whole self-confident and egocentric to an extent which recalls the jurists of the age of Trajan and Hadrian. Not for him the intricate and muted reflections of a Papinian. Forthright and uncomplicated, perhaps unsubtle, Ulpian's personal opinion is seldom unstated, though he meticulously records learned opinion to the contrary. The *disputationes*, and much besides, read like the record of an argument in which the reader himself takes part. The reader is addressed directly, told of incidents in which the author has been involved, cajoled into accepting Ulpian's views. Ulpian is careful to give reasons, generally rather summary ones, for his conclusions. He seems to assume that his scholarship, force of persuasion, and personal authority will carry the argument.

In mentioning the words and phrases which satisfy the tests described and so count as marks of Ulpian's style in the sense and to the extent explained, I have listed all instances of the word or phrase to be found in the *Digest* according to Mommsen's reading of the text. Texts by Ulpian are listed first. These are classified according to the work from which they come; first, the major treatises *ad edictum* and *ad Sabinum*; then the medium-scale works *de officio proconsulis, disputationes, de omnibus tribunalibus, ad legem Iuliam et Papiam*; then the minor works in alphabetical order. After the Ulpian texts come texts from other *Digest* authors, preceded by 'but'. After that come instances of the word or phrase taken from legal sources outside the *Digest*, and of related or analogous expressions. These are preceded by '*cf.*'. In this way the reader can count the number of Ulpianic and non-Ulpianic texts and scrutinize their distribution. When the texts are numerous, so that Ulpian by himself accounts for thirty or more instances, I have, for economy, referred to the relevant fiche in the *Concordance to the Digest Jurists*, edited by Joseph Menner and myself, instead of setting them out in full. The references take the form of the abbreviated title (*CDJ*), the number of the fiche, and the key word or phrase referred to: for example *CDJ* 67 PROINDE ET SI refers to fiche no. 67 of the *CDJ*, headed CONCORDANCE ULPIANUS POSSESSIONEM—PROPRIUS, in which all the Ulpian passages from the *Digest* containing the phrase *proinde et si* are set out. The texts from other jurists have in general been cited individually in any event, since it would be troublesome for the reader to search several fiches in *CDJ* in order to find them.

The marks of style to be listed are grouped under a number of headings: (i) conjunctions and other introductory phrases; (ii) expository phrases; (iii) phrases expressing the author's attitudes, including those which refer to himself; (iv) uses of future tenses; (v) inversions of the normal word order; (vi) verbs; (vii) adjectives and participles used as adjectives; (viii) adverbs and adverbial phrases. Appendix 1 lists in alphabetical order all the words and phrases mentioned.

(i) *Conjunctions and other introductory phrases.* Ulpian likes to link sentences by beginning each sentence except the first of a series with a conjunction or other connective phrase. In the absence of any more plausible word, he often uses *et* for this purpose. This habit, more appropriate in speech than in writing, may point to a practice of dictating. At any rate, it is a prominent feature of his writing.

Combinations of *et* and *putare* afford a good example. Thus, all 31 *Digest* texts with *et putem* come from Ulpian.[13] So do 8 of 9 texts with *et magis puto*,[14] 19 of 20 with *et non puto*,[15] all 11 with *et ego puto*[16] and all 3 with *et verum/verius puto*.[17] Even the plain *et puto* occurs in his work 112 times out of 126. Fourteen instances come from other jurists[18]: 7 from Paul, 2 from Pomponius, 1 each from Arcadius, Gaius, Marcellus, Papinian, and Tryphoninus, if we follow the inscriptions. But one of the texts attributed to Paul[19] is really Ulpian's, as I shall show. Nor is this all: *et sunt qui putent*[20] and *et putamus*[21] are also Ulpianic.

Many other expressions in which *et* functions as an introductory connective are confined, among jurists, to Ulpian. Some of these introduce verbs: *et arbitror*,[22] *et credo*,[23] *et constat*,[24] *et dico*,[25] *et dicendum erit*,[26] *et non*

---

[13] D. 19.1.13.3 (32 *ed.*), 25.4.1.9 (34 *ed.*), 27.9.5.4 (35 *ed.*), 27.9.5.12 (35 *ed.*), 47.2.52.6 (37 *ed.*), 39.3.6.2 (53 *ed.*), 40.12.18 (55 *ed.*), 42.3.6 (64 *ed.*), 42.6.1.8, 16 (64 *ed.* bis), 43.5.3.15 (68 *ed.*), 42.8.10.5 (73 *ed.*), 44.2.9 pr. (75 *ed.*), 44.4.4.24 (76 *ed.*), 44.6.1.1 (76 *ed.*), 36.3.1.11 (79 *ed.*), 38.4.3.5 (14 *Sab.*), 23.3.9.3 (31 *Sab.*), 24.1.32.28 (33 *Sab.*), 23.3.38 (48 *Sab.*), 18.4.2.10 (49 *Sab.*), 45.1.38.12 (49 *Sab.*), 48.2.7.2 (7 *off. proc.*), 50.13.1.4 (8 *off. proc.: et non putem*), 50.13.1.15 (8 *off. proc.*), 48.5.2.5 (8 *disp.*), 48.5.26.4 (2 *adult.*), 49.4.1 pr. (1 *appell.*), 40.5.24.16, 17 (5 *fid.* bis), 40.5.26.6 (5 *fid.*).
[14] D. 25.4.1.8 (34 *ed.*), 26.7.5.5 (35 *ed.*), 27.4.1.5 (36 *ed.*), 1.5.10 (1 *Sab.*), 24.1.21 pr. (32 *Sab.*), 24.1.32.14 (33 *Sab.*), 48.19.9.14 (10 *off. proc.*), 25.3.5.1 (2 *off. cons.*), all Ulp., but D. 32.64 (Afr. 6 *qu.*), cf. 19.1.13.9 (Ulp. 32 *ed.*: *et puto magis*).
[15] D. 2.2.3.4 (3 *ed.*), 4.4.3.4 (11 *ed.*), 5.3.25.6 (15 *ed.*), 50.14.2 (31/1 *ed.*), 49.17.8 (45 *ed.*), 29.4.1.5 (50 *ed.*), 47.9.3.7 (56 *ed.*), 42.6.1.1 (64 *ed.*), 28.3.6.10 (10 *Sab.*), 32.52.5 (24 *Sab.*), 23.3.9.3 (31 *Sab.*), 23.2.29 (36 *Sab.*), 26.1.6.4 (38 *Sab.*), 47.2.39 (41 *Sab.*), 47.2.43.8 (41 *Sab.*), 42.2.6.4 (5 *omn. trib.*), 40.9.14 pr. (4 *adult.*), 5.1.52.4 (6 *fid.*), 42.1.15.7 (3 *off. cons.*), all Ulp., but 43.24.21.1 (Pomp. 29 *Sab.*).
[16] D. 3.5.3.11 (10 *ed.*), 9.2.11.10 (18 *ed.*), 29.5.5.1 (50 *ed.*), 47.8.2.27 (56 *ed.*), 43.19.3.16 (70 *ed.*), 44.4.4.23, 29 (76 *ed.* bis), 7.1.13.3, 5 (18 *Sab.* bis), 34.2.27.1 (44 *Sab.*), 18.4.2.3 (49 *Sab.*).
[17] D. 35.1.10 pr. (23 *Sab.*), 1.14.3 (38 *Sab.*), 41.1.33 pr. (4 *disp.*: *et verius puto*).
[18] Ulp. texts in *CDJ* 56 but D. 48.18.10.2 (Arc. 1 *test.*), 18.6.2.1 (Gai. 2 *rer. cott.*), 17.1.49 (Marc. 6 *dig.*), 31.69.4 (Pap. 19 *qu.*), 3.4.6.2 (Paul 9 *ed.*), 4.8.32.16 (Paul 13 *ed.*), 18.5.3 (Paul 33 *ed.*), 22.1.38.14 (Paul 6 *Plaut.*), 42.1.51.1 (Paul 2 *man.*), 34.9.5.5 (Paul 1 *fisc.*), 46.1.71 pr. (Paul 4 *qu.*), 16.1.32.2 (Pomp. 1 *SCC*), 29.4.3 (Pomp. 3 *Sab.*), 37.8.7 (Tryph. 16 *disp.*).
[19] D. 3.4.6.2 (Paul 9 *ed.* = Ulp. 9 *ed.* below, nn. 765–7).
[20] D. 41.2.13.2 (72 *ed.*), 36.1.17.3 (4 *fid.*), nn. 765–7, cf. 40.5.24.19 (5 *fid.*: *s. q. putant*).
[21] D. 33.8.6.2 (25 *Sab.*).
[22] D. 13.7.24.2 (30 *ed.*), 19.1.11.18 (32 *ed.*), 27.3.1.20 (36 *ed.*), 37.4.3.9 (39 *ed.*), 38.2.12.4 (44 *ed.*), 33.7.12.14 (20 *Sab.*), 32.70.12 (22 *Sab.*), 29.1.19.2 (4 *disp.*), cf. *et magis arbitror* 18.3.4.4 (32 *ed.*), 48.5.4.2 (8 *disp.*), 36.1.18.7 (2 *fid.*).
[23] D. 28.3.6.6 (12 *Sab.*), 32.11.21 (2 *fid.*), 17.1.29.3 (7 *disp.*).
[24] D. 13.7.24.1 (30 *ed.*), 16.3.7.2 (30 *ed.*), 24.3.24 pr. (33 *ed.*), 28.2.1 (1 *Sab.*), 45.1.29.1 (46 *Sab.*).
[25] D. 38.17.1.10 (12 *Sab.*).   [26] D. 5.3.25.9 (15 *ed.*).

dubito,[27] *et eveniet,*[28] *et exstat*[29] (or *extat*[30]), *et finge,*[31] *et intererit,*[32] *et erit procedendum,*[33] *et refert,*[34] *et parvi refert,*[35] *et retineo,*[36] *et scio,*[37] *et mihi videtur,*[38] *et videtur mihi,*[39] *et visum est.*[40] In another group *et* is followed by the auxiliary *est: et est decretum,*[41] *et est dubitatum,*[42] *et est relatum,*[43] *et est rescriptum,*[44] *et est quaestio tractata.*[45] Sometimes the *est* is existential: *et est epistula,*[46] *et est actio,*[47] *et est pactio.*[48] In other cases, again, it is predicative: *et est expeditus,*[49] *et est frequentissima,*[50] *et est optimum,*[51] *et est simile,*[52] *et est utile,*[53] *et est utilius,*[54] *et est utilissima,*[55] *et est verum*[56] (or *vera*[57]), *et est verior*[58] (or *verius*[59]). This predicative form is markedly emphatic. When the *est* follows the adjective the emphasis is reduced: *et absurdum est,*[60] *et*

[27] D. 25.1.5.1 (36 *Sab.*), 47.3.2 (42 *Sab.*), 39.5.7.2 (44 *Sab.*).

[28] D. 37.6.1.19 (40 *ed.*).

[29] D. 27.7.4 pr. (36 *ed.*), 43.24.11.1 (71 *ed.*), 21.1.8 (1 *ed. cur.*), 40.5.30.6 (5 *fid.*).

[30] D. 27.8.1.2 (36 *ed.*), 39.2.15,12 (53 *ed.*), 43.20.1.27 (70 *ed.*), 43.24.11.8 (71 *ed.*), 48.18.1.27 (8 *off. proc.*).

[31] D. 5.1.18.1 (23 *ed.*).

[32] D. 18.6.4 pr. (28 *Sab.*).

[33] D. 7.8.6 (17 *Sab.: e. huc usque e. p.*).

[34] D. 4.2.9 pr. (11 *ed.*), 12.4.3.7 (26 *ed.*), 15.3.1.2 (29 *ed.*), 43.20.1.21 (70 *ed.*), 44.4.4.1 (76 *ed.*), 28.5.35.1 (4 *disp.*), 36.1.3.2 (3 *fid.*).

[35] D. 29.4.1.1 (50 *ed.*), 40.12.8.2 (55 *ed.*), 43.24.1.2 (71 *ed.*), 7.4.1 pr. (17 *Sab.*), 34.3.5.2 (23 *Sab.*), 40.7.3.1 (27 *Sab.*), 47.2.3.1 (41 *Sab.*), 45.2.3 pr. (47 *Sab.*), 46.1.6.1 (47 *Sab.*), cf. 26.7.54 (Tryph. 2 *disp.: et multum refert*).

[36] D. 35.1.92 (5 *fid.*).

[37] D. 48.13.7 (7 *off. proc.*).

[38] D. 3.1.1.10 (6 *ed.*), 3.5.5.8 (10 *ed.*), 14.5.4.4 (29 *ed.*), 25.6.1.10 (34 *ed.*), 37.4.1.7 (39 *ed.*), 38.5.1.22 (44 *ed.*), 43.24.1.5 (71 *ed.*), 10.2.49 (2 *disp.*), cf. 15.2.1.7 (29 *ed. e.m. verius v.*), 36.1.1.17 (3 *fid.: e. m. magis v.*).

[39] D. 5.3.31 pr. (15 *ed.*).

[40] D. 18.4.2.6 (49 *Sab.*).

[41] D. 36.1.1.13 (3 *fid.*), cf. 49.14.25 (19 *Sab.: est et d.*).

[42] D. 13.6.5.11 (28 *ed.*).

[43] D. 11.5.1.3 (23 *ed.*), 21.2.4 pr. (32 *ed.*), 43.24.13.5 (71 *ed.*).

[44] D. 40.5.24.5 (5 *fid.*), cf. 47.10.13.7 (57 *ed.: e. e. saepissime r.*).

[45] D. 18.4.2.7 (49 *Sab.*).

[46] D. 19.2.19.2 (32 *ed.*).

[47] D. 47.5.1.2 (38 *ed.*).

[48] D. 2.14.1.2 (4 *ed.*).

[49] D. 7.9.9 pr. (51 *ed.*).

[50] D. 42.4.7.2 (49 *ed.*).

[51] D. 43.29.3.12 (71 *ed.*).

[52] D. 43.26.1.3 (1 *inst.*).

[53] D. 49.4.1.5 (1 *appell.*).

[54] D. 43.8.2.37 (76 *ed.: e. e. hoc u.*).

[55] D. 43.26.6.4 (71 *ed.*).

[56] D. 12.4.3 pr. (26 *ed.*), 13.5.3.1 (27 *ed.*), 17.1.10.7 (31/1 *ed.*), 27.3.13 (35 *ed.*), 38.5.1.27 (44 *ed.*), 38.16.1.10 (12 *Sab.*), 7.8.4.1 (17 *Sab.*), 34.3.3.4 (23 *Sab.*).

[57] D. 15.1.3.9 (29 *ed.*).

[58] D. 14.4.7.4 (29 *ed.*).

[59] D. 4.8.21.10 (13 *ed.*), 8.5.4.2 (17 *ed.*), 11.3.1.4 (23 *ed.*), 15.1.3.5, 12 (29 *ed.* bis), 19.2.19.4 (32 *ed.*), 27.5.1.7 (36 *ed.*), 39.1.5.6 (52 *ed.*), 46.7.5.5 (77 *ed.*), 36.3.1.16 (79 *ed.*), 33.9.3.10 (23 *Sab.*), 18.6.4.2 (28 *Sab.*), 40.9.30.4 (4 *Ael. Sent.*).

[60] D. 2.13.6.9 (4 *ed.*), Citati (1927) 1 (Gradenwitz and others).

difficile est.[61] In yet other phrases it is the combination of *et* with an adverb that is distinctive: *et per contrarium,*[62] *et facilius,*[63] *et fortassis*[64] (with *dicere*), *et fortius,*[65] *et generaliter,*[66] *et regulariter,*[67] *et recte*[68] (with certain verb forms), *et rectissime,*[69] *et versa vice.*[70]

A common locution is *et ait* followed by the name of a jurist, sometimes understood, e.g. *et ait Iulianus* or *quaeritur apud Pedium . . . et ait.* This introductory phrase occurs 118 times in Ulpian in the *Digest*[71] and 5 times in other jurists.[72] One of the two instances in Paul, however, looks like a covert citation from Ulpian.[73]

A conjunction which is virtually confined to Ulpian is *proinde,* 'accordingly'.[74] All 64 instances of *proinde et si* are Ulpian's, [75] together with 84 instances out of 88 with *proinde si*[76] and all 64 cases in which *proinde* acts as a conjunction on its own.[77] In all, then, the *Digest* yields 212 texts of Ulpian in which *proinde* means 'accordingly' and 4 of other jurists: another remarkable concentration. Nor are the other four texts all true exceptions. One has a wrong inscription and should properly count as a text of Ulpian.[78] Another is probably compilatorial,[79] and a third may well be compilatorial also.[80]

Per contrarium, another conjunctive phrase, occurs 29 times in the *Digest* in Ulpian and twice in Marcianus, whose style was strongly influenced by that of Ulpian.[81]

---

[61] *D.* 21.1.38.4 (2 *ed. cur.*).

[62] *D.* 21.1.23.9 (1 *ed. cur.*).

[63] *D.* 14.1.1.5 (28 *ed.*), 42.4.3.1 (49 *ed.*: *e. f. erit*).

[64] *D.* 32.55.7 = 50.16.167 (25 *Sab.*: *e. f. quis dicet*), 40.5.24.2, 17 (5 *fid.* bis: *e. f. dixerit*).

[65] *D.* 7.9.3.4 (79 *ed.*: *e. f. dici potest*), 26.2.10.2 (36 *Sab.*: *e. f. dicendum est*).

[66] *CDJ* 56 (44 texts) but *D.* 9.4.2.8 (Afr. 6 *qu.* itp.), 21.2.24 (Gai. 1 *ed. cur.*), 24.2.6 (Iul. 62 *dig.* itp.), 21.1.41 (Paul 2 *ed. cur.*), 28.2.28.3 (Tryph. 20 *disp.*).

[67] *D.* 15.3.3.2 (29 *ed.*), 30.71.1 (51 *ed.*), 7.1.25.5 (18 *Sab.*).

[68] *D.* 29.4.4.1 (50 *ed.*), 43.24.13.5 (71 *ed.*), both *e. r. dicetur*; 36.3.1.13 (79 *ed.*: *e. r. placuit*); 4.8.21.11 (13 *ed.*), 7.6.1.3 (18 *Sab.*) both *e. r. putat*.

[69] *D.* 10.2.18.1 (19 *ed.*), 39.1.1.11 (41 *ed.*), 47.8.4.3 (56 *ed.*), 42.4.7.7 (59 *ed.*), 40.4.13.2 (5 *disp.*).

[70] *D.* 43.29.3 pr. (71 *ed.*), 44.5.1.12 (76 *ed.*), 45.1.1.3 (48 *Sab.*).

[71] *CDJ* 56.

[72] *D.* 39.6.31.3 (Gai. 8 *ed. prov.*), 8.3.35 (Paul 15 *Plaut*: compilatorial), 23.2.60.4 (Paul 1 *or. d. Ant. et Comm.*), 30.114.3 (Marci. 8 *inst.*), 29.5.15 pr. (Marci. 1 *del.*).

[73] *D.* 23.2.60.4 below, n. 773.

[74] *Proinde* can also mean 'just', as in *proinde ac si* or *proinde tamquam si.*

[75] *CDJ* 67 PROINDE ET SI.

[76] *CDJ* 67 PROINDE SI but *D.* 34.5.13.4 (Iul. 1 *ambig.*) 9.2.22 pr. (Paul 22 *ed.*), 13.7.16.1 (Paul 29 *ed.*), 47.2.21.8 (Paul 40 *Sab.*), cf. Gai. *Inst.* 2.79.

[77] *CDJ* 67 PROINDE, but Citati (1927) 70 (Vassalli, Schulz).

[78] *D.* 47.2.21.8 (Paul 40 *Sab.* = Ulp. 40 *Sab.* Mommsen).

[79] *D.* 9.2.22 pr. (intended to link the Paul text to the preceding Ulpian text).

[80] *D.* 13.7.16.1 (intended to link what follows to the correct but compilatorial statement *contrariam pigneraticiam creditori actionem competere certum est*). In that case none of the three instances attributed to Paul is genuine.

[81] *D.* 23.4.6 (4 *ed.*), 2.4.8.1 (5 *ed.*), 4.4.22 (11 *ed.*), 8.5.8.5 (17 *ed.*), 17.2.52.18 (31/2 *ed.*), 19.1.13.5, 25 (32 *ed.* bis), 25.3.1.11, 13 (34 *ed.* bis), 26.7.9.9 (36 *ed.*), 27.3.1.2 (36 *ed.*), 37.9.1.7 (41 *ed.*), 39.3.1.21

[See opposite page for n. 81 cont.]

There are many other such phrases confined or almost confined to
Ulpian's work. Some, drawing out a consequence, have much the same
meaning as *proinde: inde,*[82] *eapropter,*[83] *sic deinde,*[84] *idcircoque.*[85] Some
introduce provisos: *dummodo non,*[86] *dummodo sciamus.*[87] There is adversat-
ive force in *verumtamen,*[88] *tamenetsi . . . tamen*[89] and *attamen,* the latter
being preceded by *quamvis,*[90] *etiamsi*[91] or *qualiterqualiter,*[92] or else standing
alone.[93] Several phrases are used to reinforce what has gone before: *idem*
(and inflections) *ac si,*[94] *ceteroquin,*[95] *quin immo etiam*[96] (the latter a lapse
into pleonasm), *sed enim,*[97] *unde enim,*[98] *constat enim,*[99] *ubi enim,*[100]

(53 *ed.*), 28.1.20.2 (1 *Sab.*), 29.2.30.5 (8 *Sab.*), 7.2.8 (17 *Sab.*), 7.8.4.1 (17 *Sab.*), 33.3.1.10 (19 *Sab.*),
33.8.6.4 (25 *Sab.*), 23.2.12.2 (26 *Sab.*), 8.2.17.1 (29 *Sab.*), 24.1.11.5 (32 *Sab.*), 47.2.46.8 (42 *Sab.*),
45.1.1.6 (48 *Sab.*), 48.22.7.12 (10 *off. proc.*), 3.3.28 (1 *disp.*), 48.19.1.2 (8 *disp.*), 2.15.8.25 (5 *omn. trib.*),
21.1.23.9 (1 *ed. cur.*), but 36.1.34 (Marci. 8 *inst.*), 34.9.2.2 (Marci. 11 *inst.*). On the affinity between
Ulpian and Marcianus see ch. 9 p. 216.

[82] *CDJ* 60 INDE (30 texts with meaning 'hence') but *D.* 20.1.16.6 (Marci. 1 *hyp.*), 35.1.52 (Mod. 7
diff.), 26.7.37.2 (Pap. 11 *qu.*), 47.2.1.1 (Paul 39 *ed.*), cf. Gai. *Inst.* 2. 218, *FV* 90 (Ven.?. 1 *interd.*).

[83] *D.* 3.1.1.1 (6 *ed.*), 10.3.4.4 (19 *ed.*), 28.7.8.2 (50 *ed.*), 47.10.17.9 (57 *ed.*), 40.7.9 pr. (28 *Sab.*),
39.4.14 (8 *disp.*).

[84] *D.* 45.1.72.2 (20 *ed.*), 11.7.31 pr. (25 *ed.*), 15.1.1 pr. (29 *ed.*), 48.22.6.1 (9 *off. proc.*), 44.3.5.1 (3
disp.), 17.1.29.3 (7 *disp.*), 21.1.25.10 (1 *ed. cur.*), 36.1.6.2 (4 *fid.*), 35.1.92 (5 *fid.*).

[85] Seventeen texts of 19: *D.* 3.2.13.7 (6 *ed.*), 17.1.14 pr. (31/1 *ed.*), 26.7.9.6 (36 *ed.*), 37.4.3.4 (39 *ed.*),
37.10.3.7 (41 *ed.* bis), 37.10.5.1 (41 *ed.*), 38.5.3 pr. (44 *ed.*), 39.3.4.2 (53 *ed.*), 42.1.4.1 (58 *ed.*),
43.16.1.24 (69 *ed.*), 43.20.1.25 (70 *ed.*), 43.24.15 pr. (71 *ed.*), 25.3.5.8 (2 *off. cons.*), 47.11.7 (9 *off. proc.*),
28.3.12 pr. (4 *disp.*), 40.9.12 pr. (4 *adult.*), but 47.2.71 (Marc. 8 *dig.*), 23.2.57 (Marci. citing *divi fratres*).

[86] *D.* 50.1.25 (1 *ed.*), 16.3.7.2 (30 *ed.*), 29.4.6 pr. (50 *ed.*), 43.22.1.8, 9 (70 *ed.* bis), 7.4.5 pr. (17 *Sab.*),
47.20.3.2 (8 *off. proc.*), 48.18.1.13 (8 *off. proc.*), 50.13.1.10 (8 *trib.*), 22.1.33 pr. (1 *off. cur. reip.*), but
17.1.60.2 (Scae. 1 *resp.*).

[87] *D.* 9.3.5.5 (23 *ed.*), 16.3.1.10 (30 *ed.*), 27.9.7.4 (35 *ed.*), 43.16.3.9 (69 *ed.*), 46.2.2 (48 *Sab.*),
47.17.1 (8 *off. proc.*), 21.1.1.2 (1 *ed. cur.*), cf. Coll. 7.4.1 (8 *off. proc.*), *D.* 1.16.4.2 (1 *off. proc.: dummodo
sciat*), 42.3.6 (64 *ed.*), 46.4.6 (47 *Sab.*: both *dummodo illud sciamus*), but Citati (1927) 32 (Beseler).

[88] Twenty-nine texts of 31, 32 or 33, taking *verumtamen* and *verum tamen* together. *D.* 17.2.63.8
(31/2 *ed.*), 19.1.11.5, 18 (32 *ed.* bis), 19.1.17.7 (32 *ed.*), 4.4.4.9 (35 *ed.*), 27.2.2.2 (36 *ed.*), 28.1.22.4 (39
ed.), 37.5.8.2 (40 *ed.*), 37.5.10.2 (40 *ed.*), 38.5.1.15 (44 *ed.*), 38.2.14.4 (45 *ed.*), 38.6.1.3 (46 *ed.*),
38.11.1.1 (47 *ed.*), 42.8.10.3 (73 *ed.*), 44.4.4.33 (76 *ed.*), 44.5.1.10 (76 *ed.*), 35.3.1.12 (79 *ed.*), 36.3.1.19,
20 (79 *ed.* bis), 33.4.1.10 (19 *Sab.*), 41.1.20.1 (29 *Sab.*), 25.1.7 (36 *Sab.*), 29.1.28 (36 *Sab.*), 9.2.41 pr. (41
Sab.), 47.2.46.8 (42 *Sab.*), 28.5.35 pr. (4 *disp.*), 28.5.35.3 (4 *disp.*), 37.14.16 pr. (10 *Iul. Pap.*), 48.5.10.2
(4 *adult.*), but 48.10.6 pr. (Afr. 3 *qu.*: *verum, testamentum* Mommsen), 22.5.13 (Pap. 1 *adult.*), 20.6.8.7
(Marci. 1 *hyp.*), 33.1.19.1 (Scae. 17 *dig.*: citing will, but Mommsen *velim*): Citati (1927) 91 (Beseler).

[89] *D.* 14.6.7.11 (29 *ed.*).

[90] *D.* 24.3.24.5 (33 *ed.*), 25.4.1.11 (34 *ed.*), 27.2.1.2 (35 *ed.*), 26.7.3.3 (35 *ed.*), 11.1.16 pr. (37 *ed.*),
11.1.16.1 (37 *ed.*), 38.5.1.6 (44 *ed.*), 38.5.1.21 (44 *ed.*), 37.9.7.2 (47 *ed.*), 29.5.1.13 (50 *ed.*), 30.71.5 (51
ed.), 47.2.17.2 (39 *Sab.*), 47.1.1. pr. (41 *Sab.*), 39.5.7.4 (44 *Sab.*), 26.5.12.1 (3 *off. proc.*), 26.5.8.1 (8 *omn.
trib.*), 23.2.27 (3 *Iul. Pap.*), but 22.3.9 (Cels 1 *dig.*), 47.2.21.10 (Paul 40 *Sab.* = Ulp.: Mommsen), Citati
(1927) 12 (Beseler and many).

[91] *D.* 17.2.63 pr. (31/2 *ed.*), 29.3.8 (50 *ed.*), 39.3.4 (53 *ed.*), 42.6.1.3 (64 *ed.*), 47.2.7.1 (41 *Sab.*),
47.2.46 pr. (42 *Sab.*).

[92] *D.* 47.2.46 pr. (42 *Sab.*).   [93] *D.* 17.2.33 (31/2 *ed.*), 21.1.1.10 (1 *ed. cur.*).

[94] *D.* 46.7.5.4 (77 *ed.*), 30.33.2 (25 *Sab.*), 8.4.6.2 (28 *Sab.*), 26.8.5.4 (40 *Sab.*), 26.8.5.6 (40 *Sab.*), but
40.5.26.7 (Ulp. 5 *fid.* citing Trajan), 45.2.12.1 (Ven. 2 *stip.*).

[95] *D.* 28.5.35.3 (4 *disp.*), 49.14.29 pr. (8 *disp*).

[96] *D.* 10.3.7.13 (20 *ed.*), 9.4.35 (41 *Sab.*).

[97] Twenty-three texts of 25: *D.* 5.3.11 pr. (15 *ed.*), 6.1.1.3 (16 *ed.*), 6.2.7.13 (16 *ed.*), 37.9.7.1 (47
ed.), 40.12.7.2, 3 (54 *ed.* bis), 47.9.3.3 (56 *ed.*), 42.5.24.2 (63 *ed.*), 43.19.3.4 (70 *ed.*), 36.3.1.19 (79 *ed.*),

[*See next page for* n. 97 *cont.* 98, 99 *and* 100.]

nonnumquam enim,[101] *sane enim,*[102] *utique etiam,*[103] *sęd et si . . . aeque,*[104] *non tantum . . . autem,*[105] *non tantum . . . verum etiam,*[106] *non tantum . . . verum*[107] (without *etiam*), *non solum . . . verum etiam si,*[108] *non solum verum etiam quoque,*[109] *non solum verum quoque*[110] (without *etiam*), *non solum . . . verum omnino,*[111] and *non solummodo . . . sed et.*[112] Questions come in with *an ergo,*[113] *an vero et,*[114] *num forte,*[115] *utrum . . . autem,*[116]

46.6.4.3 (79 *ed.*), 35.2.47 pr. (79 *ed.*), 35.1.10 pr. (23 *Sab.*), 26.8.5.2 (40 *Sab.*), 47.1.1 pr. (41 *Sab.*), 39.5.7.5 (44 *Sab.*), 50.4.6.5 (4 *off. proc.*), 47.18.1.2 (8 *off. proc.*), 48.19.9.11 (10 *off. proc.*), 39.5.12 (3 *disp.*: *sed etenim* Mommsen), 36.1.23.2 (5 *disp.*), 49.14.29 pr. (8 *disp.*), 21.1.38.7 (1 *ed. cur.*), cf. Coll. 14.3.2 (9 *off. proc.*), but D. 34.3.20.1 (Mod. 10 *resp.*), 45.1.63 (Afr. 6 *qu. etenim* Mommsen).

[98] D. 44.4.4.23 (76 *ed.*).

[99] D. 26.7.3.2 (35 *ed.*), 43.20.1.13 (70 *ed.*), 28.6.2.4 (6 *Sab.*), 33.7.12.2 (20 *Sab.*).

[100] D. 6.1.9 (16 *ed.*), 38.9.1.6 (49 *ed.*), 40.5.4.5 (60 *ed.*), 43.16.1.35 (69 *ed.*), 24.3.2.2 (35 *Sab.*), 37.4.17 (35 *Sab.*), 21.1.37 (1 *ed. cur.*), but 28.6.23 (Pap. 6 *resp.*).

[101] D. 26.4.5.3 (35 *ed.*), 43.20.1.13 (70 *ed.*), 48.18.1.27 (8 *off. proc.*).

[102] D. 26.7.3.6 (35 *ed.*), 26.7.7.12 (35 *ed.*), 39.3.1.23 (53 *ed.*), 32.49.4 (22 *Sab.*), 38.1.9.1 (34 *Sab.*), cf. Coll. 12.7.8 (18 *ed.*).

[103] D. 25.6.1.11 (34 *ed.*), 37.6.1.2 (40 *ed.*), 47.8.2.10 (56 *ed.*), 40.5.4.3 (60 *ed.*), 40.5.4.14 (60 *ed.*).

[104] Twenty-five texts of 27: D. 10.3.7.13 (20 *ed.*), 11.6.1.1 (24 *ed.*), 15.1.9.6 (29 *ed.*), 15.1.30.2 (29 *ed.*), 15.3.3.1 (29 *ed.*), 27.5.15 (36 *ed.*), 9.4.38.3 (37 *ed.*), 12.1.12 pr. (38 *ed.*), 39.4.12.2 (38 *ed.*), 37.1.1.11 (40 *ed.*), 37.6.1.17 (40 *ed.*), 36.4.5.14 (52 *ed.*), 28.5.9.20 (5 *Sab.*), 30.37.1 (21 *Sab.*), 40.7.3.4 (27 *Sab.*), 18.2.4.5 (28 *Sab.*), 26.1.14.5 (37 *Sab.*), 26.8.5.5, (40 *Sab.*), 45.1.41 pr. (50 *Sab.*), 47.20.3.1 (8 *off. proc.*), 24.3.64.4 (7 *Iul. Pap.*), 40.9.12.2 (4 *adult.*), 36.1.3.5 (3 *fid.*), 36.1.9 pr. (4 *fid.*), 42.1.15.11 (3 *off. cons.*), but 7.1.60 pr. (Paul 5 *sent.*), 40.5.49 (Afr. 9 *qu.*), cf. Gai. *Inst.* 2.193 (reading uncertain).

[105] Thirteen texts of 14: D. 13.7.9.1 (28 *ed.*), 26.10.3.2 (35 *ed.*), 26.7.9.7 (36 *ed.*), 47.4.1.14 (38 *ed.*), 47.9.3.3 (56/1 *ed.*), 43.24.3.3 (71 *ed.*), 24.1.3.9 (32 *Sab.*), 26.4.3.9 (38 *Sab.*), 16.3.11 (41 *Sab.*), 45.1.1.2 (48 *Sab.*), 18.4.2.4 (49 *Sab.*), 21.1.38.10 (2 *ed. cur.*), 36.1.18.2 (2 *fid.*), but 15.1.47.4 (Paul 4 *Plaut.*).

[106] Twenty-six texts of 29: D. 26.7.9.7 (36 *ed.*), 27.4.1.5 (36 *ed.*), 37.4.3 pr. (39 *ed.*), 37.5.5 pr. (40 *ed.*), 37.9.1.15 (41 *ed.*), 37.10.1.5 (41 *ed.*), 38.3.16.8 (45 *ed.*), 38.7.2.1 (46 *ed.*), 36.4.5.28 (52 *ed.*), 8.5.10.1 (53 *ed.*), 39.3.8 (53 *ed.*), 47.10.15.19 (57 *ed.*), 28.8.7.2 (60 *ed.*), 43.22.1.1 (70 *ed.*), 43.24.15.8 (71 *ed.*), 50.17.157.2 (71 *ed.*), 42.8.10.20 (73 *ed.*), 35.3.1.11 (79 *ed.*), 7.4.10.1 (17 *Sab.*), 26.4.3.9 (38 *Sab.*), 48.18.1.23 (8 *off. proc.*), 26.5.7 (1 *omn. trib.*), 23.2.43 pr. (1 *Iul. Pap.*), 21.1.38.10 (2 *ed. cur.*), 36.1.18.2 (2 *fid.*), 25.3.5.12 (2 *off. cons.*), but 35.1.50 (Ulp. 1 *off. cons.* citing Pius), 3.5.18.4 (Paul 2 *Ner.*), 7.1.3.1 (Gai. 2 *rer. cott.*).

[107] D. 17.1.12.9 (31 *ed.*), 1.9.10 (34 *ed.*), 47.10.17.19 (57 *ed.*), 43.5.1.2 (68 *ed.*), 44.4.4.33 (76 *ed.*), 26.8.5 pr. (40 *Sab.*), 13.7.4 (41 *Sab.*), 47.2.27 pr. (41 *Sab.*), 48.19.9.13 (10 *off. proc.*), 10.2.49 (2 *disp.*), 50.16.131.1 (4 *Iul. Pap.*), 49.1.6 (2 *appell.*), but 47.2.21 pr. (Paul 40 *Sab.* = Ulp. Mommsen).

[108] D. 4.3.1.8, 3 (11 *ed.*), 15.1.11.9 (29 *ed.*), 37.5.6.4. (40 *ed.*), 37.5.8.6 (40 *ed.*), 37.9.1.14 (49 *ed.*), 42.8.3.1 (66 *ed.*), 43.16.1.33 (69 *ed.*), 40.7.3.3 (27 *Sab.*).

[109] D. 38.2.10.1 (44 *ed.*), 43.20.1.37 (70 *ed.*), 38.16.1.11 (12 *Sab.*), 1.1.1.1 (1 *inst.*).

[110] D. 9.4.5.1 (3 *ed.*), 3.3.39 pr. (9 *ed.*), 4.4.18.5 (11 *ed.*), 4.1.6 (13 *ed.*), 4.7.4.2 (13 *ed.*), 10.4.3.9 (24 *ed.*), 13.6.5.8 (28 *ed.*), 14.4.1.5 (29 *ed.*), 14.6.9.3 (29 *ed.*), 15.1.L6 (29 *ed.*), 25.5.1.1 (34 *ed.*), 37.11.2.4 (41 *ed.*), 29.5.1.7 (50 *ed.*), 36.4.5.12 (52 *ed.*), 47.10.11 pr. (57 *ed.*), 11.8.1.8 (68 *ed.*), 50.16.60.1 (69 *ed.*), 43.19.5.2 (70 *ed.*), 29.2.30.1 (8 *Sab.*), 7.8.2.1 (17 *Sab.*), 34.3.3.4 (23 *Sab.*), 46.8.20 (1 *disp.*), 15.1.3.6 (2 *disp.*), 23.2.43.4 (1 *Iul. Pap.*), but 15.1.49 (Pomp. 4 *QM*).

[111] D. 50.16.178 pr. (49 *Sab.*).

[112] D. 50.1.8 (1 *ed.*).

[113] D. 11.1.9.4 (22 *ed.*), 15.2.1.7 (29 *ed.*), 26.4.5.3 (35 *ed.*), 26.4.5.4 (35 *ed.*), 27.9.3.5 (35 *ed.*), 46.1.8.3 (47 *Sab.*), 45.3.11 (48 *Sab.*), but 37.8.7 (Tryph. 16 *disp.*).

[114] D. 17.1.8.4 (31/1 *ed.*), 37.5.8.1 (40 *ed.*), 7.8.10.2 (17 *Sab.*), 7.6.1.3 (18 *Sab.*), 26.1.3.2 (37 *Sab.*).

[115] D. 4.4.16 pr. (11 *ed.*), 10.3.7.13 (20 *ed.*), 26.2.17.2 (35 *ed.*), 43.18.1.2 (70 *ed.*), 1.7.15.2 (25 *Sab.*), but 49.16.3.7 (Mod. 4 *poen.*).

[116] Fifteen texts of 16: D. 2.14.7.8 (4 *ed.*), 7.6.5.1 (17 *ed.*), 38.5.1.6 (44 *ed.*), 29.3.2.7 (50 *ed.*), 29.5.3.14 (50 *ed.*), 39.2.30.1 (81 *ed.*), 28.1.5 (6 *Sab.*), 38.17.1.11 (12 *Sab.*), 7.8.10.3 (17 *Sab.*), 7.6.1.3 (18 *Sab.*),

[See opposite page for n. 116 cont.]

and *utrum . . . an vero*.[117] *Sive autem*,[118] *solet autem*,[119] *quia autem*,[120] and *interdum autem*[121] foreshadow a minor modification of what has gone before. *Interdum tamen*,[122] *interdum . . . licet*,[123] and *quid tamen si*[124] bring in more radical variations. *Si quidem . . . si autem*[125] points to an antithesis.

(ii) *Expository phrases*. These introduce the facts of a case, the point of law to be discussed, the opinions of a jurist, or the implications of an argument. *Finge enim*[126] is an example of the first, *quaestionis est*[127] and *quaestio in eo est*[128] of the second. The opinions of other lawyers are reported with *plane . . . inquit*[129], *alioquin . . . inquit*[130], *si*

33.8.8.8 (25 *Sab.*), 29.1.19.1 (4 *disp.*), 25.3.5.2, 20 (2 *off. cons.* bis), 36.1.11.2 (4 *fid.*), but 10.2.54 (Ner. 3 *memb.*), cf. Gai. *Inst.* 3.189.

[117] Twenty-one texts of 25: *D.* 2.8.2.5 (5 *ed.*), 4.6.28.3 (12 *ed.*), 5.3.23 pr. (15 *ed.*), 10.3.23 (32 *ed.*), 19.2.11 pr. (32 *ed.*), 37.6.1.13 (40 *ed.*), 38.5.1.14 (44 *ed.*), 29.4.10.2 (50 *ed.*), 39.2.13.2 (53 *ed.*), 42.4.5.3 (59 *ed.*), 40.5.4.3 (60 *ed.*), 46.7.5.7 (77 *ed.*), 38.4.1.8 (14 *Sab.*), 7.8.10.2 (17 *Sab.*), 41.9.1.2 (31 *Sab.*), 41.1.23.3 (43 *Sab.*), 48.19.8.7 (9 *off. proc.*), 48.19.9.14 (10 *off. proc.*), 40.9.30.4 (4 *Ael. Sent.*), 23.3.5.1, 2 (2 *off. cons.* bis), but 35.1.82 (Call. 2 *qu.*), 18.6.2.1 (Gai. 2 *rer. cott.*), 44.7.44.6 (Paul 74 *ed.*), 24.1.31.4 (Pomp. 14 *Sab.*).

[118] *CDJ* 72 SIVE AUTEM (33 texts) but *D.* 50.4.18.29 (Arc. 1 *mun. civ.*), 13.6.18.1 (Gai 9 *ed. prov.*), 16.3.14.1 (Gai. 9 *ed. prov.*), 24.2.2.3 (Gai. 11 *ed. prov.*), 39.4.13.2 (Gai. 13 *ed. prov.*), 7.2.4 (Iul. 35 *dig.*), 18.1.58 (Pap. 10 *qu.* itp.).

[119] *D.* 42.6.1.1 (64 *ed.*), 43.5.3.10 (68 *ed.*), 47.20.3.2 (8 *off. proc.*), 48.19.9.4 (10 *off. proc.*).

[120] *D.* 16.3.1.47 (30 *ed.*), 43.3.1.4 (67 *ed.*), 43.18.1.6 (70 *ed.*), 43.20.1.31 (70 *ed.*), 43.23.1.7 (71 *ed.*), 43.24.15.12 (71 *ed.*), 26.1.3.1 (37 *Sab.*), but 49.14.42.1 (Val. 5 *fid.*).

[121] *D.* 4.4.13.1 (11 *ed.*), 9.1.1.15 (18 *ed.*), 14.5.4.1 (29 *ed.*), 7.9.1.7 (79 *ed.*), 29.2.21.1 (7 *Sab.*), 26.4.1.3 (14 *Sab.*), cf. Gai *Inst.* 3.199, 4.127, *D.* 34.5.13.6 (Iul. 1 *ambig.*: *autem interdum*), but Citati (1927) 48 (Pernice etc.).

[122] Eleven texts of 13: *D.* 27.6.5 (12 *ed.*), 4.4.19 (13 *ed.*), 6.2.11.3 (16 *ed.*), 11.1.11.3 (22 *ed.*), 9.3.5.2 (23 *ed.*), 10.4.11.1 (24 *ed.*), 47.10.17.13 (57 *ed.*), 7.2.1.3 (17 *Sab.*), 7.1.25.1 (18 *Sab.*), 46.3.12.1 (30 *Sab.*), 21.1.1.9 (1 *ed. cur.*), but 11.3.14.9 (Paul 19 *ed.*), 30.12.3 (Pomp. 3 *Sab.*), cf Gai. *Inst.* 4.155.

[123] *D.* 3.3.39.1 (9 *ed.*), 4.4.13.1 (11 *ed.*), 6.2.11.3 (16 *ed.*), 9.3.5.2 (23 *ed.*), 12.6.26.12 (26 *ed.*), 38.16.1.7 (12 *Sab.*), but 36.4.15 (Val. 7 *act.* = Ven: Krueger), cf. Gai. *Inst.* 3.176 *licet . . . interdum*, *D.* 4.8.15 (Ulp. 13 *ed.*), 28.3.3.6 (Ulp. 3 *Sab.*).

[124] All 43 texts: *CDJ* 69 QUID TAMEN SI, cf. *D.* 35.2.11.6 (Pap. 29 *qu.*: *q.t. dicemus si*).

[125] Thirteen texts of 15: *D.* 14.3.1 (28 *ed.*), 15.3.3.10 (29 *ed.*), 29.4.10.2 (50 *ed.*), 49.17.2 (67 *ed.*), 43.8.2.28 (68 *ed.*), 43.24.13.7 (71 *ed.*), 42.8.10.1 (73 *ed.*), 44.4.4.17 (76 *ed.*), 46.1.33 (77 *ed.*), 46.7.5.6 (77 *ed.*), 35.3.1.4 (79 *ed.*), 7.4.10.7 (17 *Sab.*), 21.1.4.4 (1 *ed. cur.*), but 25.4.1 pr. (Ulp. 34 *ed.* citing *divi fratres*), 36.1.67.3 (Maec 5 *fid.*).

[126] Fifteen texts of 17: *D.* 4.4.3.6 (11 *ed.*), 4.4.7.11 (11 *ed.*), 4.6.23.4 (12 *ed.*), 4.8.3.1 (13 *ed.*), 5.3.31 pr. (15 *ed.*), 6.1.13 (16 *ed.*), 11.7.4 (25 *ed.*), 14.1.1.5 (28 *ed.*), 14.4.7 pr. (29 *ed.*), 17.2.52.10 (31/2 *ed.*), 7.1.17 pr. (18 *Sab.*), 36.2.14.2 (24 *Sab.*), 2.15.8.20 (5 *omn. trib.*), 48.5.24.1 (1 *adult.*), 36.1.13.3 (4 *fid.*), but 37.8.7 (Tryph. 16 *disp.*), 13.7.8 pr. (Pomp. 35 *Sab.*), Citati (1927) 40 (Appleton etc.), 33 (Schulz).

[127] Eleven texts of 12: *D.* 5.1.2.5 (3 *ed.*), 11.3.9.3 (23 *ed.*), 11.7.8 pr. (25 *ed.*), 12.1.11 pr. (26 *ed.*), 27.2.1.2 (34 *ed.*), 29.4.10.2 (50 *ed.*), 44.2.7.1 (75 *ed.*: *magnae q. e.*), 7.1.25.3 (18 *Sab.*), 18.2.2 pr. (28 *Sab.*), 15.1.3.6 (2 *disp.*), 40.5.26.6 (5 *fid.*), but 32.89 (Paul 6 Iul. Pap.), cf. *est questionis*: 15.1.9.6 (Ulp. 29 *ed.*), 15.1.11.3 (Ulp. 29 *ed.*), 47.10.9 pr. (Ulp. 57 *ed.*); *fuit questionis*: 15.2.1.7 (Ulp. 29 *ed.*), 29.4.1.12 (50 *ed.*), 29.2.24 (7 *Sab.*), 7.8.2.1 (17 *Sab.*), 36.2.12.1 (23 *Sab.*), but 37.7.9 (Tryph. 6 *disp.*); *quaestionis non est*: 50.16.164 pr. (Ulp. 15 *Sab.*).

[128] *D.* 37.6.1.21 (40 *ed.*), 43.26.6.4 (71 *ed.*), 47.2.43.11 (41 *Sab.*), 41.1.23.1 (43 *Sab.*) but 23.2.60.4 (Paul 1 *orat. d. Ant. et Comm.*), the latter perhaps derived from a work of Ulpian.

[129] *D.* 10.2.20.3 (19 *ed.*), 16.1.6 (29 *ed.*), 17.1.12.2 (31/1 *ed.*), 33.9.3.2 (22 *Sab.*), 21.2.21.3 (29 *Sab.*), cf *FV* 80 (Ulp. 17 *Sab.*).

[See next page for n. 130.]

forte . . . inquit[131], *nisi forte . . . inquit*[132] or *extat sententia.*[133] Relevant points are called to mind with *meminisse oportet,*[134]/*oportebit,*[135] *meminisse autem debemus,*[136] or *notandum quod.*[137] *Secundum quod dictum est*[138] draws an inference from a premise.

(iii) *Attitudinal phrases.* Ulpian expresses his attitude towards the points of law he discusses in a variety of distinctive ways. Half a dozen phrases disclaim doubt by using negative forms of *dubitare: non dubitamus,*[139] *quis dubitat?,*[140] *nequaquam dubium est,*[141] *nulla dubitatio est*[142]—the last two followed by the infinitive or accusative and infinitive—and, finally, *nemini dubium est*[143] and *dubio procul.*[144] *Nequaquam ambigendum*[145] and *non est ambiguum*[146] are two other expressions used to deny that the law is uncertain. *Non est incognitum*[147] denies obscurity, *non est incivile*[148] legal impropriety. The correct view is heralded in positive form by *dici*

---

[130] D. 4.7.4.2 (13 ed.), 39.2.15.12 (53 ed.), 47.10.17.19 (57 ed.), 29.2.42 pr. (4 disp.), 21.1.1.9 (1 ed. cur.), cf. FV 87 (Ulp. 17 Sab.).

[131] D. 4.2.3.1 (11 ed.), 43.23.1.8 (71 ed.).

[132] D. 3.5.5.14 (10 ed.), 4.9.3.1 (14 ed.), 6.1.1.2 (16 ed.), 17.2.63.3 (31/2 ed.), 19.1.11.18 (32 ed.), 37.10.1.8 (41 ed.), 7.1.25.5 (18 Sab.).

[133] D. 27.7.4 pr. (36 ed.), 39.2.15.12 (53 ed.), 42.4.7.16 (59 ed.) 43.20.1.17 (70 ed.), 43.24.11.1, 8 (71 ed.), 44.4.4.8 (76 ed.).

[134] D. 25.4.1.9 (34 ed.), 43.26.4.1 (71 ed.), 30.4.9.8 (23 Sab.), 24.2.11.2 (3 Iul. Pap.), 25.3.5.9 (2 off. cons.), 40.2.16 (2 Ael. Sent.), but 49.1.4.5 (Macer 1 appell.).

[135] D. 5.2.8.14 (14 ed.), 14.3.13.1 (28 ed.), 47.2.93 (38 ed.), 39.1.5.2, 10 (52 ed. bis), 47.10.7.2 (57 ed.), 47.10.15.23 (57 ed.), 39.5.7.5 (44 Sab.), 1.16.10 pr. (10 off. proc.), 39.6.37 pr. (15 Iul. Pap.), 36.1.6.1 (4 fid.).

[136] D. 43.20.1.44 (70 ed.), but Citati (1927) 13 (Berger).

[137] D. 3.4.5 (8 ed.), 9.2.25.2 (18 ed.), 11.5.1.2 (23 ed.), 13.6.1.1 (28 ed.), 25.4.1.5 (34 ed.), 39.2.15.3 (53 ed.), cf. notandum est quod: 10.4.3.2 (24 ed.), 25.3.1.5 (34 ed.), 37.4.10.3 (40 ed.), 43.15.1.6 (68 ed.), 48.5.28.16 (3 adult.), 21.1.25.7 (1 ed. cur.), but 37.4.4 pr. (Paul 41 ed.); notandum erit quod: 3.6.3.3 (Ulp. 10 ed.), 4.6.21.1 (12 ed.), but Citati (1927) 61 (Pringsheim, Beseler).

[138] D. 4.2.16.1 (11 ed.).

[139] D. 3.3.33.1 (9 ed.), 11.1.11.8 (22 ed.), 37.5.5.8 (40 ed.), 37.9.1.15 (41 ed.), 23.2.45.3 (3 Iul. Pap.), 4.6.38.1 (6 Iul. Pap.) cf. 14.4.5 pr. (19 ed.: nec nos d.)

[140] D. 39.1.5.12 (52 ed.), 39.2.24 pr. (81 ed.), 46.4.8 pr. (18 Sab.), 47.10.30 pr. (42 Sab.), 48.19.6 pr. (9 off. proc.), but Citati (1927) 31 (Bonfante).

[141] D. 19.1.13.7 (32 ed.), 29.5.3.11 (50 ed.), 45.2.3.1 (47 Sab.), 46.1.8.12 (47 Sab.).

[142] Nineteen texts: D. 27.5.1.3 (36 ed.), 28.1.22.6 (39 ed.), 37.1.3.6 (39 ed.), 37.5.8.4 (40 ed.), 37.13.1.1 (45 ed. bis), 48.19.2.1 (48 ed.), 47.10.11.9 (57 ed.), 24.1.5.15 (32 Sab.), 26.4.2 (37 Sab.), 18.1.28 (41 Sab.), 47.2.25.2 (41 Sab.), 50.2.3.2 (3 off. proc.), 48.19.8.12 (9 off. proc.), 27.9.8 pr. (2 omn. trib.), 49.15.9 (4 Iul. Pap.) 48.2.5 (3 adult.), 48.5.30.9 (4 adult.), 1.10.1.2 (2 off. cons.).

[143] D. 43.16.1.22 (69 ed.), 21.2.17 (29 Sab.), 23. 3. 5.11 (31 Sab.), 47.2.48.7 (42 Sab.), 46.1.8.6 (47 Sab.), 48.18.1.20 (8 off. proc.), 32.11.6 (2 fid.), but Citati (1927) 32 (Beseler).

[144] D. 5.3.31.2 (15 ed.), 24.3.22.7 (33 ed.), 43.12.1.5 (68 ed.), 36.1.23.5 (5 disp.), 40.9.30.2 (4 Ael Sent.).

[145] D. 44.4.4.26 (76 ed.).

[146] D. 48.2.19 pr. (4 disp.), but Citati (1927) 10 (Pringsheim).

[147] D. 5.2.8.11 (14 ed.).

[148] D. 34.1.14.1 (2 fid.).

oportet,[149] oportebit, oportere, or oporteat, and by *servari oportet*,[150] *melius dicetur*,[151] *magisque est/erit*,[152] *sciendum*,[153] put baldly, or, more expansively, *illud sciendum est*.[154] We also find *sed est verius*[155] and *est tamen verius*[156] used for this purpose and, finally, *palam est*[157] followed by the accusative and infinitive or the infinitive alone. *Credo*[158] is more tentative. The author endorses the opinions of other jurists with *placet sententia*,[159] *sententiam puto veram*[160] (or *puto veriorem*[161]), or with *sententia mihi . . . vera*[162] (or *verior*[163]) *videtur*. He underlines various virtues in the solutions espoused by the use of *benignum est*,[164] (*sententia*) *habet*

---

[149] D. 4.6.26.9 (12 ed.), 24.3.7.12 (31 Sab. bis), 17.1.29 pr. (7 disp.), 5.1.52.2 (6 fid.), all dici oportet; 30.43.1 (21 Sab.: dici oportebit), 10.4.7.4 (24 ed.), 12.4.5.4 (2 disp.), 33.4.2 pr. (5 disp.) all oportere dici, 47.2.46.5 (42 Sab.: dici oporteat) but 34.9.22 (Tryph. 5 disp.: non oportere dici).

[150] D. 27.9.11 (3 off. proc.).

[151] D. 4.8.21.10 (13 ed.), 29.4.10.2 (50 ed.), 39.2.15.13 (53 ed.), 43.16.1.38 (69 ed.), 30.41.4 (21 Sab.), 49.4.1.9 (1 appell.), but 24.1.31.3 (Pomp. 14 Sab.), cf. 27.6.6 (Paul 12 ed.: m. dicitur).

[152] D. 42.4.3.3 (59 ed.), 40.5.4.15, 16, 22 (60 ed. ter), 28.8.8 (61 ed.), 29.2.71.1, 9 (61 ed. bis), 44.2.7.3 (75 ed), 46.7.3.3, 8 (77 ed. bis), 45.3.7 pr. (48 Sab.), 37.14.16.1 (10 Iul. Pap.), 49.4.1.9 (1 appell.), but Citati (1927) 54.

[153] D. 42.8.6.7 (66 ed.), 47.15.2 (9 off. proc.).

[154] Eighteen of 19 texts: D. 29.5.1.24 (50 ed.), 7.9.9.1 (51 ed.), 42.4.7.13 (59 ed.), 5.1.19.4 (60 ed.), 42.6.1.10 (64 ed.), 42.8.6.9 (66 ed.), 43.20.1.23 (70 ed.), 43.24.3.1 (71 ed.), 2.11.4.1 (74 ed.), 44.4.4.34 (76 ed.), 46.7.5.8 (77 ed.), 46.6.4.2 (79 ed.), 7.9.1.2 (79 ed.), 24.1.7.9 (32 Sab.), 49.1.8 (4 appell.), 21.1.1.3 (1 ed. cur.), 21.1.19.4 (1 ed. cur.), 21.1.29 pr. (1 ed. cur.), but 18.6.18 (Pomp. 31 QM), cf. 14.3.15 (Ulp. 28 ed.: novissime s. e.), 28.8.3 (60 ed.: illud sciendum).

[155] All 12 texts: D. 42.9.8 (11 ed.), 4.3.7.3 (11 ed.), 6.1.15.3 (16 ed.), 27.3.1.4 (36 ed.), 28.7.8.5 (50 ed.), 44.4.4.8 (76 ed.), 7.4.29.2 (17 Sab.), 7.5.3 (18 Sab.), 34.3.5.2 (23 Sab.), 24.1.32.27 (33 Sab.), 26.2.10.3 (36 Sab.), 36.1.6.1 (4 fid.).

[156] D. 11.7.2.1 (25 ed.), 40.5.4.1 (60 ed.).

[157] D. 42.8.3 pr. (66 ed.), 43.16.1.24 (69 ed.), 43.21.1.7 (70 ed.), 44.4.2 pr. (76 ed.), 46.7.5.3 (77 ed.), 19.1.10 (47 Sab.), 18.4.2.3 (49 Sab.), 45.1.38.3 (49 Sab.), 49.4.1.11 (1 appell.), cf. 43.29.3.13 (71 ed.: p. erit), 35.3.3.3 (79 ed.: p. sit).

[158] Nineteen texts of 21: D. 4.4.7.2 (11 ed.), 11.7.14.2 (25 ed.), 18.2.16 (32 ed.), 25.6.1.11 (34 ed.), 37.5.3 pr. (40 ed.), 43.19.1.11 (70 ed.), 28.3.6.6 (10 Sab.), 30.34.4 (21 Sab.), 32.70.9, 11 (22 Sab. bis), 40.7.3.17 (27 Sab.), 24.1.33.1 (36 Sab.), 48.19.9.3 (10 off. proc.), 29.2.42 pr. (4 disp.), 17.1.29.3 (7 disp.), 32.11.21 (2 fid.), 36.1.13.3 (4 fid.), 29.1.6 (2 appell.), 48.5.18 pr. (2 Iul. Pap.), but 40.4.55 pr. (Maec. 2 fid.), 30.115 (Ulp. 2 inst. giving form of fideicommissum).

[159] D. 5.3.13.1 (15 ed.: nobis), 5.3.18 pr. (15 ed.), 10.4.19.1 (24 ed.: nobis), 19.1.13.14 (32 ed.: mihi), 42.8.10.16 (73 ed.), 1.6.6 (9 Sab.: nobis), 33.6.13 (23 Sab.: mihi), 18.4.2.7 (49 Sab.: mihi), cf. 47.2.43.5 (41 Sab.: placeat).

[160] D. 14.1.1.8 (28 ed.), 15.3.13 (29 ed.), 25.4.1.13 (34 ed.), 28.2.3.4 (1 Sab.), 7.1.7.1 (17 Sab.), 7.1.9.2 (17 Sab.), 7.1.12 pr. (17 Sab.), 7.4.10.5 (17 Sab.), 7.1.13.3 (18 Sab.), 30.44.2 (22 Sab.), but 38.1.4 (Pomp. 4 Sab.), cf. 5.3.13.8 (Ulp. 15 ed.: s. non p. v.), 11.3.11 pr. (23 ed.: s. v. puto), 15.1.11.2 (29 ed.: p. v. s.), 39.2.15.34 (53 ed.: p. s. v.), 43.19.3.16 (70 ed.: p. v. s.), 44.4.4.6 (76 ed.: p. s. v.), 21.1.33 pr. (1 ed. cur: p. s. v.), 40.7.3.2 (27 Sab.: v. putamus s.).

[161] D. 7.4.10.7 (17 Sab.), cf. 42.7.2.5 (65 ed.: p. s. veriorem), 28.5.17.1 (17 Sab. s. veriorem p.).

[162] D. 15.3.7.5 (29 ed.), 28.5.9.14 (5 Sab.), 7.8.12.1 (17 Sab.), but cf. 18.1.35.2 (Gai. 10 ed. prov.: q. s. potest . . . vera v.), 16.3.1.33 (Ulp. 30 ed.: s. v. mihi videtur), 43.8.2.42 (68 ed.: mihi videtur v. s.), 24.2.4 (26 Sab.: s. m. videtur v.), 40.7.9.2 (28 Sab.: same), 21.1.6.1 (1 ed. cur.: mihi videtur v. s.).

[163] D. 2.7.1.2 (5 ed.).

[164] D. 21.1.49 (8 disp.), 32.5.1 (1 fid.), Citati (1927) 14 (Gradenwitz etc.).

aequitatem,[165] *habet rationem*,[166] *non est sine ratione*[167] and *est tamen tutius*.[168] In warning against or rejecting wrong views or conduct, he resorts to *grave est*,[169] *nec ferendus est*,[170] and *improbum est*.[171] A currently accepted solution is endorsed by *et ita utimur*[172] or *et hodie hoc iure utimur*.[173] *Parvi refert*[174] denies a distinction. To summarize a branch of the law or a principle *generaliter dicendum est*,[175] or something akin, is a favourite.

In expressing his view on points of law Ulpian makes rather free use of the first person singular, particularly for the Severan age. His uses af *ego*, *me*, and *mihi* to refer to himself, rather than to a character in a legal example ('if I sell you a horse'), amount to 175 out of a total of 270, or 65 per cent. This is a good deal higher than the 41 per cent which Ulpian's excerpts form of the whole *Digest*, but short of the 75 per cent which would qualify the use as a mark of style according to the criteria here adopted. In the age of Trajan writers such as Iavolenus[176] and Celsus the younger[177] used the first person singular relatively more freely than Ulpian was to do later. But among his contemporaries Ulpian stands out for his ready resort to *ego*, *me*, and *mihi*. He uses these at about three times the rate of Papinian[178] and Paul[179].

---

[165] Nine of 10 texts: D. 2.2.1 pr. (3 *ed.*), 3.5.3.9 (10 *ed.*), 14.4.7.1 (29 *ed.*), 17.2.63.5 (31/2 *ed.*), 47.4.1.1 (38 *ed.*), 37.6.1 pr. (40 *ed.*), 37.10.3.13 (41 *ed.*: h. rationem et a.), 43.26.2.2 (71 *ed.*), 23.3.16 (34 *Sab.*) but 43.26.15 pr. (Pomp. 29 *Sab.*).

[166] Twenty-six of 27 texts: D. 19.1.32 (11 *ed.*), 4.8.21.4 (13 *ed.*), 9.2.27.11 (18 *ed.*), 9.4.2.1 (18 *ed.*), 10.3.7.8 (20 *ed.*), 12.2.9.6 (22 *ed.*), 11.7.2.8. (25 *ed.*), 14.5.4.5 (29 *ed.*), 17.1.12.5 (31/1 *ed.*), 18.3.4.1 (32 *ed.*), 37.10.3.13 (41 *ed.*), 42.4.3 pr. (49 *ed.*), 39.2.13 pr. (53 *ed.*), 5.1.19.2 (60 *ed.*), 20.1.21.1 (73 *ed.*), 7.9.7 pr. (79 *ed.*), 35.3.1.6 (79 *ed.*), 28.6.10.6 (4 *Sab.*), 28.5.6.4 (4 *Sab.*), 7.1.12.4 (17 *Sab.*), 7.4.3.2 (17 *Sab.*), 34.2.19.3 (20 *Sab.*), 41.9.1.4 (31 *Sab.*), 24.1.5.15 (32 *Sab.*), 27.3.5 (43 *Sab.*), 45.1.3.1 (49 *Sab.*), but 49.14.14 (Gai. 11 Iul. Pap.: nullam h. r.), cf. 13.6.7.8 (Ulp. 28 *ed.*: videtur h. r.), 27.3.17 (Ulp. 3 *off. cons*: non h. r., citing Sev. et Ant.).

[167] D. 13.7.11.4 (28 *ed.*), 14.4.9.2 (29 *ed.*), 42.4.7.11 (59 *ed.*), 16.2.13 (66 *ed.*), 28.5.9.4 (5 *Sab.*), 7.1.9.4 (17 *Sab.*), 37.4.17 (35 *Sab.*).

[168] D. 39.2.4.6 (1 *ed.*).

[169] D. 13.5.1 pr. (27 *ed.*), cf. 12.3.4 pr. (36 *ed.*: g. videbatur).

[170] Ten texts out of 11: D. 3.3.25 (9 *ed.*), 12.2.34.7 (26 *ed.*), 24.3.24.2 (33 *ed.*), 9.4.8 (37 *ed.*), 42.6.1.12, 15 (64 *ed.* bis), 23.3.33 (36 *Sab.*), 2.1.15 (2 *omn. trib.*), 26.10.5 (3 *disp.*),22.6.6 (8 Iul. Pap.), cf. FV 207 (*off. pr. tut.*) but 45.1.99 pr. (Cels. 38 *dig.*).

[171] D. 2.14.49 (36 *Sab.*), 28.7.8.6 (50 *ed.*).

[172] D. 42.7.2.5 (65 *ed.*), 18.2.9 (28 *Sab.*), 50.17.23 (29 *Sab.*), 23.3.5.9 (31 *Sab.*), 47.2.41.3 (41 *Sab.*), 45.1.38 pr. (49 *Sab.*).

[173] D. 49.1.14 pr. (14 *ed.*), 42.4.7.13 (57 *ed.*), 49.12.1 (4 *appell.*).

[174] CDJ 66 PARVI REFERT (37 texts), but D. 13.1.17 (Pap. 10 *qu.*), 3.4.6.1 (Paul 9 *ed.* = Ulp.).

[175] D. 13.3.1 pr. (27 *ed.*), 40.12.12.3 (55 *ed.*), 47.8.2.23 (56/1 *ed.*), 42.5.9.4 (62 *ed.*), 43.13.1.3 (68 *ed.*), 43.19.3.10 (70 *ed.*), 35.3.3.8 (79 *ed.*), 47.2.27 pr. (41 *Sab.*), 41.1.23.2 (43 *Sab.*), cf. g. dicendum erit 13.7.9.3 (28 *ed.*), g. erit dicendum 43.26.8.6 (71 *ed.*), g. dicimus 47.4.1.6 (38 *ed.*), 37.10.1.3 (41 *ed.*), g. dicemus 40.5.24 pr. (5 *fid.*), g. dicitur 37.11.1.9 (39 *ed.*), 48.19.8.7 (9 *off. proc.*), 48.5.16.4 (2 *adult.*), g. dici oportet 4.6.26.9 (12 *ed.*), g. potest dici 36.1.17.2 (4 *fid.*), g. poterit dici 29.1.13.2 (45 *ed.*), cf. FV 210 (*off. pr. tut.*) but Citati 41 (Eisele and many).

[176] Five texts, plus 8 in comments on Labeo.

[177] Nine texts.

[178] Seven texts.

[179] Twenty-two texts.

What is more, his uses tend to be emphatic. Thus, *ego puto*, a more categorical expression than *ego autem puto*, *ego non puto*, etc., is Ulpianic: he has 42 instances of it out of 51.[180] So are *ego . . . arbitror*,[181] *ego . . . adquiesco*,[182] *ego . . . adsentio*,[183] *ego . . . credo*,[184] *ego moveor*,[185] *ego . . . opinor*,[186] *ego quaero*,[187] and *ego . . . scio*.[188]

Papinian, a very restrained writer, does not use *ego* once. Ulpian does so on 102 occasions. He is both self-assertive and self-absorbed. Other Ulpianic phrases also make use of the first person, though without *ego*. *Mea fert opinio*[189] is one, and there are others: *invenio*,[190] *memini*,[191] *quaero*[192] (where it is the jurist, not the person consulting him, who inquiries), *retineo*,[193] 'I remember', and *volo tractare*,[194] 'I want to discuss'.

One phrase deserves special notice. *Si mihi proponas*, 'if you put it to me', comes in nine texts of Ulpian[195] and in no one else. It shows that he conceives his writings much as if he were debating with the reader. The writing reports an oral discussion, imaginary no doubt, but none the less controlling the structure of the argument. These illuminating texts are drawn not merely from the *disputationes*, where they might be expected, but from the major commentaries on the praetor's edict and on Sabinus. Other phrases, *finge enim*,[196] which we have already met, *accipe*,[197] *accipies*,[198] *dicas*,[199] point the same way.

It is a little more difficult to assess Ulpian's liking for using the plural *nos*

[180] Above, n.16 (11 texts) plus *CDJ* 54 EGO PUTO (31 other texts) but *D.* 29.2.62 (Iav. 1 *post. Lab.*), 35.1.40.3 (Iav. 2 *post. Lab.*), 40.7.39.2 (Iav. 4 *post. Lab.*), 8.1.20 (Iav. 5 *post. Lab.*), 46.3.73 (Marc. 31 *dig.: an sicut ego puto*), 4.2.4 (Paul 11 *ed.*), 17.1.58 (Paul 4 *qu.*), 46.8.15 (Paul 14 *Plaut.*), 45.1.91.6 (Paul 17 *Plaut.*).

[181] *D.* 4.3.13.1 (11 *ed.*), 41.1.44 (19 *ed.*), 16.3.1.38 (30 *ed.*), 43.26.8.5 (71 *ed.*), 33.7.12.14 (20 *Sab.*), 30.39 pr. (21 *Sab.*), 32.70.12 (22 *Sab.*), 18.4.2.17 (49 *Sab.*), 48.5.26.1 (2 *Iul. Pap.*); *ego autem arbitror* 4.4.3.4 (11 *ed.*), 10.4.11.1 (24 *ed.*), 32.55.2 (25 *Sab.*), 18.6.4 pr. (28 *Sab.*), 15.1.36 (2 *disp.*), cf. 23.4.4 (Ulp. 31 *Sab.: e. utrubique a.*), 41.1.63.3 (Tryph. 7 *disp.: e. nec . . . a.*).

[182] *D.* 38.1.7.1 (28 *Sab.*).

[183] *D.* 43.20.1.17 (70 *ed.*).

[184] *D.* 48.5.18 pr. (2 *adult*).

[185] *D.* 4.3.7.8 (11 *ed.*).

[186] *D.* 27.4.1.7 (36 *ed.*), but Citati (1927) 63 (Beseler, Levy).

[187] *D.* 3.5.9.1 (10 *ed.*), 15.4.1.2 (29 *ed.*), 33.4.1.12 (19 *Sab.*), cf. 19.1.11.6 (Ulp. 32 *ed.: e. illud q.*), 35.2.56.1 (Marc. 22 *dig.: e. quaeram*).

[188] *D.* 48.19.3 (14 *Sab.*).

[189] *D.* 27.9.7.3 (35 *ed.*), 48.19.6. pr. (9 *off. proc.*), cf. 24.1.32.4 (*m. tamen fert o.*).

[190] *D.* 39.3.1.20 (53 *ed.*), 36.1.15.4 (4 *fid.*), 27.1.15.16 (1 *excus.*).

[191] *D.* 7.8.2.1 (17 *Sab.*), 36.1.18.5 (4 *fid.*), cf. *FV* 220 (1 *off. pr. tut.*).

[192] Above, n. 187 and *D.* 12.3.4.2 (36 *ed.*).

[193] *D.* 35.1.92 (5 *fid.*).

[194] *D.* 24.1.32.14 (33 *Sab.*).

[195] *D.* 16.1.8.13 (29 *ed.*), 44.4.4.23 (66 *ed.*), 28.6.10.5 (4 *Sab.*), 32.52.7a (24 *Sab.*), 17.2.55 (30 *Sab.*), 46.3.12.3 (30 *Sab.*), 24.1.5.1 (32 *Sab.*), 49.17.6 (32 *Sab.*), 40.4.13.3 (5 *disp.*).

[196] Above, n. 127.

[197] Below, n. 385.

[198] *D.* 5.3.25.8 (15 *ed.*).

[199] *D.* 23.3.39.1 (33 *ed.*), 28.5.2.1 (2 *Sab.*), 23.4.4 (31 *Sab.: quare non d.*), 39.5.7.3 (44 *Sab.: same*).

or *nobis* of himself. Of about 58 such texts in the *Digest* 31 come from our author, which is, again, at 53 per cent, more than proportionate to the volume of his texts, but lower than for the first person. The classification of the texts creates problems. It is sometimes difficult to know whether *nos* means 'lawyers' or 'those interested in the question', or 'the author'. A range of cases runs from *quis nos sacerdotes appellet*,[200] 'one could call us (lawyers) priests' through *aliud erit nobis dicendum*,[201] 'you-and-I-and-anyone-else-interested-in-the-matter will have to say something different' to *et a nobis et a Papiniano probatum est*,[202] 'I approve, and so does Papinian'. The use of *nos* by a legal author to refer to himself does not seem to be authenticated before Pomponius[203] and Gaius.[204] There is no such use, for example, in Labeo, Iavolenus, or Celsus, and the one instance attributed to Julian in the *Digest* is palpably interpolated.[205] It is tempting to think that the habit spread to legal writing from an academic context, and that it expresses the superiority of the author to those who, by reading his work, hope to learn and so are, in a sense, his pupils. In the Antonine and Severan ages most legal authors make occasional use of the idiom.[206] What marks Ulpian, once again, is the categorical use of *nos* with the present indicative to underline his own opinion. This manner of writing does not appear, so far as I can judge, in other legal writers. Thus we have in Ulpianic texts *nos consentimus*,[207] *nec nos dubitamus*,[208] *nos opinamur*,[209] *nos probamus*,[210] and *nos putamus*,[211] expressions which would be taken as compilatorial were they not confined to Ulpian and consistent with other features of his style. Closely related to these are uses of verbs in the first person plural without *nos*, in which the subject is not specified, but the author intends, or probably intends, himself to be understood: *non dubitamus*,[212-13] *invenimus*,[214] *novimus*,[215] *opinamur*,[216] *ostendimus*,[217] *(supra) probavimus*,[218]

---

[200] D. 1.1.1.1 (1 *inst.*).

[201] D. 7.4.10.11 (7 *Sab.*).

[202] D. 24.1.32.27 (33 *Sab.*) but Citati (1927) 61 (Beseler).

[203] D. 1.2.2 pr. (1 *enchir.*: *necessarium itaque nobis videtur . . . demonstrare*).

[204] D. 44.7.1.15 (2 *rer. cott.*: *non de eo nos loqui*). This will be rejected by those who think *res cottidianae* late or post-classical, but cf. 39.4.5.1 (Gai. *ed. pr. urb.*: *quaerentibus nobis*), 1.2.1 (1 *XII tab.*: *libentius nos ad lectionem producunt*), Inst 1.188 (*nosque . . . hunc tractatum executi sumus*), 4.60.

[205] D. 9.2.51.2 (Iul. 86 *dig*) embeded in a long Tribonianic passage.

[206] Three texts in Africanus, 2 in Scaevola, 2 in Callistratus, 3 in Tryphoninus, 6 in Papinian, 4 in Paul, 2 in Macer, 1 in Modestinus.

[207] D. 17.2.29.2 (30 *Sab.*).

[208] D. 14.4.5 pr. (29 *ed.*).

[209] D. 43.21.3.2 (70 *ed.*).

[210] D. 19.1.11.3 (32 *ed.*), 28.5.9.5 (5 *Sab.*),· 35.2.82 (8 *disp.*).

[211] D. 4.8.17.4 (13 *ed.*).

[212-13] Above, n. 139.

[214] Spicil. Solesm. ed. Pitra (6 *ed. Pal.* 1.282[14]), D. 38.17.2.47 (13 *Sab.*). D. 45.3.11 (Ulp. 48 *Sab.*) and 45.3.12 (Paul 10 *qu.*) are not unequivocally self-referential.

[215] D. 45.1.26 (42 *Sab.*).

[*See opposte page for 216, 217 and 218.*]

putavimus,[219] *spectamus,*[220] *subsistimus,*[221] *vetamus.*[222]

At times it is unclear whether the subject is 'I' or 'lawyers'; the author may not himself have been sure. This is true of *addimus,*[223] *adhibemus,*[224] *admittimus*[225] (a favourite expression), *aestimamus,*[226] *animadvertimus,*[226a] *applicamus,*[227] *comparamus,*[228] *computamus,*[229] *credimus,*[230] *damus*[231] (*actionem* etc.), *defendimus,*[232] *demonstramus,*[233] *desideramus,*[234] *detrahimus,*[235] *distinguimus,*[236] *ducimus,*[237] *efficimus,*[238] *movemur,*[239] *observamus,*[240] *punimus,*[241] *quaerimus,*[242] *referimus,*[243] *requirimus,*[244] *revocamus,*[245] *solemus dicere,*[245a] *sequimur,*[245b] *tollimus,*[246] *trahimus,*[247] and

[216] *D.* 11.3.1.1 (23 *ed.*), 43.21.3.2 (70 *ed.*), 28.5.4.2 (4 *Sab.*), 12.3.1 (51 *Sab.*).

[217] Twelve texts of 13: *D.* 19.1.11.16 (32 *ed.*), 26.7.3.2 (35 *ed.*), 26.10.1.5 (35 *ed.*), 27.7.4 pr. (36 *ed.*), 38.6.1.4 (44 *ed.*), 50.16.195.3 (46 *ed.*), 28.5.4.2 (4 *Sab.*), 7.1.25.1 (18 *Sab.*), 7.1.25.6 (18 *Sab.*), 18.6.4.2 (28 *Sab.*), 28.5.35.2 (4 *disp.*), 36.1.13.1 (4 *fid.*), but 28.2.29.5 (Scae. 6 *qu.*), cf. *ostendi* 14.4.3.2 (Ulp. 29 *ed.*).

[218] *D.* 14.3.13.2 (28 *ed.*), 30.71.4 (51 *ed.*), 40.5.24.18 (5 *fid.*).

[219] *D.* 4.4.3.2 (11 *ed.*).

[220] Fourteen texts: *D.* 3.5.9.1 (10 *ed.*), 4.4.3.1 (11 *ed.*), 9.3.5.11 (23 *ed.*: ? *expectamus*), 15.1.11.2 (29 *ed.*), 5.3.3.6 (29 *ed.*), 17.2.63.6 (31/2 *ed.*), 38.2.3.20 (41 *ed.*), 49.17.8 (45 *ed.*), 47.8.2.22 (56/1 *ed.*), 42.4.7.15 (59 *ed.*), 43.29.3.1 (71 *ed.*), 34.2.19.13, 20 (20 *Sab.* bis), 24.1.32.14 (33 *Sab.*).

[221] *D.* 3.3.33 pr. (9 *ed.*).

[222] *D.* 3.3.33 pr. (9 *ed.*).

[223] *D.* 41.2.13.1 (72 *ed.*), 1.1.6 pr. (1 *inst.*).

[224] *D.* 25.4.1.3 (34 *ed.*), 28.1.22.5 (39 *ed.*).

[225] *D.* 3.3.33 pr. (9 *ed.*), 14.1.1.5 (28 *ed.*), 37.5.1.2 (40 *ed.*), 37.9.1.5 (41 *ed.*), 37.11.2.4 (41 *ed.*), 38.6.1.6 (46 *ed.*), 47.8.4.3 (56 *ed.*), 43.24.9 pr. (71 *ed.*), 43.24.11.13 (71 *ed.*), 38.16.2.5 (13 *Sab.*), 38.17.2.17 (13 *Sab.*), 38.4.3.2 (14 *Sab.*), 24.1.32.18 (33 *Sab.*), 25.1.5 pr. (36 *Sab.*), 26.1.3.1 (37 *Sab.*), 48.5.28.2 (3 *adult.*).

[226] *D.* 9.2.21.2 (18 *ed.*).

[226a] *FV* 156 (1 *excus.*).

[227] *D.* 33.8.8.8 (25 *Sab.*).

[228] *D.* 1.5.10 (1 *Sab.*), 50.17.209 (4 *Iul. Pap.*).

[229] *D.* 41.3.6 (11 *ed.*), 42.1.4.5 (56 *ed.*), 42.8.6.14 (66 *ed.*), 32.52.1 (24 *Sab.*), 24.3.7.8 (31 *Sab.*), 49.4.1.5 (1 *appell.*).

[230] *D.* 28.5.1.5 (1 *Sab.*), 24.1.5.15 (32 *Sab.*).

[231] Eleven texts: *actionem D.* 3.6.5.1 (10 *ed.*), 47.12.3.9 (25 *ed.*), 14.1.1.20 (28 *ed.*), 43.18.1.4 (70 *ed.* = 50.17.156.1), 47.2.12.2 (29 *Sab.*), 47.2.14.17 (29 *Sab.*), cf. 14.4.9.2 (29 *ed.* = 50.17.44 *actionem* understood), *annum ad restitutionem* 4.6.28.3 (12 *ed.*); *ius removendi* 26.10.1.3 (35 *ed.*), *electionem* 13.4.2.3 (27 *ed.*); *debitam partem* 38.2.3.20 (42 *ed.*).

[232] *D.* 24.1.32.14 (33 *Sab.*), 40.5.26.1 (5 *fid.*).

[233] *D.* 50.16.195.2 (46 *ed.*), 15.1.41 (43 *Sab.*).

[234] *D.* 50.16.199 (8 *omn. trib.*).

[235] *D.* 15.3.10.8 (29 *ed.*), 33.8.8.8 (25 *Sab.*), 1.1.6 pr. (1 *inst.*).

[236] *D.* 28.6.10.6 (4 *Sab.*), 7.1.22 (18 *Sab.*).

[237] *D.* 23.3.23 (35 *Sab.*).

[238] *D.* 1.1.6 pr. (1 *inst.*).

[239] *D.* 4.4.3.4 (11 *ed.* = *nec eo m. quod*).

[240] *D.* 17.2.63.8 (31/2 *ed.*), 36.4.5.3 (52 *ed.*).

[241] *D.* 38.17.2.34 (13 *Sab.*).

[242] *D.* 9.2.5.2 (18 *ed.*), 38.5.1.1 (42 *Sab.*).

[243] *D.* 15.1.41 (43 *Sab.*).   [244] *D.* 38.5.1.1 (42 *Sab.*).

[245] *D.* 37.14.16.1 (10 *Iul. Pap.*).

[245a] *D.* 2.14.10.2 (4 *ed.*), 16.3.1.18 (30 *ed.*), 19.1.13.31 (32 *ed.*), 37.1.3 pr. (39 *ed.*), 47.9.1.2 (56 *ed.*), 47.10.7.1 (57 *ed.*), 50.16.46 pr. (59 *ed.*), 43.12.1.14 (68 *ed.*), 44.1.2.4 (74 *ed.*), 28.5.6.2 (4 *Sab.*), 35.1.9

[See next page for 245a continued and 245b, 246 and 247].

videmus.[248] There are also some future forms: *accomodabimus,*[249] *adsumemus,*[250] *aestimabimus,*[251] *cogemus,*[252] *contribuemus,*[253] *convertemus,*[254] *deliberabimus,*[255] *excusabimus,*[256] *exigemus,*[257] *eximemus,*[258] *exsequemur,*[259] *numerabimus,*[260] *observabimus,*[261] *restituemus,*[262] *sequemur,*[263] *servabimus,*[264] *subveniemus.*[265] The number and variety of these categorical forms in which Ulpian thinks of himself as speaking for lawyers or for the Roman government in general is a measure both of his self-confidence and of his self-regard.

These traits emerge most clearly in those texts in which the author treats his own opinions about the law, rather than the law itself, as the primary object of the debate. Here are some of them:

haec utique nemo credet nos esse probaturos[266]
nec quisquam putet hoc nos existimare[267]
secundum nostram sententiam etiam divus Marcus rescripsit[268]
apud eum [Marcellus] notavi non de omni iniuria hoc esse dicendum me putare[269]
ut in iunctura argentea scio me dixisse[270]
et retineo me dixisse defici eos a petitione fideicommissi[271]
eleganter apud me quaesitum est . . . an habeat contrariam pigneraticiam[272]

(20 *Sab.*), 34.3.5 pr. (23 *Sab.*), 45.1.38.9 (49 *Sab.*), 50.16.178.2 (49 *Sab.*), cf. 2.14.7.5 (4 *ed.: s. enim d.*), 28.5.3.4 (3 *Sab.: s . . . d*), 5.1.61 pr. (26 *ed.*; same), 29.3.2.1 (50 *ed.*: same). *Dicere solemus* is in *D.* 50.16.111 (Iav. 6 *Cass.*), 47.10.1 pr. (Ulp. 56 *ed.*).

[245b] *D.* 36.4.5.21 (52 *ed.*), 39.3.1.23 (53 *ed.*), 50.17.9 (15 *Sab.*), 26.2.10.1 (36 *Sab.*), 50.17.34 (45 *Sab.*), 45.1.41 pr. (50 *Sab.*).

[246] *D.* 15.3.10.8 (29 *ed.*).

[247] *D.* 13.5.16.4 (27 *ed.*), 24.1.3.3 (32 *Sab.*).

[248] *D.* 33.7.12.27 (20 *Sab.*), 23.3.9.3 (31 *Sab.*), 1.1.1.3 (1 *inst.*).

[249] *D.* 40.5.30.4 (5 *fid.: mentem senatusconsulti*).

[250] *D.* 45.1.41 pr. (50 *Sab.*).

[251] *D.* 42.3.6 (64 *ed.*).

[252] *D.* 39.3.1.23 (53 *ed.*), 25.3.5.4 (2 *off. cons.*).

[253] *D.* 29.4.6.2 (50 *ed.*).

[254] *D.* 29.4.2.1 (7 *Sab.*).

[255] *D.* 3.1.1.5 (6 *ed.*).

[256] *D.* 9.4.2.1 (18 *ed.*).

[257] *D.* 14.1.1.16 (28 *ed.*) 37.11.1.4 (39 *ed.*), 37.5.10.1 (40 *ed.*).

[258] *D.* 47.10.17.7 (57 *ed.*).

[259] *D.* 3.1.1.10 (6 *ed.*).

[260] *D.* 9.2.21.1 (18 *ed.*).

[261] *D.* 38.5.1.13 (44 *ed.*).

[262] *D.* 42.2.6.6 (5 *omn. trib*).

[263] *D.* 16.3.1.1 (30 *ed.*), 33.1.3.3 (24 *Sab.*), 45.1.41 pr. (50 *Sab.*).

[264] *D.* 44.4.4.31 (76 *ed.*).

[265] *D.* 42.6.1.6 (64 *ed.*).

[266] *D.* 32.1.1 (1 *fid.*).

[267] *D.* 6.2.7.17 (16 *ed.*), cf. 9.2.27.9 (18 *ed.*), 11.7.4 (25 *ed.*), 26.7.3.2 (35 *ed.*), 26.7.9.1 (36 *ed.*).

[268] *D.* 29.1.3 (2 *Sab.*), cf. 13.7.36 pr. (11 *ed.*), 47.9.3.78 (56 *ed.*), Pernice (1885) 382.

[269] *D.* 47.10.11.7 (57 *ed.*).

[270] *D.* 34.2.19.8 (20 *Sab.*).

[271] *D.* 35.1.92 (5 *fid.*).   [272] *D.* 13.7.24. pr (30 *ed.*).

Ulpian uses *nos* and *me* about equally in these texts. It would be hard to find any parallel to them in the legal literature. But a qualification is called for. As will appear in chapter 7,[273] this assured sense of superiority is a feature of the early, rather than the middle and late, period of his writing.

(iv) *Future tenses.* A feature of discourse about law which is not shared by other branches of learning is that statements of law can be made at choice in the present and future tenses. 'The contract is binding' and 'the contract will be binding' (sc. if the subject-matter and price are agreed) are equivalent, and the tense has no temporal connotation. At most one might surmise that the future draws attention more firmly to the hypothetical character of statements of law in relation to given facts. They presuppose that the facts are found to be such-and-such. Another nuance which may be conveyed by the use of the future is that of a forward-looking, perhaps optimistic, outlook, even if the optimism is by implication no more than that of a lawyer who is confident that the correct view will be accepted by the parties or, if not, applied at the trial or on appeal.

Ulpian is a partisan of the future tenses. Whether he is so to a greater extent than any other jurist in the *Digest* could not be determined without a labour that seemed excessive for purposes of the present study. Nevertheless, it is clear that Ulpian often uses, at least as a variant, the future form of a verb, when others confine themselves to the present.

A good example is *dicendum erit*,[274] 'it will have to be said', viz. that the law is so-and-so. Whereas *dicendum est* is commonly found in juristic writing, *dicendum erit* and *erit dicendum* come 179 times in texts of Ulpian and only 15 in other writers.[275] Confined to Ulpian are the forms *et dicendum erit*,[276] *et ita erit dicendum*,[277] *et generaliter dicendum erit*,[278] *et generaliter erit dicendum*,[279] and *et ideo dicendum erit*.[280] *Idem erit dicendum* comes[281] in 81 texts of Ulpian and 6 of other jurists,[282] *dicendum erit* or *erit*

---

[273] Below, pp. 165–6.

[274] *CDJ* 53 DICENDUM. The texts with *erit dicendum* number 11: *D.* 2.14.7.5 (4 *ed.*), 3.4.2 (8 *ed.*), 3.3.33.5 (9 *ed.*), 4.4.11.1 (11 *ed.*), 6.1.5.1 (16 *ed.*), 40.5.4.2 (60 *ed.*), 43.3.1.9 (67 *ed.*), 37.6.5 pr. (79 *ed.*), 7.4.10.1 (17 *Sab.*), 22.3.18.2 (6 *disp.*), 34.1.14.2 (2 *fid.*).

[275] *CDJ* 53 DICENDUM ERIT (77 texts), 55 ERIT DICENDUM (102 texts) but *D.* 2.8.15.5 (Marci. 1 *appell.*: *idem d. erit.*), 34.5.15 (Marci. 2 *reg.*: *idem erit ex eventu d.*), 20.1.16.8 (Marci. 1 *hyp.*: *quod e. d.*), 38.2.42.2 (Pap. 13 *qu.*: *idem e. d.*), 41.3.44.4 (Pap. 23 *qu*: *idem d. e.*), 33.9.4.5 (Paul 4 *Sab.*: *idem e. d.*), 4.2.17 (Paul 1 *qu.*: *d. e.*), 31.82 pr. (Paul 10 *qu.*: *d. e.*), 18.1.15.2 (Paul 5 *Sab.*: *idem d. e.*), 28.5.48 pr. (Afr. 4 *qu.*: *idem e. d.*), 39.2.29 (Gai. 28 *ed. prov.*: *idem e. d.*), 13.6.13.2 (Pomp. 11 *Sab.*: *idem . . . e. d.*), 23.2.48 pr. (Ter. 8 *Iul. Pap.*: *idemque d. e.*), 48.19.10.2 (Macer 2 *pub. iud.*: *d.e.*), 36.1.67.1 (Maec. 5 *fid.*: *d.e.*).

[276] *D.* 5.3.25.9 (15 *ed.*), cf. 43.21.3.6 (70 *ed.*: *et erit dicendum*).

[277] *D.* 4.4.3.3 (11 *ed.*).

[278] *D.* 13.7.9.3 (28 *ed.*).

[279] *D.* 43.26.8.6 (71 *ed.*).

[280] *D.* 38.17.2.9 (13 *Sab.*).

[281] *CDJ* 59 IDEM.

[282] Above, n. 275.

dicendum[283] (without *et* or *idem*) in 92 texts of Ulpian out of 96. *Probandum erit*[284] is parallel. Of 35 texts with *erit probandum* or *probandum erit* 34 are Ulpian's.[285] For the commonest form, *idem erit probandum*, all 22 texts are his; so are the 2 texts with *idemque erit probandum*. There is a contrast between *cessat*, 'does not apply', and *cessabit*, 'will not apply'. According to our criteria, the former is not Ulpianic, since, though 81 texts out of 101 come from him,[286] there are 21 from other jurists, including 12 from Paul.[287] *Cessabit* is a different matter. Here 44 texts out of 46 are Ulpian's;[288] there are also three texts, all his, with *cessabunt*.[289] *Accipere* is another illustrative verb. Here the Tyrian has all 20 texts with *accipiendum erit* and *erit accipiendum*,[290] together with 25 instances of *accipiemus*[291] out of 28, and all 7 of *accipietur*.[292] He has the only texts with *erit admittendum*[293] and *erit notandum*.[294] All 13 instances of *consequenter dicemus*[295] and 26 of 27 with *consequens erit dicere*[296] come from him. So do

[283] Above, nn. 274, 275.
[284] *CDJ* 67 PROBANDUM.
[285] *Idem e. p.* D. 17.1.8.6 (31/1 *ed.*), 38.5.1.6 (44 *ed.*), 38.5.1.20 (44 *ed.*), 47.10.5.3 (56/2 *ed.*), 47.10.13.5 (57 *ed.* bis incl. *i. ergo e. p.*), 42.1.5.1 (59 *ed.*), 40.5.4.17 (60 *ed.*), 42.6.1.10 (64 *ed.*), 41.2.4 (67 *ed.*), 43.17.4 (70 *ed.*), 43.24.3.4 (71 *ed.*), 43.24.11.8, 13 (71 *ed.* bis), 20.6.4.1 (73 *ed.*), 42.8.2 (73 *ed.*), 44.2.7 pr. (75 *ed.*), 44.2.7.5 (75 *ed.*), 44.5.1.6 (76 *ed.*), 29.2.6.2 (6 *Sab.*), 18.2.4.6 (28 *Sab.*), 24.2.11.1 (3 *Iul. Pap.*); *idemque e. p.* 43.3.1.12 (67 *ed.*), 11.8.1.3 (68 *ed.*), 42.8.10.20 (73 *ed.*); 49.9.1 (4 *appell.*); *quod magis e. p.* 48.22.7.11 (10 *off. proc.*), 40.5.4.5 (60 *ed.*); *quod ita e. p.* 15.1.11.7 (29 *ed.*); *erit p.* 39.2.15.34 (53 *ed.*), 43.24.15.11 (71 *ed.*), 48.22.7.11 (10 *off. proc.*); *tantundem e. p.* 45.3.11 (48 *Sab.*); *Idem p. e.* 44.4.4.21 (76 *ed.*); all Ulp., cf. 28.5.85.1 (Paul 23 *qu.*: *idem p. e.*).
[286] *CDJ* 51 CESSAT but Citati (1927) 16–17 (Beseler etc).
[287] *CDJ* 30 CESSAT.   [288] *CDJ* 51 CESSABIT.
[289] D. 2.1.7.2 (3 *ed.*), 25.3.5.19 (2 *off. cons.*), 42.1.15.6 (3 *off. cons.*).
[290] D. 4.4.9.5 (11 *ed.*), 12.2.7 (22 *ed.*), 21.2.37.1 (32 *ed.*), 27.3.1.15 (36 *ed.*), 38.8.1.8 (46 *ed.*), 39.2.15.35 (53 *ed.*), 42.6.1.13 (64 *ed.*), 28.6.2 pr. (6 *Sab.*), 38.16.2 pr. (13 *Sab.*), 38.17.2.43 (13 *Sab.*), 30.34.4 (21 *Sab.*), 33.9.3.6 (22 *Sab.*), 18.6.4.2 (28 *Sab.*), 25.1.5 pr. (36 *Sab.*), 30.74 (4 *disp.*), 9.2.49.1 (9 *disp.*), 39.6.37 pr. (15 *Iul. Pap.*), 48.5.24.4 (1 *adult.*), 36.1.18.3 (2 *fid.*), 36.1.18.4 (2 *fid.*), cf. 4.6.26.5 (12 *ed.*: *e. accipienda*), 6.2.9.1 (16 *ed.* same), 40.4.13.3 (5 *disp.*: *erunt accipienda*). All but three texts have *erit* preceding.
[291] D. 2.8.2.3 (5 *ed.*), 3.2.2.1 (6 *ed.*), 4.9.1.5 (14 *ed.*), 5.3.20.15 (15 *ed.*), 9.2.5.1 (18 *ed.*), 9.2.27.17 (18 *ed.*), 14.1.1.21 (28 *ed.*), 50.16.185 (18 *ed.*), 37.11.1.6 (39 *ed.*), 38.8.1.4 (46 *ed.*), 48.19.2.2 (48 *ed.*), 40.12.22.1 (55 *ed.*), 47.8.2.11 (56 *ed.*), 47.8.4.3 (56 *ed.*), 50.16.45 (58 *ed.*), 40.5.4.11 (60 *ed.*), 46.7.3.6 (77 *ed.*), 7.9.3.1 (79 *ed.*), 23.3.33 (6 *Sab.*), 23.2.43.8 (1 *Iul. Pap.*), 21.1.23.2 (1 *ed. cur.*), 21.1.27 (1 *ed. cur.*), 21.1.31.12 (1 *ed. cur.*), 40.16.2.1 (2 *off. cons.*), 1.12.1.8 (1 *off. pr. urb.*), cf. Coll. 2.4.1 (18 *ed.*), FV 188 (*off. pr. tut.*), but D. 24.2.9 (Paul 2 *adult.*), 48.16.13 pr. (Paul 3 *adult.*), 13.6.18 pr. (Gai. 9 *ed. prov.*).
[292] D. 4.6.21.3 (12 *ed.*), 5.2.8.9 (14 *ed.*), 38.8.1.5 (Ulp. 46 *ed.*), 47.9.1.2 (56/1 *ed.*), 33.6.11 (23 *Sab.*), 46.1.8.7 (47 *Sab.*), 28.5.35 pr. (4 *disp.*).
[293] D. 50.2.2.5 (1 *disp.*), 43.24.13.4 (71 *ed.*), cf. 5.4.1.4 (15 *ed. e. admittenda*).
[294] D. 3.6.3.3 (10 *ed.*), 4.6.21.1 (12 *ed.*).
[295] D. 12.2.11.1 (22 *ed.*), 17.1.10.3 (31/1 *ed.*), 25.2.17 pr. (34 *ed.*), 27.9.5.14 (35 *ed.*), 37.5.3.5 (40 *ed.*), 43.16.3.15 (69 *ed.*), 30.49.1 (23 *Sab.*), 18.6.1 pr. (28 *Sab.*), 24.1.7.3 (32 *Sab.*), 48.22.7.13 (10 *off. proc.*), 10.2.49 (2 *disp.*), 28.5.35.1 (4 *disp.*), 4.6.38 pr. (6 *Iul. Pap.*), cf. 37.6.5 pr. (79 *ed.*: *c. erit dicendum*).
[296] D. 11.1.9.4 (22 *ed.*), 26.10.1.4 (35 *ed.*), 26.10.3.6 (35 *ed.*), 27.9.5.3 (35 *ed.*), 29.1.11 pr. (45 *ed.*), 29.6.1.1. (48 *ed.*), 47.10.3.1 (56/2 *ed.*), 47.10.17.1 (57 *ed.*), 42.1.4.4 (58 *ed.*), 42.4.7.3 (59 *ed.*), 40.5.4.5 (60 *ed.*), 43.4.3 pr. (68 *ed.*), 43.24.15.12 (71 *ed.*), 46.7.3.7 (71 *ed.*), 43.32.1.4 (73 *ed.*), 44.2.7.3 (75 *ed.*), 39.5.19.3 (76 *ed.*: *erit c. d.*), 44.6.1.1 (76 *ed.*), 46.7.5.3 (77 *ed.*), 46.6.4.7 (79 *ed.*), 39.2.30.1 (81 *ed.*), 18.4.2.11 (49 *Sab.*), 18.4.2.16 (49 *Sab.*), 46.4.13.1 (50 *Sab.*), 2.12.1.1 (4 *omn. trib.*), 36.1.17.9 (4 *fid.*), cf. FV 269 (46 *Sab.*) but 29.1.41.5 (Tryph. 18 *disp.*: *c erit hoc d.*).

all 3 with *definiemus*,[297] all 5 with *dicet quis*,[298] 6 of 7 with *melius dicetur*,[299] all 7 with *officium . . . erit*[300] (of the praetor etc.). He has the only passages with *accedendum*,[301] *recedendum*[302] and *distinguendum erit*.[303] He alone writes *in ea erit causa*,[304] as opposed to *in ea causa est*. *Aequissimum est* is found in other writers, but *aequissimum erit*,[305] 26 times, only in Ulpian. *Nullius momenti est* occurs in others, *nullius erit momenti*[306] only in our author. *Meminisse oportet* is in others, *meminisse oportebit*[307] is Ulpianic. *Locus est*, 'there is room for . . .', is fairly common in legal writing, *erit locus*[308] and *locus erit*,[309] with 22 mentions between them, are confined to Ulpian. The catalogue includes *dubium non erit*,[310] *fortasse* or *fortassis*[311] with the future indicative, *gravabitur*,[312] and *difficile erit*.[313–14] We have already met *et eveniet*,[315] *et intererit*,[316] and *et erit procendendum*.[317]

Ulpian's liking for future tenses is not a constant. As will be seen in chapter 8, it follows an upward curve to a peak and then declines. This variation helps to plot the course and order of his works.

(v) *Inversion of the normal word order.* In what has been said so far the attentive reader will have noticed many inversions of the normal Latin word order. Thus, the auxiliary often comes before the main verb, *erit*

---

[297] *D.* 37.1.3.2 (39 *ed.*), 25.1.3.1 (36 *Sab.*), 26.1.3.1 (37 *Sab.*).

[298] *D.* 27.9.7 pr. (35 *ed.*), 38.17.2.41 (13 *Sab.*), 32.55.7 (25 *Sab.*), 50.16.167 (25 *Sab.*), 41.1.33.1 (4 *disp.*).

[299] Above, n. 151.

[300] *D.* 39.2.4 pr. (1 *ed.*), 6.1.9 (16 *ed.*), 7.6.5.6 (17 *ed.*), 10.3.6.9 (19 *ed.*), 26.7.5.8 (35 *ed.*), 36.4.5.22 (52 *ed.*), 39.3.6.6 (53 *ed.*).

[301] *D.* 42.1.4.3 (58 *ed.*).

[302] *D.* 43.29.3.7 (71 *ed.*).

[303] *D.* 44.2.11.10 (75 *ed.*).

[304] *D.* 2.11.4.1 (74 *ed.*), 45.1.38.22 (49 *Sab.*), cf. 42.4.7.5 (59 *ed: in ea tamen erit causa*).

[305] *D.* 3.5.13 (10 *ed.*), 4.8.13.4 (13 *ed.*), 5.3.13.9 (15 *ed.*), 5.3.37 (15 *ed.*), 4.9.7.3 (18 *ed.*), 14.3.11 pr. (18 *ed.*), 14.3.11.5 (28 *ed.*), 16.3.1.27 (30 *ed.*), 17.1.12.9 (31/1 *ed: a. enim erit*), 25.4.1.8 (34 *ed.*), 26.10.3.7 (35 *ed.*), 27.3.1.11 (36 *ed.*), 37.4.3.4 (39 *ed.*), 37.5.3.6 (40 *ed.*), 36.4.5.30 (52 *ed.*), 39.1.5.10 (52 *ed.*), 47.10.7.2 (57 *ed.*), 43.14.1.7 (68 *ed.*), 43.18.1.5 (70 *ed*) 30.53.8. (25 *Sab.*), 2.15.8.22 (5 *omn. trib.*), 36.1.23.3 (5 *disp.*), 21.1.17.19 (1 *ed. cur.*), 36.1.6.3 (4 *fid.*), 40.5.24.14 (5 *fid.*), 42.1.15.9 (3 *off. cons.*).

[306] *D.* 29.1.15.1 (45 *ed.*), 26.8.5.2 (40 *Sab.*), 46.4.13.1 (50 *Sab.* bis), 2.15.8.17 (5 *omn. trib.*), 26.5.8.1 (8 *omn. trib.*), cf. 50.9.4.2 (1 *off. cur. reip: ullius erit momenti*).

[307] Above, n. 134.

[308] *D.* 9.1.1.7 (18 *ed.*), 9.2.7.4 (18 *ed.*), 38.5.1.17 (44 *ed.*), 10.2.49 (2 *disp.*), 21.1.1.5 (1 *ed. cur.*), 36.1.17.9 (4 *fid.*).

[309] *D.* 4.2.9.1 (11 *ed.*), 14.6.7.12 (29 *ed.*), 26.7.5.3 (35 *ed.*), 27.4.1.3 (36 *ed.*), 13.1.10.2 (38 *ed.*)́, 47.4.1.11 (38 *ed.*), 39.2.15.33 (53 *ed.*), 43.12.1.15 (68 *ed.*), 43.20.1.14 (70 *ed.*), 39.1.20.2, 7 (71 *ed.* bis), 43.24.9 (71 *ed.*), 43.22.1.5 (73 *ed.*), 18.4.2.11 (49 *Sab.*), 36.1.1.12 (3 *fid.*), 37.14.16.1 (10 *Iul. Pap.*), cf. *locus non erit* 40.4.12 (50 *ed.*), 39.1.20.13 (71 *ed.*).

[310] *D.* 12.2.11.3 (22 *ed.*).

[311] *D.* 6.1.15.1 (16 *ed.*), 15.1.30.6 (29 *ed.*), 37.10.5.3 (41 *ed.: fortasse*), 32.55.7 (25 *Sab.*), 50.16.167 (25 *Sab.*), 50.13.1.3 (8 *omn. trib.*)

[312] *D.* 43.16.1.15. (69 *ed.*).

[313–14] *D.* 50.16.99.2 (1 *off. cons.*).

[315] Above, n. 28.

[316] Above, n. 32.

[317] Above, n. 33.

admittendum for *admittendum erit*, *est decretum* for *decretum est*. Similarly the object often follows the verb *habet aequitatem*[317a] *rationem* for *aequitatem trationem habet*.[317b] This feature of Ulpian's discourse rests, no doubt, on his liking for a manner that is relaxed, conversational, *décousu*. It is a pervasive feature of his writing.

Thus, if we begin with inversions of *erit* and the gerund or gerundive, we find, apart from *erit accipiendum*,[318] *admittendum*,[319] *dicendum*,[320] *notandum*,[321] *probandum*,[322] and *procedendum*,[323] uses, confined to Ulpian, of *erit agendum*,[324] *audiendus*,[325] *cavendum*,[326] *cogendus*,[327] *conveniendus*,[328] *concedendum*,[329] *danda* (*actio*[330] etc.), *decurrendum*,[331] *defendendum*,[332] *descendendum*,[333] *detrahendum/a*,[334] *excipiendum*,[335] *exigenda*,[336] *faciendum/a*,[337] *innovandum*,[338] *inspiciendum/a*,[339] *interponendum/a*,[340] *interpretandum*,[341] *intuenda*,[342] *invidendum*,[343] *ignoscendum*,[344] *liberandus*,[345] *movendum*,[346] *obicienda*,[347] *observandum*,[348] *permittendum*,[349]

[317a] *D.* 3.5.3.9 (10 ed.), 14.4.7.1 (29 ed.), 17.2.63.5 (31/2 ed.), 37.10.3.13. (41 ed.).

[317b] *D.* 9.2.27.11 (18 ed.), 9.4.2.1 (18 ed.), 12.2.9.6 (22 ed.), 14.5.4.5 (29 ed.), 37.10.3.13 (41 ed.), 42.4.3 pr. (59 ed.), 7.9.7 pr. (79 ed.), 28.5.6.4 (4 Sab.), 28.6.10.6 (4 Sab.), 7.1.12.4 (17 Sab.), 7.4.3.2 (17 Sab.), 34.2.19.3 (20 Sab.), 41.9.1.4 (31 Sab.), 24.1.5.15 (32 Sab.), Citati (1927) 42 (de Francisci etc.). Other positive uses of *habet/habent* with an abstract noun following: *disceptationem D.* 26.2.10.2 (36 Sab.), 2.15.8.24 (5 omn. trib.), *dubitationem* 44.5.1.6 (76 ed.), cf. 4.4.25 (Gai. 4 ed. prov.: *nullam h. d.*), *publicam exsecutionem* 47.10.7.1 (Ulp 57 ed.), *humanitatem* 44.4.7.1 (76 ed.), *liberationem* 46.3.7 (43 Sab.), *mentionem* 37.15.5.1 (10 ed.), 4.8.31 (13 ed.), *necessitatem* 25.1.1.1 (36 Sab.), *praestationem* 35.3.3.1 (79 ed.), *quaestionem* 32.50.4 (23 Sab.), *reputationem* 25.1.1.2 (36 Sab.), *tractatum* 12.1.9.3 (26 ed.), *voluntatem* 14.4.1.3 (29 ed.), 47.6.1.1 (38 ed.), 44.4.4.10 (76 ed.), 33.8.6.1 (25 Sab.).

[318] Above, n. 290.   [319] Above, n. 293.   [320] Above, n. 275.

[321] Above, n. 294.   [322] Above, n. 285.   [323] *D.* 7.8.6 (17 Sab.).

[324] *D.* 2.7.3 pr (5 ed.), 9.2.27.17, 28 (18 ed. bis), 13.6.3.4 (28 ed.), 47.10.15.29 (57ed.). 43.5.3.5 (68 ed.), 10.3.12 (71 ed.), 19.5.14.3 (41 Sab.).

[325] *D.* 3.3.25 (9 ed.), 38.5.1.15 (44 ed.), 36.1.13.2 (4 fid.), 1.12.1.5 (1 off. pr. urb.).

[326] *D.* 39.2.15 pr. (53 ed.), 46.7.3.3 (77 ed.), 39.1.21.6 (81 ed.), cf. 39.2.15.31 (53 ed.: *erit ei cavendum*).

[327] *D.* 4.8.17.4 (13 ed.), 40.5.24.12 (5 fid. bis).

[328] *D.* 4.9.3.3 (14 ed.), 15.2.1.7 (29 ed.), 17.1.6.1 (31/1 ed.), 29.4.10.2 (50 ed.).

[329] *D.* 40.2.20.2 (2 off. cons.).

[330] *D.* 3.3.27.1 (9 ed.), 3.5.11.1 (10 ed.), 4.3.7.9 (11 ed.), 4.3.13 pr (11 ed.), 9.2.7.3 (18 ed.), 9.2.11.8 (18 ed.), 42.8.6.11 (66 ed.) cf. 24.3.64.9 (7 Iul. Pap: *erit . . . d*); *erit dandum* 47.12.3.11 (25 ed.), 43.17.4 (70 ed.), but *erit dandus* 40.5.37 (6 fid. citing Marcus).

[331] *D.* 11.6.5 pr. (24 ed.).

[332] *D.* 50.2.3. pr. (3 off. proc.).

[333] *D.* 4.6.26.9 (13 ed.), 7.5.11 (18 Sab.), cf. 43.33.2 (73 ed: *erit eis d.*)

[334] *D.* 44.4.4.16 (76 ed.), 39.5.12 (3 disp.).

[335] *D.* 44.4.4.16 (76 ed.).

[336] *D* 36.4.3.2 (52 ed.).

[337] *D.* 4.4.7.8 (11 ed.), 37.6.1.17 (40 ed.).

[338] *D* 49.7.1.1 (4 appell.).

[339] *D* 46.3.24 (47 ed.), 43.13.1.8. (68 ed.).

[340] *D.* 37.6.1.11 (40 ed.), 7.5.10.1 (79 ed.).

[341] *D.* 43.3.1.11 (67 ed.).

[342] *D.* 43.13.1.8 (68 ed).

[343] *D.* 7.8.4 pr. (17 Sab.: *non erit ei i.*).

[344] *D* 34.3.5.4 (23 Sab.).

[345] *D.* 38.17.2.44. (13 Sab.: *erit matri ignoscendum?*).

[See *opposite page for n. 346, 347, 348, 349.*]

plectendus,[350]   *praestandum,*[351-2]   *prospiciendum,*[353]   *provocandus,*[354] *quaerendum,*[355]   *ratum   habendum,*[356]   *redhibendus,*[357]   *reducenda,*[358] *referendum,*[359]   *repellendus,*[360]   *requirendum,*[361]   *restituendus/a,*[362] *revocanda,*[363]   *satisdandum,*[364]   *sequendus/a,*[365]   *servandum,*[366] *spectandus/um,*[367]   *statuendum,*[368]   *subveniendum,*[369]   *transeundum,*[370] *transferendum/a,*[371]   *tribuendum,*[372]   *utendum.*[373] Indeed, the use of this construction is itself a mark of Ulpian's style. It occurs in his work at least 250 times,[374] against 35 for all other jurists—9 for Paul, 7 for Papinian, mainly in the negative form *non erit . . .*, and 6 for Pomponius.[375] Its use in a given text may therefore be taken as a pointer, though not of course a conclusive one, to Ulpian's authorship.

Another set of inversions involve putting *est* as an auxiliary before the main verb or, when used as a copulative, before the subject: *est decretum,*[376]

[346] *D.* 43.29.3.13 (71 *ed.*).

[347] *D.* 21.1.59.1 (74 *ed.*).   [348] *D.* 26.7.3.5 (35 *ed.*), 43.15.1.6 (68 *ed.*).

[349] *D.* 42.5.15 pr. (62 *ed.*).

[350] *D.* 48.19.9.15 (10 *off. proc.*), 48.5.30.2 (4 *adult.*), cf. 11.7.8.2 (25 *ed.: erit . . . p.*).

[351-2] *D.* 19.1.13 pr. (32 *ed.*), 30.47.1 (22 *Sab.*), 37.11.5.1 (4 *disp.*).

[353] *D.* 37.10.3.12 (41 *ed.*).

[354] *D.* 49.3.1 pr., 1, 49.4.1.4 (all 1 *appell.*).

[355] *D.* 26.10.3.7 (35 *ed.*).

[356] *D.* 12.2.5 pr. (22 *ed.*).

[357] *D.* 21.1.12.1 (1 *ed. cur.*).

[358] *D.* 13.3.3 (27 *ed.*).

[359] *D.* 37.9.7.1 (47 *ed.*), 33.4.1.4 (19 *Sab.*).

[360] *D.* 38.2.14.11 (45 *ed.*), 36.2.14.2 (24 *Sab.*).

[361] *D.* 2.15.8.9 (5 *omn. trib.*).

[362] *D.* 4.4.3.4 (11 *ed.*), 24.1.7.3 (32 *Sab.*).

[363] *D.* 42.8.10.11 (73 *ed.*).

[364] *D.* 36.4.3.2 (52 *ed.: erit ei s.*).

[365] *D.* 48.19.32 (6 *ed.*), 29.4.6.1 (50 *ed.*), 30.39.1 (21 *Sab.*).

[366] *D.* 3.2.19 (8 *ed.*).

[367] *D.* 6.2.7.13 (16 *ed.*), 13.3.3 (27 *ed.*).

[368] *D.* 2.11.2.8 (74 *ed.*).

[369] *D.* 38.2.8.1 (43 *ed.*), 2.11.2.2 (74 *ed.*) both *erit ei s.*

[370] *D.* 39.1.1.1 (52 *ed.*).

[371] *D.* 3.3.25 (9 *ed.*), 21.1.38.3 (2 *ed. cur.*).

[372] *D.* 14.4.5.9 (29 *ed.*).   [373] *D.* 43.13.1.12 (68 *ed.*).

[374] Texts in nn. 275, 285, 290, 293, 294, 324–73.

[375] Above, n. 275 and *D.* 3.5.28 (Call. 3 *ed. mon.: e. agendum*), 35.1.68 (Iav. 2 *Cass.: e. exspectandum*), 38.5.6 (Iul. 26 *dig.: e. inhibenda*), 41.2.51 (Iav. 5 *post. Lab.: e. aestimanda*), 41.1.65.3 (Lab. 6 *pith.: e. instruenda*), 20.6.8.14 (Marci. 1 *hyp.: non e. quaerendum*), 32.13 (Maec. 2 *fid.: non e. dubitandum*), 40.5.32 pr. (Maec. 15 *fid.: non e . . . compellendus*), 48.5.6 (Pap. 1 *adult.: nec e. deneganda*), 36.3.5.3 (Pap. 28 *qu.: non e. . . . remittendus*), 24.3.40 (Pap. 28 *qu.: non e. impediendus*), 46.1.51.2 (Pap. 3 *resp.: non e. prohibendus*), 31.77.16 (Pap. 8 *resp.: non e. quaerendum*), 31.76 pr. (Pap. 7 *resp.: non e. trahendum*), 3.4.6 pr. (Paul 9 *ed.: e. servandum* = Ulp. 9 *ed.*), 12.2.30.2 (Paul 18 *ed.: non e. quaerendum*), 10.1.4.1 (Paul 23 *ed.: e. facienda*), 10.2.29 (Paul 23 *ed.: e. damnandus*), 15.1.26 (Paul 30 *ed.: non e. condemnandus*), 17.2.65.3 (Paul 32 *ed.: non e. communicandum*), 3.3.61 (Paul 1 *Plaut.: idem e. observandum*), 48.20.7.1 (Paul 1 *port. lib. damn.: e. vindicanda*), 28.6.16 pr. (Pomp. 3 *Sab.: e. spectanda*), 21.2.16 pr. (Pomp. 9 *Sab.: e. agendum*), 34.2.34.2 (Pomp. 9 *Sab.: non. e. utendum*), 31.43.1 (Pomp. 3 *Q M: e. accipienda*), 36.1.72.1 (Pomp. 2 *fid.: e. persequendum*), 27.1.45.4 (Tryph. 13 *disp.: e. subcumbendum*).   [376] Above, n. 41

est constitutum,[376a] *est quaesitum,*[376b] *est rescriptum,*[376c] *est . . . ex-pressum,*[376d] *est . . . tractatum,*[376e] *est . . . agitatum,*[376f] or again *est autem manumissio de manu missio.*[377] The phrases which are used to begin sentences or clauses with *et est,* listed above,[378] involve inversions of one of these sorts. The initial *est et,* found in 13 texts, is confined, among *Digest* jurists, to Ulpian.[379] Initial *est hoc,* also Ulpianic, comes 3 times.[380]

Of inversions of object and verb we have mentioned *habet aequitatem*[380a] and *habet rationem.*[380b] It would be tedious to list more. The reader will be on the look-out for this trait.

All these forms of inversion may be regarded as aspects of one of two techniques. Ulpian tries to avoid concentrations of verbs at the end of a sentence, in order to keep the various clauses of which it is composed, and their meaning, separate. This involves putting the verb at the beginning or in the middle, rather than at the end, of a clause. He also wishes to emphasize the most important word, which must therefore, by way of climax, come at the end of a clause or sentence.

(vi) *Verbs.* A verb which *VIR* notes as Ulpianic[381] is *accipere* in the sense 'take', 'construe', 'interpret'. We have come across *erit accipiendum,*[382] *accipiemus,*[383] and *accipietur.*[384] A number of other forms of *accipere* count as marks of style. One is *accipe,*[385] of which all 14 instances

---

[376a] *D.* 2.13.4.5 (4 *ed.*), 3.6.5 pr. (10 *ed.*), 4.1.6 (13 *ed.*), 17.1.12.9 (31/1 *ed.*), 28.3.6.8, 10 (10 *Sab.* bis), 50.12.3 pr. (4 *disp.* bis) but 50.16.244 (Lab. 4 *pith.* itp.), 47.22.1.2 (Marci. 3 *inst.*, derivative) 3.5.27 (Tryph. 2 *disp.*), cf. 42.8.10.13 (73 *ed.: e. saepissime c.*), 40.5.24.21 (5 *fid.*: same), 48.1.5.1 (8 *disp.: e. enim c.*), 22.1.37 (10 *ed.: est . . . c.*), 4.4.3.1 (11 *ed.: est et c.*), 13.6.5.2 (28 *ed.:* same), but 16.3.24 (Pap. 9 *qu.: est quidem c.*, really a note).

[376b] *D.* 3.3.37.1 (9 *ed.*), 14.4.5.7 (29 *ed.*), 43.3.1.8 (67 *ed.*), 43.24.1.3 (71 *ed.*), 28.2.6 pr. (3 *Sab.*), 7.1.13.5 (18 *Sab.*), 34.2.19.2 (20 *Sab.*), 47.2.17.1 (40 *Sab.*) but 36.1.46.1 (Marc. 15 *dig.?* note), cf 41.9.1.2 (31 *Sab:* est quaestio volgata).

[376c] *D.* 4.6.26.9 (12 *ed.*), 13.7.13 pr. (28 *ed.*), 29.1.9.1 (9 *Sab.*), 30.41.7 (21 *Sab.*), 26.8.5.3 (40 *Sab.*), 48.18.4 (3 *disp.*), 49.1.10.4 (8 *disp.*), 42.1.59.1 (4 *omn. trib.*), 50.13.1.12 (8 *omn. trib.*), 40.5.24.5 (5 *fid.*), cf. *est saepissime r.* 3.2.2.2 (6 *ed.*), 4.4.20.1 (11 *ed.*), 13.7.36 pr. (11 *ed.*), 47.10.13.7 (57 *ed.*), 34.3.9 (24 *Sab.*) est et r. 4.2.16.2 (11 *ed.*), 36.1.19.1 (15 *Sab.*) est . . . et r. 38.16.1.1. (12 *Sab.*) est. saepe r. 29.2.25.2 (8 *Sab.*).

[376d] *D.* 4.4.19 (13 *ed.*), 28.3.6.9 (10 *Sab.*).

[376e] *D.* 34.3.7 pr. (23 *Sab.*).

[376f] *D.* 15.1.36 (2 *disp.*).

[377] *D.* 1.1.4 (*inst.*).   [378] Above, nn. 41–59.

[379] *D.* 3.2.2.2 (6 *ed.*), 3.3.39.6 (9 *ed.*), 37.12.1.4 (45 *ed.*), 43, 24.7.4 (71 *ed.*), 49.14.25 (19 *Sab.*), 8.2.3 (29 *Sab.*), 12.7.1 pr. (43 *Sab.*), 50.15.1.2, 3 bis, 5, 10, 11 (all 1 *cens.*).

[380] *D.* 1.19.1.2 (16 *ed.*), 47.10.7.1 (57 *ed.*).

[380a] Above, n. 165.

[380b] Above, n. 166.

[381] *VIR* I. 94.34–5.

[382] Above, n. 290.

[383] Above, n. 291.

[384] Above, n. 292.

[385] *D.* 11.4.1.5 (1 *ed.*), 39.2.4.1 (1 *ed.*), 2.4.4.2 (5 *ed.*), 3.1.1.9 (6 *ed.*), 3.2.6 pr. (6 *ed.*), 3.5.3.2 (10 *ed.*), 4.8.21.3 (13 *ed.:* =*iudex*), 39.2.15.5 (53 *ed.*), 43.20.1.39 (70 *ed.*), 43.30.3.6 (71 *ed.*), 29.2.30.1 (8 *Sab.*), 28.2.12 pr. (9 *Sab.*), 7.1.13.8 (18 *Sab.*), 21.1.25.2 (1 *ed. cur.*), cf. *FV* 321 (8 *ed.*).

come from Ulpian's texts. Others are *accipias*,[386] *accipies*,[387] *accipere debemus*,[388] for which Ulpian has 82 texts of 87, *accipere debes*,[389] *accipere nos debere*,[390] *accipere nos oportet*,[391] and *accipere debeamus*.[392] For *accipimus*[393] he has 60 texts out of 62, and for *sic accipiendum est* and variants (*accipienda sunt, est accipiendum, sunt accipienda*), 20 instances out of 21.[394] It is a remarkable concentration.

Putare is another verb which elicits Ulpian's favour. The forms *et puto, et putem, et magis puto, et ego puto, et non puto*, and *et verum/verius puto* have been mentioned already.[395] To these can be added *ut puta*, which occurs in the Tyrian's excerpts 298 times out of 315.[396] Of the remaining 17 texts Paul has 11. Despite this distribution, several authors have had the temerity to list it as non-classical.[397] Other Ulpianic forms of *putare* include *puto tamen*,[398] *putavimus tamen*,[399] *puto autem*,[400] and *et putat*[401] or *et recte putat*[402] followed by the jurist etc.

No other verbs are as Ulpianic as *accipere* and *putare*. But there are a

---

[386] D. 15.1.3.7 (29 ed.), 28.1.20.3 (1 Sab.), 29.2.30.1 (8 Sab.), 21.1.19.4 (1 ed. cur.).

[387] D. 5.3.25.8 (15 ed.).

[388] CDJ 49 ACCIPERE DEBEMUS but D. 35.2.74 (Gai. 3 leg. ed. urb.), 6.1.78 (Lab. 4 Pith. = Paul), 20.6.8.11 (Marci. I hyp.), 46.3.98.3 (Paul 15 qu.), 27.1.45.3 (Tryph. 13 disp.).

[389] D. 43.23.1.8 (71 ed.).

[390] D. 4.8.11.2 (13 ed.), cf. 11.5.1.2 (23 ed.: nos accipere debere).

[391] D. 26.2.3.1 (35 ed.), 38.5.1.4 (44 ed.), 38.8.1.6 (46 ed.), 50.16.99.1 (1 off. cons.).

[392] D. 14.6.7.3 (29 ed.), 38.17.1.12 (12 Sab.: ? debemus).

[393] CDJ 49 ACCIPIMUS but D. 9.2.45 pr. (Paul 10 Sab.), 43.3.2.1 (Paul 63 ed.).

[394] D. 50.16.3 pr. (2 ed.), 9.4.3 (3 ed.), 50.16.6.1 (3 ed.), 2.14.7.5 (4 ed.), 3.5.3.1 (10 ed.: s. sunt a.), 11.1.4.1. (22 ed.), 13.5.1.1. (27 ed.), 19.2.19.2 (32 ed.), 27.4.3 pr. (36 ed.), 37.5.8 pr. (40 ed.), 37.6.1.23 (40 ed.), 39.4.3.1 (55 ed.), 40.12.10 (55 ed. s. est. a.), 42.1.5.1 (59 ed.), 43.8.2.32 (68 ed.), 39.2.24 pr. (81 ed.), 28.1.21.2 (2 Sab.), 29.2.30.3 (8 Sab.), 49.3.1 pr. (1 appell.), 27.1.3 (1 off. pr. tut.), cf. VF 186 (1 off. pr. tut.) but 47.2.4 (Paul 9 Sab.).

[395] Above, nn. 13 – 17, 20 – 1.

[396] CDJ 74 UT PUTA and cf. FV 177 (17 Sab.) but D. 14.2.4.2 (Call. 2 qu.), 11.7.4.3 (Pap. 8 qu.), 22.1.3.2 (Pap. 20 qu.), 45.2.9 pr. (Pap. 27 qu.), 48.5.39 pr. (Pap. 36 qu.), 5.1.45 pr. (Pap. 3 resp.: Mommsen), 2.7.4 pr. (Paul 4 ed.), 4.8.19.2 (Paul 13 ed.), 4.8.28 (Paul 13 ed.), 10.1.4.8 (Paul 23 ed.), 2.14.9 (Paul 62 ed.), 19.1.4.1 (Paul 5 Sab.), 12.6.15 pr. (Paul 10 Sab.), 9.4.31 (Paul 7 Plaut.: del. Mommsen), 31.8.3 (Paul 9 Plaut.), 45.1.91.1 (Paul 17 Plaut.), 28.6.38.1 (Paul 1 sec. tab.), cf. ut . . . puta 47.2.22.1 (Paul 9 Sab.), 12.6.31 (Paul 3 qu.); puta ut 19.5.5.2 (Paul 5 qu.).

[397] Citati (1927) 72 (Eisele, Bonfante, Pringsheim, Donatuti, and others).

[398] Eight of 9 texts: D. 5.3.25.5 (15 ed.), 5.3.25.15 (15 ed.), 11.7.14.11 (25 ed.), 16.3.1.12 (30 ed.), 49.14.6 pr. (63 ed.), 33.9.1 (24 Sab.), 48.3.4 (9 off. proc.), 49.1.3.3 (1 appell.), cf. FV 71 (17 Sab.), 198 (1 off. pr. tut.), but D. 4.6.13.1 (Paul 12 ed.).

[399] D. 4.4.3.2 (11 ed.).

[400] D. 50.1.27.2 (2 ed.), 3.1.6 (6 ed.), 6.1.37 (17 ed.), 15.3.3.10 (29 ed.), 19.5.20.1 (32 ed.), 44.4.4.22 (76 ed.), 38.17.2.37 (13 Sab.), 7.1.70.4 (17 Sab.).

[401] D. 2.2.3.1 (3 ed.), 3.1.1.10 (6 ed.), 9.3.13.4 (15 ed.), 12.6.26.13 (26 ed.), 16.3.1.11 (30 ed.) 39.1.3.2 (52 ed.), 28.5.17.4 (7 Sab.), 38.17.2.44 (13 Sab.), 38.4.5.1 (14 Sab.), 7.1.12.5 (17 Sab.), 7.2.1.1 (17 Sab.), 47.2.12.2 (28 Sab.)

[402] D. 4.8.21.11 (13 ed.), 7.6.1.3 (18 Sab.).

number which occur once or more in his excerpts and not in other *Digest*
writers. I list them alphabetically:

adaequo,[403] *addo,*[404] *arto,*[405] *capesso,*[406] *causor,*[407] *commoneo,*[408]
commoveo,[409] *commundo,*[410] *comcumbo,*[411] *confringo,*[412] *coniveo,*[413]
conqueror,[414] *conscisco,*[415] *(boni) consulo,*[416] *dehonesto,*[417] *delitesco,*[418]
demereo,[419] *demoror,*[420] *(satis) desidero,*[421] *devoco,*[422] *diffindo,*[423]
dilapido,[424] *discutio*[425] (= *diiudico*), *disicio,*[426] *(ratione) ducor,*[427] *(obviam)
eo,*[428] *effervesco,*[429] *eloquor,*[430] *evoco*[431] *(ad praetorem), exaggero,*[432]
exorior,[433] *exorno,*[434] *(recte) exprimo,*[435] *facesso,*[436] *flagito,*[437] *(ante
oculos) habeo,*[438] *illicio,*[439] *immergo,*[440] *immoror,*[441] *imprecor,*[442]

[403] D. 30.41.13 (21 Sab.).
[404] D. 3.2.6.6 (6 ed.), 19.2.13.5 (32 ed.), 19.2.19 pr. (32 ed.), 47.8.2.23 (56/1 ed.), 41.2.13.1 (72 ed.), 16.3.11 (41 Sab.).
[405] D. 42.1.2 (6 ed.), 38.9.1.12 (49 ed.), 43.24.5.1 (71 ed.), 2.11.2.8 (74 ed. bis), 48.19.8.7 (9 off. proc.), but Citati (1957) 12 (Beseler, H. Krueger).
[406] FV 155 (1 excus.).
[407]. Nine texts of 11: D. 14.3.11.3 (28 ed.), 16.3.3 (30 ed.), 42.6.1.12 (64 ed.), 43.24.13.5 (71 ed.), 2.11.2.8 (74 ed.), 30.50.1 (24 Sab.), 32.11.8 (2 fid.), 36.1.13 pr. (4 fid.), 40.5.24.14 (5 fid.), but 2.15.12 (Cels. 3 dig.), 40.7.34.1 (Pap. 21 qu.)
[408] D. 13.6.12.1 (29 Sab.).
[409] D. 9.1.1.4 (18 ed.), 11.7.6 pr. (25 ed.), 39.6.2 (32 Sab.).
[410] D. 34.2.25.10 (44 Sab.)
[411] D. 1.6.6 (9 Sab.).
[412] D. 9.2.27.31 (18 ed.), 10.4.9 pr. (24 ed.), 39.2.24.9 (81 ed.).
[413] D. 40.1.4.1 (6 disp.).
[414] D. 29.5.1.3 (50 ed.), 47.10.7.2 (57 ed.).
[415] D. 21.1.17.4 (1 ed. cur.), 21.1.23.3 (1 ed. cur.).
[416] D. 23.4.4 (31 Sab.), 23.3.12.1 (34 Sab.), 50.2.3 pr. (3 off. proc.).
[417] D. 50.13.1.5 (8 omn. trib.).
[418] D. 11.4.1.2 (1 ed.).   [419] D. 16.1.2.3 (29 ed.).   [420] D. 5.1.2.4 (3 ed.).
[421] D. 3.3.35.3 (9 ed.), 36.4.1.1 (52 ed.), 36.4.3.2 (52 ed.).
[422] D. 37.10.1.11 (41 ed.).
[423] D. 2.11.2.3 (74 ed.).
[424] D. 4.4.11.6 (11 ed.), 5.3.25.11 (15 ed.), 26.4.1 pr. (14 Sab.).
[425] D. 4.8.13.2 (13 ed.), 4.8.25.1 (13 ed.), 48.2.6 (2 off. proc.).
[426] D. 43.24.7.6 (71 ed.).
[427] D. 11.3.5. pr. (23 ed.), 40.12.12.3 (55 ed.), 29.2.30.3 (8 Sab.), 47.14.1.4 (8 off. proc.).
[428] D. 1.18.13.1 (7 off. proc.), 47.11.6 pr. (8 off. proc.).
[429] D. 21.1.17.4 (1 ed. cur.).
[430] D. 3.2.13.6 (6 ed.), 22.5.12 (37 ed.), 46.8.12.2 (80 ed.).
[431] D. 25.4.1.2, 9 (34 ed. bis).
[432] D. 43.19.3.15 (70 ed.), 50.2.3.1 (3 off. proc.).
[433] D. 1.15.2 (1 off. pr. vig.).
[434] D. 15.3.3.4 (29 ed.), 11.8.1.6 (68 ed.), 32.49 pr. (22 Sab.), 25.1.7 (36 Sab.).
[435] D. 34.2.19.13 (20 Sab.), 50.15.3.1 (2 cens.).
[436] D. 48.2.4 (2 adult.).
[437] D. 47.1.2.5 (43 Sab.).
[438] D. 13.4.4.1 (27 ed.), 27.2.3.2 (1 omn. trib.), 48.5.14.5 (2 adult.).
[439] D. 25.4.1.8 (34 ed.).
[440] D. 29.2.20.2 (61 ed.).
[441] D. 39.2.13.21 (53 ed.).
[442] D. 47.20.3.1 (8 off. proc.).

inaugeo,[443] *incresco*,[444] *inrepo*,[445] *insinuo*,[446] *interfrigesco*,[447] *intermisceo*,[448] *intribuo*,[449] *invalesco*,[450] *obduro*,[451] *operor*[452] (with the dative), *recolo*,[453] *reconduco*,[454] *recorrigo*,[455] *relaxo*,[456] *relevo (reum)*,[457] *remeo*,[458] *remoror*,[459] *resilio*,[460] *retorqueo*,[461] *revereor*,[462] *rodo*,[463] *sapio*,[464] *seduco*,[465] *sopio*,[466] *sortior*[467] (metaphorical), *studeo*[468] (= take pains), *subterfugio*,[469] *tracto*[470] (intransitive, = debate), *transformo*,[471] *transvolo*,[472] *vigeo*,[473] *vitupero*.[474]

There are two more widespread verbal constructions. *In ea condicione est, ut . . .*, 'he it is in the position that . . .', occurs 13 times,[475] and there are 7 variants,[476] all confined to Ulpian. *In ea causa est, ut . . .*, which means the same, occurs 16 times in his work,[477] and there are another 18 Ulpianic

[443] D. 40.12.27.2 (2 off. cons.).   [444] D. 39.3.1.16 (53 ed.), 33.7.12.27 (20 Sab.).
[445] D. 13.5.14.1 (27 ed.), cf. Coll. 15.2.2 (7 off. proc.).
[446] D. 37.10.3.5 (41 ed.), 32.11.2 (2 fid.).
[447] FV 155 (1 excus.), but Citati (1927) 48 (Albertario).
[448] D. 28.1.21.3 (2 Sab.).
[449] D. 14.4.9.2 (29 ed.).
[450] D. 33.7.12.27 (20 Sab.).
[451] D. 48.5.28.11 (3 adult.).
[452] D. 50.13.1.11 (8 omn. trib.), 48.5.16.1 (2 adult).
[453] D. 47.10.11.1 (57 ed.).
[454] D. 19.2.13.11 (32 ed. bis.).
[455] D. 49.1.1. pr. (1 appell.).
[456] D. 4.2.14.11 (11 ed.).
[457] D. 16.1.8.10 (29 ed. bis), 17.1.12.9 (31/1 ed. bis), 46.3.24 (47 Sab.).
[458] D. 50.16.141 (8 Iul. Pap.).
[459] D. 28.3.6.9 (10 Sab.), 38.16.3.9 (14 Sab.), but Citati (1927) 78 (Albertario).
[460] D. 18.2.9 (28 Sab.).
[461] D. 38.2.14.6 (45 ed.).
[462] D. 3.1.15 (6 ed.).
[463] D. 19.2.13.6 (32 ed.), 37.11.1.11 (39 ed. bis.).
[464] D. 23.2.9 pr. (26 Sab.), 24.3.2.2 (35 Sab.), 26.2.10.3 (36 Sab.).
[465] D. 43.29.3.5 (71 ed.).
[466] D. 38.17.1.12 (12 Sab.), 48.5.30.5 (4 adult.), but Citati (1927) 83 (Kalb).
[467] D. 37.4.3.5 (39 ed.), 42.8.10.1 (73 ed.), 48.5.18.6 (2 Iul. Pap), 1.9.8 (6 fid.), 40.2.20.2 (2 off. cons.).
[468] D. 3.5.5.5 (10 ed.), 9.3.1.2 (23 ed.), 1.7.15.2 (26 Sab.).
[469] D. 42.5.36 (45 Sab.).
[470] Nine out of 11: D. 10.4.3.14 (24 ed.), 15.2.1.8 (29 ed.), 15.3.10.2 (29 ed.), 17.2.58 pr. (31/2 ed.), 30.39.6 (21 Sab.), 34.3.7 pr. (23 Sab.), 48.19.9.10 (10 off. proc. bis), 36.1.18.5 (2 fid.), but 18.1.57.2 (Paul 5 Plaut.), 37.14.17 pr. (Ulp. 11 Iul. Pap. citing divi fratres).
[471] D. 7.1.13.7 (18 Sab.).
[472] D. 41.1.44 (19 ed.).
[473] D. 38.2.12.5 (44 ed.), 47.2.46 pr. (42 Sab.).
[474] D. 4.7.4.1 (13 ed.).
[475] D. 18.7.1 (32 ed.), 26.7.7 (35 ed.), 29.1.13.3 (45 ed.), 38.8.1.8 (46 ed.), 38.8.1.9. (46 ed.), 47.9.3 pr. (56/1 ed.), 43.19.1.2 (70 ed.), 44.2.7.2 (75 ed.), 40.7.2 pr. (4 Sab.), 26.2.16 pr. (39. Sab.), 40.5.45.2 (5 disp.), 40.1.4.12 (6 disp.), 23.2.27 (3 Iul. Pap.).
[476] D. 42.1.4.1 (58 ed.: sunt ut), 42.8.6.1 (75 ed.: est ne), 39.5.7.6 (44 Sab.: sunt ut), 50.4.6.1 (4 off proc.: in ea sunt c. ut), 10.2.49. (2 disp.: est ne), 28.5.35.3 (4 disp.: in ea sunt c. ut), 33.4.2.1 (5 disp.: in ea esse c. ut).
[477] D. 11.1.11.4 (22 ed.), 37.4.1.5 (39 ed.), 37.12.1 pr. (45 ed.), 29.4.1.1 (50 ed.), 5.1.19.2 (60 ed.), 29.2.20.1 (61 ed.), 12.6.9 (66 ed.), 41.2.6 pr. (70 ed.), 39.1.20.5 (71 ed.), 43.29.3.3 (71 ed.), 21.1.59 pr. (74 ed. bis), 26.8.5.3 (40 Sab.), 45.1.1.2 (48 Sab.), 45.1.38.22 (49 Sab.), 49.1.1.3 (1 appell.).

texts with variants of this phrase in the present or future indicative.[478]
Other writers use the expression *in ea causa esse* in the infinitive or
subjunctive.[479] This illustrates once more the categorical character of
Ulpian's writing, in contrast with his more tentative rivals and colleagues.

(vii) *Nouns and nominal phrases.* Nothing special need be noted except
for a certain liking for diminutive forms: *alicula*,[480] *domuncula*,[481]
frivusculum,[482] *loculus*,[483] *operula*,[484] *sarcinula*,[485] *signaculum*,[486]
tabernula,[487] *viaticulum*,[488] *vulnusculum*.[489] The remaining nouns may be
listed alphabetically:

> *abusus*,[490-1] *adfirmator*,[492] *adgressus*,[493] *adiutorium*,[494] *adparitio*,[495]
> *adpendix*,[496] *adpulsus*,[497] *adsessorium*,[498] *alternatio*,[499] *apertura*,[500]
> *apex*,[501] *audacia*,[502] *calculator*,[503] *calliditas*,[504] *colloquium*,[505]
> *commendatio*,[506] *comminatio*,[507] *concubitus*,[508] *contaminatio*,[509]

---

[478] *Non est in ea causa ut* D. 37.4.8.11 (40 *ed.*), 40.12.12.3 (55 *ed.*), 47.10.13.2 (57 *ed.*), 42.8.6.2 (66 *ed.*), 47.2.17.2 (40 *Sab.*), 48.5.14.7 (2 *adult.*); *in ea causa sunt ut* 28.3.6.7 (10 *Sab.*), 26.1.3 pr. (37 *Sab.*), 26.5.12 pr. (3 *off. proc.*), 40.5.26.10 (5 *fid.*); *in ea causa est ne* 14.5.4.5 (29 *ed.*), 47.10.3.4 (56/2 *ed.*); *in ea erit causa ut* 2.11.4.1 (74 *ed.*), 45.1.38.22 (49 *Sab.*); *in ea sunt causa ut* 5.1.5 (5 *ed.*); *in ea est causa ut* 50.2.3.1 (3 *off. proc.*); *in ea causa non est ut* 4.7.4.3 (13 *ed.*); *in hac causa est ut* 26.10.3.18 (35 *ed.*); cf. *in ea . . . erit ne* 42.4.7.5 (59 *ed.*); *in ea causa est ac si* 29.5.3.12 (50 *ed.*).

[479] D. 38.2.25 (Iul 1 *Urs.: sit*), 14.6.14 (Iul. 12 *dig.: esset*), 41.4.7.4 (Iul. 44 *dig.: fuerit*), 19.1.7 (Pomp. 10 *Sab.: esse coeperit*), 20.4.9 pr. (Afr. 8 *qu.: esse coeperit*), 16.1.13.2 (Gai. 9 *ed. prov.: sit*), 27.10.5 (Gai. 9 *ed. prov.: sit*), 26.2.1.1 (Gai. 12 *ed. prov.: sint*), 26.7.57.1 (Scae. 10 *dig.: esset*), 40.5.29 (Paul 3 *fid.: esse coeperit*), 46.5.5 (Paul 48 *ed.: esse coepit*).

[480] D. 34.2.23.2 (44 *Sab.*).

[481] D. 47.12.3.11 (25 *ed.*).

[482] D. 24.1.32.12 (33 *Sab.*).

[483] D. 32.52.9 (24 *Sab.*).

[484] D. 50.14.3 (8 *omn. trib.*).

[485] D. 4.6.15.3 (72 *ed.*).   [486] D. 16.3.1.36 (30 *ed.*).

[487] D. 5.1.19.2 (60 *ed.*).

[488] D. 5.1.18.1 (23 *ed.*), but Citati (1927) 91 (Solazzi).

[489] D. 21.1.1.8 (1 *ed. cur.*).

[490-1] D. 12.2.11.2 (22 *ed.*), 7.8.12.1 (17 *Sab.*), 7.5.5.1, 2 (18 *Sab.* bis).

[492] D. 4.4.13 pr. (11 *ed.*), 27.7.4.3 (36 *ed.*).

[493] D. 36.1.18.7 (2 *fid.*).

[494] D. 47.2.50.3 (37 *ed.*).

[495] D. 21.2.50 (25 *ed.*).

[496] D. 29.2.35 pr. (9 *Sab.*).

[497] D. 8.3.5.1 (17 *ed.*), 43.20.1.18 (70 *ed.* bis), 34.1.14.3 (2 *fid.*), 8.3.1.1 (2 *inst.*).

[498] D. 2.14.12 (4 *ed.*), 47.10.5.8 (56/2 *ed.*).

[499] D. 11.3.9. pr. (23 *ed.*), 13.4.2.3 (27 *ed.* bis), 47.10.7.4 (57 *ed.*).

[500] D. 28.5.3.4 (3 *Sab.*).

[501] D. 17.1.29.4 (7 *disp.*).

[502] D. 39.4.12 pr. (38 *ed.* bis).

[503] D. 38.1.7.5 (28 *Sab.*), 50.13.1.6 (8 *omn. trib.*).

[504] Below, n. 582.

[505] D. 48.5.10.2 (4 *adult.*).

[506] D. 4.1.1 (11 *ed.*), 1.16.4.3 (1 *off. proc.*).

[507] D. 26.7.7.7 (35 *ed.*), 37.14.1 (9 *off. proc.*).

[508] D. 35.1.15 (35 *Sab.*).

[509] D. 48.5.2.3 (8 *disp.*).

corruptela,[510] *corruptor,*[511] *curiositas,*[512] *decus,*[513] *dedecus,*[514] *(vera)*
distinctio,[515] *dulcitudo,*[516] *efficacia,*[517] *elatio,*[518] *elocutio,*[519] *excessus*[520]
(death), *exhortatio,*[521] *exiguitas,*[522] *experimentum,*[523] *fervor,*[524] *fons*
(metaphorical),[525] *fortitudo,*[526] *frivolum,*[527] *fulcimentum,*[528] *gestus,*[529]
imminutio,[530] *immunditiae,*[531] *impostor,*[532] *impostura,*[533] *inceptum,*[534]
incolumitas,[535] *incredibilitas,*[536] *indevotio,*[537] *indicatio,*[538] *insolentia,*[539]
instigatus,[540] *instinctus,*[541] *intellegentia,*[542] *interrogator,*[543] *interventio,*[544]
interventor,[545] *nervus,*[546] *obscaenitas,*[547] *obventio,*[548] *occultatio,*[549]
occursus,[550] *ostentatio,*[551] *paratio,*[552] *pedester,*[553] *penuarius,*[554]

[510] D. 11.3.9.1 (23 *ed.*), 49.14.29 pr. (8 *disp.*).
[511] D. 11.3.9.3 (23 *ed.*), 11.3.11.1 (23 *ed.*), 49.14.20 pr. (8 *disp.*).
[512] D. 22.6.6 (18 *Iul. Pap.*).
[513] D. 3.1.1 pr. (6 *ed.*), 39.1.20.10 (71 *ed.*).
[514] D. 4.6.10 (12 *ed.*), 37.4.3.5 (39 *ed.*).
[515] D. 2.14.7.14 (4 *ed.*), 4.3.9.3 (11 *ed.*) cf. 12.1.11 pr. (26 *ed.*: *d. verissima*).
[516] D. 42.8.10.10 (73 *ed.*).
[517] D. 22.1.33 pr. (1 *off. cur. reip.*).
[518] D. 11.7.14.3 (25 *ed.*).
[519] D. 22.5.12 (37 *ed.*), 46.8.12.2 (80 *ed.*).
[520] D. 24.1.32 pr. (33 *Sab.*).
[521] D. 1.1.1.1 (1 *inst.*).
[522] D. 19.2.15.5 (32 *ed.*).
[523] D. 19.5.20 pr., 1 (32 *ed.* bis).
[524] D. 19.2.15.2 (32 *ed.*), 48.5.16.6 (2 *adult.*).
[525] D. 50.16.195.4 (46 *ed.*).
[526] D. 21.1.38.7 (2 *ed. cur.*).
[527] D 13.7.11.5 (28 *ed.*)., cf. above, n. 482.
[528] D. 33.7.12.19 (20 *Sab.*).
[529] Eight texts: D. 26.7.23 (9 *ed.*), 3.5.5.13 (10 *ed.*), 26.10.3.9 (35 *ed.*), 26.7.5.2 (35 *ed.*), 26.10.3.10 (35 *ed.*), 27.3.1.13 (36 *ed.*), 27.5.1.5 (36 *ed.* itp.), 46.3.14.1 (30 *Sab.*).
[530] D. 28.5.35.2 (4 *disp.*).
[531] D. 43.23.1.2 (71 *ed.*).
[532] D. 50.13.1.3 (8 *omn. trib.*), 21.1.4.2 (1 *ed. cur.*).
[533] D. 47.20.3.1 (8 *off. proc.*) cf. Coll. 15.2.1 (2 *off. proc.*).
[534] Coll. 15.2.1 (7 *off. proc.*).
[535] FV 123 (1 *excus.*).   [536] D. 48.5.30 pr. (4 *adult.*).   [537] D. 33.9.1 (24 *Sab.*).
[538] D. 19.1.13.3 (32 *ed.*).
[539] D. 22.1.33 pr. (1 *off. cur. reip.*).
[540] D. 9.1.1.6 (18 *ed.*).
[541] D. 47.11.5 (5 *off proc.*), cf. Coll. 15.2.5 (7 *off. proc.*).
[542] D. 28.1.20.9 (1 *Sab.*).
[543] D. 11.1.11.7 (22 *ed.*).
[544] D. 4.4.7.3 (11 *ed.*).
[545] D. 37.15.7.5 (10 *ed.*), 15.1.3.9 (29 *ed.*).
[546] D. 48.18.1.20 (8 *off. proc.*).
[547] D. 1.12.1.8 (1 *off. pr. urb.*).
[548] D. 22.1.3.4 (15 *ed.*), 14.1.1.15 (28 *ed.*), 27.9.5.9 (35 *ed.*), 7.1.7.1 (17 *Sab.*).
[549] 42.4.7.4 (59 *ed.*).
[550] D. 42.4.7.13 (59 *ed.*).
[551] D. 13.6.3.6 (28 *ed.*).
[552] D. 30.39.7 (21 *Sab.*).
[553] D. 43.12.1.14 (68 *ed.*).
[554] D. 33.9.3.11 (22 *Sab.*).

ratiocinatio,[555]   *recisio*,[556]   *redemptura*,[557]   *redditio*,[558]   *remotio*,[559]
repertorium,[560] *repositorium*,[561] *repudiatio*,[562] *resolutio*,[563] *revocatio*,[564]
sepositio,[565] *series*,[566] *sobrietas*,[567] *socordia*,[568] *solitudo*,[569] *somnus*,[570]
stupratio,[571] *suasor*,[572] *suasus*,[573] *sustenatio*,[574] *taciturnitas*,[575] *tarditas*,[576]
territio,[577] *tumor*,[578] *variatio*,[579] *vaticinatio*,[580] *vituperatio*.[581]

All 25 texts with *calliditas* are attributed to Ulpian,[582] and, even if a few of
them are compilatorial, this is a striking mark of his style. Presumably he
specially disliked craftiness, and thought of himself as a candid person.[583]

(viii) *Adjectives.* Ulpianic adjectives or participles used as adjectives
include:

accusatorius,[584]   *acerbus*,[585]   *adsuetus*,[586]   *ambitiosus*,[587]   *amicalis*,[588]

[555] *D.* 14.4.5.16 (29 *ed.*).
[556] *D.* 28.5.35.1 (4 *disp.*).
[557] *D.* 14.3.5.2 (28 *ed.*).
[558] *D.* 16.1.8 pr. (29 *ed.*), 21.1.21 pr. (1 *ed. cur.*).
[559] *D.* 50.16.10 (6 *ed.*), 26.10.4.2 (1 *omn. trib.*).
[560] *D.* 26.7.7 pr. (35 *ed.*).
[561] *D.* 24.2.19.10 (20 *Sab.*).
[562] Eleven texts of 12: *D.* 38.6.1.3 (44 *ed.*), 38.9.1.7,11 (49 *ed.* bis), 29.2.13 pr., 2 (7 *Sab.* bis),
29.2.17.1 (7 *Sab.*), 29.2.21.3 (7 *Sab.*), 38.16.2.7 (13 *Sab.*), 24.1.5.13 (32 *Sab.*), 49.17.9 (4 *disp.*),
36.1.15.5 (4 *fid.*), but 19.2.25.2 (Gai. 10 *ed. prov.*).
[563] *D.* 41.2.13.2 (72 *ed.*).
[564] *D.* 5.1.2.3 (3 *ed.*).
[565] *D.* 50.12.2.2 (1 *disp.*).
[566] *D.* 37.11.2.4 (41 *ed.*), 50.15.1 pr. (1 *cens.*).
[567] *D.* 1.7.17.4 (26 *Sab.*).
[568] *D.* 2.12.1.1 (4 *omn. trib.*).
[569] *D.* 47.10.7.8 (57 *ed.*), 47.14.1.1 (8 *off. proc.*).
[570] *D.* 26.8.1.1 (1 *Sab.*), 34.2.25.10 (44 *Sab.*), 21.1.14.4 (1 *ed. cur.*).
[571] *D.* 23.2.43.1 (1 *Iul. Pap.*).
[572] *D.* 4.4.13 pr. (11 *ed.*), but Citati (1927) 83 (Pringsheim).
[573] *D.* 9.2.9.1 (18 *ed.*).
[574] *D.* 24.3.22.8 (33 *ed.*).
[575] *D.* 19.2.13.11 (32 *ed.*), but Citati (1927) 86 (Kalb etc.).
[576] *D.* 26.7.7.3 (35 *ed.*), but Citati (1927) 86 (Beseler, Kunkel).
[577] *D.* 47.10.15.41 (57 *ed.*).
[578] *D.* 9.2.27.17 (18 *ed.*), 21.1.14.8 (1 *ed. cur.*).
[579] *D.* 14.3.11.5 (28 *ed.*).   [580] *FV* 148 (1 *excus.*).
[581] *D.* 34.2.23.2 (44 *Sab.*).
[582] *D.* 2.14.7.9 (4 *ed.*), 4.1.1 (11 *ed.*), 4.3.1 pr., 2 (11 *ed.* bis), 4.3.7.10 (11 *ed.*), 4.4.3.1 (11 *ed.*), 11.3.3
pr. (23 *ed.*), 10.4.11.1 (24 *ed.*), 15.3.3.9 (29 *ed.*), 16.1.2.3 (29 *ed.*), 50.17.47 pr. (30 *ed.*), 17.1.6.7 (31/1
ed.), 50.14.2 (31/1 *ed.*), 24.3.22.8 (33 *ed.*), 47.4.1.1 (38 *ed.*), 29.4.1 pr. (50 *ed.*), 40.12.12.3 (55 *ed.*),
40.12.14 pr. (55 *ed.*), 42.6.1.5 (64 *ed.*), 43.24.1.1 (71 *ed.*), 43.29.3.5 (71 *ed.*), 47.20.3.1 (8 *off. proc.*),
17.1.29.5 (7 *disp.*), 49.4.1 pr. (1 *appell.*), 21.1.1.2 (1 *ed. cur.*).
[583] See also nn. 603 (*dolosus*), 679 (*callide*), 683 (*dolose*).
[584] *D.* 48.5.18.1 (2 *adult.*), 48.5.30.8 (4 *adult.*).
[585] *D.* 22.1.33 pr. (1 *off. cur. reip.*).
[586] *D.* 19.2.15.2 (32 *ed.*)
[587] *D.* 4.4.3 pr. (11 *ed.*), 22.1.33 pr. (1 *off. cur. reip.*), 50.9.4 pr. (1 *off. cur. reip.*), cf. 36.1.67.2 (Maec. 5
fid.: *ambitiose*), but Citati (1927) 10 (Vassalli).
[588] *D.* 17.1.10.7 (31/1 *ed.*).

armipotens,[589] *authenticus,*[590] *calcitrosus,*[591] *captus* (deceived),[592] *cavus,*[593] *clivosus,*[594] *consimilis,*[595] *consuetus,*[596] *contemptibilis,*[597] *contestatorius,*[598] *contumeliosus,*[599] *crassus,*[600] *delatorius,*[601] *docilis,*[602] *dolosus,*[603] *exclusorius,*[604] *exemptilis,*[605] *facinorosus,*[606] *fanaticus,*[607] *feriaticus,*[608] *fessus,*[609] *formalis,*[610] *fluviatilis,*[611] *gulosus,*[612] *gutturosus,*[613] *impetiginosus,*[614] *impetrabilis,*[615] *inaequus,*[616] *inargutus,*[617] *incautus,*[618] *incogitabilis,*[619] *incultus,*[620] *incuriosus,*[621] *indemnatus,*[622] *indoctus,*[623] *inexcusabilis,*[624] *infaustus,*[625] *inscius* . . . *invitus,*[626–7] *intimus,*[628] *inutilis*

---

[589] D. 50.15.1 pr. (1 *cens.*).

[590] D. 10.2.4.3 (19 *ed.*), 10.2.8 pr. (19 *ed.*). Used as noun in 29.3.12. (Ulp. 13 *Iul. Pap.*) and PS 5.12.11.

[591] D. 9.1.1.4 (18 *ed.*), 21.1.4.3 (1 *ed. cur.*).

[592] Twenty-eight texts of 29: D. 4.4.3.3, 4, 5, 7, 10 (11 *ed.* quinq.), 4.4.5 (11 *ed.*), 4.4.7.1, 4, 5, 7 (11 *ed.* quat.), 4.4.9.2 (11 *ed.*), 4.4.13 pr. (11 *ed.*), 4.4.11.2, 3, 4, 5, 6, 6 (11 *ed.* sex.), 4.4.18.1 (11 *ed.*), 13.7.36.1 (11 *ed.*), 4.6.28.1 (12 *ed.*), 4.1.6 (13 *ed.*), 12.2.9.4 (22 *ed.* bis), 15.1.5 pr. (29 *ed.*), 16.3.1.42 (30 *ed.*), 15.1.36 (2 *disp.* bis) but 4.4.29 pr. (Mod. 2 *resp.*).

[593] D. 43.23.1.4 (71 *ed.*).

[594] D. 43.8.5.32 (68 *ed.*).

[595] D. 34.2.23.2 (44 *Sab.*).

[596] D. 26.1.23.3 (5 *disp.*).

[597] D. 21.2.37.1 (32 *ed.*), 1.16.9.2 (2 *off.cons.*).

[598] FV 156 (1 *excus.*).

[599] D. 47.10.7.7 (57 *ed.*), 22.1.33 pr. (1 *off. cur. reip.*), 1.12.1.10 (1 *off. pr. urb.*)

[600] D. 22.6.6 (18 *Iul. Pap.*).

[601] D. 22.6.6 (18 *Iul. Pap.*).

[602] D. 21.1.37 (1 *ed. cur.*).

[603] D. 4.3.1 pr. (11 *ed.*).

[604] D. 44.1.2.2 (74 *ed.*).

[605] D. 34.2.25.11 (44 *Sab.*).

[606] D. 2.1.3 (2 *off. qu.*)

[607] D. 21.1.1.9 (1 *ed. cur.*).

[608] D. 2.12.2 (5 *ed.*).

[609] D. 39.6.5 (2 *inst.*).

[610] D. 35.2.62.1 (1 *Iul. Pap.*).

[611] D. 14.1.1.6 (28 *ed.*).

[612] D. 21.1.4.2 (1 *ed. cur.*).

[613] D. 21.1.12.2 (1 *ed. cur.*).

[614] D. 21.1.6.1 (1 *ed. cur.*).

[615] D. 43.20.1.43 (70 *ed.*).

[616] D. 33.1.3.2 (24 *Sab.*).

[617] D. 7.5.5.1 (18 *Sab.*).

[618] Coll. 12.5.2 (8 *off. proc.*).

[619] FV. 75.5 (17 *Sab.*), but Citati (1927) 46 (Beseler).

[620] D. 28.8.7.3 (60 *ed.*).

[621] D. 22.1.33 pr. (1 *off. cur. reip.*).

[622] D. 28.1.9 (45 *ed.*).

[623] D. 21.1.19.4 (1 *ed. cur.*).

[624] D. 5.1.50.1 (6 *fid.*).

[625] D. 34.9.9.1 (14 *Iul. Pap.*).

[626–7] D. 9.2.27.30 (18 *ed.*), 23.3.34 (43 *ed.*), 43.24.15 pr. (71 *ed.*), but 46.3.78 (Iav. 11 *Cass.*), cf. FV. 269 (Ulp. 46 *Sab.*).

[628] D. 4.8.3.1 (13 *ed.*), 7.1.13.8 (18 *Sab.*).

(invalid),[629] *notabilis*,[630] *nugatorius*,[631] *obsequens*,[632] *occultus*,[633] *olitorius*,[634] *opacus*,[635] *par(atque)*,[636] *pavidus*,[637] *reprobus*,[638] *spatiosus*,[639] *squalidus*,[640] *subsidiarius*,[641] *subsimilis*,[642] *succedaneus*,[643] *sumptuosus*,[644] *superstitiosus*,[645] *supervacaneus*,[646] *suppellecticarius*,[647] *suspendiosus*,[648] *tempestivus*,[649] *venatorius*,[650] *vindemiatorius*.[651]

Comparative adjectives include *audacior*,[652] *cautior*,[653] *contumeliosor*,[654] *cultior*,[655] and *durior* (*sententia*)[656]; superlatives *aequissimus*,[657] *angustisssimus*,[658] *antiquissimus*,[659] *audacissimus*,[660] *durissimus*,[661] *exploratissimus*,[662] *facillimus*,[663] *frequentissimus*,[664] *improbissimus*,[665] *splendidissimus*,[666] *usitatissimus*,[667] and *verissima* (*sententia*).[668] Of these *aequissimus* is the most important. In its various inflections, particularly

[629] D. 45.1.1.5 (48 Sab. bis), 46.4.8 pr. (48 Sab.), 37.11.6 (8 disp.).
[630] D. 3.1.1.5 (6 ed.).
[631] D. 21.1.17.14 (1 ed. cur.).
[632] D. 1.16.9.3 (2 off. proc.).
[633] D. 11.1.11.8 (22 ed.), 14.4.7 pr. (29 ed.), 37.6.1.11 (40 ed.), 18.6.4 pr. (28 Sab.), 29.3.10.2 (13 Iul. Pap.).
[634] D. 7.1.13.4 (18 Sab.).
[635] D. 50.13.1.11 (8 omn. trib.), 48.5.16.1 (2 adult.).
[636] D. 43.8.2.42 (68 ed. = 50.17.150).
[637] D. 21.1.4.3 (1 ed. cur.).
[638] D. 13.7.24.1 (30 ed. ter).
[639] D. 39.2.15.13 (53 ed.), 7.8.4 pr. (17 Sab.).
[640] D. 47.10.15.27 (57 ed.).
[641] D. 27.8.1 pr., 4 (36 ed. bis).
[642] D. 35.3.1.5 (79 ed.).
[643] D. 26.7.3.8 (35 ed.); 27.8.4 (3 disp.).
[644] D. 28.8.5.1 (60 ed.).
[645] D. 21.1.4.9 (1 ed. cur.).
[646] D. 26.7.9.6 (36 ed.).
[647] D. 33.7.12.31 (20 Sab.).
[648] D. 3.2.11.3 (6 ed.).
[649] D. 36.1.13.4 (4 fid.).
[650] D. 48.19.8.11, 12 (9 off. proc. bis).
[651] D. 3.3.78 pr. (20 Sab.).
[652] D. 47.4.1.1 (38 ed.).
[653] D. 46.5.1.4 (70 ed.).
[654] D. 47.10.7.7 (57 ed.).
[655] D. 33.7.8.1 (20 Sab.).
[656] D. 3.2.13.7 (6 ed.).
[657] Below, nn. 669–71.
[658] D. 40.9.12.6 (4 adult.).
[659] D. 50.3.1 pr. (3 off. proc.), 50.15.1 pr. (1 cens.), 1.13.1 pr. (1 off. qu.).
[660] D. 37.10.1.5 (41 ed.).
[661] D. 5.1.19.2 (60 ed.), 38.2.1 (42 ed.).
[662] D. 39.1.5.4 (52 ed.).
[663] D. 12.2.3 pr. (22 ed.).
[664] D. 42.4.7.2 (59 ed.).
[665] D. 3.1.1.5 (6 ed.).
[666] D. 50.15.1 pr. (1 cens.).
[667] D. 27.1.19 (35 ed.).
[668] D. 19.1.11.16 (32 ed.), 32.11.20 (2 fid.), 36.1.15.3 (4 fid.).

aequissimum erit[669] and *aequissimum est*,[670] Ulpian accounts for 80 *Digest* instances out of 86.[671] *Utilissimus* occurs 5 times.[672]

(ix) *Adverbs and adverbial phrases.* Many of these are related to verb or noun forms already mentioned. Thus, *abusive*[673] is related to *abusus*,[674] *acerbe*[675] to *acerbus*,[676] *benigne dicere*[677] to *benignum est*,[678] *callide*[679] to *calliditas*,[680] *contumeliose*[681] to *contumeliosus*,[682] *dolose*[683] to *dolosus*,[684] *minus dubitanter*[685] and *indubitanter*[686] to a number of expressions rejecting doubt,[687] *incaute*[688] to *cautior*,[689] *notabiliter*[690] to *notabilis*,[691] *sobrie*[692] to *sobrietas*,[693] *sumptuose*[694] to *sumptuosus*.[695]

There is a group of negative adverbs: *non difficile*,[696] *gravate*,[697] *idonee*,[698] *mediocriter*,[699] *passim*,[700] *plene*,[701] *principilater*,[702] *secure*,[703]

---

[669] Above, n. 305 (26 texts).

[670] Fifteen texts: *D.* 4.6.26.9 (12 *ed.*). 11.1.11.8 (22 *ed.*), 10.4.11 pr. (24 *ed.*), 13.6.7.1 (28 *ed.*), 14.5.2.1 (29 *ed.*), 19.1.13.20 (32 *ed.*), 47.6.1.2 (38 *ed.*), 37.4.3.4 (39 *ed.*), 37.8.1.1 (40 *ed.*), 38.2.8 pr. (43 *ed.*), 43.19.3.7 (70 *ed.*), 2.11.2.1 (74 *ed.*), 36.3.1.19 (79 *ed.*), 42.1.57 (2 *disp.*), 17.1.29.6 (7 *disp.*), cf. *est aequissimum* 3.1.1.6 (6 *ed.*), 14.4.5.13 (29 *ed.*), 19.2.9.1 (32 *ed.*), 29.5.3.17 (50 *ed.*).

[671] *CDJ* 49 AEQUISSIMA, AEQUISSIMUM but *D.* 16.2.5 (Gai. 9 *ed. prov.: a. est*), 17.1.22.4 (Paul 32 *ed.: a. esse*), 14.2.2 pr. (Paul 34 *ed.: a. enim est*), 48.20.7 pr. (Paul 1 *port. lib.: a. existimatum est*), 38.17.5 pr. (Paul 1 *SC Tert.: a. visum est*), 36.1.1.2 (Ulp. 3 *fid.* citing SC Trebellianum: *esset a.*), but Citati (1927) 8 (Bonfante, Wylie).

[672] *D.*47.6.1 pr. (38 *ed.*), 43.15.1.1 (68 *ed.*), 43.21.1.1 (70 *ed.*), 43.26.6.4 (71 *ed.*), 10.3.21 (30 *Sab.*).

[673] *D.* 50.1.1.1 (2 *ed.*), 50.16.15 (10 *ed.*), 29.3.2.1 (50 *ed.*), 47.10.15.40 (57 *ed.*).

[674] Above, n. 491.

[675] *D.* 43.30.1.5 (71 *ed.*), but Citati (1927) 1 (Eisele).

[676] Above, n. 585.

[677] *D.* 38.2.14.2, 8 (45 *ed.* bis), 36.4.1 pr. (52 *ed.*), 42.5.24.3 (63 *ed.*), 7.4.1.2 (17 *Sab.*), 35.1.10 pr. (23 *Sab.*), 24.1.34 (43 *Sab.*), 50.2.2.3 (1 *disp.*), but *Citati* (1927) 14 (Beseler etc.).

[678] Above, n. 164.

[679] *D.* 4.3.9.1 (11 *ed.*), 4.8.31 (13 *ed.*), 16.1.2.3 (29 *ed.*), 47.8.2.8 (56/1 *ed.*), 26.8.5.4 (40 *Sab.*).

[680] Above, n. 504.

[681] *D.* 7.1.27.1 (18 *Sab.*) but Gai. *Inst.* 1.141.

[682] Above, n. 599.

[683] *D.* 4.4.3.1 (11 *ed.*), 4.8.31 (13 *ed.*), 5.3.25.5 (15 *ed.*), 10.4.9.2 (24 *ed.*), 11.6.3 pr. (24 *ed.*), 44.4.2.5 (76 *ed.*), 42.5.31.2 (2 *omn. trib.*).

[684] Above, n. 603.

[685] *D.* 15.1.9.5 (28 *ed.*).   [686] *D.* 37.11.2.7 (41 *ed.*).   [687] Above, nn. 139–144.

[688] *D.* 28.4.1.1 (15 Sab.) cf. *Coll.* 12.5.2 (8 *off. proc.: incautus?*).

[689] Above, n. 653, and *incautus* above, n. 618.

[690] *D.* 47.10.15.26 (56/2 *ed.*).

[691] Above, n. 630.

[692] *D.* 4.4.11.4 (11 *ed.*), 26.5.12.1 (3 *off. pro.*).

[693] Above, n. 567.

[694] *D.* 39.2.37 (42 *Sab.*).

[695] Above, n. 644.

[696] *D.* 1.18.13 pr. (7 *off. proc.*).

[697] *D.* 1.17.7 pr. (2 *off. proc.*).

[698] *D.* 27.8.1.17 (36 *ed.*).

[699] *D.* 47.10.7.2 (57 *ed.*) but Citati (1927) 56 (Beseler).

[700] *D.* 4.4.11.3 (11 *ed.*), 27.9.5.9, 14 (35 *ed.* bis), 37.9.7.1 (47 *ed.*).

[701] *D.* 11.1.9.4 (22 *ed.*), 34.4.7 (24 *Sab.*).

[702] *D.* 47.10.7.1 (57 *ed.*).

[703] *D.* 18.2.11 pr. (28 *Sab.*).

specialiter,[704] *turpiter*.[705] Some of these are used, by way of meiosis, with a double negative: *non improprie*,[706] *inconsulte*,[707] *indigne*,[708] *infavorabiliter*,[709] *inhoneste*,[710] *insuptiliter*.[711]

There is exaggeration in Ulpian's use of *saepissime*, 'very often', and *cottidie*, 'every day'. The former cannot strictly be listed as a mark of his style, since there are, besides 29 Ulpianic texts, 3 of Marcianus.[712] But this can be safely accepted as an example of the writer's influence on his younger contemporary. Despite one text of Gaius, *cottidie*, used in this loose manner, counts as Ulpianic.[713] The same writers feature in the profile of *eleganter*. Ulpian is a neat and lucid, not an elegant, writer, but he clearly admired elegance. He uses the adverb in 39 texts out of 42 in which it occurs in the *Digest*, there being also 2 instances in Gaius and 1 in Marcianus.[714]

Other adverbs confined to Ulpian include: *avare*,[715] *circa*,[716] *collusorie*,[717] *congruenter*,[718] *criminaliter*,[719] *destricte*,[720] *diverse*,[721] *frugaliter*,[722] *generaliter*,[723] *immoderate*,[724] *imperite*,[725] *impotenter*,[726] *incolorate*,[727] *inconsideranter*,[728] *incunctanter*,[729] *indifferenter*,[730] *hoc animo*

---

[704] *D.* 19.1.17.6 (32 *ed.*), 18.1.24 (28 *Sab.*) cf. 7.1.43 (7 *reg.*: *non . . . s.*).

[705] *D.* 12.5.4.3 (26 *ed.*).

[706] *D.* 38.16.1 pr. (12 *Sab.*), 50.16.130 (2 *Iul. Pap.*).

[707] *D.* 4.4.11.4 (11 *ed.*).

[708] *D.* 40.2.20.1 (2 *off cons.*).

[709] *D.* 50.2.2.6 (1 *disp.*), but Citati (1927) 47 (Albertario).

[710] *D.* 50.16.46.1 (59 *ed.*).

[711] *D.* 2.14.7.6 (4 *ed.*), 28.5.1.5 (1 *Sab.*).

[712] *D.* 3.2.2.2 (6 *ed.*), 4.4.20.1 (11 *ed.*), 13.7.36 pr. (11 *ed.*), 4.6.26.9 (12 *ed.* bis), 4.1.6 (13 *ed.*), 5.2.8.2 (14 *ed.*), 11.7.6 pr. (25 *ed.*), 27.2.1.3 (34 *ed.*), 12.3.4 pr. (36 *ed.*), 26.7.9 pr. (36 *ed.*), 27.3.1.15 (36 *ed.*), 47.4.1.7 (38 *ed.*), 37.5.5.6 (40 *ed.*), 47.10.13.7 (57 *ed.*), 43.24.13.5 (71 *ed.*), 42.8.10.13 (73 *ed.*), 42.8.10.14 (73 *ed.*), 44.4.4.26 (76 *ed.*), 28.3.6.8 (10 *Sab.*), 34.2.9 (24 *Sab.*), 47.2.12.2 (29 *Sab.*), 48.18.1.7 (8 *off. proc.*), 13.7.26 pr. (3 *disp.*), 29.7.1 (4 *disp.*), 37.14.16 pr. (10 *Iul. Pap.*), 49.2.1.4 (1 *appell.*), 50.15.4.10 (3 *cens.*), 40.5.24.21 (5 *fid.*) but 39.4.16.4 (Marci. 1 *del.*), 48.15.3 pr. (Marci. 1 *Iul. Pap.*), 48.24.2 (Marci. 2 *pub. iud.*).

[713] *D.* 4.4.7.8 (11 *ed.*), 12.1.9.8 (26 *ed.*), 26.10.1 pr. (35 *ed.*), 43.26.6.4 (71 *ed.*), 23.1.4.1 (35 *Sab.*), but 20.1.15.1 (Gai. 1 *hyp.*), and Citati (1927) 23 (Pernice etc.).

[714] *CDJ* 54 ELEGANTER (39 texts) but *D.* 22.1.19 pr. (Gai. 6 XII *tab.*), 2.2.4 (Gai. 1 *ed. prov.*), 15.1.40 pr. (Marci. 5 *reg.*), cf. 46.3.103 (Maec. 2 *fid.*: *elegantissime*), 26.7.61 (Pomp. 20 *epist*: *elegantius*).

[715] *D.* 1.16.6.3 (1 *off. proc.*).

[716] *D.* 43.13.1.4 (68 *ed.*).

[717] *D.* 30.50.2 (24 *Sab.*).

[718] *D.* 45.1.1.6 (41 *Sab.*).

[719] *D.* 47.2.93 (38 *ed.*), but Citati (1927) 24 (Albertario).

[720] *D.* 3.3.13 (8 *ed.*), 4.4.7.8 (11 *ed.*), 4.8.15 (13 *ed.*), 48.18.1.26 (8 *off. proc.*).

[721] *D.* 33.6.9.3 (23 *Sab.*).   [722] *D.* 27.2.3.3 (36 *ed.*).

[723] See above, nn. 61 (*et g.*), 443 (*g. dicendum est* etc.).

[724] *D.* 21.1.17.3 (1 *ed. cur.*).

[725] *D.* 9.2.7.8 (18 *ed.*), 11.6.1.1 (24 *ed.*).

[726] *D.* 1.16.9.5 (2 *off. proc.*).

[727] *D.* 4.4.18.1 (11 *ed.*).

[728] *D.* 26.10.3.17 (35 *ed.*).

[729] *D.* 40.2.20 pr. (2 *off. cons.*).

[730] *D.* 1.13.1.3 (1 *off. qu.*), but Citati (1927) 47 (Pringsheim).

(followed by *quasi*,[731] *quod*,[732] or standing alone[733]), *pecuniarie*,[734] *regulariter*,[735] *secure*,[736] *sordide*,[737] *sufficienter*,[738] *tamdiu* (with *donec*[739] or *quoad*[740] or standing by itself[741]), *usquam*,[742] *verecunde*,[743] *versa vice*,[744] and *vigilanter*.[745]

Some adverbs appear in the comparative: *civilius*,[746] *solutius*,[747] *subtilius*,[748] *timidius*,[749] and *violentius*;[750] or superlative: *atrocissime*,[751] *consultissime*,[752] *diligentissime*,[753] *rectissime* (*ait*,[754] *rescripsit*,[755] *scribit*,[756] *videtur*,[757]), and *tardissime*.[758]

The foregoing account could not, in the nature of things, be very lively. Yet Ulpian himself is a vivacious and enthusiastic author. To bring this out, I now reproduce a typical passage from his work. It is concerned with gifts between husband and wife. These were in principle invalid, but a proposal (*oratio*) of Caracalla to the senate during his father's lifetime changed the law to the extent that an unrevoked gift was valid unless the donee spouse predeceased the donor. Ulpian discusses the hypothesis that husband and wife are both captured in war, capture in war being in many respects equivalent to death. Can it be said that the donee spouse has predeceased, or

---

[731] D. 11.7.14.7, 11 (25 *ed.* bis), 29.2.20.1 (61 *ed.*), 32.11.13 (2 *fid.*), 40.5.24.8 (5 *fid.*).

[732] D. 24.1.22 (3 *Sab.*).

[733] D. 12.4.3.8 (26 *ed.*), 29.2.20.1 (61 *ed.*), 42.6.1.10 (64 *ed.*), 43.16.3.6 (69 *ed.*), 38.4.1.6 (14 *Sab.*), 24.1.32.5 (33 *Sab.*), 33.4.2 pr. (5 *disp.*).

[734] D. 16.2.10.2 (63 *ed.*).

[735] D. 5.3.9 (15 *ed.*), 15.3.3.2 (29 *ed.*), 30.7.1.1 (51 *ed.*), 7.1.25.5 (18 *Sab.*) but Citati (1927) 77 (de Francisci).

[736] D. 5.2.8.6 (14 *ed.*).

[737] D. 26.7.7.2 (35 *ed.*), 26.10.3.5 (35 *ed.*).

[738] D. 7.1.15.2 (18 *Sab.*), 24.3.14 pr. (36 *Sab.*).

[739] D. 13.1.10.2 (38 *ed.*), 34.1.14 pr. (2 *fid.*).

[740] D. 42.4.5.1 (59 *ed.*).

[741] D. 48.19.6 pr. (9 *off. proc.*).

[742] D. 1.9.1.1 (62 *ed.* usquam . . . umquam).

[743] D. 39.2.4.5 (1 *ed.*), 24.3.21.6 (3 *disp.*), 1.12.1.8 (1 *off. pr. urb.*), but Citati (1927) 90 (Albertario).

[744] D. 39.3.6.3 (53 *ed.*), 40.12.1.1 (54 *ed.*), 43.29.3 pr. (71 *ed.*), 44.5.1.12 (76 *ed.*), 36.3.1.11 (79 *ed.*), 24.1.33.1 (36 *Sab.*), 45.1.1.3 (48 *Sab.*).

[745] D. 27.9.5.10 (20 *Sab.*).

[746] D. 25.5.1.2 (34 *ed.*).

[747] D. 11.7.14.14 (25 *ed.*).

[748] D. 12.4.3.8 (26 *ed.*), 49.15.15 (12 *Sab.*).

[749] D. 29.2.42 pr. (4 *disp.*).

[750] D. 9.2.29.7 (18 *ed.*).

[751] D. 1.6.2 (8 *off. proc.*).

[752] D. 28.7.8 pr. (50 *ed.*).

[753] D. 37.10.3.5 (41 *ed.*), cf. Coll. 11.7.5 (8 *off. proc.*).

[754] D. 10.2.18.1 (19 *ed.*), 17.1.12.14 (31/1 *ed.*), 29.4.10 pr. (50 *ed.*), 47.8.4.3 (56/1 *ed.*), 23.3.5.9 (31 *Sab.*), 40.4.13.2 (5 *disp.*), 23.2.43.3 (1 *Iul. Pap.*).

[755] D. 17.1.6.7 (31/1 *ed.*).

[756] Eight texts of 10: D. 13.7.36 pr. (11 *ed.*), 9.2.23.4 (18 *ed.*), 19.2.19.6 (32 *ed.*), 37.9.1.11 (41 *ed.*). 37.10.3.13 (41 *ed.*), 39.2.15.10 (53 *ed.*), 42.4.7.7 (59 *ed.*), 39.2.40.1 (43 *Sab.*) but 35.1.62.1 (Ter. 4 *Iul. Pap.*), 34.2.34.2 (Pomp. 9 *QM*).

[757] D. 4.2.14.5 (11 *ed.*).

[758] D. 43.23.15.4 (71 *ed.*), cf. above, n. 576.

is it the other way round? He goes on to a more general discussion of simultaneous death, the problem of *commorientes*, and concludes that, in the case he puts, the donation is valid because it cannot be shown that the donee has predeceased the donor:[759]

> Si ambo ab hostibus capti sunt et qui donavit et cui donatum est, quid dicimus? et prius illud volo tractare. oratio, si ante mors contigerit ei, cui donatum est, nullius momenti donationem esse voluit: ergo si ambo decesserint, quid dicemus, naufragio forte vel ruina vel incendio? et si quidem possit apparere, quis ante spiritum posuit, expedita est quaestio. sin vero non appareat, difficilis quaestio est. et magis puto donationem valuisse et [hoc] his ex verbis orationis defendimus: ait enim oratio 'si prior vita decesserit qui donatum accepit': non videtur autem prior vita decessisse qui donatum accepit, cum simul decesserint. proinde rectissime dicetur utrasque donationes valere, si forte invicem donationibus factis simul decesserint, quia neuter alteri supervixerit, licet de commorientibus oratio non senserit.

It is a passage which exemplifies a number of points of style to which attention has been drawn. Three sentences begin with *et*. *Proinde* appears as a connective. The movement is from the present to the future: *quid dicemus? rectissime dicetur*. The first person singular (*volo tractare, magis puto*) gives way to the first person plural, *defendimus*. The structure is that of a dialogue between the author and himself. He asks himself a question, searches for the answer, suddenly finds the decisive reason, and pounces. There is a sharp contrast between the rather formal expression of the *oratio*, which suggests Papinian's hand (*vita decesserit*)[760] and the eager, even ebullient, attempt by Ulpian to pick its meaning to pieces.

Zest is the quality which infuses Ulpian's mind, except on rare occasions—for example in the first five books of the edictal commentary—when a shadow seems to cloud his enthusiasm. There was a controversy whether the legacy of a farm 'as equipped' (*instructus*), was more comprehensive than one of a farm 'with its equipment' (*cum instrumento*). Sabinus held that it was. Ulpian supports him. 'We see this opinion daily gaining ground and support' he says: *quam sententiam cottidie increscere et invalescere videmus.*[761] Daily? Only a man soaked in the law could put it like that.

With the help of the guidance I have tried to give, the alert reader should not find it too hard to recognize what is genuine Ulpian and what spurious. The next two chapters deal with the various works attributed to the Tyrian and try to set up two lists, one of genuine, the other of spurious compositions. It may be of interest here to sketch—no more—one or two other ways in which the study of Ulpian's style can be applied.

[759] D. 24.1.32.14 (33 *Sab.*).
[760] *CDJ* 27 VITA; below, ch. 8 n. 24a.
[761] D. 33.7.12.27 (20 *Sab.*).

One is that a grasp of the elements of style enables us to recognize as Ulpianic passages which the *Digest* attributes to other authors.

A title of the *Digest* deals with actions by and against bodies such as municipalities and *civitates* (local authorities).[762] There was a rule that a two-thirds majority was needed to authorize someone to bring or defend an action in the name of the authority. How was the two-thirds reckoned? A text from Ulpian on the edict says that, according to Pomponius, a father can vote for a son and a son for his father.[763] The sentence continues, in the *Digest* version, with an excerpt from Paul on the edict,[764] which says that persons in the same power (e.g. two sons both in their father's power) can vote for one another, since their act is done as councillors (*decuriones*) not in a domestic capacity. The text attributed to Paul then goes on to say that the same (viz. voting rule) applies to appointments to local office (*honores*):

D. 3.4.5   *ULPIANUS libro octavo ad edictum* Illud notandum Pomponius ait, quod et patris suffragium filio proderit et filii patri,

3.4.6   *PAULUS libro nono ad edictum* item eorum, qui in eiusdem potestate sunt: quasi decurio enim hoc dedit, non quasi domestica persona. quod et in honorum petitione erit servandum.

These last remarks are more naturally taken as a continuation of Ulpian's text than of Paul's. The construction *erit* followed by the gerund is common in Ulpian but rare in Paul.[765] The passage in question continues with other Ulpianic phrases. For instance, we find, a little lower down, *parvi refert*, which occurs in thirty-seven texts of Ulpian and otherwise only once in Papinian and once (this text) in Paul.[766] There is a sentence beginning *et puto*[767] and another short sentence (*et constitui ei potest*) beginning with *et*.

The whole passage, from *quasi decurio enim . . .* to the end of the *lex*, is in reality a passage from Ulpian's edictal commentary, not from Paul. It is a continuation of *D.* 3.4.5. The mistake is due to Justinian's compilers. Their practice, as I have shown elsewhere,[768] was to take Ulpian's commentary as the fundamental text and to insert in it shorter passages from Paul and Gaius when it seemed to them that these authors had something valuable to add. At the end of the insertion it was of course necessary to repeat the original inscription before resuming the text of Ulpian. In this case the repetition was overlooked, through the fault of the commissioner in charge of the excerpting (Theophilus) or of the secretary who was copying out the text.[769]

---

[762] *D.* 3.4.   [763] *D.* 3.4.5 (Ulp. 8 *ed.* = 9 *ed. Lenel*).
[764] *D.* 3.4.6 pr. (Paul 9 *ed.*).
[765] Above, nn. 318–73.
[766] Above, n. 174.   [767] Above, n. 18.
[768] Honoré (1970) 250, (1978) 151–70.
[769] Honoré (1978) 166–70. Perhaps a later copier is responsible. If *D.* 3.4.5 was (mistakenly) ascribed to Ulpian book 8, 3.4.6 *pr.* to Paul book 9, and 3.4.6 (continuation) to Ulpian book 9, a copier might think that in the third inscription 'Ulpian' was a mistake for Paul.

This example throws light on the proceedings of Justinian's commissioners. The next tells us something unsuspected about Paul himself. A resolution of the senate at the instance of Marcus and Commodus laid down that a *tutor* (guardian) could not marry off his female ward to his son. Paul wrote a single-book commentary on this enactment (*liber singularis ad orationem divi Antonini et Commodi*), from which Justinian's compilers included two excerpts.[770] The longer of the two is in Paul's style, apart from a passage which comes in the middle of section 4.[771] As the discussion of this passage in chapter 3 shows,[772] there is reason to suppose that in this text Paul is drawing on a lost work of Ulpian. He does not say so. But neither Paul nor Ulpian, famous contemporaries, overtly cites the other.

Another application of criteria of style is to the problem of post-classical alterations in the texts and Justianic interpolations. This vast and controversial topic would need a book to itself if real progress were to be made. But one can at least see how in principle what we have learned about Ulpian's ways could be brought to bear on the problems. Take a famous text on agency, *D.* 19.1.13.25:

> Ulp. 32 ed. . . . . Si procurator vendiderit et caverit emptori, quaeritur an domino vel adversus dominum actio dari debeat. et Papinianus libro tertio responsorum putat cum domino ex empto agi posse utili actione ad exemplum institoriae actionis, si modo rem vendendam mandavit: ergo et per contrarium dicendum est utilem ex empto actionem domino competere.

The owner's general agent sells property and promises security to the buyer. Papinian thought the buyer could sue the owner in an analogous action on sale, if the owner had authorized his general agent to sell. 'So conversely we must say that the owner can sue the buyer in an analogous action on sale.' Is this genuine Ulpian? The proposition stated, though perfectly fair, is rather bold. So it is suspect. But the fact that *per contrarium* is found twenty-nine times in Ulpian and only twice in any other jurist (both in Marcianus, who was influenced by Ulpian) tells in favour of its genuineness. If the phrase came in a jurist other than Ulpian, we should be more suspicious.

Take another text from the same book on the edict which has often been held interpolated.[773] A man selling a slave who is in fact a thief honestly asserts that the slave is reliable. Can he be sued for damages in an action on sale?

> Ulp. 32 *ed.* Quid tamen si ignoravit quidem furem esse, adseveravit autem

---

[770] *D.* 23.2.20, 23.2.60; *Pal.* 1.1145−6.
[771] *D.* 23.2.60.4.
[772] Ch. 3 p. 104.
[773] *D.* 19.1.13.3 (32 *ed.*).

bonae frugi et fidum et caro vendidit? videamus, an ex empto teneatur, et putem teneri. atqui ignoravit: sed non debuit facile quae ignorabat adseverare.

Does Ulpian really hold that an action on sale lies for making a false statement, which raises the price, in good faith? In favour of the view that he does is the use of *et putem*, all thirty-one instances of which occur in his texts. The form of this text is, in any case, highly Ulpianic: question, answer, objection, reply. Of course a post-classical editor, or one of Justinian's commissioners, *might* have hit on *et putem* as a phrase to be inserted into the texts of Ulpian (and no one else). But such pastiche, requiring a profound knowledge of the texts and great literary skill, is hardly probable. The writers of the later empire compose in the manner of their own time. The fact that a text reads like a text of Ulpian must therefore be a strong argument in favour of its genuineness.

CHAPTER 3

Genuine Works

In this chapter the analysis given in the last chapter is presented in a different form. The material is arranged according to the works in which the listed marks of style appear. The object of this is to show which works attributed to Ulpian are genuine, and, to a lesser extent, what writings of Ulpian not attributed to him in the sources may be regarded as his.

The method adopted is to cite, work by work and book by book, the footnotes in the last chapter in which reference is made, by direct citation or via the *Concordance to the Digest Jurists*, to the works and books in question. The reader who refers to these notes will be able to judge for himself the strength of the evidence that a given book was composed by Ulpian. Clearly, the argument is based upon coherence of style. Assuming, for example, that the main commentaries *ad edictum* and *ad Sabinum* are genuine, the evidence tends to show that a number of other works commonly attributed to Ulpian are in a similar style. These may therefore also be regarded as genuine.

Clearly this argument would not satisfy a critic, if there is one, who thought that substantially the whole of the Ulpianic corpus was composed by someone else, an Ulpianic Bacon. On the other hand, it should, in appropriate cases, be convincing to a reader who is troubled about the existence in the body of Ulpian's work of extraneous elements, for example citations of imperial constitutions not drafted by the author, post-classical glosses or alterations, and interpolations by Justinian's compilers. For the arguments here adduced go to show that, despite these intrusions in the texts, and despite mistakes in copying before and after Justinian, whatever the extent of the change, the style of many of the works remains recognizably Ulpianic. No attempt is made to quantify the genuine and spurious matter in any given work or book, but merely to show that the spurious matter, whether voluminous or sparse, does not obliterate the style of the original. In regard to a particular text, on the other hand, the argument for total authenticity may be stronger. If the text contains a phrase such as *ut putem* or *idem erit probandum*, it is unlikely to be by any hand other than that of the Tyrian, though, even so, a coincidence or clever pastiche is not entirely ruled out. The case for the genuineness of certain works presented in this chapter, if cogent, establishes genuineness in a sense different from that of the spuriousness of certain works for which a case is made in the next. In chapter 4 it is argued that works such as the *opiniones*, though attributed to Ulpian, are wholly spurious, viz. that they contain no elements of Ulpian's writing at all. The present chapter does not purport to show that any work attributed to Ulpian is wholly genuine in the sense that it contains *nothing* by another hand. That would be a most implausible view. The thrust of an argument, however, is one thing; its strength another. Readers may feel that the positive case for genuineness in the sense explained, at least when there are numerous indications of it, is stronger than the negative case for spuriousness, which is based on the complete absence from certain works of expressions typical of Ulpian. My own opinion is that the positive and negative arguments are about equally strong when we are dealing with several hundred lines of text from the same work. When the volume of text is relatively small, on the other hand, the positive argument is stronger.

How many expressions characteristic of Ulpian rather than of other jurists are to be expected in a genuine passage? If the commentary *ad edictum* is treated as a standard example of a genuine work, the answer is as follows. On an average something typical—not just a hapax legomenon or other rare turn of phrase—turns up every fifteen or twenty lines. (Lines are counted as printed in Lenel's *Palingenesia*.) Ten or a dozen lines will often contain nothing idiosyncratic. On the other hand, it is rare to find as many as thirty lines without a characteristic expression. It is true that such expressions are entirely missing from one book of edictal commentary, book 78, but this yields only thirteen lines of excerpts.

To show the coherence of Ulpian's style, I set out, beginning with the major commentaries *ad edictum* and *ad Sabinum*, book by book, the number of lines in each book and the various footnote references to it in chapter 2. These enable the reader to ascertain, if he wishes, which Ulpianic expressions are found in each book. Some of these are pervasive features of Ulpian's style, some occur a few times in his works, others are hapax legomena. Obviously the more pervasive the feature the greater the weight its presence in a given work or book will carry. But hapax legomena and other rarities are not omitted, because, as mentioned earlier, they sometimes provide examples of general traits of style (e.g. the use of certain grammatical forms, or a fondness for certain roots) and, in any case, they are useful as a measure of the relative idiosyncrasy of the author's style in a given work or book. Where they do not illustrate a general trait, however, they can, in assessing the strength of the evidence for genuineness, be disregarded.

I. THE MAJOR COMMENTARIES

1. *Ad edictum praetoris urbani (81 books)*

Book	Lines	Footnotes in chapter 2
1	148	86, 112, 168, 300, 385, 388, 418, 743
2	111	394, 396, 400, 673
3	183	15, 18, 76, 110, 128, 165, 289, 393, 394, 401, 420, 564, 714
4	369	48, 60, 66, 81, 116, 118, 245a, 274, 376a, 394, 396, 498, 504, 515, 582, 671, 711, 714
5	213	81, 117, 163, 288, 291, 324, 385, 388, 393, 396, 478, 608
6	374	38, 66, 83, 85, 118, 174, 214, 255, 259, 274, 291, 365, 376c, 379, 385, 388, 393, 396, 400, 401, 404, 405, 430, 462, 513, 559, 630, 648, 656, 665, 670, 671
7	72	18, 393, 671
8	81	137, 274, 366, 385, 388, 396, 720
9	268	71, 110, 123, 139, 212, 221, 225, 274, 325, 330, 371, 376b, 379, 396, 421, 529
10	361	16, 18, 38, 66, 71, 132, 137, 165, 180, 187, 192, 220, 231, 274, 281, 294, 305, 317a, 317b, 330, 376a, 385, 394, 396, 468, 529, 545, 671, 673, 714
11	1001	15, 18, 34, 66, 71, 75, 76, 77, 81, 108, 110, 115, 121, 123, 127, 131, 138, 155, 158, 166, 170, 181, 185, 219, 220, 229, 239, 274, 277, 281, 288, 290, 309, 330, 337, 362, 376a, 376c, 393, 396, 399, 456, 492, 504, 506, 515, 544, 572, 582, 587, 592, 603, 679, 683, 692, 700, 707, 713, 714, 720, 727, 756, 757
12	343	18, 66, 71, 76, 117, 122, 127, 137, 149, 175, 231, 288, 290, 292, 294, 376c, 393, 396, 514, 592, 670, 671
13	423	18, 59, 68, 71, 75, 76, 77, 82, 110, 122, 123, 127, 130, 151, 166, 174, 211, 299, 305, 317b, 327, 333, 376a, 376d, 385, 388, 390, 396, 402, 425, 474, 478, 592, 628, 677, 683, 714, 720
14	393	18, 75, 76, 82, 132, 135, 147, 173, 174, 274, 281, 288, 291, 292, 328, 388, 396, 736
15	631	15, 18, 26, 39, 71, 76, 97, 117, 118, 127, 144, 159, 160, 174, 198, 274, 276, 281, 291, 293, 305, 387, 396, 398, 401, 424, 548, 671, 683, 735
16	369	18, 77, 97, 100, 122, 123, 127, 132, 155, 267, 274, 281, 290, 300, 311, 367, 380, 396
17	343	18, 59, 71, 81, 116, 274, 281, 300, 388, 400, 497
18	660	16, 66, 71, 75, 76, 82, 102, 118, 121, 137, 166, 174, 180, 226, 242, 256, 260, 274, 281, 288, 291, 305, 308, 317b, 324, 330, 388, 396, 409, 412, 540, 573, 578, 591, 626, 671, 725, 750, 756
19	377	18, 66, 69, 71, 83, 118, 129, 139, 181, 300, 472, 590, 714, 754

Book	Lines	Footnotes in chapter 2
20	100	84, 96, 104, 115, 166, 274, 281, 288, 396, 671, 714
21	35	388
22	396	71, 76, 113, 122, 139, 274, 281, 290, 295, 296, 310, 371b, 356, 388, 394, 396, 477, 543, 592, 633, 663, 670, 671, 701
23	402	31, 43, 59, 71, 75, 87, 122, 123, 128, 138, 160, 180, 216, 220, 274, 281, 388, 390, 393, 427, 468, 488, 499, 504, 510, 511, 582
24	315	71, 75, 76, 82, 104, 110, 122, 137, 149, 159, 181, 274, 281, 331, 388, 393, 412, 470, 504, 582, 670, 671, 683, 714, 725
25	393	66, 71, 84, 127, 128, 156, 158, 166, 181, 231, 288, 330, 350, 388, 396, 398, 409, 481, 495, 518, 671, 731, 747
26	404	18, 34, 56, 71, 75, 118, 123, 128, 170, 245a, 317b, 393, 396, 401, 515, 705, 713, 733, 748
27	283	18, 56, 66, 71, 76, 77, 169, 175, 231, 247, 288, 358, 367, 394, 438, 445, 499
28	678	42, 63, 66, 71, 75, 76, 105, 110, 126, 127, 135, 154, 160, 166, 167, 174, 175, 180, 181, 218, 225, 231, 257, 274, 278, 281, 288, 291, 305, 324, 376a, 376c, 388, 393, 396, 407, 527, 548, 551, 557, 579, 611, 670, 671, 685
29	1296	18, 34, 38, 57, 58, 59, 67, 71, 75, 76, 77, 84, 89, 104, 108, 110, 113, 118, 121, 126, 127, 128, 129, 160, 162, 165, 166, 167, 174, 187, 192, 195, 208, 220, 235, 246, 274, 281, 285, 288, 309, 311, 317a, 317b, 328, 372, 376b, 386, 388, 392, 393, 396, 400, 419, 424, 434, 449, 457, 470, 504, 545, 555, 558, 560, 582, 592, 593, 612, 613, 614, 623, 633, 670, 671, 679, 714, 735
30	400	22, 24, 71, 75, 76, 82, 86, 87, 120, 162, 181, 245a, 263, 272, 305, 398, 401, 407, 486, 582, 592, 638, 671, 714
31	633	15, 56, 71, 75, 76, 81, 82, 85, 88, 91, 93, 107, 114, 127, 129, 132, 165, 166, 220, 240, 274, 281, 285, 288, 295, 305, 317a, 328, 376a, 396, 457, 470, 504, 582, 588, 671, 754, 755
32	772	13, 18, 22, 46, 59, 71, 76, 81, 88, 117, 132, 141, 158, 159, 180, 187, 210, 217, 245a, 274, 281, 290, 351, 388, 394, 396, 400, 404, 454, 463, 475, 538, 575, 586, 597, 668, 670, 671, 704, 714, 756
33	222	18, 24, 43, 90, 118, 144, 170, 199, 504, 574, 582
34	447	13, 14, 38, 71, 81, 90, 103, 107, 110, 125, 128, 134, 137, 158, 160, 224, 295, 305, 388, 396, 431, 439, 671, 714, 746
35	779	13, 14, 18, 56, 71, 75, 76, 87, 88, 90, 99, 101, 102, 105, 113, 115, 174, 189, 217, 231, 274, 281, 288, 295, 296, 298, 300, 305, 309, 348, 355, 388, 391, 393, 396, 475, 478, 507, 529, 548, 576, 643, 667, 671, 706, 713, 737
36	490	14, 18, 22, 29, 30, 59, 71, 75, 77, 81, 85, 88, 104, 105, 106, 133, 142, 169, 174, 186, 192, 217, 290, 305, 309, 394, 396, 492, 529, 641, 646, 671, 698, 722

Book	Lines	Footnotes in chapter 2
37	233	13, 75, 90, 104, 170, 174, 396, 430, 494, 519
38	345	47, 66, 76, 77, 104, 105, 118, 135, 165, 175, 180, 288, 309, 388, 393, 502, 504, 582, 652, 670, 671, 672, 714, 739
39	288	22, 38, 76, 77, 85, 88, 106, 142, 175, 224, 245a, 257, 274, 281, 291, 297, 305, 314, 388, 463, 467, 477, 514, 670, 671
40	626	18, 28, 71, 77, 88, 103, 104, 106, 108, 114, 117, 125, 137, 139, 142, 158, 165, 225, 257, 274, 281, 288, 295, 305, 337, 340, 394, 478, 633, 670, 671, 714
41	491	66, 69, 71, 81, 85, 106, 110, 132, 139, 165, 166, 174, 175, 220, 225, 281, 311, 317a, 317b, 353, 388, 422, 446, 566, 646, 660, 671, 753, 756
42	84	75, 231, 661
43	72	369, 396, 626, 670, 671
44	239	18, 22, 38, 56, 71, 75, 85, 88, 90, 109, 116, 117, 217, 261, 274, 285, 308, 325, 388, 391, 393, 396, 473, 562
45	267	15, 18, 66, 77, 88, 106, 142, 175, 220, 274, 296, 306, 360, 379, 461, 475, 477, 622, 671, 677
46	195	88, 106, 217, 225, 233, 290, 291, 391, 396, 475
47	40	88, 90, 97, 339, 359, 700
48	36	142, 291, 296, 388
49	138	50, 63, 66, 77, 100, 108, 166, 405, 562
50	652	15, 16, 35, 68, 71, 75, 83, 86, 90, 91, 110, 116, 117, 126, 128, 141, 151, 154, 155, 171, 174, 180, 245a, 253, 274, 281, 299, 309, 328, 365, 388, 393, 396, 414, 477, 478, 504, 582, 670, 671, 673, 714, 752, 754
51	71	49, 67, 90, 154, 218, 671, 735
52	422	18, 59, 71, 75, 76, 82, 104, 106, 110, 118, 135, 140, 240, 245b, 300, 305, 336, 364, 370, 388, 393, 401, 421, 662, 671, 677
53	622	13, 18, 30, 66, 71, 75, 81, 82, 85, 91, 102, 106, 117, 118, 130, 133, 138, 151, 160, 166, 180, 190, 245b, 252, 274, 281, 285, 288, 290, 299, 300, 309, 326, 385, 441, 444, 639, 671, 714, 744, 756
54	87	97, 274, 281, 744
55	175	13, 18, 35, 66, 75, 76, 174, 175, 288, 291, 388, 393, 394, 427, 478, 504, 582
56	424	15, 16, 66, 69, 71, 76, 97, 103, 105, 118, 125, 175, 180, 220, 225, 229, 245a, 285, 288, 291, 292, 296, 388, 393, 396, 404, 475, 478, 498, 679, 690, 754
57	517	44, 71, 75, 76, 77, 83, 106, 107, 110, 122, 130, 135, 142, 173, 174, 245a, 258, 269, 285, 296, 305, 317b, 324, 376c, 380, 388, 393, 396, 414, 453, 478, 499, 569, 577, 599, 640, 654, 671, 673, 699, 702
58	72	71, 85, 291, 296, 301, 388, 476

Book	Lines	Footnotes in chapter 2
59	209	18, 69, 71, 77, 117, 133, 152, 154, 167, 180, 220, 245a, 274, 281, 285, 288, 296, 304, 317b, 388, 394, 478, 549, 550, 664, 710, 740, 756
60	239	18, 75, 100, 103, 106, 117, 125, 152, 154, 156, 166, 274, 285, 288, 291, 296, 477, 487, 620, 644, 661
61	158	66, 75, 118, 152, 274, 281, 393, 396, 440, 477, 731, 733
62	158	71, 175, 180, 349, 742
63	117	77, 174, 288, 393, 396, 398, 677, 734
64	166	13, 15, 18, 87, 91, 119, 154, 170, 251, 265, 285, 290, 407, 504, 582, 671, 733
65	45	161, 172
66	125	71, 77, 108, 153, 154, 156, 167, 195, 229, 330, 388, 477, 478
67	141	120, 126, 274, 281, 285, 288, 341, 376b, 388, 393, 671
68	666	13, 18, 66, 75, 76, 77, 82, 107, 110, 118, 119, 126, 137, 144, 162, 175, 245a, 285, 288, 296, 305, 309, 314, 339, 342, 348, 373, 388, 393, 394, 434, 553, 593, 636, 671, 672, 716
69	459	66, 75, 85, 87, 100, 108, 110, 118, 143, 151, 156, 174, 295, 299, 312, 393, 671, 733
70	635	16, 30, 34, 66, 71, 75, 77, 82, 85, 86, 97, 99, 101, 106, 109, 110, 115, 118, 120, 133, 136, 156, 158, 160, 175, 180, 181, 209, 216, 231, 274, 276, 281, 285, 305, 309, 330, 385, 393, 396, 432, 475, 477, 497, 615, 653, 670, 671, 672
71	924	29, 30, 35, 38, 43, 51, 55, 66, 68, 70, 71, 75, 76, 85, 105, 106, 118, 120, 126, 128a, 131, 133, 134, 154, 157, 165, 174, 175, 180, 181, 220, 225, 279, 281, 285, 293, 296, 302, 309, 324, 346, 376b, 379, 385, 389, 393, 396, 405, 407, 426, 465, 577, 504, 513, 531, 582, 626, 671, 672, 675, 713, 744, 758
72	75	18, 20, 76, 180, 223, 388, 404, 485, 563
73	273	13, 18, 75, 76, 77, 88, 106, 126, 159, 166, 274, 285, 296, 309, 333, 363, 376a, 393, 396, 467, 516
74	168	71, 77, 180, 245a, 304, 347, 368, 369, 388, 396, 405, 407, 423, 477, 478, 604, 670
75	148	13, 66, 71, 75, 76, 128, 152, 274, 285, 296, 303, 396, 475, 476
76	483	13, 16, 18, 34, 54, 66, 70, 71, 75, 77, 88, 98, 107, 118, 126, 133, 145, 154, 155, 156, 160, 174, 180, 264, 274, 281, 285, 296, 317b, 334, 335, 400, 671, 683, 744
77	201	59, 71, 94, 117, 126, 152, 154, 156, 274, 291, 296, 326, 388
78	13	—
79	467	13, 18, 59, 65, 66, 68, 71, 76, 88, 97, 106, 121, 126, 154, 157, 166, 175, 274, 288, 291, 295, 296, 317b, 340, 393, 642, 670, 671, 744
80	86	71, 118, 180, 393, 430, 519
81	181	116, 140, 180, 296, 326, 394, 412

Apart from book 78 which, as noted, has no marks of Ulpian's style, all the books contain some typical feature, though book 21 has only one (*accipere debemus*). But this book yields only thirty-five lines.

Broadly speaking, the number of footnote references is proportionate to the number of lines excerpted by the *Digest* commissioners. But it is interesting to note that the proportion of idiosyncratic features increases as the edictal commentary continues. The following table, in which the work is divided up in a way whose significance will become clear in chapter 5, shows this:

Books	Lines	Number of references	References per 100 lines
1—5	1024	55	5.4
6—31	11031	672	6.1
32—56	8217	530	6.5
57—81	6726	482	7.2

Towards the end of the work there are more footnote references per line. Thus Ulpian, presumably like other authors, becomes more himself as his writing continues. He gradually shakes off derivative traits.

Nevertheless, there are, quite apart from this interesting trend, points at which his style varies from time to time during the course of the edictal commentary. These provide clues to the method and rate of composition of his work and are discussed in chapter 6. But the variations, though significant, are minor in relation to the style as a whole. The over-all impression is one of uniformity. Thus, *ut puta* occurs in 39 different books of the edictal commentary, *proinde* (meaning 'accordingly') in 50, and *et ait* (*Iulianus* etc.) in 43. Apart from the first five books, written when the author had not quite got into his stride, the tone is remarkably even.

2. *Ad Masurium Sabinum* (51 books)

Much the same is true of Ulpin's other major comentry, on Sabinus and the *ius civile*. Here, too, the coherence of style is remarkable.

Book	Lines	Footnotes in chapter 2
1	185	14, 24, 81, 160, 228, 230, 386, 542, 570
2	81	18, 199, 268, 394, 396, 448
3	100	18, 245a, 376b, 396, 500, 732
4	180	166, 195, 216, 217, 245a, 236, 317b, 396, 475
5	141	104, 162, 167, 210, 396
6	138	99, 116, 285, 290, 291
7	169	97, 121, 128, 201, 254, 396, 401, 562
8	156	81, 110, 376c, 385, 386, 394, 427
9	56	159, 274, 281, 376c, 385, 411, 496
10	123	15, 76, 18, 158, 376a, 376d, 396, 459, 478
11	7	—

Book	Lines	Footnotes in chapter 2
12	165	23, 25, 56, 77, 109, 116, 123, 274, 281, 376c, 388, 392, 396, 466, 706, 748
13	286	18, 174, 214, 225, 241, 274, 280, 281, 290, 298, 345, 388, 393, 400, 401, 562
14	178	13, 18, 82, 117, 121, 188, 225, 274, 281, 388, 396, 401, 424, 459, 753
15	111	71, 75, 128, 245b, 376c, 688
16	37	—
17	622	18, 33, 35, 56, 71, 75, 76, 77, 81, 86, 106, 110, 114, 116, 117, 122, 126, 128, 129, 130, 155, 160, 161, 162, 166, 167, 174, 180, 191, 274, 281, 317b, 323, 343, 352, 396, 398, 400, 401, 490, 548, 619, 639, 677, 714
18	398	16, 18, 66, 67, 68, 71, 76, 77, 82, 114, 116, 122, 127, 132, 140, 155, 160, 180, 217, 236, 274, 281, 333, 376b, 385, 393, 396, 402, 471, 490, 617, 628, 634, 671, 681, 735, 738
19	153	18, 41, 71, 76, 81, 88, 180, 187, 192, 288, 359, 379
20	462	18, 22, 71, 76, 77, 82, 99, 166, 180, 181, 220, 245a, 248, 270, 274, 281, 317b, 376b, 393, 435, 444, 450, 528, 561, 647, 651, 655, 744
21	244	18, 75, 77, 82, 104, 149, 151, 158, 181, 274, 282, 290, 299, 365, 376c, 403, 470, 552
22	256	22, 77, 102, 118, 129, 158, 160, 174, 181, 274, 290, 351, 434, 490, 554
23	324	17, 18, 35, 56, 59, 71, 75, 76, 82, 110, 128, 134, 155, 159, 174, 245a, 274, 281, 292, 295, 317b, 344, 376e, 470, 677, 721
24	294	15, 18, 71, 75, 77, 82, 127, 195, 229, 263, 274, 281, 360, 376c, 396, 398, 407, 483, 537, 616, 671, 701, 714, 717
25	202	18, 21, 64, 71, 76, 81, 94, 115, 116, 227, 235, 274, 288, 298, 305, 311, 317b, 393, 671
26	139	75, 81, 162, 464, 468, 567
27	208	18, 35, 77, 82, 104, 108, 158, 160, 174
28	426	18, 32, 59, 66, 71, 76, 82, 83, 94, 104, 162, 172, 174, 182, 217, 274, 285, 290, 295, 393, 396, 460, 503, 633, 703, 704, 714
29	323	19, 71, 81, 82, 88, 129, 143, 172, 231, 274, 379, 401, 408, 478, 714
30	231	18, 71, 118, 122, 195, 207, 274, 281, 288, 388, 396, 529, 672, 714
31	315	13, 15, 71, 76, 117, 143, 149, 166, 172, 180, 181, 199, 229, 248, 288, 317b, 376b, 388, 416, 754
32	443	14, 75, 76, 81, 105, 142, 154, 166, 195, 230, 247, 295, 317b, 362, 396, 409, 522, 523, 524, 562, 714
33	226	13, 14, 75, 76, 77, 118, 155, 193, 202, 220, 225, 232, 274, 281, 388, 396, 482, 520, 733

34	128	18, 82, 102, 165, 396, 416
35	68	18, 100, 167, 237, 274, 393, 464, 508, 713, 728
36	208	15, 27, 65, 76, 77, 88, 155, 158, 170, 171, 225, 245b, 290, 297, 314, 317b, 396, 434, 464, 714, 738, 744
37	64	71, 104, 114, 120, 142, 225, 297, 314, 478
38	97	15, 17, 76, 105, 106, 719
39	41	75, 90, 274, 281, 475
40	150	94, 97, 104, 107, 306, 376b, 376c, 477, 478, 679
41	320	15, 35, 66, 71, 77, 82, 88, 90, 91, 96, 97, 105, 107, 142, 159, 172, 174, 175, 324, 396, 404, 714, 718
42	278	27, 71, 77, 81, 88, 91, 92, 140, 143, 149, 180, 215, 242, 244, 388, 393, 473, 694
43	229	71, 76, 117, 128a, 166, 175, 233, 243, 274, 281, 317b, 379, 437, 671, 677, 714, 756
44	157	16, 27, 90, 97, 135, 180, 199, 410, 476, 480, 570, 581, 593, 605
45	35	245b, 296, 468
46	151	24, 274, 281, 296, 525, 626
47	165	35, 87, 113, 141, 143, 157, 174, 288, 292, 457
48	203	13, 18, 70, 75, 76, 81, 87, 105, 113, 152, 214, 274, 281, 285, 393, 477, 629, 744
49	309	13, 16, 40, 49, 71, 105, 111, 157, 159, 172, 180, 181, 245a, 274, 281, 296, 304, 309, 396, 477, 478, 671
50	115	18, 104, 245b, 250, 263, 296, 306
51	45	216, 396

The authenticity of Ulpian's *ad Sabinum* is not in doubt. Two books, however, 11 and 16, which contain seven and thirty-seven lines respectively, lack listed marks of the author's style. But, in general terms, the excerpts from book 16 conform to style. There are, for instance, four instances of the future in these thirty-seven lines: *locum habebit, repetetur, erit . . . necessarius, valebit.*

It is interesting that the trend, noticed in the edictal commentary, towards greater idiosyncrasy as the work progresses is found also in *ad Sabinum*. If we divide the work into two roughly equal parts, the proportion of footnotes increases slightly:

Books	*Lines*	*Number of references*	*References per 100 lines*
1—26	5336	355	6.65
27—51	4935	335	6.79

The total for the first 26 books includes 139 lines from *Frag. Vat.* in book 17. In comparison with *ad edictum*, the increase in the proportion of references in *ad Sabinum* is small.

II. THE MEDIUM-SCALE WORKS

There is good evidence for the authenticity of the treatises in ten and twenty books: *de officio proconsulis, disputationes, de omnibus tribunalibus*, and *ad legem Iuliam et Papiam*.

3. *De officio proconsulis* (10 books)

Book	Lines	Footnotes in chapter 2
1	74	87, 506, 714, 715
2	87	274, 425, 533, 632, 697, 726
3	60	90, 142, 150, 332, 416, 432, 478, 659, 692
4	69	97, 388, 476
5	37	541, 627
6	24	—
7	170	13, 37, 428, 445, 534, 541, 626, 696
8	288	13, 30, 71, 77, 86, 87, 97, 101, 104, 106, 119, 143, 427, 428, 442, 504, 533, 546, 569, 582, 628, 688, 720, 751, 753
9	207	77, 84, 85, 97, 117, 140, 142, 153, 175, 189, 396, 398, 405, 507, 650, 741
10	195	14, 81, 97, 107, 117, 119, 135, 158, 285, 295, 350, 388, 396, 470

Only book 6 lacks a mark of Ulpian's style, but as the excerpts from it amount only to twenty-four lines, the lacuna is not surprising. The two references from book 5 are insubstantial, but, again, only thirty-seven lines survive from this book. All the other books contain adequate indications that Ulpian is the author. Though Schulz says that the style of this (highly original) work departs considerably from the classical,[1] the references listed in chapter 2 do not bear this out. Their density, indeed, at first sight appears rather high:

Books	Lines	Number of references	References per 100 lines
10	1211	87	7.2

But this includes some references to texts drawn from the *Collatio*. When an adjustment is made for these, the number of references per line is only 6.3, which is about the average for the edictal commentary.

---

[1] Schulz (1946) 245. His statement that *D.* 47.11.9 (9 *off. proc.*) was not by Ulpian because it concerns only Arabia, an imperial province, is mistaken: *ut puta* shows that it is genuine. Schulz's opinion that law special to the imperial provinces was excluded from the work must therefore be wrong.

4. *Disputationes* (10 books)

Book	Lines	Footnotes in chapter 2
1	129	77, 81, 110, 274, 293, 388, 565, 677, 709
2	210	38, 76, 107, 110, 128, 149, 181, 288, 295, 308, 376f, 476, 592, 670, 671
3	198	18, 84, 97, 170, 274, 281, 334, 376c, 643, 743
4	372	17, 18, 22, 34, 75, 76, 85, 88, 95, 116, 130, 146, 158, 217, 274, 281, 290, 292, 295, 298, 351, 376a, 396, 476, 530, 556, 562, 714, 749
5	278	69, 71, 75, 76, 77, 97, 144, 149, 195, 274, 281, 290, 305, 393, 475, 476, 596, 671, 733, 754
6	162	18, 76, 77, 118, 274, 288, 413, 475
7	253	18, 23, 76, 77, 82, 84, 149, 274, 281, 501, 504, 582, 670, 671
8	304	13, 18, 22, 75, 76, 81, 82, 95, 97, 164, 210, 274, 281, 376a, 376c, 509, 510, 511, 629, 714
9	13	290
10	9	—

Book 10, with nine lines of excerpts, contains no mark of Ulpian's style. The other books all do. Beseler stated dogmatically that this work was not by Ulpian.[2] Schulz argued that the text reached the compilers much altered by post-classical editing, and that 'this for practical purposes comes to much the same thing for the legal historian' as Beseler's opinion.[3] But the surviving excerpts contain over 100 words and phrases typical of Ulpian rather than other jurists. There are indeed some alterations in the texts,[4] but Schulz's approach is mistaken. The texts are largely genuine, and they conform in style to the rest of Ulpian's work, taking account of the fact that disputation, oral debate on points of law, has its own conventions. The passages and phrases which are post-classical have to be winkled out one by one.

The proportion of references in *disputationes* to the footnotes of chapter 2 is a little above the average for the edictal commentary:

Books	Lines	Number of references	References per 100 lines
10	1928	127	6.6

5. *De omnibus tribunalibus* (10 books)

Books	Lines	Footnotes in chapter 2
1	77	106, 438, 559
2	58	18, 77, 142, 170, 393, 683

[2] Beseler (1925) 225[1]; (1930) 190; (1936) I. 313.
[3] Schulz (1946) 240.
[4] Of which Schulz gives an example—D. 15.1.32 pr. (*sed licet hoc iure contingat, tamen aequitas dictat. .*)

Book	Lines	Footnotes in chapter 2
3	18	—
4	61	296, 376c, 568
5	183	15, 81, 127, 262, 274, 281, 288, 305, 306, 317b, 361, 671
6	0	—
7	0	—
8	100	18, 77, 86, 90, 234, 306, 311, 376c, 388, 393, 417, 452, 484, 503, 532, 635
9	9	—
10	0	—

The five books which lack marks of style have either no or very few lines of text. There can be no doubt about the authenticity of this work, since the remaining books contain plenty of indications that Ulpian is the author. The density of references is on the high side:

Books	Lines	Number of references	References per 100 lines
10	506	40	7.9

6. *Ad legem Iuliam et Papiam* (20 books)

Book	Lines	Footnotes in chapter 2
1	99	76, 77, 106, 110, 180, 291, 388, 393, 571, 610, 754
2	26	158, 181, 467, 706
3	96	76, 77, 90, 134, 139, 285, 388, 393, 475
4	30	107, 142, 228
5	13	—
6	25	139, 295
7	43	104, 330, 393
8	37	170, 274, (281), 396, 458
9	6	—
10	29	88, 152, 245, 309
11	47	274, (281)
12	0	—
13	38	274, (281), 633
14	10	274, (281), 625
15	12	135, 290
16	7	—
17	0	—
18	40	388, 512, 600, 601
19	5	—
20	9	—

There are no less than seven books which lack marks of style, but this is accounted for by the fact that none of these books yields more than 13 lines of excerpt. The style is highly Ulpianic, as the density of references shows:

Books	Lines	Number of references	Lines per reference
20	572	51	8.9

III. MINOR WORKS

The two major commentaries and the four medium-scale works attributed to Ulpian can be shown, therefore, to be substantially genuine. The same is not true of all the minor works which stand in the *Digest* and the *Index Florentinus* in his name. They fall into four classes. Some are demonstrably genuine. Some, again, are consistent in style with Ulpian's authorship and so, given that they are attributed to him, are probably genuine. In some cases the evidence is so scanty that no conclusion can be drawn from the texts themselves. Any inference of genuineness rests on the inscriptions in the *Digest* or the attribution of the *Index Florentinus* alone. Others, lastly, are clearly or probably spurious.

De fideicommissis falls in the first class.

7. *De fideicommissis* (6 books)

Book	Lines	Footnotes in chapter 2
1	105	76, 164, 266, 274, 281, 388
2	294	18, 22, 23, 76, 105, 106, 143, 148, 158, 274, 290, 407, 446, 470, 493, 497, 668, 731, 739
3	159	34, 38, 41, 82, 104, 309
4	329	20, 77, 82, 84, 104, 116, 127, 135, 155, 158, 175, 180, 190, 191, 217, 274, 281, 296, 305, 308, 325, 407, 562, 649, 668, 671, 714
5	404	13, 29, 36, 44, 64, 71, 75, 76, 77, 128, 175, 193, 218, 232, 249, 271, 274, 281, 305, 327, 376a, 376c, 407, 478, 671, 714, 731
6	112	15, 149, 396, 467, 624

There is ample evidence of authenticity from all six books, but the density of references is relatively low, and corresponds to that of the early part of the edictal commentary:

Books	Lines	Number of references	Lines per references per 100 lines
6	1403	84	6.0

8. *De appellationibus* (4 books)

Book	Lines	Footnotes in chapter 2
1	188	13, 18, 53, 75, 151, 152, 157, 229, 299, 338, 354, 393, 394, 396, 398, 455, 477, 504, 582
2	10	107, 158
3	2	—
4	76	66, 154, 173, 285

The only books from which more than ten lines are drawn contain ample marks of Ulpian's style and the authorship of this treatise on appeals is not in doubt. The density of footnote references is high:

Book	Lines	Number of references	References per 100 lines
4	276	26	9.4

9. *Ad legem Iuliam de adulteriis* (5 books)

Book	Lines	Footnotes in chapter 2
1	46	127, 290
2	200	13, 18, 66, 76, 175, 184, 393, 396, 435, 438, 452, 478, 524, 584, 635
3	79	77, 137, 142, 225, 451
4	120	15, 85, 88, 104, 118, 142, 350, 388, 466, 505, 536, 584, 685
5	26	77, 388, 393

Expressions typical of Ulpian are found in all five books. The density of reference is, again, on the high side:

Books	Lines	Number of references	References per 100 lines
5	471	38	8.1

10. *De officio consulis* (3 books)

Book	Lines	Footnotes in chapter 2
1	55	313, 388, 391, 393
2	218	14, 18, 85, 106, 116, 117, 134, 142, 252, 289, 291, 329, 388, 443, 467, 597, 708, 729
3	136	15, 104, 166, 289, 305, 671

All three books present signs of Ulpian's authorship. The density of idiosyncratic references is about average:

Books	Lines	Number of references	References per 100 lines
3	409	28	6.3

11. *Ad edictum aedilium curulium* (2 books)

Books	Lines	Footnotes in chapter 2
1	749	18, 29, 62, 71, 75, 76, 77, 81, 84, 87, 93, 97, 100, 122, 126, 130, 154, 160, 162, 180, 274, 281, 288, 291, 305, 308, 357, 385, 386, 388, 393, 396, 415, 429, 489, 504, 533, 558, 570, 578, 582, 591, 602, 607, 631, 637, 645, 671, 724
2	104	61, 105, 106, 118, 371, 526

The density of references is about average:

Books	Lines	Number of references	References per 100 lines
2	853	55	6.4

12. *Institutiones* (2 books)

Book	Lines	Footnotes in chapter 2
1	93	52, 109, 223, 235, 238, 248, 377, 396, 521, 714
2	27	497, 609, 671

The evidence of genuineness is adequate, but, with so few lines of excerpts, it ceases to be meaningful to calculate the proportionate density of the references.

13. *Ad legem Aeliam Sentiam* (4 books)

Book	Lines	Footnotes in chapter 2
1	3	—
2	14	134
3	0	—
4	20	59, 117, 144

Despite the shortage of texts, the presence in these few lines of *meminisse oportet*[5], *dubio procul*[6], *et est verius*,[7] and *utrum . . . an vero*[8] would seem to guarantee the genuineness of this work.

Two at least of the *libri singulares* are, on linguistic grounds, clearly genuine.

14. *De officio curatoris reipublicae* (1 book)

Book	Lines	Footnotes in chapter 2
1	67	77, 86, 306, 393, 517, 539, 585, 587, 599, 621

---

[5] D. 40.2.16 (2 *leg. Ael. Sent.*), ch. 2 n. 134.
[6] D. 40.9.30.2 (4 *leg. Ael. Sent.*), ch. 2 n. 144.
[7] D. 40.9.30.4 (4 *leg. Ael. Sent.*), ch. 2 n. 59.
[8] D. 40.9.30.4 (4 *leg. Ael. Sent.*), ch. 2 n. 117.

15. *De officio praetoris tutelaris* (1 book)

Book	Lines	Footnotes in chapter 2
I	19	76, 170, 175, 191, 291, 394, 398

To the nineteen lines from the *Digest* must be added some 320 lines, often fragmentary, from the *Vatican Fragments*. It would, again, be unprofitable to try to calculate the density of references in view of the shortage of text with a clear reading. But the authenticity of the work is not in doubt; it contains a number of leading marks of Ulpian's style.

16. *De excusationibus* (1 book)

Book	Lines	Footnotes in chapter 2
I	8	190, 226a, 406, 447, 535, 580, 598

To the eight lines from the *Digest* must be added some 206 from *FV*, again sometimes fragmentary. The linguistic arguments for the genuineness of this work are not conclusive. Of the distinctive features, only *invenio* is found both here and elsewhere[9]. However, the general impression created by the texts is consistent with Ulpian's manner. Thus, *quia est iniquum*[10] followed by the accusative and infinitive is a striking inversion. *Non computabitur*[11] and *non oberit*[12] are plausible uses of the future. The texts from *de excusationibus* fall into the second class mentioned above. They are consistent with Ulpian's authorship but do not point unequivocally to it. But since two texts from this work are virtually common to it and to *off. pr. tut.*,[13] its genuineness need not depend on marks of style alone.

Indeed, when all the evidence is taken into account, we are justified in classing it among Ulpian's authentic works.

17. *De officio praefecti urbi* (1 book)

Book	Line	Footnote in chapter 2
I	72	291, 325, 547, 599, 743

The presence of *accipiemus*[14] and of *erit audiendus*[15] is probably enough to justify our accepting this work as genuine.

---

[9] D. 27.1.15.6 (1 *excus.*), ch. 2. n. 190.

[10] FV 153 (1 *excus.*) but D. 39.3.11.2 (Paul 49 *ed.*: *et est iniquum* . . .).

[11] FV 161 (1 *excus.*), cf. D. 24.3.7.12 (Ulp. 31 *Sab.*).

[12] FV 165 (1 *excus.* = *n. o. si.*) cf. D. 6.2.7.12 (16 *ed.*: *n. o. mihi si*), 2.11.2.9 (74 *ed.*), but 35.1.78.1 (Pap. 9 *resp.*), 12.6.59 (Pap. 2 *def.*).

[13] D 27.1.7 (1 *excus.*) = FV 240 (1 *off. pr. tut.*) almost exactly. D. 27.1.15.16 (1 *excus.*) is a slightly shortened version of FV 189 (1 *off. pr. tut.*). FV 145 (1 *excus.*) = FV 222 (1 *off. pr. tut.*) almost exactly.

[14] D. 1.12.1.8 (1 *off. pr. urb.*), ch. 2 n. 291.

[15] D. 1.12.1.5 (1 *off. pr. urb.*), ch. 2 n. 325, 374.

18. *De officio quaestoris* (1 or 2 books)

Book	Lines	Footnotes in chapter 2
I	29	606, 659, 730

The presence of *indifferenter*[16], one of a group of similar adverbs[17] and of *antiquissimus*[18] afford arguments for genuineness, but they are inconclusive. The excerpts read as if Ulpian might have composed them, but his authorship must be treated as probable rather than certain.

19. *De censibus* (6 books)

Book	Lines	Footnotes in chapter 2
I	30	379, 566, 589, 659, 666
2	18	435
3	40	—
4	6	—
5	2	—
6	0	—

The argument for genuineness, though weighty, is inconclusive. It rests on the presence in book 1 of the *et est . . .* construction, which occurs five times,[19] and in book 2 of *recte expressum est*, referring to a rescript of Caracalla, which exhibits a certain form of condescension peculiar to Ulpian.[20] On the other hand, the forty lines of excerpts from book 3 contain no characteristic mark. Much of this passage is in my view taken either from the official *forma census* or from another author. *Saepissime* is, however, close to being a mark of Ulpian's style,[21] and the work as a whole may be regarded as probably genuine. This is just as well, since it is from it alone that we learn of the Ulpian's connection with Tyre.[22]

In three instances when textual evidence is lacking, no conclusion can be reached, and any presumption of genuineness must rest solely on the ascription of the work to Ulpian in the *Digest* and the *Florentine Index*.

20. *De officio praefecti vigilum* (1 book)

Book	Lines	Footnotes in chapter 2
I	I	433

The reference does not help the argument since the verb (*exoriri*) is a *hapax legomenon*.[23]

---

[16] D. 1.13.1.3 (1 *off. qu.*), ch. 2 n. 730.

[17] Cf. D. 40.2.20 pr. (2 *off. cons.: incuntanter*); below, ch. 7 p. 177.

[18] D 1.13.1 pr. (1 *off. qu.*) ch. 2 n. 659.

[19] D. 50.15.1.2, 3, 5, 10, 11 (all 1 *cens.*), ch. 2 n. 379.

[20] D. 50.15.3.1 (2 *cens.*), ch. 7 p. 165.

[21] Ch. 2 n. 712.

[22] D. 50.15.1 pr. (1 *cens.*).

[23] D. 1.15.2 (1 *off. pr. vig.*), ch. 2 n. 433.

21. *De officio consularium* (1 book)

Book	Lines	Footnotes in chapter 2
I	3	—

The three lines, though the author does not say so, are taken from a constitution of Marcus.[24] The construction is non-Ulpianic, and, if the source were not known, might lead to the inference that the work was spurious. As it is, no conclusion can be drawn.

22. *De sponsalibus* (1 book)

Book	Lines	Footnotes in chapter 2
I	7	—

No conclusion can be drawn from these few lines, either. In the upshot, the works which, on the basis of stylistic analysis, are clearly genuine, comprise:

Major: ad edictum praetoris urbani 81
ad Masurium Sabinum 51

Medium: de officio proconsulis 10
disputationes 10
de omnibus tribunalibus 10
ad legem Iuliam et Papiam 20

Minor: de fideicommissis 6
ad legem Iuliam de adulteriis 5
de appellationibus 4
ad legem Aeliam Sentiam 4
de officio consulis 3
institutiones 2
ad edictum aedilium curulium 2
de officio curatoris reipublicae 1
de officio praefecti urbi 1
de officio praetoris tutelaris 1

The works which turn out to be probably genuine comprise:

de censibus 6
de excusationibus 1
de officio quaestoris 1 or 2

Those which are neutral from a stylistic point of view, and which can be assigned to Ulpian only in so far as the sources make this attribution and the evidence of the texts does not contradict it, comprise:

de officio praefecti vigilum 1
de officio consularium 1
de sponsalibus 1

[24] D. 42.5.24.1 (Ulp. 63 *ed.*).

This list of Ulpian's writings is not necessarily complete. There is some evidence that he wrote a monograph about the *oratio* of Marcus and Commodus concerning marriage between a tutor and his female ward. The *Digest* contains two excerpts from a one-book work by Paul *ad orationem divi Antonini et Commodi*.[25] It is not suggested that these are not genuine excerpts from Paul, but the second of them contains a passage that is strongly reminiscent of Ulpian:

D. 23.2.60.4   Quid ergo si, cum se vellet excusare aliquo titulo nec in promptu probationes haberet, excusationis negotium fuerit dilatum et inter moras pupilla adolveverit, an ad senatusconsultum pertineat? *quaestio in eo est*, an et post pubertatem officio finito excusationem eius recipi oporteat: nam si recipitur et excusaverit [excusatus erit Mommsen] impune potest ducere: si vero non debeat recipi post officium finitum, non recte ducit. *et ait Papinianus* libro quinto responsorum. . . .

Et ait . . . occurs in 117 texts of Ulpian and in only one text of Paul apart from this one.[26] *Quaestio in eo est* occurs, apart from this text, only in four texts of Ulpian.[27] The suspicion must be that, in this passage, Paul has drawn from a work of Ulpian on the same subject. This he may well have done, since Paul survived into the reign of Alexander[28] and this particular monograph cannot be independently dated.

Ulpian is known to have annotated the *digesta* of Marcellus and the *responsa* of Papinian. He himself twice mentions notes on the former.[29] In three other passages excerpted in the *Digest*, a note of his on Marcellus is recorded.[30] In at least one other passage his hand may be suspected[31].

Eight passages in Papinian's *responsa* record a note of Ulpian.[32] These notes, and his notes on Marcellus, are short sentences, which, in general, show no particular marks of his style, though they are often couched in the future indicative.[33] In some other instances, where the *Digest* text does not say that the passage is a note, the style, nevertheless, points to the Tyrian. Thus, Lenel thought that Ulpian perhaps annotated Papinian's *questiones* as

[25] D. 23.2.20, 23.2.60.
[26] Ch. 2 n 71–2.
[27] Ch. 2 n. 128a.
[28] D. 31.87.3.4 (14 *resp.*), 49.1.25 (20 *resp.*).
[29] D. 9.2.41 pr. (Ulp. 41 *Sab.*), 47.10.11 (*Ulp.* 57 *ed.*).
[30] D. 20.1.27 (Marc. 5 *dig.*), 26.7.28.1 (Marc. 8 *dig.*), 29.7.9 (Marc. 9 *dig.*) cf. Reggi (1951).
[31] D. 44.3.2 (Marc. 6 *dig.*: *mihi contra videtur*) but this might be Scaevola. The note in 29.7.19 (14 *dig.*: *immo dumtaxat* . . .) might be Ulpian's.
[32] D. 50.8.4 (Pap. 1 *resp.*), 3.5.30.2 (Pap. 2 *resp.*), 37.6.9 (5 *resp*: ZRG 15, 85); ZRG 15.88 (5 *resp.*); ZRG 15.89 (5 *resp.*); ZRG 18.171, 176 (9 *resp.*); ZRG 18.171, 177 (9 *resp.*); D. 40.4.50 (9 *resp.*: ZRG 18.173, 179); Santalucia (1965).
[33] D. 20.1.27 (Marc. 5 *dig.*: *tenebitur* . . . *non tenebitur*), 29.7.9 (Marc. 9 *dig*: *valebit*), 3.5.30.2 (Pap. 2 *resp*: *aget, poterit*).

well as his *responsa*.[34] This seems correct. In one of the two texts he cited,[35] the passage which he suspects of being a note of Ulpian is followed by *et est quidem constitutum in bonae fidei iudiciis*, which is decidedly Ulpianic.[36] The *epistulae* of Iavolenus also bear traces of Ulpian's intervention. Thus, in D. 38.5.12 (Iav. 3 *epist*.) a variation of the facts is introduced, contrary to Iavolenus' manner, with a question and answer in the future indicative (*quid enim dicemus? . . . non dubitabimus*). As Eckardt notes,[37] the text incorporates a gloss on this variation. *Non dubitabimus* is found, apart from this text, only in another text of Ulpian,[38] and one must suspect his hand. This is the more likely since the theme which he introduces (the possible absence of *dolus*) is also the theme of one of his notes on Marcellus.[39] In this instance it looks as if the manuscript which the *Digest* commissioners used was descended from one in the possession of Ulpian. Clearly Ulpian, like Tribonian later, had a good law library. There may be other *Digest* works which passed at an earlier stage through his hands. So it is worth asking, when we find an normally Ulpianic expression attributed to another jurist, whether the passage in question could be an annotation by the former.

[34] *Pal.* 2.950⁶.
[35] D. 16.3.24 (Pap. 9 *qu*.: note begins *quod ita verum est* . . .).
[36] Cf. ch. 2 n. 41 (*et est decretum*), 43 (*et est relatum*), 44 (*et est rescriptum*).
[37] Eckardt (1978) 132 f.
[38] D. 27.8.1.2 (36 *ed*.) and cf. ch. 2 n. 139.
[39] D. 20.1.27 (Marc. 5 *dig*.).

CHAPTER 4

Spurious Works

The argument presented in this chapter is that the following works attributed to Ulpian are spurious:

> regularum libri 7
> regularum liber 1
> opinionum libri 6
> pandectarum liber 1 (or libri 10)
> responsorum libri 2.

If this is right, of the total of 235 (or 244, depending on how many books of *pandectae* are counted) books attributed to our author 17 (or 26) were not written by him. This is a significant, though not overwhelming, proportion. It suggests that it was possible, in the Roman empire, to pass off, as written by a well-known jurist, spurious works, at least on a fairly small scale.

The works listed above are all attributed to Ulpian in the *Florentine Index* to the *Digest*, ch. XXIV, except that the *Index* speaks of πανδέκτου βιβλία δέκα,[1] whereas the two excerpts in the *Digest* itself purport to come from a *liber singularis pandectarum*.[2] Although a few *responsa* of Ulpian are cited in other sources,[3] none of these works is mentioned as such outside the *Digest*, with the exception of the *liber singularis regularum*. From this are taken three texts in the *Romanorum et Mosaicarum legum collatio*,[4] a compilation which in its present form seems to date from somewhere between AD 390 and 428,[5] but which is based on a collection of material apparently made, in the first instance, about AD 320.[6] *Liber singularis regularum* or *LSR* (as I shall call it) was therefore known in the fourth century. We can tell this in another way. Two of the *Collatio* texts,[7]

---

[1] *Ind. Flor.* XXIV 7

[2] *Pal.* 2.1013; D. 12.1.24, 40.12.34; below, nn. 127–42.

[3] D. 19.1.43 (Paul 5 *qu.*), 50.5.5 (Macer 2 *off. praes.*), CJ 8.37.4 (Alex. 31 March 222).

[4] P. Krueger–Th. Mommsen–G. Studemund (1878–90) vol. III; literature in Schulz (1961) 394[1].

[5] *Coll.* 5.3 cites a constitution of 14 May 390 but this may be a later addition to a work originally compiled in the early fourth century. The *Codex Theodosianus* (438) is not cited.

[6] *Coll.* 15.3, the latest constitution, perhaps, in the original edition, is a constitution of the tetrarchs of 31 March 297 or, better, 302.

[7] *Coll.* 6.2.1–4, 16.4.1–2.

together with one text in the *Digest*[8] from *LSR*, occur in almost identical form[9] in a manuscript found in the sixteenth century, bound together with the Visigothic *breviarium*. This manuscript began *incipiunt tituli ex corpore Ulpiani* and was named by Schulz *Epitome Ulpiani* (*EU*).

(a) Liber singularis regularum[10]

It is convenient to discuss the authenticity of *LSR* first. The question is a complicated one. *EU* appears to be a fourth-century version of the text. Schulz, whose views have won and with certain reservations deserve acceptance, argued that it was composed between AD 320 and 342.[11] The earlier date is that of Constantine's legislation relieving childless persons and the unmarried from the penalties imposed on them by Augustus.[12] The editor of *EU* has tried, though clumsily, to take account of this. On the other hand, he has not taken account of the repeal by Constantius II in 342 of the legislation permitting marriage with a brother's daughter,[13] originally passed to enable Claudius to marry Agrippina. The first of these dates is stronger evidence than the second, since arguments from omission to notice recent legislation are notoriously unreliable. But, since *EU* contemplates gifts by will to pagan gods,[14] a date in the third century is in any event more likely than one in the fourth.

The editor of *EU* does not seem to have made many changes in the text before him.[15] The question is what this text was. Schulz held that it was the work known as *LSR*.[16] The argument in favour of this hypothesis is the close verbal similarity of *EU* to *LSR* in the three texts mentioned above. Alternatively, *LSR* might have been one among two or several sources used by the editor of *EU*. It seems to me that Schulz's opinion, if not free from doubt, is the more likely.

The next question, and the most difficult, is what the source or sources and dates of *LSR* were. If Ulpian is the author, then of course he must have composed the work during his lifetime, though it need not have been published until later. a second possibility is that, though Ulpian did not compose it, someone after his death put *LSR* together out of material written by him. A third view is that the posthumous compiler used some

---

[8] *D.* 22.5.17.

[9] *Ulp.* 5.6–7, 26.1–1a.

[10] Schulz (1926); *Ind. Flor.* XXIV 15; *Pal.* 2.1016; *RE* 5.1448; Mommsen (1905) II 2 47; Fitting (1908) 116; Schulz (1946) 180–2, (1961) 220–3; Sciascia (1952); Schönbauer (1956) 303; Rotondi (1922) I 1453; Müller (1969) 197 (not convincing); Cancelli (1973) 392.

[11] Schulz (1926) 8–9; cf. Buckland (1922) 38, *contra* Arangio-Ruiz (1921) 178, Albertario (1922) 73.

[12] *CTh.* 8.16.1 (31 Jan. 320).

[13] *CTh.* 3.12.1 (31 March 342).

[14] *Ulp.* 22.6.

[15] Schulz (1926) 14–16, 18.

[16] Schulz (1926) 17.

material from Ulpian together with the work of other authors, such as Gaius or Modestinus. Schulz himself opted for this view,[17] and held that the compilation of *LSR* was post-classical. He thought it belonged to the same period and genre as the *Sententiae* of Paul, which are generally assigned to the late third or early fourth century.[18] A fourth view is that the compilation, whatever its period, is entirely derived from sources other than Ulpian. It is to this last view that I incline.

The *LSR* as preserved by *EU* does not much resemble other collections of *regulae*, but is more of an institutional work. Though we have only about a third of it,[19] and do not know whether it was ever completed, we can see that it is, as it were, a rival to the *Institutes* of Gaius, though a great deal shorter and more succinct. Opinions differ as to the merits of its style. Mommsen was deeply impressed by it.[20] Schulz pointed to many defects, not all of them explicable by the vicissitudes of the manuscript. It is a pedestrian handbook, to which the theoretical preoccupations of Gaius are foreign. The modern counterpart would be a student 'nutshell'. The latest law mentioned in *EU* is the provision, in a constitution of Antoninus, that lapsed gifts in a will (*caduca*) go to the imperial treasury rather than to close relatives.[21] This is plausibly identified with the legislation of Caracalla, of which Dio speaks with disapproval,[22] when he says that the emperor changed the order of succession in order to enrich himself and his soldiers. But it is curious, in that case, that *EU* appears to be unaware of the *constitutio Antoniniana* which conferred citizenship on free inhabitants of the empire with certain exceptions, notably *dediticii*.[23] On the contrary, it reads as if the old law relating to foreigners (*peregrini*) was in full force.[24] Nor can this be explained away, as Schulz,[25] citing Kuebler,[26] tries to do, by pointing to the survival of the categories of *dediticii* and *Latini*. No one, especially a jurist, could after AD 212 (to accept the traditional date for the sake of argument) have been unaware that, for example, a marriage between a Roman man and a peregrine woman had now become a rarity instead of a matter of daily concern.

A certain ineptitude on the part of the compiler of *LSR* is to be seen also in the fact that he speaks indifferently of Pius,[27] Marcus,[28] and Caracalla[29]

---

[17] Schulz (1926) 17.
[18] Schulz (1946) 176; Kunkel (1972) 149; E. Levy (1954); M. Kaser–F. Schwarz (1956).
[19] It stops at succession to freedmen and omits the whole law of obligations.
[20] Mommsen[2] (1905) II 48.
[21] *Ulp.* 17.2.
[22] Dio 78 (77).9
[23] D. 1.5.17 (Ulp. 22 *ed.*).
[24] e.g. *Ulp.* 5.8, 7.4, 10.3, 19.4, 20.14.
[25] Schulz (1926) 9[6].
[26] Kuebler (1925) 227 *contra* Fitting (1908) 116.
[27] *Ulp.* 8.5.
[28] *Ulp.* 26.7.
[29] *Ulp.* 17.2.

as 'Antoninus'. All in all, this is a lowly piece of work, though often well expressed. What of its sources? It is generally accepted that the *Institutes* of Gaius was a principal source.[30] Thus, as Schulz points out, the unusual phrase *paenitentia actus* is common to *EU*[31] and the *Institutes*,[32] and there are passages in which *EU* seems to copy mistakes or repeat omissions in the Gaian original or fails to correct Gaius.[33] But the compiler of *LSR* has taken some trouble to change or rephrase Gaius, presumably so as not to make his copying too obvious. Another likely source, listed by Schulz, is the *liber singularis pandectarum* of Modestinus.[34] It is indeed true that there are some striking parallels between the two.[35] Schulz also took 'Ulpiani' *regularum* 7 as a likely source,[36] mainly because the word *voluptuosus* is found both in this[37] and in *LSR*.[38] He recognized, of course, that the word used by Ulpian for 'luxury' expenses is not *voluptuosus* but *voluptarius*, which is to be found in four Ulpianic texts of unassailable pedigree.[39] Schulz argued, rather, that in *reg.* 7 *voluptuosus* was a copyist's mistake, which the author of *LSR* had in turn copied.[40] This reasoning is, however, forced. The natural conclusion, and the one which I draw, is that, while the compiler of *LSR* may indeed have used *reg.* 7, what this shows is that neither *reg.*7 nor *LSR* is a work of Ulpian. Why should such a strange mistake occur in a genuine work of Ulpian, and, by an odd coincidence, in a genuine work which has a title similar to that of a spurious work?

The truth is that there is nothing in the language of *LSR* to suggest a connection with Ulpian.[40a] The Tyrian's favourite phrases are notably absent, with one exception. This is *ut puta*, which occurs four times in *EU*. This expression comes from Ulpian in 229 *Digest* texts out of 244, so that, generally speaking, it can confidently be taken as a mark of his style.[41] But it also occurs, though rarely, in Callistratus,[42] Papinian,[43] and Paul.[44] A

[30] Schulz (1926) 13–14; Fitting (1908) 52; Grupe *ZS* 20 (1899) 90; Buckland (1922), (1926), (1937); Mommsen (1905) II 48.

[31] *Ulp.* 22.30.

[32] Gaius *Inst.* 2.168.

[33] *Ulp.* 22.17 with *Inst.* 2.124; *Ulp.* 24.16 with *Inst.* 2.232; *Ulp.* 23.6, 28.6 with *Inst.* 2.147, 119; *Ulp.* 8.5 with *Inst.* 1.102; *Ulp.* 29.2 with *Inst.* 3.43.

[34] Schulz (1926) 17.

[35] *Ulp.* 19.8 with *D.* 41.3.3 (Mod. 5 *pand.*).

[36] Schulz (1926) 17–18.

[37] *D.* 25.1.14.2 (5 *reg.*).

[38] *Ulp.* 6.14, 17.

[39] *D.* 25.1.1, 25.1.7, 25.1.9, 25.1.11. pr. (all 36 *Sab.*), 7.1.13.4 (17 *Sab.*: *voluptarium praedium*)

[40] Schulz (1926) ad 6.14–17.

[40a] Unconvincing Müller (1969), who tries to show that *EU* resembles Ulp. *ed.*, but without an adequate range of criteria.

[41] Ch. 3 n. 71.

[42] *D.* 14.2.4.2 (Call. 2 *qu.*).

[43] *D.* 11.7.43 (Pap. 8 *qu.*), 48.5.39 pr. (36 *qu.*), 5.1.45 pr. (3 *resp.* but the insertion is due to Mommsen), 22.1.3.2 (20 *qu.*), 45.2.9 pr. (27 *qu.*).

[44] *D.* 4.8.28 (Paul 13 *ed.*), 10.1.4.8 (23 *ed.*), 2.14.9 (62 *ed.*), 12.6.15 pr. (10 *Sab.*), 2.7.4 pr. (4 *ed.*), 4.8.19.2 (13 *ed.*), 19.1.4.1 (5 *Sab.* ? itp.), 28.6.38.1 (1 *sec. tab.*).

single trait pointing to Ulpian is not, in the circumstances, enough to establish that his work was used as a source.

It is possible to supplement Schulz's analysis by pointing to another possible source. *LSR* contains a number of expressions which, among the jurists, are associated with Paul. Thus, *abalienare* is found, apart from *EU*,[45] only in three Paul texts[46] and one of Paul's teacher, Scaevola,[47] where Scaevola cites it as part of a will. *Infinite* is found, apart from *EU*,[48] only in a *Digest* text where Paul comments on a proposition put forward by Labeo.[49] Only Paul, among the jurists, agrees with *EU*[50] in calling the Sabinian school *Cassiani*.[51] Where *EU* has *sed tutius est*,[52] which Schulz regards as a sign of interpolation or post-classical alteration,[53] one might point to the occurrence of *sed longe tutius est*[54] in the *Institutes* of Gaius, and *sed tutius erit*[55] in a *Digest* text from Paul. The similarity of style of Gaius and Paul is unmistakable, but we do not know how this resemblance is to be accounted for. It would be no surprise if the compiler or at least a principal source of *LSR* were some minor lawyer in Paul's circle who tried to provide a substitute for Gaius *Institutes*, intended for those whose tastes ran to simple summaries.

Of course this is not to say that Paul himself played any part in the enterprise. The compiler had his own turns of phrase. Thus, he speaks of the *praetor urbis*[56] where the jurists use *praetor urbanus*.[57] He is fond of the preposition *per*[58]: *per eminentiam*,[59] *per consequentiam*,[60] *per similitudinem*.[61] He notes that a person giving a gift by will can do so *imperative*[62] or *precative*[63] (*precativo modo*).[64] Neither word is found in the *Digest*. He is certainly not to be identified with any third-century author of legal writings or rescripts otherwise known to us. Nor, despite the parallels with Modestinus, is it clear whether the compilation is to be assigned to

---

[45] *Ulp.* 2.4.

[46] D. 10.3.14.1 (Paul 3 *Plaut.*), 41.1.48 pr. (17 *Plaut.*), 4.7.8.5 (12 *ed.*).

[47] D. 32.38.7 (Scae. 19 *dig.*).

[48] *Ulp.* 5.6.

[49] D. 22.3.28 (Lab. 7 *pith. Paul. epit.*).

[50] *Ulp.* 11.28.

[51] D. 47.2.18 (Paul 9. *Sab.*), 39.6.35.3 (6 *leg. Iul. Pap.*).

[52] *Ulp.* 22.22.

[53] Schulz (1926) *ad* 22.22; Beseler (1910–20) 2.164, 4.159; Gradenwitz (1887) 133; Rotondi (1922) 2.254.

[54] Gaius *Inst.* 2.181.

[55] D. 19.5.5.4 (Paul 5 *qu.*).

[56] *Ulp.* 11.20,24.

[57] *VIR* 3.1498.27–9.

[58] e.g. *Ulp.* 11.3–5, 19.16.

[59] *Ulp.* 11.3.

[60] *Ulp.* 11.3.

[61] *Ulp.* 11.5.

[62] *Ulp.* 24.1.

[63] *Ulp.* 25.1.

[64] *Ulp.* 24.1.

Caracalla's reign or to some later date in the third or even the early fourth century. But it is certain that Ulpian is not its author, and there is no strong argument for supposing that the compiler made use of Ulpian's work. It is a second-rate effort by a purported rival of Gaius, which must at least have had a modest success, since it was used by the author of the *Collatio*. How it came to be attributed to Ulpian is a mystery, though of course it was tempting to try to pass off an inferior work as that of a major jurist. But it may be that the attribution is derived from that of 'Ulpiani' *reg.* 7, to which we may now turn.

(b) *Regularum libri 7*[65]

The *Digest*, in Lenel's reconstruction, contains 107 lines attributed to this work. The order in which topics are treated is obscure. There are no references to jurists or emperors from which the date could be inferred. Some of the *Digest* texts excerpted from the work are famous. An instance is the definition of *iustitia* as *constans et perpetua voluntas ius suum cuique tribuendi*[66] and of *lata culpa* as *nimia neglegentia, id est non intellegere quod omnes intellegunt.*[67]

Unfortunately there is no ground for attributing these and other texts from the *regulae* to Ulpian. They contain none of his characteristic phrases. On the contrary, they make use of expressions or constructions which are foreign to his style.

One that has already been noted is *voluptuosus*,[68] which occurs in 5 *reg.* The real Ulpian writes *voluptarius* for 'luxury' (expenses).[69]

Another inappropriate expression is *benigna interpretatione*; as in:[70]

> benigna interpretatione potius a plerisque respondetur nullum exheredatum esse.

Apart from the fact that the assonance *potius a plerisque* is foreign to Ulpian, the piling of one qualification on another is alien to his method. He might perhaps have written *a plerisque respondetur* or *potius respondetur*,[71] or (perhaps) *benigna interpretatione respondetur*, but not two, still less three of these together. And in fact *benigna interpretatione* and similar phrases are absent from Ulpian's genuine works. There is one apparent exception. A person condemned to fight with beasts[72]

---

[65] *Ind. Flor.* xxiv 8; *Pal.* 2.1013–15; *RE* (1905) 5.1448; Schulz (1946) 180, (1961) 220. On *regulae* Stein (1966) Schmidlin (1970).
[66] *D.* 1.1.10 or (Ulp. 1 *reg.*).
[67] *D.* 50.16.213.2 (Ulp. 1 *reg.*).
[68] Above, n. 37.
[69] Above, n. 39.
[70] *D.* 28.2.2 (6 *reg.*), cf. 39.5.16 (2 *resp.*).
[71] But in fact *respondetur* is not in Ulpian apart from this text.
[72] *D.* 38.17.1.6 (Ulp. 12 *Sab.*).

ex senatus consulto Orphitiano ad matris hereditatem non admittebatur: sed humana interpretatione placuit eum admitti. Idem erit dicendum et si hic filius in eius sit potestate qui in causa supra scripta sit, posse eum ex Orphitiano admitti.

This is visibly a text in which the compilers have altered the decision,[73] so that persons who (or whose sons) were not allowed to succeed under the *SC Orphitianum* (AD 178, allowing a woman's children to succeed to her in certain events), may now do so. The phrase *sed humana interpretatione placuit eum admitti* is an interpolation, as is the final clause *posse eum ex Orphitiano admitti*, which is in addition loosely and awkwardly attached to *Idem*. We may conclude, then, that in the surviving texts Ulpian never uses *benigna* (*humana, subtili etc.*) *interpretatione* in order to explain or justify a decision, apart from these two texts from *reg.* 7. This must cast further doubt on the authenticity of *reg.* 7.

Another text speaks of a husband having alternative remedies against his wife:[74]

et in potestate est, qua velit actione uti

He can choose. This way of saying that a choice is open is not found in other texts of Ulpian. In all other passages *in potestate est* means 'he is in the legal power of'.[75] The phrase is ungrammatical. It should run *in potestate eius est . . .*

In order to discover the accomplices of a slave who has committed a wrong, one can bring an action claiming that he should be produced:[76]

Quaestionis habendae causa ad exhibendum agitur ex delictis servorum ad vindicandos conscios suos

Quite apart from the use of *suos* for *eorum*, this is clumsy. The sentence should have been split, and Ulpian would have split it, into two or three separate clauses.

Again, *praeterquam quod* for 'apart from the fact that' is found in 2 *reg.*[77] but not elsewhere in Ulpian except for a citation from the praetor's edict.[78] It is too clumsy a conjunctive phrase for him. One may conclude that both the absence of positive marks of Ulpian's style and the presence of discordant elements tell against *reg.* 7 being a genuine work.

The style of *reg.* 7 is indeed marked by a number of positive features. One is a fondness for asyndetion:

Iuris praecepta haec sunt; honeste vivere, alterum non laedere, suum cuique tribuere[79]

---

[73] *Index Interp.* 3.72.   [74] *D.* 25.2.24 (5 *reg.*).
[75] *CDJ* 60 IN POTESTATE EST (17 texts).
[76] *D.* 10.4.20 (2 *reg.*).
[77] *D.* 46.3.43 (2 *reg.*).   [78] *D.* 43.8.2 (68 *ed.*).   [79] *D.* 1.1.10.1 (1 *reg.*).

Impensae necessariae sunt . . . veluti aggeres facere, flumina avertere, aedificia vetera fulcire[80]

nam et bonorum possessionem dare potest et in possessionem mittere, pupillis non habentibus tutores constituere, iudices litigantibus dare[81]

Another is a tendency to invert the conditional, thus:

Communis servus etiamsi . . .[82]

Procurator si quidem . . .[83]

Servus communis ab extero heres institutus si . . .[84]

Servum meum heredem institutum cum libertate si vivus vendidero . . .[85]

and there are analogous inversions:

Statulibera quidquid peperit[86]

This makes, as we have seen, for somewhat clumsy phrases. It may be noted that inversion of the conditional is very rare in Ulpian's genuine works. One jurist of the Severan age who likes to use this construction is Arrius Menander,[87] who was Caracalla's secretary *a libellis* in 212–13.[88] This, while it may have some relevance to the date of composition of *reg.* 7, cannot be used as an argument for Menander's authorship. Whoever he was, the author was a jurist much superior to the compiler of *LSR*, who used his work as a source, but he was certainly not of the first rank.

(c) *Responsorum libri 2*[89]

The two books of *responsa* attributed to Ulpian are generally regarded as consisting of excerpts from genuine *responsa* by the jurist. Jörs says they are taken from Ulpian's private archive.[90] Schulz argues that the collection is post-classical, but remarks that the editor does not seem to have altered the substance of the law as stated by Ulpian.[91] A text in the *Vatican Fragments* corresponds closely to a surviving excerpt in the *Digest*.[92] Hence the collection must have existed by the first half of the fourth century.[93]

---

[80] *D.* 25.1.14 pr. (5 *reg.*).
[81] *D.* 2.1.1 (1 *reg.*).
[82] *D.* 41.2.42 pr. (4 *reg.*).
[83] *D.* 41.2.42.1 (4 *reg.*).
[84] *D.* 29.2.67 (1 *reg.*).
[85] *D.* 28.5.51 pr. (6 *reg.*).
[86] *D.* 40.7.16 (4 *reg.*).
[87] *Pal.* 1.695–700: Giuffrè (1974) 362.
[88] Honoré (1981) 65–7.
[89] *Ind. Flor* XXIV 17; *Pal.* 2.1016–19; *RE* 5.1438, 1446; Fitting (1908) 116; Schulz (1946) 241, (1961) 307.
[90] *RE* 6.1446.
[91] Schulz (1946) 241, (1961) 307.
[92] *FV* 44.
[93] Though there were isolated later additions, the *Frag. Vat.* collection seems to have been made between 318 (*FV* 287 Licinio V et Crispo conss.) and AD 324 when the memory of Licinius was condemned (*CTh.* 15.14.1); Schulz (1946) 311, (1961) 393.

If the date of the edition is left on one side for the moment, there remain obstacles in the way of accepting that the 141 lines of excerpts in the *Digest* are derived even indirectly from any genuine writing of Ulpian. In the first place they do not contain a single phrase which is characteristic of his style, as judged from writings which are unquestionably genuine. But the objections are more serious than this.

A text from the second book of *responsa* refers to a *societas universarum fortunarum*.[94] This is, of course, a universal partnership, usually called a *societas omnium bonorum*, the partner being a *socius omnium bonorum*. These are, indeed, the phrases which Ulpian himself uses in his edictal commentary.[95] *Societas universarum fortunarum*, on the other hand, is not found, apart from these two instances, in any jurist or imperial constitution. It is not easy to see how an editor could turn Ulpian's *societas omnium bonorum* into a *societas universarum fortunarum*. If anything, an editor shortens and condenses the text he is editing.

In the second book of *responsa*, again, the word *persolvere* is twice used for *solvere*, to pay.[96] Apart from these texts, *persolvere* is attributed to Ulpian only twice. In one of these it means not to 'pay' but to 'pay back'. In a certain event the seller has a choice:[97]

> utrum malit de pretio remittere an potius rem quam vendidit recipere persoluto pretio

The other text has plainly been altered.[98] Two people go surety for ten, the debtor pays three, and then the sureties pay five each. The surety paying last can recover three

> quia tribus a reo solutis septem sola debita supererant, quibus persolutis tria indebita soluta sunt

As the text stands, *quibus persolutis* means 'if the seven remaining are paid', whereas the sense of the text requires the meaning 'if ten (viz. five each) are then paid'. The use of *persolvere*, therefore, cannot be attributed with any confidence to Ulpian. On the contrary, it seems likely that he did not use this word for 'to pay'. Such restraint would accord with his general preference for shorter words. The use of *persolvere* in the *responsa* text therefore points rather to another hand. There is, in addition, no reason why an editor should change *solvere* into *persolvere*.

In the *responsa* we find one sentence beginning and two ending with ablative absolutes.[99] This is a construction which Ulpian avoids at the

---

[94] D. 17.2.73 (1 *resp.*).

[95] *Socius omn. bon.* D. 17.2.52.16, 17, 18 (31 *ed.*), 47.2.52.18 (38 *ed.*), 42.1.16 (63 *ed.*); *societas omn. bon.* 17.2.5 pr. (31 *ed.*).

[96] D. 43.26.20 (2 *resp.*).   [97] D. 38.5.1.13 (44 *ed.*).

[98] D. 12.6.25 (47 *Sab.*).

[99] D. 30.120 pr., 1 (2 *resp.*), 32.68 pr. (1 *resp.*).

beginning and end of sentences, though it would be going too far to say that he never uses it. But certainly he never uses the ablative absolute termination with *salvo* or *salva* to express a proviso, as in the following texts from the *responsa*:

salvo scilicet iure debitoris[100]

salva tamen causa legati[101]

A text which Huschke[102] and Lenel[103] regard as an excerpt from Ulpian's *responsa*, but which Mommsen does not accept,[104] runs:

Festo respondit, si ancilla fuit, ad libertatem perductam non videri neque per fideicommissi relicti sibi probationem nec quod alimenta sunt ut nutrici praestita

This is too clumsy for the real Ulpian, but, if Mommsen is right, it does not bear on the genuineness of the *responsa*.

Most of the texts in the *responsa* do not purport to be composed by Ulpian himself. They, like the *responsa* of some other jurists,[105] are in the form *Maximino respondit*,[106] *Iunianio respondit*[107] etc, followed by the accusative and infinitive. In other cases the accusative and infinitive alone is recorded, with no governing *respondit*.[108] In three cases Ulpian himself is by implication the subject of the sentence. In these instances the relevant sentence ends as follows:

habere posse respondi[109]

non habere respondi[110]

habere respondi[111]

Such a termination, in which two or three verbs are juxtaposed, is of course untypical of Ulpian. One may ask why he should have changed his word order so drastically when composing *responsa*.

The fact is that there is nothing except the name to connect these excerpts with Ulpian. It is, indeed, far from clear that Ulpian gave any substantial number of *responsa*. If we go by internal evidence from the works which are clearly genuine, he is recorded as giving opinions only in three contexts, none of them technically appropriate to *responsa*.

---

[100] *D.* 32.68 pr (1 *resp.*).
[101] *D.* 30.120 pr. (2 *resp.*).
[102] *D.* 22.3.30 (1 *resp.*); Huschke (1875) 95.
[103] *Pal.* 2.1016⁵.
[104] *Corp. Iur. Civ.* 2.327⁶.
[105] e.g. Modestinus: *Pal.* 1.740−55; Paul: *Pal.* 1.1223−51.
[106] *D.* 17.2.73 (1 *resp.*).
[107] *D.* 32.68 (1 *resp.*).
[108] *D.* 22.1.31, 22.3.22, 23.4.25, 26.7.19, 27.3.19, 27.4.5 (all 1 *resp.*), etc.
[109] *D.* 27.4.5 (1 *resp.*).
[110] *D.* 27.1.23 (2 *resp.*).
[111] *D.* 27.1.23.1 (2 *resp.*).

In the first place, he writes letters to those who consult him. One famous example is his letter to Modestinus about the man who used someone else's horses to service his mares:[112]

> quod et Herennio Modestino studioso meo rescripsi circa equos . . .

Note that the word used is *rescripsi* and not *respondi*. Ulpian is in any case not here composing a *responsum* in the technical sense of advice given to a judge or magistrate trying a case on a point of law arising in it. He is simply corresponding with a pupil.

Another context concerns disputations. In his work of that title and also in *de fideicommissis* the jurist mentions opinions expressed by himself in the course of argument. He generally introduces these with *dicebam*[113] or *dixi*,[114] more rarely with *dicebamus*[115] or *referebam*.[116] But though Jörs treats these texts as evidence of Ulpian's responsal activity,[117] the opinions referred to are of course oral, whereas *responsa* must be in writing. Even if we knew nothing about disputations in the ancient world, the use of the imperfect is generally a sign of oral discussion.[118] These passages, therefore, add nothing to the evidence for Ulpian's activity in the field of *responsa*.

Thirdly, Ulpian mentions advice given by him as assessor to the praetor.[119] In a number of cases where he does not explicitly state that this is the context, we can understand him most readily by assuming that he is advising a magistrate.[120] He is, of course, often thought to have been assessor to Papinian.[121]

All the cases in which Ulpian records an opinion given by himself, apart from the texts from 'Ulpiani' *responsa*, can therefore be explained in other ways. It is notable that, again outside 'Ulpiani' *responsa*, Ulpian never speaks of himself as engaged in *respondere*; the words *respondi*, *respondimus*, etc. are not found at all. This is a surprise, since other jurists who gave *responsa* use these words even in collections of material which are not entitled *responsa*.[122] This is true, for example, of Paul. Why do we not find these expressions in Ulpian?

---

[112] *D.* 47.2.52.20 (Ulp. 37 *ed.*).

[113] *D.* 27.8.2, 44.3.5.1 (both 3 *disp.*), 28.4.2, 28.5.35 pr. 29.1.19 pr., 49.17.9 bis (all 4 *disp.*), 33.4.2.1, 36.1.23 pr. (5 *disp.*), 46.7.13 pr. (7 *disp.*), 35.2.82 (8 *disp.*), 34.1.14.3 (2 *fid.*).

[114] *D.* 26.1.7 (2 *disp.*), 28.5.35.5 (4 *disp.*), 36.1.23.4 (5 *disp.*), 2.1.19 pr. (6 *fid.*) 47.2.39 (41 *Sab.*), cf. *probavi D.* 38.5.35.1 (4 *disp.*).   [115] *D.* 29.2.42 (4 *disp.*).

[116] *D.* 49.17.9, 29.1.19 pr. (4 *disp.*), 35.1.92 (5 *fid.*).   [117] *RE* 5.1438.

[118] Honoré (1962) xvi. Thus *quidam consulebat* (*D.* 42.1.57; 2 *disp.*) refers to an oral consultation.

[119] *D.* 4.2.9.3 (11 *ed.*). *Adsidere* means here to act as a member of the praetor's *consilium*, not to hold the junior post of *adsessor*.

[120] e.g. *D.* 47.2.39 (41 *Sab.*: *ex facto dixi*); 4.4.3.2 (11 *ed.*: *contradicebatur, putavimus*).

[121] HA *Niger* 7.4; *Alexander Severus* 26.6; Kunkel (1967) 245–6: unreliable but not impossible. Dorotheus in *Bas.* (ed. Heimbach) IV 624 also refers to Ulpian as assessor to a praetor, but this may be derived from *D.* 4.2.9.3.

[122] e.g. Paul *D.* 31.68 (11 *qu.*), 34.1.11 (10 *qu.*), 28.6.43.2 (9 *qu.*), 24.3.45 (6 *qu.*), etc.

I am not suggesting that Ulpian gave no *responsa*, or did not possess the *ius respondendi ex auctoritate principis*, if indeed that institution existed in his time. Undoubtedly he gave some *responsa*. Three of these are recorded in the texts, one in Paul,[123] one in Macer[124] and one in a rescript of Alexander of AD 222.[125] The Paul text concerns a case on *fideicommissa* in which *lectum est responsum Domitii Ulpiani, quo continebatur* . . . Paul's correspondent is asking about a point arising in a *cognitio* in which Ulpian gave a *responsum* contrary to the view of Julian. Paul approved Julian's opinion. So Ulpian did give *responsa*. But, for whatever reason, neither he nor his pupil Modestinus seems to have attached great importance to them. Modestinus cites no actual *responsum* of his teacher, at least so far as the surviving texts go. Ulpian's interest seems to have lain more in public life, scholarship and teaching than in responsal practice. In this he differs from his contemporaries Papinian and Paul.

Why, then, was a rather mediocre collection of opinions, expressed without distinction or elegance, attributed to the Tyrian? Perhaps because some contemporary or successor, seeing this gap in his *oeuvre*, was tempted to take advantage of it, if only to the modest extent of two books, and to pass off opinions which were his own or which he wanted to cite in court under an illustrious name. We have no clue to the identity of the real author, but, as the law recorded is orthodox, he may be a minor jurist of the first half of the third century. He shares the expression *benigna interpretatione* with the author of *reg.* 7.[126]

(d) Liber singularis pandectarum

The *Digest* contains two fragments inscribed to Ulpian's alleged *liber singularis pandectarum*.[127] The *Florentine Index* does not record such a *liber singularis*, but instead mentions ten books of pandect (πανδέκτου βιβλία δέκα).[128] Trying to explain this, Lenel suggests that only one book of the ten survived to be available to Justinian's compilers.[129] Schultz[130] thinks that the compilers may have possessed the complete work, but did not draw on it for the *Digest*. Instead they used a short abridgement.

But though it may be that the *Digest* fragments are taken from an abridgement of a larger work, they are not derived from any work of Ulpian. What is more, in this instance we can form a good idea of their actual provenance.

---

[123] D. 19.1.43 (Paul 5 *qu.*).
[124] D. 50.5.5 (Macer 2 *off. praes.*).
[125] CJ 8.37.4 (Alex. 31 March 222).
[126] Above, n. 70.
[127] Pal. 2.1013; RE 5.1447; Fitting (1908) 120; Schulz (1946) 222, (1961) 280–1.
[128] Ind. Flor. XXIV 7.
[129] Pal. 2.1013[5].
[130] Schulz (1946) 222, (1961) 281.

The first text is about the accounts of a freeman who has been treated as a slave:[131]

> Imperator Antoninus constituit non alias ad libertatem proclamationem permittendam, nisi prius administrationum rationes reddiderit, quas cum in servitute esset gessisset.

The compilers have substituted *proclamatio in libertatem* for *libertatis adsertio* or some such phrase.[132] But when the latter is restored the text remains inconsistent with Ulpian's authorship. In the first place he avoids the sort of assonance represented by *esset gessiset*, and also avoids juxtaposing two verbs as here, one from a relative clause and one from the clause to which it relates. *Non alias nisi prius* is not found in genuine works of Ulpian.

Finally, the sequence of long words (*administrationum rationes reddiderit*) is foreign to Ulpian, and the sentence too complex. It should have been split into two.

The other *Digest* text[133] from this alleged work is no better:

> Si quis certum stipulatus fuerit, ex stipulatu actionem non habet, sed illa condicticia actione id persequi debet, per quam certum petitur.

Here *condicticia* is naturally a prime suspect for a gloss or interpolation.[134] There are certainly texts in which *condicticius* is compilatorial, but not all mentions of it are spurious. Thus, Ulpian cites Julian to the effect that one who takes an oath that he has not committed a theft:[135]

> videri de toto iurasse, atque ideo neque furti neque condicticia tenetur, quia condicticia, inquit, solus fur tenetur

Condicticia (*actione*) is perfectly natural here, because it parallels *furti* (*actione*), and *condictione* would be out of place. But it is another matter to defend, as Ulpianic, *illa condicticia actio per quam certum petitur*. Firstly, this states the obvious. If (as one must suppose) the stipulation was for a *certum*, the *condictio* must also be. But above all the phrase is circumlocutory. You do not sue by bringing an action, *petere per actionem*. The bringing of the action *is* the suit. The *petitio* is (the concrete manifestation of) an *actio*. This periphrastic turn of phrase cannot be paralleled in any genuine text of Ulpian.

These two texts have affinities of style not with any *Digest* jurist but to certain rescripts of AD 222, issued when Ulpian was, or was in the process of becoming, a prefect under the young Alexander to whom he stood in something of the relation of a guardian. The composer of these rescripts,

---

[131] *D.* 40.12.34 (1 *pand.*).
[132] *Pal.* 2.1013.
[133] *D.* 12.1.24 (1 *pand.*).
[134] *Index Interp.* ad loc. (Seckel, Triantaphyllopoulos, Naber, Pernice, Lenel, Beseler, *VIR*).
[135] *D.* 12.2.13.2 (Ulp. 22 *ed.*).

like the author of *'Ulpiani' pandectae*, favoured assonances, particularly sibiliant sounds:[136]

Si servum alienum non inutilem constitutum aegrum curastis et negotium utiliter gessistis, competenti vobis actione sumptus recuperare potestis

The sequence of sounds *curastis . . . gessistis . . . potestis* resembles the *esset gessisset* of *D.* 40.12.34. Notice also the clumsiness of the phrase *servum alienum non inutilem constitutum aegrum*. The *Digest* text has *non alias nisi prius*. This is not found in the rescripts of 222, but the similar phrase *non aliter nisi prius*, not otherwise in Ulpian, is:[137]

Qui crimen publicum instituere properant, non aliter ad hoc admittantur, nisi prius inscriptionum pagina processerit . . .

The latter phrase is also found in one *Digest* text of Marcellus,[138] and, apart from this, only in the *opiniones* of Ulpian,[139] a work which, we shall see, is also spurious.

The rescripts of AD 222 also contain a text[140] with a circumlocution similar to that in *D.* 12.1.24:

Promissae tibi pecuniae a servo tuo, ut eum manumitteres, si, posteaquam manumisisti, stipulatus ab eo non es, adversus eum petitionem per in factum actionem habes.

Here, as there, a *petitio* is brought by means of an *actio*. The straightforward and Ulpianic way to express this is to say *in factum actionem habes* or *habes actionem in factum*. To treat the action as a means of giving effect to the *petitio* is conceptually wrong. It is the other way round. The *petitio* gives effect to or realises the *actio*.

In another study I have shown that between 19 February 222 (possibly somewhat earlier) and 1 October 222 the office *a libellis* was held by a secretary, designated no. 6, whose somewhat inept style is marked by a fondness for assonances and for awkward phrases involving the preposition *per*.[141] It looks as if this secretary *a libellis* might well be the author of *'Ulpiani' pandectae*, whether in one book or ten. Holding office when he did, during the last months of Elagabal, at a time when Alexander had been adopted by the senior Augustus in order to facilitate the civil administration of the empire, and during the first months of Alexander's sole rule,[142] he must have enjoyed Ulpian's confidence. Who would be better

---

[136] *CJ* 2.18.10 (20 Nov. 222) cf. 7.56.1 (7 May 222 mandasti, habuisti), 7.8.4 (10 May 222 *fuisti, potuisti*), 3.32.3 (30 Oct. 222 *consensisti, amisisti*).

[137] *CJ* 9.1.3 (3 Feb. 222)..   [138] *D.* 33.2.15.1 (Marc. 13 *dig.*).

[139] *D.* 8.4.13.1 (Ulp. 6 *op.*).

[140] *CJ* 4.14.3 (13 Sept. 222).   [141] Honoré (1981) 70–2.

[142] Herodian 5.7. Alexianus (Alexander) was possibly adopted by Elagabal on 26 June 221 (Whittaker, *Herodian* 2.581) and Elagabal was murdered on 13 March 222. Alexander exercised power of some sort (Herodian 5.7.5 κοινωνὸν τῆς ἀρχῆς before his cousin's death.

placed, when during the course of AD 223 Ulpian was murdered, to slip in spurious works as genuine compositions.

(e) *Libri opinionum 6*[143]

As printed in Lenel's *Palingenesia*, we have 645 lines from texts attributed to the *opiniones* of Ulpian, in six books. The title itself is unique in juristic literature. The authenticity of the work has been in doubt since Gothofredus first questioned it.[144] Lenel,[145] followed by the majority of Romanists, held it to be a post-classical compilation from genuine writings of Ulpian. Rotondi[146] argued that it was an anthology composed in the fourth century on the basis of fragments of Ulpian. More recently Santalucia,[147] in a thorough and lucid study, has argued that the *opiniones* are a genuine work of the Tyrian jurist. The view I shall propose is different again. Though the work itself may belong to the third century—possibly even to the age of Alexander Severus—it was not composed by, nor does it contain excerpts from the writings of, Ulpian.

The main ground on which doubts have been expressed about the work has been its style. This, both on a casual reading and after prolonged scrutiny, seems to be and is very different from that of the classical jurists, and in particular, Ulpian, in any of their normal writings. Santalucia concedes this point, but seeks to circumvent it.

He argues, first,[148] that the *opiniones* are not really a work in the nature of *regulae*, as is generally supposed, nor do they conform to the order of the praetor's edict, as Lenel maintained.[149] They are in effect a manual of instruction for provincial governors, intended as a practical guide in the performance of their duties. They are more akin to books *de officio proconsulis* than to other types of legal literature. Though the praetor and the urban prefect are each mentioned on one occasion,[150] this does not detract from the fact that the work as a whole centres round the duties of the provincial governor. The *opiniones* are not directed to any particular type of governor, imperial or senatorial, but cater for all.

This analysis can be accepted. The points on which the *opiniones* concentrate, like the incidence of municipal offices, are those which were most likely to be troublesome to a provincial governor. What is more, many of the precepts contained in them are expressly directed to governors, and takes some such form as *praeses provinciae iubeat* or the like.

---

[143] *Pal.* 2.1001–13; *RE* 5.1450; Schulz (1946) 182; (1961) 223; Rotondi (1922) 1.453.
[144] Santalucia (1971) I 1–2.
[145] *Pal.* 2.1001[2].
[146] Rotondi (1922) 1.453.
[147] Santalucia (1971), Contra Liebs (1973), cf. Wieacker (1973).
[148] Santalucia (1971) I 17–73.
[149] *Pal.* 2.1001[2].
[150] *D.* 2.1.17 (2 *op.*), 37.15.1.2 (1 *op.*).

Santalucia next argues[151] that scholars, and in particular Rotondi, put the date of composition unrealistically late. Texts in the *opiniones* assume that the *oratio Severi* concerning the alienation of land belonging to *pupilli* is in force.[152] Hence the work must date from after AD 195.[153] There is a strong case for supposing that the rule, stated in the *opiniones*, that those who give elementary instruction to boys (*qui pueros primas litteras docent*) are not entitled to exemption from civil burdens,[154] reflects a constitution of Caracalla which is mentioned by Modestinus.[155] The wording is almost identical in the two texts. The reign of Caracalla, or possibly Severus, may therefore be taken as the earliest possible period of composition. The *terminus ante quem* presents more difficulty.

The age from which young people can be called on to perform personal *munera* is taken in the *opiniones* to be 25.[156] Hence the author was not aware of the constitution of 4 August 331[157] which treats seventeen as the minimum age. Fathers of five children are treated as *ipso facto* exempt from personal *munera*[158] without the qualification introduced by a constitution of 19 June 324[159] that, if there is a son of sufficient age, he is to replace the father. The *decaprotia* is taken to be a largely patrimonial burden[160] (*patrimonii magis onus*). This may indicate that the author did not know of the constitution of the tetrarchs which treated it as *purely* patrimonial (*tantum patrimonii esse non ambigitur*).[161] The flat statement that women by the nature of their sex cannot be liable for personal *munera*[162] shows, it is argued, that the author did not know of the constitution of Philip, which states that there are frequent rescripts to the effect that women can perform those personal *munera* of which their sex is capable, or of the later constitution of the tetrarchs to the same effect.[163] According to the *opiniones* a veteran who voluntarily assumes a *munus* or *honor* does not thereby lose his right to exemption,[164] whereas a constitution of Alexander denies this for the decurionate[165] and one of Diocletian and

---

[151] Santalucia (1971) I 75–131; above, n. 146.

[152] *D.* 27.9.9 (5 *op.*) 27.9.10 (6 *op.*).

[153] *D.* 27.9.1 pr.–2 (Ulp. 35 *ed.*).

[154] *D.* 50.5.2.8 (3 *op.*).

[155] *D.* 50.4.11.4 (Mod. 11 *pand.*).

[156] *D.* 50.5.2 pr. (3 *op.*).

[157] *CTh.* 12.1.19 (4 Aug. 331).

[158] *D.* 50.4.3.6 (2 *op.*).

[159] *CTh.* 12.17.1 pr. (19 June 324) = *CJ* 10.52.6 pr. But it is not clear that this really changed the existing law.

[160] *D.* 50.4.3.10 (2 *op.*). But this text could be taken to state as a firm principle that the *decaprotia* is patrimonial.

[161] *CJ* 10.42.8 (Dio. et Max. AA et CC). This too could be taken as declaratory of existing law.

[162] *D.* 50.4.3.3 (2 *op.*).

[163] *CJ* 10.64.1 (Philip); 10.52.5 (Dio et Max. AA et CC).

[164] *D.* 49.18.2 (3 *op.*).

[165] *CJ* 10.44.1 (Alex.).

Maximian for other burdens.[166] Indeed a text of Paul *de cognitionibus* says the same so far as the decurionate is concerned.[167]

These arguments are not all of equal weight, since in the Roman empire even a reasonably well-informed lawyer could be ill informed about recent changes in the law, particularly when they took place by rescript and not by general enactment. One has also to be wary of the possibility of retrospective changes in the texts, which make them appear earlier than they really are. Nevertheless, the author of *opiniones* intended his work to be used by provincial governors, so far as we can tell, and had every motive for making it as up-to-date as he could. On one view the evidence cited by Santalucia tends to show that the compilation probably belongs to the third, not, as Rotondi thought, to the fourth century. He would date the composition to the period running from the reign of Caracalla to that of Alexander Severus.[168] But Liebs has produced counter-arguments in favour of the fourth century.[168a] The matter could only be settled by a thorough comparison of the language and style of the *opiniones* with that of legal and administrative texts of both centuries, and this lies beyond the scope of the present study.

Whatever the date of composition may be, the *opiniones* contain passages which are characteristic of imperial rescripts of the Severan age and the later third century.[169] To take but a few examples from a period when, in fact, Modestinus was head of the office *a libellis*,[170] the *praeses provinciae provideat* and *providebit* of 5 *op.*[171] runs parallel to the *competens iudex providebit* of a rescript of 224.[172] *Ad sollicitudinem suam praeses provinciae revocet* in 1 *op.*[173] is like *ad sollicitudinem suam revocabit praeses provinciae* in another constitution of 224.[174] *Execrandam praedam* in 1 *op.*[175] is an expression similar to *exsecrabile delictum* in yet another *CJ* text of 224.[176] *Ex forma restituatur* in 2 *op.*[177] is like *forma est . . . ut . . . restituatur*[178] in a rescript of 225. In 5 *op.* we have *res suae aequitati per praesidem provinciae restituitur*;[179] in a rescript of 224 *praeses . . . rem ad suam aequitatem*

---

[166] *CJ* 10.44.2 (Dio. et Max. AA). But perhaps all these texts merely mean that the veteran does not lose his immunity in general, though he is bound by his waiver in the particular instance.

[167] *D.* 49.18.5.2 (Paul 1 *cogn.*).

[168] Santalucia (1971) I 129.

[168a] Liebs (1973).

[169] Santalucia (1971) I 133−93.

[170] Honoré (1981) 78−80.

[171] *D.* 1.18.6 pr., 5 (1 *op.*).

[172] *CJ* 6.54.5 (11 Aug. 224).

[173] *D.* 1.18.6.4 (1 *op.*).

[174] *CJ* 8.52.1 (27 March 224).

[175] *D.* 47.9.10 (1 *op.*).

[176] *CJ* 4.55.4.1 (21 June 224).

[177] *D.* 50.7.3 (2 *op.*).

[178] *CJ* 10.4.1 pr. (26 Sept. 225).

[179] *D.* 4.2.23.1 (5 *op.*).

rediget.[180] It would be pointless to multiply examples. Although by no means all the texts in *opiniones* reflect the language of imperial constitutions, there are many which do. It seems justifiable to conclude that imperial constitutions of the third century formed a major source of the *opiniones* and, in particular, it looks as if rescripts of AD 224 and 225 may have been used in its compilation.

It is another matter to conclude, as does Santalucia, that Ulpian himself was the author. There are many counter-indications. In the first place, Ulpian composed a ten-book work *de officio proconsulis*,[181] which must have been intended for the use of provincial governors. Why should he write a further work on the same lines? Why, again, if he is the author of *opiniones*, are they written without citation of authority, either from juristic writings or imperial constitutions? For it is clear, and Santalucia himself emphasizes, that the reflections in *opiniones* of the language of imperial constitutions are implicit, not explicit. Apart from an occasional *placuit*[182] or *responsum est*[183] the author of *opiniones* gives no indication of his source. It may be that, as Santalucia says, he had no need to do so, since Ulpian's name guaranteed the authenticity of the opinions stated.[184] But this does not explain why Ulpian himself should have followed a method so foreign to his normal practice.

No doubt Ulpian's administrative experience was such that he could have complied such a work.[185] Indeed he did compile one, *de officio proconsulis*, a more scholarly and better written work than the pedestrian manual we are now considering. And when would he have written the *opiniones*? If, as seems likely, they contain echoes of rescripts of the age of Alexander, Ulpian by then held high office. He was murdered before the end of 223, before, that is, the constitutions of 224 and 225, whose echoes we seem to notice in the texts of the *opiniones*, were issued.

There is a still more fundamental objection to Santalucia's hypothesis. For it presupposes not merely the abandonment by the prefect of his normal standards of scholarship and his intellectual pretensions, but a change in his vocabulary and syntax too radical to be contemplated.

Obviously when an author turns to a different genre of literary composition he changes his style. If he is composing imperial rescripts rather than writing a commentary on the praetor's edict, he adopts some of the vocabulary and turns of phrase customary in the rescript office. He

[180] *CJ* 8.1.1 (26 March 224).
[181] *Pal.* 2. 966–91
[182] D. 2.14.52.1 (1 *op.*), 50.4.3.10 (2 *op. pridem placuit*), 50.1.6.2 (2 *op.*), 3.5.44.2 (4 *op.*), 4.3.33 (4 *op.*), 49.15.21.1 (5 *op.*), 12.1.26 (5 *op.*), 5.2.27.3 (6 *op.*), 5.4.6 pr. (6 *op.*).
[183] D. 4.7.11 (5 *op.*).
[184] Santalucia (1971) I 219.
[185] Santalucia (1971) I 195–209 though the details of his account cannot be accepted as correct.

reads the work of his predecessors and is influenced by it. But the extent of this influence must not be exaggerated. An author does not radically change his word-order, or his favoured constructions, merely because he changes the genre of composition. What is striking about the comparison between the works of jurists such as Papinian,[186] Ulpian,[187] Menander,[188] and Modestinus[189] writing on their own account and composing imperial rescripts is the fact that, despite the different context, the author can be recognized.

We know that Ulpian normally avoids juxtaposing verbs, especially those drawn from different clauses. It is therefore striking that the author of *opiniones* adopts a word order so orthodox that it often results in three, four or even five verbs coming together at the end of a clause or sentence. Here are some examples:

Si inter debitorem et eum, qui fundum pigneratum a creditore, quasi debitoris negotium *gereret, emerit, placuit,* ut . . .[190]

Cessatio unius legati ei, qui munus ut *oportet obiit,* non *nocet*[191]

Qui ad munera vocantur, vivorum se liberorum numerum habere tempore, quo propter eos *excusari desiderant, probare debent:*[192]

quod de his est, qui pecuniam, ut negotium *facerent* aut non *facerent, accepisse dicerentur, restitui iubeat*[193]

adversarius movere coepit et posteaquam opportunitatem emptoris, cui *venumdari potuit, peremit, destitit.*[194]

tamen quae solutioni debitarum ab eo quantitatium *profecerunt, revocare incivile est.*[195]

aut quod *habuerunt amiserint,* aut quod acquirere emolumentum *potuerunt omiserint,* aut se oneri, quod non *suscipere licuit, obligaverunt.*[196]

actionibus se exuere, quibus ante sententiam *subiectus fuerat,* non *poterit.*[197]

ex bonis, quae non *erant adempta, probatum fuerit* suae causae restituendum est.[198]

Altius aedes suas extollendo, ut luminibus domus minoris annis viginti quinque vel impuberis, cuius curator vel tutor *erat, officiatur, efficit:* . . .[199]

---

186 Honoré (1981) 57–9.
187 Honoré (1981) 61–4; below, ch. 9.
188 Honoré (1981) 66–7.
189 Honoré (1981) 78–80.
190 *D.* 2.14.52.1 (1 *op.*).
191 *D.* 50.7.2.2 (2 *op.*).
192 *D.* 50.5.2.2 (3 *op.*).
193 *D.* 3.6.8 (4 *op.*).
194 *D.* 4.3.33 (4 *op.*).
195 *D.* 4.2.23.3 (5 *op.*).
196 *D.* 4.4.44 (5 *op.*).
197 *D.* 48.23.2 (5 *op.*).
198 *D.* 4.6.40.1 (5 *op.*).
199 *D.* 8.5.15 (6 *op.*).

si iam solutione liberatas receptasque eas is qui *susceperat tenet, exhibere iubendus est.*[200]

These verb clusters are therefore to be found in all six books of the *opiniones*. It is simply not conceivable that Ulpian, influenced by chancery style, would have changed his word order in so radical a fashion. Indeed none of the composers of rescripts in the third century write like this, so that the influence of chancery style would be inadequate to account for the change. One or two of them, for instance the secretary *a libellis* of the later part of the reign of Gordian III and of a large part of Philip's,[201] adopt a relatively orthodox word-order, in which the main verb comes regulularly at the end of the sentence. But they do not carry this policy to the extreme lengths of the author of *opiniones*.

Not only is the word order inconsistent with Ulpian's hand, but the words are too long. Ulpian avoids strings of long words and complicated nominal phrases. There are, however, a number of these in the *opiniones*. Thus, we find:

Honeste sacramento solutis data immunitas[202]

illicita ministeria sub praetextu adiuvantium militares viros ad concutiendos homines procedentia[203]

a quibusdam propria sibi commoda inique vindicantibus[204]

praetextu humanae fragilitatis delictum decipientis in periculo homines innoxium esse non debet[205]

Curator operum creatus praescriptione motus ab excusatione perferenda . . .[206]

sumptus honeste ad honores per gradus pertinentes factus.[207]

These complex expressions make use of present or past participles in order to construct phrases which would be better expressed with the use of relative clauses.

The *opiniones* admit assonances which are foreign to Ulpian's style. Examples are:

tam callidum commentum . . .[208]

calumniosis criminibus insectentur innocentes[209]

solitum solacium[210]

onera sollemnia omnes sustinere oportet[211]

---

[200] *D.* 13.7.27 (6 *op.*).
[201] Honoré (1981) 90–3.
[202] *D.* 49.18.2 (3 *op.*).
[203] *D.* 1.18.6.6 (1 *op.*).
[204] *D.* 1.18.6.6 (1 *op.*).
[205] *D.* 1.18.6.7. (1 *op.*).
[206] *D.* 50.10.1 pr. (2 *op.*).
[207] *D.* 3.5.33 pr. (4 *op.*).
[208] *D.* 27.9.9 (5 *op.*).
[209] *D.* 1.18.6.2 (1 *op.*).
[210] *D.* 8.4.13.1 (6 *op.*).
[211] *D.* 49.18.2 (3 *op.*).

The *opiniones*, to a far greater extent than the real Ulpian, admit ablative absolutes at the beginning or end of a sentence:

> ... usuris pecuniae, quam constiterit ex tutela deberi, reputatis et cum quantitate fructuum perceptorum compensatis.[212]
> ... oculisque suis subiectis locis.[213]

Illicite post senatus consultum pupilli vel adulescentis praedio venumdato[214]

None of these features can be explained away on the basis that they are the result of adopting a chancery style. Indeed none of them occur at all commonly in third-century rescripts. The style of the author of *opiniones* corresponds neither to that of Ulpian or some other jurist, nor to the rescripts of the third century in general, or to a particular secretary *a libellis* of that period. It is true, as Santalucia has shown, that the rescripts of the third century formed an important source of the *opiniones*. But this does not mean that the style, in its general and syntactical features, corresponds to that of any of those who composed those rescripts.

The author, whoever he was, had his own idiosyncratic manner. Thus, he likes the preposition and prefix *prae*. Ulpian does not use *prae* as a preposition, whereas in *opiniones* we find *prae manu*,[215] and also *praepostere visum est*,[216] another expression foreign to Ulpian. Santalucia,[217] following Arangio-Ruiz,[218] points to some passages which read as if they were the work of a classical jurist. Indeed, if we postulate a late classical jurist of the second or third rank, one may agree that there are texts which conform to the pattern to be expected from such a writer. But even these are not in Ulpian's manner. In *D.* 3.5.44 we have:

> in quibus est etiam *sumptus honeste ad honores per gradus pertinentes factus* . . .[2] . . . *quamvis* animo gerendi sororis negotia id fecisset, *veritate tamen filiorum defuncti, qui sui heredes patri sublato testamento erant, gessisset*: . . . *placuit*

The first clause has a portmanteau nominal phrase of the sort delineated earlier.[219] The second is barely grammatical, since *veritate tamen* 'but in truth' destroys the contrast between *quamvis* . . . and *placuit*. The collocation *erant, gessisset* illustrates the habit of placing alongside one another the verb of a relative and of a main clause. In *D.* 8.4.13 we find:

> *solitum solacium* . . . ita tamen lapides caedere debet . . . ut neque usus necessarii lapidis *intercludatur* neque commoditas rei iure domino *adimatur*.

---

212 *D.* 4.4.40 (5 *op.*).
213 *D.* 10.1.8.1 (6 *op.*).
214 *D.* 27.9.10 (6 *op.*).
215 *D.* 13.7.27 (6 *op.*).
216 *D.* 50.10.1.1 (2 *op.*).
217 Santalucia (1971) I 174, 183, 190.
218 Arangio-Ruiz (1946/1970) 181–2.
219 Above, nn. 202–7.

There are two rhymes or assonances here of the sort which the author of *opiniones* likes but Ulpian does not. In *D.* 8.4.15 we find:

> Altius aedes suas extollendo, ut luminibus domus minoris annis viginti quinque vel impuberis, cuius curator vel tutor *erat, officiatur, efficit*: . . . ut quod non iure *factum est tollatur.*

This text contains, from an Ulpianic point of view, objectionable verb clusters. In addition the syntax of the first sentence is mysterious.

At two points in his argument Santalucia[220] points to an expression in *opiniones* as one that is common in Ulpian but not in other jurists. In a text of 5 *op.* we have:[221]

> sed cum ei facultas oblata esset a principe bona quoque sua reciperandi, maluerit ea derelinquere, actionibus *exuere se*, quibus ante sententiam *subiectus fuerat, non poterit.*

Exuere is said to be an Ulpianic word. But as *VIR*[222] makes clear, this is the only text with the reflexive *exuere se*. Apart from it there are four texts of Ulpian, one each of Paul and Venuleius with *exuere bonis (commercio, facultatibus* etc.). The proportion of texts, four out of six, would not, even so, make the expression Ulpianic according to the criteria for listing marks of style adopted in this book.[223] One may also note, in regard to the text cited, that the verb cluster is inconsistent with Ulpian's authorship, and that the text is awkward in that it requires a conjunction such as *sed* before *maluerit* in order to read smoothly.

Another text from the same book has *qui neque iurisdictioni praeest.* . . .[224] Here again there are three texts from Ulpian (apart from this controversial one) which use this expression, one from Ulpian citing the praetor's edict, one from Paul and one from Julian.[225] Again, this is not a high enough proportion of texts to make the expression Ulpianic, even if it were not in addition highly contextual.

Indeed, the *opiniones* contain a number of grammatical ineptitudes. Here is one:[226]

> In civilibus dissensionibus quamvis saepe per eas res publica laedatur, non tamen. . . .

'As regards civil disturbances, though the *respublica* often suffers harm as a result of them . . .'. This should have read *quamvis per civiles dissensiones res*

---

[220] Santalucia (1971) I 185, 187.
[221] *D.* 48.23.2 (5 *op.*).
[222] *VIR* 2.734. 4–8.
[223] Above, ch. 2 pp. 47–8.
[224] *D.* 5.1.81 (5 *op.*).
[225] *VIR* 3(1) 1391. 37–8.
[226] *D.* 49.15.21.1 (5 *op.*), cf. *D.* 1.18.7 (3 *op.*) *inspectis aedificiis* . . . *ea = inspecta aedificia.*

publica saepe laedatur. . . . The actual text is the result of slapdash composition, in which civil dissensions are mentioned before the author sees how they fit into the syntax of the sentence. Here is an example of confused tenses:[227]

> Qui neque iurisdictioni praeest neque a principe potestate aliqua praeditus est . . . iudex esse non potuit.

It should be *praeerat* . . . *praeditus erat* . . . *potuit* or *praeest* . . . *praeditus est* . . . *potest*. Another example of careless composition, or a sort of which Ulpian would not have been guilty.

It is not only the parts of *opiniones* that betray the influence of a chancery style, then, that are not in the Ulpianic manner. Other texts, which state the law more in the fashion of a jurist writing privately, are also composed in a way which fails to meet Ulpian's standards of scholarship, brevity, lucidity, and smooth flow, and which violate his canons of taste in regard to assonances, verb clusters and nominal phrases.

Santalucia has raised doubts as to period of composition of the *opiniones* but he has not established its authorship. The real author, whoever he may be, is not Ulpian.

In this chapter I have used criteria of style to draw more radical conclusions about the authenticity of disputed works than most scholars have been apt to do. I think that Ulpian's name was falsely attached to a number of works in which he had no part, mainly no doubt in order to make them acceptable for citation in court. These spurious works were not all by the same hand. The style of *LSR* is simple and elementary. That of *opiniones* is cumbersome and marked by verbal clustering. Perhaps *responsa* and *reg.* 7 are by the same author.[228] Only in the case of *pandectae* can one hazard a reasonable guess as to who the author was: the secretary *a libellis* of March to October 222.[229] Presumably he belonged to Ulpian's circle. Did the others do so too? Apart perhaps from *opiniones*, none of the spurious works seems to derive, in its original form, from later than the third century. Most of them could belong to the reign of Alexander Severus. Greater certainty will be difficult to achieve.

---

[227] *D.* 5.1.81 (5 *op.*).
[228] Above, nn. 70, 126.
[229] Above, nn. 131–41.

CHAPTER 5

ad edictum: Dates and Segments

In this and the next two chapters an attempt is made to fix the dates of Ulpian's various works, their order of composition and the rate at which the author wrote them. The best plan is to begin with Ulpian's eighty-one books *ad edictum praetoris*. Once these are assigned to the correct period and once the segments or divisions in which Ulpian composed them are determined, the other works can be fitted in.

In order to discover the dates and segments of *ad edictum*, as the *magnum opus* is called for short, we have, apart from a few clues in individual texts, two methods of investigation. One is afforded by the existence of references in the edictal commentary to the reigning or recently deceased emperors. These, if carefully studied, are seen to reflect political conditions at the moment of composition. They can therefore be used to date, within limits, the different parts of the commentary. A second method is derived from the study of Ulpian's style. This naturally evolved over the period of time required to complete such a large-scale work as *ad edictum*. Had Ulpian composed it in one continuous tract, it would still be useful to note how, as time went by, he discarded certain expressions and adopted others. This would help in fixing the dates of other works by their relation to the different parts of the edictal commentary. But in fact we can go further. Instead of being gradual, changes in the style of the edictal commentary are in places abrupt. They occur between one book and the next, or even in the middle of a book. Such abrupt changes indicate a discontinuity in composition. Ulpian has, for a time, left *ad edictum* on one side in order to do or compose something else. This is hardly surprising, given the tedium involved in writing of such diuturnity. The breaks which can be detected in this way enable us to fix the segments of composition of the edictal commentary. These, in turn, provide a clue to Ulpian's method of composition, and suggest a hypothesis, to be expounded in the next chapter, by which to date the majority of his works and fix the rate and order in which he wrote them.

The *Index Florentinus*[1] ascribes to Ulpian eighty-three books *ad edictum*.

---

[1] Ch. xxiv 1.

This is a mistake. The inscriptions to the *Digest* texts record no number higher than eighty-one.[2] The two books *ad edictum aedilium curulium* formed a separate commentary. Texts from these books are inscribed *ad edictum aedilium curulium libro primo* or *secundo*. They are not treated in the inscriptions as if they formed the 82nd and 83rd books *ad edictum*. It was, I believe, a mistake on Lenel's part to treat them as such in his *Palingenesia*.[3] As will appear later,[4] these two books were probably composed at a time when Ulpian had not got beyond book 31 of his commentary *ad edictum praetoris*. They were not left till the end, as Lenel's numbering implies.

I. REFERENCES TO EMPERORS

We have therefore eighty-one books to consider. From the point of view of references to contemporary and recently deceased emperors, the eighty-one books can be divided into five groups, on the assumption, hardly a rash one, that book 1 was composed before book 2, book 44 before book 45, etc. These six groups are:

1. Books   1 to   8
2. Books   9 to 19
3. Books 22 to 57
4. Books 61 to 73
5. Books 74 to 81

These divisions do not represent segments of composition. They are intended to reflect the political conditions obtaining at the time of composition of various books or groups of books. In regard to each group in turn I set out the relevant references and then attempt an interpretation.

1. *Books 1 to 8*

There is one reference to a living or recently deceased emperor:

6 *ed.*   *D.* 3.2.24   Imperator Severus rescripsit

These first eight books contain no indication of who the reigning emperor may be. We cannot conclude from the phrase *imperator Severus* that Severus was alive at the time of composition of book 6. Although Mommsen, on the basis of his epigraphic studies, advanced the theory that *imperator* is properly used only of a living emperor,[5] Fitting pointed out[6] that, on Mommsen's own showing, the practice of the jurists often did not

---

[2] *D.* 21.2.52, 39.1.21, 39.2.24, 26, 28, 30.
[3] *Pal.* 2.884−98.
[4] Ch. 7 pp. 172−3.
[5] Mommsen (1905) II 156−7, cf. d'Ors (1942−3).
[6] Fitting (1908) 5−6.

conform to this pattern. A treatise by a lawyer is not like an inscription on a column, in which it is important to adhere to the exact titulature and to observe the constitutional convention that a deified emperor should be called *divus*. Mommsen admitted[7] and Fitting emphasized[8] that the jurists often failed to observe the convention. When a jurist gives an exact citation from the constitution of a deceased emperor, he often introduces it with a shortened form of the original titles, as in this text of Marcianus written after Caracalla's death:[9]

Imperatores Severus et Antoninus in haec verba rescripserunt:

Again, the *quaestiones* of Papinian, composed under Severus, consistently violate the supposed convention and refer to deceased emperors as *imperator* so-and-so, as in:[10]

Imperator Titus Antoninus rescripsit non laedi statum . . .

Papinian's *responsa*, on the other hand, apart from one text,[11] call dead emperors *divus*.[12] What factors influence the choice between *divus* and *imperator* in relation to a dead emperor? If the jurist has consulted the actual text of the constitution he cites, he is more likely to favour *imperator*. If, again, he is writing in a less formal mode (*quaestiones* being less formal than *responsa*), or if he wishes to evince particular respect towards the emperor, he is more likely to adopt the *imperator* form. But, as Papinian's examples show, the practice is not rigid. A writer may want to vary the form of reference in order to avoid monotony. Perhaps for this reason jurists sometimes give the dead emperor's name without any title: just Traianus,[13] Hadrianus, etc. Apart from these instances, Mommsen listed twenty-one miscellaneous violations of his convention in the *Digest*, culled from writers as various as Callistratus,[14] Menander, Ulpian, Paul, Macer,

---

[7] Mommsen (1905) 157−61.

[8] Fitting (1908) 6−8.

[9] *D.* 28.1.5 (Ulp. 6 *Sab.*).

[10] *D.* 22.1.3 pr. (20 *qu.*), 31.67.10 (19 *qu.*), 35.2.11.2 (29 *qu.*), 36.3.5.1 (28 *qu.*), 31.64 (15 *qu.*), 48.5.39.8 (36 *qu.*), 48.5.39.4−6 (36 *qu.*), *FV* 224 (11 *qu.*), *D.* 1.5.8 (3 *qu.*), 1.7.32.1 (31 *qu.*), 3.1.8 (2 *qu.*), 12.6.3 (20 *qu.*), 36.1.57.1 (20 *qu.*), 36.3.3−4 (28 *qu.*), 50.1.11 pr. (2 *qu.*).

[11] *D.* 20.2.1 (10 *resp.*).

[12] e.g. *D.* 29.2.86 pr. (6 *resp: divus Pius*).

[13] There are a number of examples from early emperors: Augustus *D.* 1.17.1 (Ulp. 15 *ed.*), *D.* 23.2.14.4 (Paul 35 *ed.*), 40.1.14.1 (Paul 16 *Plaut.*), 49.16.12.1 (Macer 1 *re mil.*), 50.15.1.1 (Ulp. 1 *cens.*): Claudius: Gai. *Inst.* 1.32 c, *D.* 4.4.3.4 (Ulp. 11 *ed.*), 16.1.2 pr. (Ulp. 29 *ed.*); Trajan: Gai. *Inst.* 1. 34, *D.* 26.7.12.1 (Paul 38 *ed.*), 29.1.1 pr. (Ulp. 45 *ed.*), 49.14.13.6 (Paul 7 *leg. Iul. Pap.*), 49.14.16 (Ulp. 18 *leg. Iul. Pap;*)); Hadrian: Gai. *Inst.* 1.47, Ulp. 24.28, Coll. 1.6.1 (Ulp. 7 *off. proc.*), 11.8.3 (Ulp. 8 *off. proc.*), 27.1.6.8 (Mod. 2 *excus.*), 34.1.14.1 (Ulp. 2 *fid.*, bis), 36.1.31.5 (Marci. 8 *inst.*), 40.12.27.1 (Ulp. 2 *off. cons.*), 42.4.7.16 (Ulp. 59 *ed.*), 47.14.1.3 (Ulp. 8 *off. proc.*), 49.14.13.5 (Paul 7 *leg. Iul. Pap.*), 49.16.5.6 (Men. 2 *re mil.*), 49.17.19.3 (Tryph. 18 *disp.*), 50.8.12.3 (Papir. 2 *const.*).

[14] *D.* 4.4.45.1 (1 *ed. mon.: imperator Titus Antoninus*).

and Modestinus. [15] In these texts the author wrote *imperator* for *divus* when speaking of a dead emperor. Fitting added a further two instances, taken from Paul and Marcianus respectively. [16] Given this number of exceptions, it was indeed bold of Mommsen to argue that his rule remained intact. Indeed he relied on it in order to elaborate a hypothesis about the composition of Ulpian's edictal commentary. [17]

The safe course is rather to assume that, while the use of *divus* is a sign that the emperor is dead (though, in view of the possibility of retrospective alterations of the texts, not an infalliable one) its absence is no sure indication that the emperor is alive.

The reference to *imperator Severus* in book 6, then, does not tell us whether Severus was then alive or dead.

2. Books 9 to 19

9 *ed.*	*D.* 3.3.33.2	quod et ex rescripto imperatoris nostri apparet
10 *ed.*	*D.* 3.6.1.3	sed et constitutio imperatoris nostri . . . prohibuit
11 *ed.*	*D.* 4.2.9.3	sed ex facto scio rescriptum esse ab imperatore nostro
11 *ed.*	*D.* 4.4.3 pr.	Denique divus Severus et imperator noster . . . interpretati sunt
11 *ed.*	*D.* 4.4.7.10	et divus Pius rescripsit et imperator noster
11 *ed.*	*D.* 4.4.11 pr.	et hoc rescripto divi Sevari continetur
11 *ed.*	*D.* 4.4.11.2	Aetrius Severus quia dubitabat ad imperatorem Severum rettulit
11 *ed.*	*D.* 4.4.18.1	denique Glabrionem Acilium divus Severus et imperator Antoninus non audierunt
11 *ed.*	*D.* 4.4.18.2−3	Sed et Percennio Severo . . . divus Severus et imperator Antoninus permiserunt in auditorio suo examinari . . . Idem imperator Licinnio Frontoni rescripsit
11 *ed.*	*D.* 4.4.18.3	Idem imperator Licinnio Frontoni rescripsit
11 *ed.*	*D.* 4.4.22	Calpurnio Flacco Severus et Antoninus rescripserunt
15 *ed.*	*D.* 5.3.20.12	sed imperator Severus epistula ad Celerem idem videtur fecisse

[15] *D.* 49.16.6.7 (Men. 2 *re. mil.*), 4.4.45.1 (Call. 1 *ed. mon.*), 48.15.3 pr. (Marci. 1 *iud. pub.*), 40.5.12 pr. (Mod. 1 *man.*), 25.3.6.1 (Mod. 1 *man.*), 27.1.6.8, 17 (Mod. 2 *excus.*), 27.1.13.6, 7 (Mod. 4 *excus.*), 27.1.15. pr. (Mod. 6 *excus.*), 19.2.49 pr. (Mod. 6 *excus.*), 5.3.43 (Paul 2 *Plaut.*), 40.4.56 (Paul 1 *fid.*), 4.6.8 (Paul 3 *brev.*), 34.9.5.9 (Paul 1 *iur. fisc.*), 49.14.49 (Paul 1 *resp.*), 1.5.1.8 (Ulp. 21 *Sab.*), 49.14.25 (Ulp. 19 *Sab.*), 23.1.16 (Ulp. 3 *leg. Iul. Pap.*), 42.8.10.1 (Ulp. 73 *ed.*), *FV* 119 (Ulp. 2 *off. proc.*), Ulp. Epit. 26.7.

[16] *D.* 40.9.15 (Paul 1 *leg. Iul. Pap.*), 49.14.30 (Marci. 3 *inst.*), to which can be added *D.* 49.14.34, 48.21.2 pr. (both Macer 2 *iud. pub.*).

[17] Mommsen (1905) ii 159.

16 *ed.*	*D.* 36.1.38.1	divus Severus in persona Arri Honorati pupilli decrevit
16 *ed.*	*D.* 6.2.11. pr.	imperator Severus rescripsit
17 *ed.*	*D.* 8.4.2	sed rescripto imperatoris Antonini ad Tullianum adicitur
18 *ed.*	*Coll.* 12.7.6	cuius sententia et rescripto divi Severi comprobata est in haec verba:
18 *ed.*	*D.* 9.2.29.1	ex rescripto imperatoris Severi
19 *ed.*	*D.* 10.2.18.3	secundum rescriptum imperatorum Severi et Antonini
19 *ed.*	*D.* 10.2.20.1	et ita imperator noster rescripsit

In book 11[18] the phrase *divus Severus et imperator noster* implies that Caracalla is sole emperor at the time of writing, since his father is dead and there is a single reigning emperor. The *imperator noster* of book 9[19] is surely also Caracalla. It is true that there may have been an interval between the composition of book 9 and book 11. But between 198 and the end of AD 211 there was always more than one emperor. Hence, if the *imperator noster* of book 9 is not Caracalla, the book must have been composed fourteen years before book 11. This seems implausible.

Throughout the period which separates book 9 from book 19, then, Caracalla is reigning as sole emperor. But Ulpian still respects the seniority of Severus. This is shown by the fact that, when father and son are mentioned in the same text, the father is mentioned first. Ulpian uses the following formulae:

> divus Severus et imperator noster[20]
> divus Severus et imperator Antoninus[21]
> Severus et Antoninus[22]
> imperatorum Severi et Antonini[23]

The formulae vary, Severus being alternatively *divus*, *imperator* and without title, but the order of the *Augusti* does not.

During this period Severus is six times *divus*,[24] five times *imperator*,[25] and is once mentioned without title.[26] If we approach the matter without preconceptions, Ulpian appears flexible, indeed indifferent, in his nomenclature.

[18] *D.* 4.4.3 pr.
[19] *D.* 3.3.33.2.
[20] *D.* 4.4.3 pr. (11 *ed.*).
[21] *D.* 4.4.18.1, 3 (11 *ed.*).
[22] *D.* 4.4.22 (11 *ed.*).
[23] *D.* 10.2.18.3 (19 *ed.*).
[24] *D.* 4.4.3 pr. (11 *ed.*), 4.4.11 pr. (11 *ed.*), 4.4.18.1 (11 *ed.*), 4.4.18.3 (11 *ed.*), 36.1.38.1 (16 *ed.*), *Coll.* 12.7.6 (18 *ed*).
[25] *D.* 4.4.11.2 (11 *ed.*), 5.3.20.12 (15 *ed.*), 6.2.11 pr. (16 *ed.*), 9.2.29.1 (18 *ed.*), 10.2.18.3 (19 *ed.*).
[26] *D.* 4.4.22 (11 *ed.*).

The part of Caracalla's sole rule during which Ulpian, in joint citations, treats Severus as senior to his son, will be called Caracalla A.

3. *Books 22 to 57*

There is a reference in book 21 which may or may not belong to Caracalla A:

21 *ed.*	D. 28.5.30	imperator Severus rescripsit

The next texts, from book 22, clearly belong to a new period, which will be called Caracalla B:

22 *ed.*	D. 1.5.17	ex constitutione imperatoris Antonini
22 *ed.*	D. 12.2.13.6	imperator noster cum patre rescripsit
24 *ed.*	D. 11.6.7.3	nam et divus Severus . . . decrevit
25 *ed.*	D. 11.7.12 pr.	Imperator Antoninus cum patre rescripsit
25 *ed.*	D. 47.12.3.3	ut rescripto imperatoris Antonini cavetur
25 *ed.*	D. 47.12.3.4	edicto divi Severi continetur
25 *ed.*	D. 47.12.3.7	ut divus Severus rescripsit
25 *ed.*	D. 11.7.14.7	et ita imperator noster rescripsit
26 *ed.*	D. 12.5.2.2	et non ita pridem imperator noster constituit (= *CJ* 7.49.1, 19 Dec. 212)
26 *ed.*	D. 12.6.26 pr.	divus Severus rescripsit
26 *ed.* (= 1 *ed. de rebus creditis*)	FV 266	imperator noster rescripsit in haec verba
28 *ed.*	D. 13.7.11.6	quod constitutum est ab imperatore nostro
29 *ed.*	D. 16.1.2.3	hoc enim divus Pius et Severus rescripserunt . . . et est et Graecum Severi tale rescriptum
29 *ed.*	D. 16.1.4	et ita divus Pius et imperator noster rescripserunt
31 *ed.*	D. 17.1.12.10	et ita imperator Severus Hadriano Demostrati rescripsit
31 *ed.*	D. 17.2.52.5	et imperator Severus Flavio Felici in haec verba rescripsit:
32 *ed.*	D. 18.2.16 pr.	imperator Severus rescripsit
32 *ed.*	D. 18.3.4 pr.	ut rescriptis imperatoris Antonini et divi Severi declaratur
32 *ed.*	D. 19.2.9.1	et ita imperator Antoninus cum divo Severo rescripsit
32 *ed.*	D. 19.2.9.4	imperator Antoninus cum patre ita rescripsit
32 *ed.*	D. 19.2.15.5	rescripto divi Antonini continetur
32 *ed.*	D. 19.2.15.6	rescriptum est ab Antonino Augusto
32 *ed.*	D. 19.2.19.9	imperator Antoninus cum divo Severo rescripsit . . . in haec verba:

34 *ed.*	D. 23.3.40	divus Severus rescripsit Pontio Lucriano in haec verba
34 *ed.*	D. 23.4.11	ita interpretandum divus Severus constituit
34 *ed.*	D. 49.14.27	divus Severus rescripsit
34 *ed.*	D. 27.2.1.1	imperator Severus rescripsit
34 *ed.*	D. 27.2.1.3	et ita divus Severus saepissime statuit
35 *ed.*	D. 26.7.3.4	imperator noster cum patre rescripsit
35 *ed.*	D. 26.7.7.4	et ita divus Severus decrevit
35 *ed.*	D. 27.9.1 pr.	imperatoris Severi oratione . . . quae oratio in senatu recitata est (13 June 195)
35 *ed.*	D. 27.9.3 pr.	secundum constitutionem imperatoris nostri et divi patris eius
35 *ed.*	D. 26.10.1.4	sed imperator Antoninus cum divo Severo rescripsit
35 *ed.*	D. 26.10.1.7	et rescriptum exstat divi Severi
35 *ed.*	D. 26.10.3 pr.	et ita divus Severus rescripsit
35 *ed.*	D. 26.10.3.13	Severus et Antoninus rescripserunt Epicurio
36 *ed.*	D. 27.3.1.3	nam divus Severus decrevit
36 *ed.*	D. 26.7.9.6	imperator Antoninus cum patre prohibuit
36 *ed.*	D. 27.3.1.13	constitutum est a divo Pio et ab imperatore nostro et divo patre eius
36 *ed.*	D. 27.3.1.15	et ita imperator noster Ulpio Proculo rescripsit
36 *ed.*	D. 12.3.4 pr.	rescriptis imperatoris nostri et divi patris eius continetur
36 *ed.*	D. 12.3.4.1	et ita constitutionibus expressum est imperatoris nostri et divi patris eius
36 *ed.*	D. 27.5.1.2	divus Severus rescripsit
38 *ed.*	D. 47.4.1.7	est autem saepissime et a divo Marco et ab imperatore nostro cum patre rescriptum
45 *ed.*	D. 29.1.13.4	imperator noster cum divo Severo rescripsit
50 *ed.*	D. 48. 18.3	constitutione imperatoris nostri et divi Severi placuit
52 *ed.*	D. 36.4.5.16	Imperator Antoninus Augustus rescripsit
52 *ed.*	D. 36.4.5.25	Constitutio autem divi Antonini pertinet
57 *ed.*	D. 47.10.7.6	imperator noster rescripsit

The mark of the period which has been termed Caracalla B is that Caracalla is sole emperor, and that, when he is mentioned in conjunction with his father, his father comes second. It is this that distinguishes Caracalla B from Caracalla A.

In books 22[27] and 50[28] constitutions of *imperator noster* and his father Severus are mentioned. *Imperator noster* comes in thirteen intermediate

---

[27] D. 12.2.13.6 (22 *ed.*).
[28] D. 48.18.3 (50 *ed.*).

texts,[29] and *imperator Antoninus* in eight,[30] *Antoninus Augustus* in a ninth.[31] It can be deduced that Caracalla was sole emperor during the whole period between the composition of these books. Doubt surrounds only the last three texts, two from book 52 and one from book 57.

In the first text from book 52[32] *imperator Antoninus Augustus* is said to have given a rescript to the effect that a legatee or fideicommissary could in certain circumstances get an order putting him in possession of the heir's own property. In the second text[33] this same rescript is referred to as a *constitutio divi Antonini*. Fitting argued[34] that the first sentence was written at the very end of Caracalla's reign. His death then caused Ulpian to put his pen aside—and, by the time he resumed, Caracalla was referred to as *divus Antoninus*. But the two texts both occur in the course of a continuous passage, as printed in the *Palingenesia*, of fifty lines.[35] It is most unlikely that the shock of Caracalla's death, however traumatic, would have interrupted Ulpian in the middle of writing this passage. The correct explanation, surely, is that of Mommsen.[36] In the second text *divus* is a retrospective insertion. A person copying a text is tempted to insert *divus* if by the time he is copying it the emperor in question has been deified. This he is specially likely to do if the emperor is referred to in the original without title. So the likelihood here is that the original read *constitutio autem Antonini*. The later copier has inserted *divi* before *Antonini*. The reason why we might well find bare *Antonini* in the original at this point is that Caracalla has just previously been called *imperator Antoninus Augustus*,[37] which, in a juristic text, is a trifle elaborate. A formal reference can properly be followed by an informal one.

This presupposes that *imperator Antoninus Augustus* is indeed Caracalla, not Elagabal. The constitution is that referred to in a rescript of Alexander of 225,[38] and attributed to *divus Antoninus pater meus*. It was of course Caracalla, not the discredited Elagabal, from whom Alexander claimed descent.[39] Hence book 52 of the edictal commentary was composed during the reign of the former. In any case Caracalla's deification came not

---

[29] D. 11.7.14.7 (25 ed.), 12.5.2.2 (26 ed.), FV 266 (26 ed.), D. 13.7.11.6 (28 ed.), 16.1.4 (29 ed.), 26.7.3.4 (35 ed.), 27.9.3 pr. (35 ed.), 27.3.1.13 (36 ed.), 27.3.1.15 (36 ed.), 12.3.4 pr. (36 ed.), 12.3.4.1 (36 ed.), 47.4.1.7 (38 ed.), 29.1.13.4 (45 ed.).

[30] D. 11.7.12 pr. (25 ed.), 47.12.3.3 (25 ed.), 18.3.4 (32 ed.), 19.2.19.1 (32 ed.), 19.2.9.4 (32 ed.), 19.2.19.9 (32 ed.), 26.10.1.4 (35 ed.), 26.7.9.6 (36 ed.).

[31] D. 19.2.15.6 (32 ed.).

[32] D. 36.4.5.16 (52 ed.).

[33] D. 36.4.5.25 (52 ed.).

[34] Fitting (1908) 107; Karlowa I (1885) 743.

[35] Pal. 2.741–2.

[36] Mommsen (1905) II 169.

[37] D. 36.4.5.16 (52 ed.).

[38] CJ 6.54.6 (8 Jan. 225).

[39] Herodian 5.3.10, 5.7.3, CJ 12.35.4 (*Antoninus pater meus*), 6.50.5 (17 Nov. 223 *constitutio divi Severi avi mei*).

at once, but after an interval, at the end of the reign of Macrinus or the beginning of that of Elagabal.[40] If, therefore, *divus* were genuine in the second text, we should still have to suppose the sort of traumatic break which Fitting proposed—a year's interval between the beginning and the end of the text.

The third text (*D.* 47.10.7.6) presents more difficulty. Fitting held[41] that the *imperator noster* in this text is Alexander. D'Ors follows him.[42] Gualandi, however, points out[43] that their arguments, drawn as they are from the use of *divus* in book 52, are unreliable. One cannot rule out the possibility that the emperor referred to was Caracalla.

In my view *imperator noster* is indeed Caracalla. But it must be conceded that the argument for preferring a later emperor can be strengthened. This later emperor could not be Alexander, because during the short time that he lived under Alexander, between AD 222 and 223, Ulpian, as a prefect, did not have time for literary composition on the scale implied by the suggestion that the last twenty-five books of his edictal commentary were written in this reign. One could, however, adapt the view of Fitting and d'Ors by substituting Elagabal for Alexander. One could point to the fact that, as explained later in this chapter,[44] there appears to be a break in Ulpian's edictal commentary in the middle of book 56. This break occurs, therefore, just before the text in book 57 we are now considering. Hence there may have been a considerable interval between the composition of book 52, when we have concluded that Caracalla was still reigning, and book 57. It might then be the case that book 57 was composed under Elagabal.

My reason for not accepting this suggestion is twofold. First, there is no positive sign that the text refers to Elagabal. Indeed, there is no positive evidence that Ulpian composed anything in the reign of Elagabal. So it seems simpler not to introduce a complicating hypothesis, the ground for which falls away once we accept Mommsen's explanation of *divus Antoninus* in book 52.[45] Secondly, there is positive evidence, to be detailed in a moment,[46] that certain books of edictal commentary later than book 57 were composed in the reign of Macrinus. If this is accepted, book 57 cannot have been composed under Elagabal, unless it was written out of order, which there is no reason to suppose. I therefore adopt as a firm conclusion the tentative suggestion of Gualandi, that in this text *imperator noster* is still Caracalla.

[40] Dio 79.9.2; 79.17.2; 80.2.6; *RE* 2.2437.
[41] Fitting (1908) 107.
[42] d'Ors (1942–3) 68.
[43] Gualandi (1963) 2. 197.
[44] Below, pp. 145–6.
[45] Mommsen (1905) II 169.
[46] Below, pp. 141–2.

But if Caracalla is reigning as sole emperor during the period of composition of books 22 to 57, his relation to Severus has changed from what it was up to book 19. Ulpian now treats him as senior to Severus, in the sense that he is consistently mentioned first. Various formulae are used:

> imperator noster cum patre[47]
> imperator Antoninus cum patre[48]
> imperator Antoninus et divus Severus[49]
> imperator Antoninus cum divo Severo[50]
> imperator noster et divus pater eius[51]
> imperator noster cum divo Severo[52]
> imperator noster et divus Severus[53]

In contrast with Caracalla A, in which we found four texts in all of which Severus preceded his son, we now come across seventeen texts, in sixteen of which one of the listed formulae are employed.[54] There is one exception,[55] which occurs in book 35. Here the text runs

> Severus et Antoninus rescripserunt Epicurio

Whatever the exact explanation of this exception, with its absence of titles, it cannot obscure the contrast between Caracalla B and Caracalla A. Respect for or fear of the tyrant now made it imperative to mention him first. Other jurists, such as Paul, do the same.[56] It is not easy to say whether this change (which, I shall argue, occurred about the middle of 213) corresponds to some striking political event,[57] or whether it merely reflects the growing insistence of Caracalla that the achievements of his father's reign were in substance his own. At any rate the change points to a new political climate.

When Severus is mentioned as joint emperor with Caracalla, his title, if he is given one, is *divus*, not *imperator*. He is called *divus* in ten such joint texts; on the other hand, seven refer to him merely as *Severus* or *pater*.[58]

---

[47] *D.* 12.2.13.6 (22 *ed.*), 26.7.3.4 (35 *ed.*), 47.4.1.7 (38 *ed.*).

[48] *D.* 11.7.12 pr. (25 *ed.*), 19.2.9.4 (32 *ed.*), 26.7.9.6 (36 *ed.*).

[49] *D.* 18.3.4 (32 *ed.*).

[50] *D.* 19.2.9.1 (32 *ed.*), 19.2.19.9 (32 *ed.*), 26.10.1.4 (35 *ed.*).

[51] *D.* 27.9.3 pr. (35 *ed.*), 27.3.1.13 (36 *ed.*), 12.3.4 pr. (36 *ed.*), 12.3.4.1 (36 *ed.*).

[52] *D.* 29.1.13.4 (45 *ed.*).

[53] *D.* 48.18.3 (50 *ed.*).

[54] Above, nn. 47–53.

[55] *D.* 26.10.1.13 (35 *ed.*).

[56] *D.* 27.1.46.2 (1 *cogn.*), 40.8.7 (1 *lib. dand.*), 27.9.13 pr. (1 *Orat. d. Sev.*) 47.15.6 (1 *pub. iud.*), cf. *D.* 27.1.44 pr. (Tryph. 2 *disp.*), 49.15.12.17 (Tryph. 4 *disp.*).

[57] Quite possible. In 213 we first find inscriptions which call Caracalla *magnus imperator* (*CIL* v 28, x 5286). The *fratres arvales* call him *Germanice max(ime)* as early as 19 May 213: *CIL* vi 2086(2) 15.

[58] *Divus: D.* 18.3.4 (32 *ed.*), 19.2.9.1 (32 *ed.*), 19.2.19.9 (32 *ed.*), 27.9.3 pr. (35 *ed.*), 26.10.1.4 (35 *ed.*), 27.3.1.13 (36 *ed.*), 12.3.4 pr. (36 *ed.*), 12.4.3.1 (36 *ed.*), 29.1.13.4 (45 *ed.*), 48.18.3 (50 *ed.*); *Severus: D.* 26.10.3.13 (35 *ed.*); *pater: D.* 12.2.13.6 (22 *ed.*), 11.7.12 pr. (25 *ed.*), 12.2.9.4 (32 *ed.*), 26.7.3.4 (35 *ed.*), 26.7.9.6 (36 *ed.*), 47.4.1.7 (38 *ed.*).

When Severus stands on his own as the author of a constitution, he is *imperator* on five occasions,[59] *divus* thirteen times[60] and twice is mentioned without title.[61] Whereas in Caracalla A there is an even balance between Severus, standing on his own, as *imperator* and *divus*, in Caracalla B the *divus* texts outweigh the *imperator* texts by somewhere between three and five to one, depending on whether one counts in the joint references.[62]

Mommsen pointed out that the references to Severus as *imperator* cease after book 35.[63] Since, in his view, *imperator* is only properly used of a reigning emperor, Ulpian must, he supposed, have drafted his commentary up to book 35 during the reign of Severus, and then revised it under Caracalla. This would account for the mixture of references to Severus, some calling him *imperator*, some *divus*. But jurists do not invariably confine the title *imperator* to reigning emperors.[64] If Ulpian really proceeded in the way supposed, why did he not revise the references to *imperator Severus* when he later inserted references to *divus Severus*? Why did he not make them all *divus*? As Fitting pointed out,[65] this slapdash method of revision is hardly consistent with a strict adherence to the constitutional convention that Mommsen takes as the basis for his argument. It must be added that, on the face of the texts, there is no evidence that *ad edictum* has been subjected to revision. In this respect it contrasts with Ulpian's *ad Sabinum* and *de officio proconsulis* which, we shall see,[66] do present marks of a revision, albeit a limited one.

In favour of the revision theory, Mommsen cites a text from book 11,[67] which, beginning *divus Severus et imperator Antoninus permiserunt*, goes on in the next sentence *Idem imperator rescripsit*. He supposes that in the earlier version, composed under Severus, the text ran *imperator Severus permisit*.[68] The reference to Caracalla has been added in the revised draft, and *imperator Severus* has been changed to *divus Severus*. But, if Ulpian went to that trouble to revise the text, why did he not change *Idem imperator rescripsit* in the second sentence into *Idem imperatores rescripserunt*? A simpler explanation lies at hand. An enactment of joint emperors is often treated as that of the senior Augustus, who alone normally had power to make law. In this text, which comes from Caracalla A, Ulpian treats Severus as the senior

---

[59] D. 17.1.12.10 (31 *ed.*), 17.2.52.5 (31 *ed.*), 18.2.16 (32 *ed.*), 27.2.1.1 (34 *ed.*), 27.9.1 pr. (35 *ed.*).

[60] D. 11.6.7.3 (24 *ed.*), 47.12.3.3 (25 *ed.*), 47.12.3.7 (25 *ed.*), 12.6.26 pr. (26 *ed.*), 23.3.40 (34 *ed.*), 23.4.11 (34 *ed.*), 49.14.27 (34 *ed.*), 27.2.1.3 (34 *ed.*), 26.7.7.4 (35 *ed.*), 26.10.1.7 (35 *ed.*), 26.10.3 pr. (35 *ed.*), 27.3.1.3 (36 *ed.*), 27.5.1.2 (36 *ed.*).

[61] D. 16.1.2.3 (29 *ed.* bis).

[62] Fourteen to 5; 24 to 5.

[63] Mommsen (1905) II 158–9; Jörs (1905) 1505; Karlowa (1885) 1 743; Pernice (1885) 444.

[64] Above, nn. 6–17.

[65] Fitting (1908) 8.

[66] Ch. 6 p. 156.

[67] D. 4.4.18.2, 3 (11 *ed.*).

[68] Mommsen (1905) II 159[23].

Augustus and the real author of the permission in question. A formal reference to both emperors is followed by an informal reference which encapsulates the substance of the matter. No doubt, had he been writing these sentences during Caracalla B, Ulpian would have expressed himself differently.

Even Fitting, who is sceptical of Mommsen's views, thinks that the whole work went through two drafts, one during the reign of Severus and a second under Caracalla and his successors.[69] Kipp[70] would extend the initial draft beyond book 35 to the whole edictal commentary, every part of which was, he thinks, worked over twice. Indeed Mommsen's argument that the initial draft stopped at book 35 is a weak one. It is based on the fact that references to *imperator Severus* stop there. But between books 36 and 57 there are in all only two references to constitutions of Severus on his own. Different considerations apply to the references to Severus from book 61 onwards.[71] The two earlier texts occur in book 36, and both speak of *divus Severus*.[72] There are also seven texts between books 36 and 50 which mention Severus jointly with Caracalla.[73] All of these have *divus Severus, divus pater* or *pater*, none *imperator*. But this is hardly surprising, since none of the earlier joint references make Severus an *imperator* either.[74] As for the two texts in which *divus Severus* is mentioned on his own, there is no reason why they should be balanced by a text in which Severus is called *imperator*, since the ratio of *divus* to *imperator* references in this whole period is, as we have seen, at least three to one.[75] In the upshot there is no reason to suppose that the method of composition of the edictal commentary changed at or about book 35.

An argument of Fitting[76] in favour of the revision theory deserves mention. In both 10 *ed.* and 26 *ed.* Ulpian cites a constitution of Caracalla of 19 December 212 which penalizes a litigant who attempts to corrupt the judge or his opponent.[77] In the second of these texts it is said that the constitution was issued *non ita pridem*, 'not so long ago'. It is impossible, says Fitting, that in this brief period Ulpian could have composed for the first time the intervening sixteen books—and possibly more, since there is no guarantee that 10 *ed.* was written immediately after 19 December 212. So Ulpian must have been revising a first draft during this brief interval, not composing a wholly new commentary.

---

[69] Fitting (1908) 8.
[70] Kipp (1919) II 122[53].
[71] Below, pp. 141–2.
[72] D. 27.5.1.2, 27.3.1.3 (both 36 *ed.*).
[73] Texts above, nn. 56–7.
[74] The only such text in *ed.* is D. 10.2.18.3 (19 *ed.*) from Caracalla A.
[75] Above, n. 62.
[76] Fitting (1908) 106.
[77] *CJ* 7.49.1 (to Cassius Sabinus, or Gaudius).

But this argument is also a weak one. It is not certain that the phrase *non ita pridem* represents a very short period of time. Up to, say, a year, it would surely remain appropriate. The idea that Ulpian could not compose sixteen books of commentary in that period is absurd. It is reminiscent of the similar theories once held about the composition of Justinian's *Digest*, which, some scholars thought,[78] could not have been completed in three years unless there had been earlier drafts or partial codifications to work on. The falsity of this view has been amply demonstrated,[79] and it is no more plausible in regard to Ulpian. Ulpian's literary activity is best understood, I shall suggest, if we suppose that when he was writing legal commentaries or treatises he, on the average, composed a book a week. This means that, again on average, he set down each week about 12,000 words or the equivalent of thirty pages of modern print. It is perfectly possible for a methodical man to keep up this rhythm week after week, provided that two conditions are fulfilled. One is that the source material must have been gathered beforehand. What has to be supposed about Ulpian's scholarly activity in the reign of Severus is, not that he was engaged in drafting the whole or the first thirty-five books of the edictal commentary, but that he was collecting together and analysing the material he intended to use later, and making notes of the points that were relevant to particular titles. Secondly, we must suppose that Ulpian had secretarial assistance, and, perhaps, dictated to scribes, who were trained to follow legal technicalities. Given these two conditions, a fluent writer can have had no difficulty in advancing from book 10 to book 26 in the time represented by the expression *non ita pridem*.

There is no solid basis, then, for the theory that the edictal commentary, or the first thirty-five books of it, were drafted first under Severus and later revised under Caracalla. So far as books 22 to 57 are concerned, the evidence from references to emperors shows rather that they were drafted in that part of Caracalla's reign which we have termed Caracalla B. This began 'not long after' 19 December 212. What is more, it began after the *constitutio Antoniniana*, which is mentioned in book 22.

4. *Books 61 to 73*

In the next period Caracalla is plain Antoninus, without title, and Severus, in the majority of texts, is also plain Severus:

61 *ed.*	*D.* 26.5.18	et ita Severus rescripsit
64 *ed.*	*D.* 42.6.1.3	et ita Severus et Antoninus rescripserunt
68 *ed.*	*D.* 43.4.3.1	constitutum est ab Antonino
71 *ed.*	*D.* 43.30.1.3	et divus Pius decrevit et a Marco et a Severo rescriptum est

[78] Peters (1913), Arangio-Ruiz (1932), Collinet (1952), Guarino (1957), Volterra (1967).
[79] Diosdi (1971); Honoré (1970), (1978).

73 *ed.*   D. 42.8.10.1   et ab imperatore Severo et Antonino rescriptum est

Again it is clear from the mention of Severus and Antoninus together that Antoninus means Caracalla. He is now, however, not called *imperator*, *noster*, *Augustus*, or *princeps*. There is no indication that he is presently reigning. On the other hand, he is not *divus* either. He has not been deified.

An isolated text in which Caracalla was plain Antoninus would be consistent with the hypothesis that he was still reigning, or alternatively, had been deified. Three successive texts in which he is called Antoninus without more call for a different interpretation. They point to the reign of Macrinus, during which Caracalla's status was a source of perplexity to the equestrian emperor. Dio explains[80] that Macrinus found himself in a dilemma. When writing to the senate, says the historian, himself a senator, 'he made no reference to Tarautas [viz. Caracalla] either favourable or unfavourable but simply called him emperor. He dared neither declare him a god nor call him a public enemy. He hesitated to take the first course, I think, because of (Caracalla's) actions and the hatred felt for him by many, the second because of the soldiers. Some thought he acted in this (hesitant) way because he wished the senate and people to take the step of dishonouring Tarautas themselves, the emperor being surrounded by troops.' It is this dilemma of Macrinus, surely, that Ulpian in his own way reflects. Unsure how to refer to Caracalla, he cannot call him *divus*, since he has not been deified and perhaps never will be. Since he is dead, he cannot be *noster*, *Augustus*, or *princeps*. *Imperator* might do, but in the writings of a jurist that title, when used of a dead emperor, is perhaps unduly respectful. So, although Macrinus selected it in his letter to the senate as a non-committal expression, Ulpian cannot easily follow suit. His solution is to adopt the plain form Antoninus. As to Severus, though he is not in disgrace, he, too, suffers to some extent from his association with Caracalla, and, in three texts out of four,[81] becomes plain Severus. In the fourth,[82] on the other hand, he is *imperator Severus*. The text runs *ab imperatore Severo et Antonino*. This is not necessarily ungrammatical. Severus is an *imperator*. Caracalla is, at least for the time being, neither *imperator* nor *divus*.

That Caracalla is dead is clear from the fact that Severus is now mentioned before him,[83] in contrast with the practice in the period we have called Caracalla B. Severus resumes his natural seniority.

During this fourth period of edictal commentary, as Fitting pointed out,[84] the number of citations of jurists and constitutions falls and, in

[80] Dio 79.17.2–3. What follows develops a theme in Honoré (1962) 209.
[81] D. 26.5.18 (61 *ed.*), 42.6.1.3 (64 *ed.*), 43.30.1.3 (71 *ed.*).
[82] D. 42.8.10.1 (73 *ed.*).
[83] D. 42.6.1.3 (64 *ed.*).
[84] Fitting (1908) 107.

contrast with the first fifty-two books, Ulpian no longer cites authors by work and book as he often does earlier. An instance of the earlier practice is:

ut est apud Iulianum tractatum libro trigesimo tertio digestorum.[85]

Such references, with one uncertain exception (*Sabinus in adsessorio ait*[86]), are missing in the later books. Jörs thought that the whole commentary was first drafted during the lifetime of Severus, in this skeletal form, then revised under Caracalla.[87] If the theory of revision is rejected, what account can be given of the change in the mode of citation? Two factors may have contributed. As Ulpian drew towards the end of his great undertaking he may have wanted to save space. In Paul's edictal commentary, which runs to seventy-eight books, references of this sort, to work and book, cease at book 41.[88] Alternatively, or in addition, Justinian's compilers may have wished to save space. The middle section of edictal commentary was read by the Sabinian committee, the last by the edictal committee.[89] The division falls, according to Bluhme and Krueger, in the middle of Ulpian book 52 and Paul book 48. It might therefore be the case that the edictal committee, when they came to read these books, decided to reduce the volume of excerpts by omitting these references. Unfortunately for this explanation, two references occur in the second half of Ulpian book 52 *ad edictum*,[90] which Bluhme and Krueger assign to the edictal committee. Otherwise there are no such references from either Ulpian or Paul in the materials excerpted by the committee from these late books. Bluhme may conceivably have made a mistake about this half-book. In that case the apparent change of style was largely due to the compilers. But even if we suppose that Ulpian did make some changes in order to finish in the space available—and we shall see that the edictal commentary had to finish at book 81[91]—this would not explain the omission of Caracalla's titles. The explanation of this is not stylistic, but political.

5. *Books 74 to 81*

There are no references to contemporary or recently deceased emperors in these books, so that, while they cannot be earlier than the reign of Macrinus, they cannot, from this evidence alone, be more closely dated.

---

[85] *D.* 34.3.7 pr. (Ulp. 23 *Sab.*).
[86] *D.* 47.10.5.8 (Ulp. 56 *ed.*).
[87] *RE* 5.1.439–1440.
[88] *D.* 37.6.2.5 (Paul 41 *ed.*).
[89] Bluhme (1820), *Corp. Iur. Civ.* II. 927–9 (Krueger); Honoré (1978) 258–9, 270–2.
[90] *D.* 39.1.5 pr. (Ulp. 52 *ed.*–Iul. 12 *dig.*), 39.1.1.10 (Ulp. 52 *ed.*–Cels. 12(22) *dig.*).
[91] Below, pp. 144–8.

In the upshot we can draw the following conclusions from the references to emperors in the edictal commentaries:

- (i) Books 9 to 19 were composed during the sole rule of Caracalla but at a time when he did not insist that joint constitutions and other acts of his father and himself should be attributed primarily to himself.
- (ii) Books 22 to 57 were also composed during the sole rule of Caracalla but at a time after Caracalla came to insist on being regarded as the principal author of these joint acts. This period began not long after (within a year or so of) December 212.
- (iii) Books 61 to 73 were composed in the reign of Macrinus.

In order to take the matter further we must form an idea of the number of books of edictal commentary which Ulpian composed in a given period, such as a year. For this purpose it is necessary to return to a study of his style, and mark those points in the commentary at which new expressions are introduced or old ones fall out of use.

II. THE SEGMENTS OF ULPIAN'S COMMENTARY

Close attention to the language of Ulpian in his edictal commentary enables us to detect three breaks in the process of composition. From the point of view of segments of composition, the edictal commentary falls into groups of books which do not correspond with the groupings set out above on the basis of references to emperors. The four groups of books, arranged from the point of view of style, are:

- (i) Books 1 to 6.
- (ii) Book 7 to the middle of book 31.
- (iii) Middle of book 31 to the middle of book 56.
- (iv) Middle of book 56 to book 81.

Though this may not appear a logical proceeding, ease of exposition suggests that I should begin with the break in the middle of book 31 and then work forwards and backwards to the other two breaks.

The first part of book 31 is devoted to friendly services (*actio*) *mandati vel contra*, the second to partnership (*actio*) *pro socio*.[92]

Odd though it may seem, certain expressions occur, so far as the edictal commentary is concerned, for the first time in the second half of book 31, which will be designated book 31/2. Thus:

verumtamen (or verum tamen)[93]   *ed.* 31/2, 32, 32, 32, 35, 36, 39, 40, 40, 44, 45, 46, 47, 73, 76, 76, 79, 79.

[92] Lenel (1927) III 295–9.
[93] Ch. 2 n. 88.

One may notice a bunching of thirteen texts between book 31/2 and book 47, then a second bunching of five texts between books 73 and 79. A second example is

per contrarium quoque[94]   *ed.* 31/2, 32, 32, 34.

The four texts which contain this expression fall within $3\frac{1}{2}$ books, beginning with book 31/2. Certain other expressions begin soon after book 31/2, at book 32 or 33:

et putem[95]   *ed.* 33, 34, 35, 35, 37, 53, 55, 64, 64,
                          64, 68, 73, 75, 76, 76, 79
et magis puto[96]   *ed.* 32, 34, 35, 36
in ea condicione esse ut/ne[97]   *ed.* 32, 35, 45, 46, 46, 56, 58, 66, 70,
                          75
ostendimus[98]   *ed.* 32, 35, 35, 36, 44, 46
quamvis . . . attamen[99]   *ed.* 33, 34, 34, 35, 37, 37, 44, 44,
                          47, 50, 51

The seven examples show that Ulpian introduced a number of expressions of a non-technical sort into his edictal commentary in those books which are numbered in the early thirties. To be precise, he began to introduce these phrases in the second half of book 31. Hence, although it may seem surprising, we should assume, until evidence to the contrary turns up, that the break in style occurred in the middle rather than at the beginning of book 31.

If we bisect the number of books between the middle of book 31 and the end of commentary (book 81) we arrive at book 56. Here, as one would expect, the evidence is less clear, because by book 56 Ulpian has already used the great majority of turns of phrase of a non-technical sort which he has the inclination to use. Nevertheless, there are two characteristic expressions which display a bunching from the second half of book 56:

idem erit probandum[100]   *ed.* 31, 44, 44, 56/2, 56/2, 57, 57, 59,
                          60, 68, 71, 71, 73, 75, 76, 76, 77,
                          79, 81.

The other expression which shows bunching from book 56/2 is:

consequens erit dicere[101]   *ed.* 22, 35, 35, 35, 45, 48, 56/2, 57,
                          58, 59, 60, 68, 71, 71, 73, 75, 76,
                          77, 79, 81.

[94] Ch. 2 n. 81.
[95] Ch. 2 n. 13.
[96] Ch. 2 n. 14.
[97] Ch. 2 n. 475.
[98] Ch. 2 n. 217.
[99] Ch. 2 n. 90.
[100] Ch. 2 n. 285.
[101] Ch. 2 n. 296.

Note that the texts from *ad Sabinum* in which this phrase is found are also bunched. They occur in *Sab.* 46, 49, 49 and 50. The Sabinian commentary ends at book 51. This suggests that the end of the Sabinian commentary is closely related to the beginning of the last segment of edictal commentary at book 56/2.

So far, then, we have two segments of edictal commentary, one running from the middle of book 31 to the middle of book 56 and comprising 25 books, and one running from the middle of book 56 to the end and comprising 25½ books. This suggests that the module adopted by Ulpian for his edictal commentary was one of 25 or 25½ books. If, then, we apply this module to the books preceding book 31/2, we shall expect a break in the middle or at the beginning of book 6.

There is in fact a break between books 5 and 6. This break is obvious, even at a first reading, to a scholar with a sense of style, whereas the later ones are not. When I first read Ulpian's *ad edictum* systematically, I marked this break, though I then had no idea that this would fit in with the other breaks which came to light later and were, in themselves, much less obvious.

The striking difference between books 1–5 and the books from 6 on is that the writing in the first five books is relatively constrained. From book 6, on the other hand, Ulpian sounds a confident, even exuberant note. He adopts a more flexible word order, for instance. One example of this is the use of *non* with a future verb, followed by the object, participle or infinitive. This construction is not found in the first five books. Here are some examples from book 6 onwards:

6 *ed.*	*D.* 48.19.32	non erit notatus
6 *ed.*	*D.* 3.2.2. pr.	non dubitabis eum esse notatum
7 *ed.*	*D.* 2.10.1.3	non habebit reus actionem
8 *ed.*	*D.* 3.4.2	non erit dicendum sic haberi
9 *ed.*	*D.* 3.3.40.2	nonne ratum non videbitur habere?
9 *ed.*	*D.* 3.3.40.3	non compelletur ad cautionem
10 *ed.*	*D.* 12.2.16	non compelletur iurare
10 *ed.*	*D.* 3.6.3.3.	non habebit ipse repetitionem
11 *ed.*	*D.* 4.2.9.6	non sine ratione dicetur . . . finiri actionem
11 *ed.*	*D.* 4.4.3.4	non erit restituendus

Contrast these expressions with those to be found in the first five books:

3 *ed.*	*D.* 5.1.2 pr.	non erit eius iurisdictio
3 *ed.*	*D.* 2.2.3.3	mandati actionem non habebis

Here the future verb is followed by a subject noun, or the *non* follows the object. Again, the verbs which express the author's activity in the first five books are limited and conventional. They comprise *accipere debemus*,[102]

[102] *D.* 39.2.4.5 (1 *ed.*), 2.4.10.5 (5 *ed.*), 2.8.2.3 (5 *ed.*).

dicimus,[103] *accipimus*,[104] *putamus*,[105] *solemus dicere*,[106] *accipiemus*,[107] *dabimus*,[108] *videamus*.[109] The use of *accipere* is indeed characteristic of Ulpian,[110] but these verbs remain modest and restrained. Far more outgoing are those to be found from book 6 onwards:

6 ed.	D. 3.1.5.5	deliberabimus
6 ed	D. 3.1.1.10	exsequemur
9 ed.	D. 3.3.33 pr.	subsistimus . . . admittimus . . . vetamus
9 ed.	D. 3.3.33.1	non dubitamus
9 ed.	D. 3.3.39.4	non exigimus
10 ed.	D. 3.5.9.1	spectamus
11 ed.	D. 41.3.6	computamus

The turn of phrase *ut est* (*rescriptum* etc.) is not found in the first five books.[111] It occurs regularly from book 6 onwards:

6 ed.	D. 3.2.2.2	ut est saepissime rescriptum
10 ed.	D. 22.1.37	ut est in bonae fidei iudiciis constitutum
11 ed.	D. 4.4.3.1	ut est et constitutum
11 ed.	D. 4.4.20.1	ut est saepissime rescriptum
11 ed.	D. 13.7.36 pr.	ut est saepissime rescriptum
11 ed.	D. 4.2.16.2	ut est et rescriptum
13 ed.	D. 4.4.19	ut est edicto expressum

The relative orthodoxy of Ulpian's word order in the first five books is shown by the number of sentences ending in the present indicative of *esse* (*sum, est, sunt*, etc.). Thus, one finds a sequence such as the following:

3 ed.	D. 2.1.7 pr.	populare est . . . complexus est . . . ad haec . . . torquendum est.

Three sentence endings out of four in this sequence are in *est*. This is never repeated in later books of the edictal commentary. The statistics for sentences ending in *est* etc. are as follows:

ed. books	Sentences in est etc.	Lines (Pal.)	Sentences in est etc. per 1,000 lines
1–5	50	1024	49
6–31/1	308	10753	29
31/2–56/1	240	8287	29
56/2–81	269	6934	39

[103] D. 39.2.4.8 (1 ed.), 50.1.1.1 (2 ed.).
[104] D. 2.2.1.2 (3 ed.), 2.4.10.2 (5 ed.), 2.4.10.9 (5 ed.).
[105] D. 2.2.1.2 (3 ed.).
[106] D. 2.14.7.5 (4 ed.), 2.14.10.2 (4 ed.).
[107] D. 2.8.2.3 (5 ed.).
[108] D. 2.8.2.3 (5 ed.). [109] D. 2.8.2.5 (5 ed.). [110] Ch. 2 nn. 381 f.
[111] The closest to it is D. 2.13.4.5 (4 ed.: *et hoc est constitutum*).

The tendency to end a sentence in this way falls away sharply from book 6, but returns, to a limited extent, in the last segment of edictal commentary.

A habit of Ulpian which appears from book 6 on but not in the first five books is that of using *diximus* to refer back to what he has written previously.[112] For example:

6 *ed.*	*D.* 3.1.1.7	ut initio huius tituli diximus
6 *ed.*	*D.* 3.1.1.11	sub titulo de in ius vocando plenius diximus
9 *ed.*	*D.* 3.3.17	quae supra diximus
11 *ed.*	*D.* 4.2.7.1	ea quae diximus
11 *ed.*	*D.* 4.2.14.4	secundum quod supra diximus
11 *ed.*	*D.* 4.2.14.10	quatenus autem diximus
11 *ed.*	*D.* 4.2.16 pr.	quod diximus

The break between books 5 and 6 of the edictal commentary is, to my mind, clear beyond doubt. The reason for it may be left aside for the present. Given a break at that point, it looks as if the author, from then on, adopted a module of 25 or 25½ books for the remaining segments of his edictal commentary. The first of these ran from book 6 to the middle of book 31. A word which is found only in this segment is:

$$\text{luxuriosus}^{133} \qquad ed. \text{ 11, 31/1}$$

Why Ulpian should have chosen a module of this strange, irregular length, will emerge later. For the moment it is enough to summarize the results so far reached, putting together the information derived from a study of reference to emperors with that drawn from changes in style.

The first segment of edictal commentary (books 1 to 5) cannot be dated exactly, though it must be earlier than 213, perhaps a good deal earlier. The second segment (books 6 to 31/1) belongs, at least from book 9, to Caracalla's sole reign. Book 10 was composed after, book 22 not long after 19 December 212, and book 22 was written after the *constitutio Antoniniana*, which is itself not earlier than 212. This segment therefore seems to belong to the year 213, and perhaps a few months before and after. It straddles Caracalla A and B. During the course of it Ulpian moves from treating Severus as the senior to giving Caracalla priority over his father. The third segment (book 31/2 to 56/1) also belongs to Caracalla's sole reign, and must therefore be fitted in to all or parts of 214, 215, and 216. The fourth segment (books 56/2 to 81) begins in the sole reign of Caracalla (book 57) but books 61 to 73 were composed under Macrinus. This segment therefore belongs to 217 and perhaps also 218.

Useful in themselves, though only approximate, these results provide the springboard for something more ambitious; a detailed hypothesis about Ulpian's survey of Roman law. Exactly when and how was this composed?

---

[112] There is one reference back in the earlier books: *D.* 2.14.7.18 (4 *ed.*: *et supra rettulimus*). *Rettuli/-imus* returns in three much later texts: *D.* 24.1.7.6 (32/31 *Sab.*: *rettuli*), 24.1.32 pr. (32 *Sab.*: *rettulimus*), 41.1.23.3 (43 *Sab.*: *rettuli*).   [113] *D.* 4.3.11.1 (11 *ed.*), 17.1.12.11 (31 *ed.*).

CHAPTER 6

Ulpian's Five-Year Plan: A Hypothesis

What is the relation between the edictal commentary and Ulpian's *ad Sabinum* in fifty-one books? That these two major works were, broadly speaking, written at the same period, is clear from the many references to Caracalla as reigning emperor, and to Severus, in *ad Sabinum*.[1]

6 *Sab.*	D. 28.6.2.4	quae sententia rescripto imperatoris nostri ad Virium Lupum Britanniae praesidem comprobata est
6 *Sab.*	D. 29.2.6.3.	ut divus Pius et imperator noster rescripserunt
6 *Sab.*	D. 24.1.23	Papinianus recte putabat orationem divi Severi . . .
12 *Sab.*	D. 38.16.1.1	ut est a divis Marco et Vero et imperatore nostro Antonino Augusto rescriptum
12 *Sab.*	D. 38.17.1.3	secundum rescriptum imperatoris nostri et divi patris eius ad Ovinium Tertullum (= *CJ* 8.50.1, Impp. Severus et Antoninus undated)
13 *Sab.*	D. 38.17.2.2	idque et Iulianus scripsit et constitutum est ab imperatore nostro
13 *Sab.*	D. 38.17.2.47	et invenimus rescriptum ab imperatore nostro Antonino Augusto et divo patre eius (12 April 203)
19 *Sab.*	D. 49.14.25	est et decretum ab imperatore Severo et constitutum
21 *Sab.*	D. 30.37 pr.	quae sententia rescripto imperatoris nostri et divi Severi iuvatur
21 *Sab.*	D. 30.41.3	et ita imperator noster et divus Severus rescripserunt
21 *Sab.*	D. 30.41.5	Papinianus refert . . . imperatorem nostrum et divum Severum constituisse
25 *Sab.*	D. 33.8.6.4.	sed huic sententiae adversatur rescriptum imperatoris nostri et patris eius
25 *Sab.*	D. 33.8.8.7	imperator igitur noster cum patre rescripsit

---

[1] Fitting (1908) 111–12, who omits three of these texts; Krueger (1912) 243.

31 *Sab.*	*D.* 23.3.9.3	ut divus Marcus et imperator noster cum patre rescripserunt
32 *Sab.*	*D.* 24.1.3 pr.	haec ratio et oratione imperatoris nostri Antonini Augusti electa est
32 *Sab.*	*D.* 24.1.3.1	divus temen Severus . . . contra statuit
32 *Sab.*	*D.* 24.1.7 pr.	idque imperator noster cum patre rescripsit
32 *Sab.*	*D.* 24.1.7.5	remedium monstravit imperator noster cum divo patre suo rescripto
32 *Sab.*	*D.* 24.1.7.6	imperator noster cum patre suo rescripsit
33 *Sab.*	*D.* 24.1.32 pr.	imperator noster Antoninus Augustus ante excessum divi Severi patris sui oratione in senatu habita auctor fuit
33 *Sab.*	*D.* 24.1.32.1	oratio autem imperatoris nostri
33 *Sab.*	*D.* 24.1.32.19	secundum rescriptum imperatoris nostri cum patre
35 *Sab.*	*D.* 24.3.2.2	et est ab imperatore Antonino rescriptum
37 *Sab.*	*D.* 26.1.3.1	et ita imperator Antoninus Augustus rescripsit
40 *Sab.*	*D.* 26.8.5.3.	et ita est rescriptum a divo Severo et Antonino
43 *Sab.*	*D.* 12.6.23.1	hoc enim imperator Antoninus cum patre suo rescripsit
43 *Sab.*	*D.* 46.3.5.2	Imperator Antoninus cum divo patre suo rescripsit . . . Imperator Antoninus cum divo patre suo rescripsit

The first text, from 6 *Sab.*, refers to an *imperator noster*, who is not identified. The *imperator noster* of book 12 must be Caracalla, since his father, the co-author of the rescript cited, is *divus*. Presumably the *imperator noster* of book 6 is also Caracalla. Otherwise we should have to suppose that the interval between the composition of books 6 and 12 was at least fourteen years, the previous sole emperor, Severus, having ceased to be so in AD 198. In book 43 Caracalla is still emperor, and hence books 6 to 43 *ad Sabinum* fall into his sole rule. But which part of it do they belong to?

Between 12 *Sab.* and 43 *Sab.* there are fifteen texts in which, when a joint constitution is cited, Caracalla is mentioned before Severus. The only example to the contrary comes from book 40. It is safe to conclude that books 12 to 43 *ad Sabinum* fall into the period Caracalla B, which ran from books 22 to 57 on the edict.[2] The references to Severus do not add anything useful to this. He is once called *imperator*, in book 19,[3] otherwise always *divus*, whether mentioned on his own, as in two texts, or together with his son.[4] In the upshot the books before book 6 *might* be earlier than 212, and

---

[2] Mommsen (1905) II 163.

[3] *D.* 49.14.25 (19 *Sab.*).

[4] Alone: *D.* 24.1.23 (6 *Sab.*), 24.1.3.1 (32 *Sab.*). Together: *D.* 38.17.1.3 (12 *Sab.*), 38.17.2.47 (12 *Sab.*), 30.37 pr. (21 *Sab.*), 30.41.3 (21 *Sab.*), 30.41.5 (21 *Sab.*), 33.8.6.4 (25 *Sab.*), 33.8.8.7 (25 *Sab.*),

[*See opposite page for n. 4 cont.*]

the books after book 43 *might* belong in the reign of Macrinus or later. But there is no positive evidence of this. At least a very substantial part of *ad Sabinum* was composed in Caracalla B, and was thus roughly contemporaneous with a large part of the edictal commentary.

A correct explanation of the relation between the edictal and Sabinian commentaries must take account of two other bits of evidence. In *Sab.* 33 Ulpian, dealing with a donation made to a fiancée when the subsequent marriage is invalid, for instance because the woman is under age, endorses his own opinion, together with that of Labeo and Papinian, to the effect that a preceding engagement, if there has been one, must be deemed to continue despite the invalid marriage:[5]

> sed est verius, quod Labeoni videtur et a nobis et a Papiniano libro decimo quaestionum probatum est . . .

The context makes it clear that Ulpian is referring to his own opinion as expressed in a legal treatise, such as Papinian's *quaestiones*. The text which fits this best comes from book 35 of Ulpian's edictal commentary:[6]

> et semper Labeonis sententiam probavi existimantis, si quidem praecesserint sponsalia, durare ea, quamvis in domo loco nuptae esse coeperit

The relation between the two works was therefore probably such that in 33 *Sab.* Ulpian could refer to 35 *ed.*, which must in that case have been composed earlier. The other piece of evidence is more important. The Sabinian commentary stops, incomplete, at fifty-one books. It breaks off at the point which Lenel designates chapter 20[7] and leaves the last ten chapters, in Lenel's notation, unfinished. These last ten chapters were dealt with by Paul in books 13 to 16 *ad Sabinum*,[8] and by Pomponius at books 29 to 36.[9] They include the acquisition of ownership, its vindication, possession, usucapion, donations, servitudes, interdicts, and *postliminium*. Not all these topics are dealt with by Ulpian in his edictal commentary, though the latter is, along its own lines, complete. For example, in regard to donations, the edictal work discusses only the defence to a claim for a donation based on the *lex Cincia*.[10] These missing topics should, in the interest of completeness, have been dealt with somewhere, especially as in general Ulpian aims to give a synoptic view of the whole area he is dealing with. Not only that, but he has no aversion to duplicating a topic. Thus, he

23.3.9.3 (31 *Sab.*), 24.1.7 pr. (32 *Sab.*), 24.1.32 pr. (33 *Sab.*), 24.1.32.19 (33 *Sab.*), 26.8.5.3 (40 *Sab.*), 12.6.23.1 (43 *Sab.*), 46.3.5.2 (43 *Sab.*) bis.
[5] D. 24.1.32.27 (33 *Sab.*); Krueger (1912) 245.
[6] D. 23.1.9 (35 *ed.*).
[7] *Pal.* 2. 1257–60; Krueger (1912) 244.
[8] *Pal.* 1.1286–93.
[9] *Pal.* 2.137–48.
[10] D. 44.4.7 (76 *ed.*).

writes about theft twice, once in books 37 and 38 *ad edictum*[11] and again at
40 to 42 *ad Sabinum*.[12] Why should he not have planned to make his
commentary *ad Sabinum* as comprehensive as those of Paul and
Pomponius? Why does he break off at book 51?

The reason becomes plain when we consider that for the edictal
commentary Ulpian adopted a module of 25 or 25½ books. Fifty-one
books amounts to two modules of this sort, appropriate, in the author's
mind, to a large-scale opus. *Ad Sabinum* stopped at book 51 because Ulpian
had then completed two segments of his work on it. Perhaps he planned a
third. This would have extended to a further 25 or 25½ books. We cannot
be sure. At any rate, the extra books were not written.

In the light of this explanation, the relation between the Sabinian and
edictal commentaries is clarified. The Sabinian modules were intercalated
between the edictal modules. Between segments of edictal commentary
Ulpian composed a segment of Sabinian commentary. It is this that
accounts for the changes in style in the edictal work which we noticed in
the middle of books 31 and 56. Between the composition of the first and
last halves of these books a substantial time elapsed while the author turned
his attention to another project. When he returned to the praetor's edict his
habits of expression had to some extent changed; he had come to use some
words more, others less.

If we use M 1, M 2, etc. for the different modules of 25 or 25½ books, we
can express the method of composition as follows:

M 1	6−31/1 *ed.*
M 2	1−26/1 *Sab.*
M 3	31/2−56/1 *ed.*
M 4	26/2−51 *Sab.*
M 5	56/2−81 *ed.*

In this way the points which were puzzling are cleared up. The changes in
style in the edictal commentary are explained. The impression that the two
major works were written in parallel is shown to be a half-truth. We see
how it was possible for Ulpian in 33 *Sab.* to refer to what he had written
previously in 35 *ed.*[13] Though the book number is lower, that part of the
Sabinian work comes later than the part of *ad edictum* with the higher
number of books.

So far so good. To take the matter further it is necessary to introduce the
hypothesis which gives its name to this chapter. Suppose that the 25- or
25½-book modules are interpreted as annual stints. Suppose that Ulpian's

---

[11] *Pal.* 2.675−83.

[12] *Pal.* 2.1160−70.

[13] Above, nn. 5, 6. It is not necessary to suppose with Krueger (1912) 245 that the reference was
inserted in the second edition of *Sab.*

plan required him to compose that number of books of major commentary a year. In that case the five modules would occupy five years: *quinquennium Ulpiani*.

I do not think the suggestion is particularly startling. We know that the bulk of both great works belongs to Caracalla's sole rule, which ran from the last days of 211 to April 217. The end of the edictal commentary, or much of it, falls in the reign of Macrinus in 217–18.[14] All I suggest is that the actual limits in time were slightly narrower and the operation more methodical than these dates might suggest. The substance of the work, all but the first five books *ad edictum*, was compressed into the years 213 to 217. On this hypothesis, the time schedule was as follows:

213	6–31/1 *ed.*
214	1–26/1 *Sab.*
215	31/2–56/1 *ed.*
216	26/2–51 *Sab.*
217	56/2–81 *ed.*

Thus, for module 1, read 213; for module 2, 214, etc. The first module cannot be earlier than 213, if it was composed in a single year, because it has texts which refer to the rescript of 19 December 212[15] and to the *constitutio Antoniniana*, which is not earlier than 212.[16] But neither can the first module be later than 213. This is because the fifth module begins with Caracalla as sole emperor, but continues in the reign of Macrinus,[17] and so must belong to 217, the year in which Macrinus succeeded. The first module therefore belongs to 213, and there is only one possible chronology.

The medium-scale works

Can the hypothesis of a module of literary composition, representing a year's task, be applied to those of Ulpian's works which were composed in ten books or a multiple of ten? If Ulpian composed his major commentaries over a five-year period in slices of 25 or 25½ books, did he also compose a series of lesser but still substantial treatises in annual stints of ten books? Do we know of works which divide neatly into five groups of ten books? We do. There are four relevant works, *de officio proconsulis*, *disputationes*, *de omnibus tribunalibus*, and *ad legem Iuliam et Papiam*. The first three are in ten books, the last in twenty. There are therefore fifty books in all, or five modules, as the hypothesis requires. Will these five modules fit the years 213–17? Could the medium and large scale works have been written in parallel?

---

[14] Ch. 5 p. 142.
[15] *D.* 3.6.1.3 (10 *ed.*), 12.5.2.2 (26 *ed.*).
[16] *D.* 1.5.17 (22 *ed.*).
[17] Ch. 5 p. 142.

The first work to consider is *de officio proconsulis*.[18] It contains no less than 22 references to Caracalla, to his father or to both together:

1 *off. proc.*	*D.* 1.16.4. pr.	ut imperator noster cum patre rescripsit
1 *off. proc.*	*D.* 1.16.4.5	ut imperator noster Antoninus Augustus rescripsit . . . necessitatem impositam
1 *off. proc.*	*D.* 1.16.6.3	quam rem divus Severus et imperator Antoninus elegantissime epistula sunt moderati
2 *off. proc.*	*FV* 119	Imperatores Augusti Iulio Iul . . .
3 *off. proc.*	*D.* 50.2.3.1	Imperator enim Antoninus edicto proposito statuit (= *CJ* 10.61.1, 11 July 212)
3 *off. proc.*	*D.* 50.2.3.3	divi Severus et Antoninus permiserunt
4 *off. proc.*	*D.* 50.4.6.2	ita enim imperator noster cum divo patre suo rescripsit
4 *off. proc.*	*D.* 27.1.6.6	imperator noster cum patre rescripsit
4 *off. proc.*	*D.* 50.7.7	imperator noster cum patre Claudio Callisto rescripsit
5 *off. proc.*	*D.* 50.12.6.1	imperator noster Antoninus rescripsit
5 *off. proc.*	*D.* 50.12.6.2	et ita rescripto imperatoris nostri et divi patris eius continetur
5 *off. proc.*	*D.* 50.12.6.3	rescriptis imperatoris nostri et divi patris eius continetur
8 *off. proc.*	*D.* 48.18.1.10	imperator noster cum divo patre suo rescripsit
8 *off. proc.*	*D.* 48.18.1.15	et ita imperator noster cum divo patre suo rescripsit
8 *off. proc.*	*D.* 48.18.1.16	item Severus Spicio Antigono ita rescripsit
8 *off. proc.*	*D.* 48.18.1.17	Divus Severus rescripsit
8 *off. proc.*	*D.* 48.18.1.18	imperator noster cum divo patre suo id non admiserunt
8 *off. proc.*	*D.* 47.9.12 pr.	idque imperator Antoninus cum divo patre suo rescripsit
9 *off. proc.*	*Coll.* 14.3.3	imperator Antoninus constituit . . . constitutione imperatoris Antonini
9 *off. proc.*	*D.* 48.19.8.5	epistula divi Severi ad Fabium Cilonem exprimitur

[18] *Pal.* 2.966−91; Schulz (1946) 139, 243−6, (1961); *RE* 5.1452.

9 *off. proc.*	*D.* 48.19.8.12	imperator Antoninus rectissime rescripsit
9 *off. proc.*	*D.* 48.22.6.1	hoc enim epistula divi Severi ad Fabium Cilonem expressum est
10 *off. proc.*	*D.* 48.22.7.10	sed imperator noster cum divo patre suo huic rei providerunt

Caracalla is mentioned with his father in both the first and last books of this treatise. There are thirteen such allusions in all. In the first three books two texts out of three place Severus before Antoninus, but in the remaining books Caracalla consistently precedes his father. Is the inference that the first three books belong to the Caracalla A period, and the last seven to Caracalla B? If so, *de officio proconsulis* must belong to the same year as books 6–31/1 *ad edictum*, viz. 213. For in that segment of the edictal commentary Caracalla A runs to book 19, and Caracalla B starts from book 22.

But do the citations in the first three books point to Caracalla A? Of the two texts in which Severus precedes Antoninus, the first presents no problem. It comes from book 1[19] and runs *divus Severus et imperator Antoninus . . . sunt moderati.* Severus is dead, Caracalla is sole ruler, but Severus' seniority has not yet been displaced. The other text in which Severus is senior, from book 3,[20] does present a problem. It runs *divi Severus et Antoninus . . . permiserunt.* This implies that Caracalla and Severus are both dead. But in the later books Caracalla is consistently *imperator noster*[21] and so alive. Mommsen is surely right in thinking that *divi* is here a gloss.[22] Originally the text ran *Severus et Antoninus permiserunt.* Thinking this too bald, the copyist, at a time when Caracalla was in fact dead and deified, inserted *divi.* The original reference is indeed a little bleak. But though Ulpian does not often refer to emperors without some title (*imperator, divus, noster*) he occasionally does so.[23] At any rate, the order in which the emperors appear is not open to debate. When book 3 was composed, Ulpian gave Severus precedence. These two texts, then, show Severus as senior, and indicate that books 1 and 3 fall in Caracalla A. But what of the other text from book 1?[24]

---

[19] *D.* 1.16.6.3 (1 *off. proc.*).

[20] *D.* 50.2.3.3 (3 *off. proc.*).

[21] *D.* 50.4.6.2 (4 *off. proc.*), 27.1.6.6 (4 *off. proc.*), 50.7.7 (4 *off. proc.*), 50.12.6.1 (5 *off. proc.*), 50.12.6.2 (5 *off. proc.*), 50.12.6.3 (5 *off. proc.*), 48.18.1.10 (8 *off. proc.*), 48.18.1.15 (8 *off. proc.*), 48.18.1.16 (8 *off. proc.*), 48.18.1.18 (8 *off. proc.*), 48.22.7.10 (10 *off. proc.*).

[22] Mommsen (1905) II 169–70.

[23] *D.* 4.4.3.4 (11 *ed.*), 1.17.1 (15 *ed.*), 50.15.1.1 (1 *cens.*), 16.1.2 pr. (29 *ed.*), 49.14.16 (18 *leg. Iul. Pap.*); *Coll.* 1.6.1 (7 *off. proc.*); *Coll.* 8.3 (8 *off. proc.*); *FV* 235 (1 *off. praet. tut.*); *D.* 34.1.14.1 (2 *fid.*), 40.12.27.1 (2 *off. cons.*), 42.4.7.16 (59 *ed.*), 47.14.1.3 (8 *off. proc.*), none of which relates to Severus or Caracalla.

[24] *D.* 1.16.4 pr. (1 *off. proc.*).

Observare autem proconsulem oportet, ne in hospitiis oneret provinciam, ut imperator noster cum patre Aufidio Severo rescripsit.

Ulpian does not usually end a sentence with a citation of authority in the form *ut . . . rescripsit*. Normally, in order to end on a stronger note, he employs a phrase such as *et ita rescripsit*[25], *idque rescripsit*[26] etc., or he gives the substance of the rescript in the accusative and infinitive after *rescripsit*. This is what he has done in the second of the listed texts from *off. proc.*[27] A final clause with *ut . . . rescripsit, ut . . . videtur* or the like is a sign that we have to do with an after thought (or gloss or interpolation). There is an example in 6 *Sab.*, where a text ends with the clause *ut Marciano videtur*.[28] It is fairly clear that this cannot have been part of Ulpian's original text. Book 6 *Sab.*[29] is known to have been written under Caracalla. Marcianus is not thought to have published any work until after Caracalla's death and deification.[30] Tribonian mentions that there was a second edition of Ulpian's *ad Sabinum*.[31] This may have been later than AD 217. I think it can be assumed that the phrase *ut Marciano videtur* was put in either as part of the revision for the second edition, or on some later occasion.

The same could well be true of the phrase *ut imperator noster cum patre Aufidio Severo rescripsit* in the text we are considering.[32] It is not necessary to postulate a second edition of *off. proc.*, though of course there is nothing to rule it out. Ulpian may simply have gone through the text of the whole work when he had completed it. The completion took place in Caracalla B. If the rescript to Aufidius was issued after the draft of book 1 but before the completion of the whole work, it would have been natural to add a mention of it. In doing so the appropriate form of citation was now that in which Caracalla preceded his father. So explained, the citation does not stand in the way of the hypothesis that the first three books on the proconsul were composed in Caracalla A, the last seven in Caracalla B, during which the text as a whole was read through and revised.

It seems reasonable, therefore, to conclude that, like books 6–31/1 *ad edictum*, the treatise *de officio proconsulis* belongs to the period straddling Caracalla A and B. If, among Ulpian's medium-range works, it represents a year's stint, it must be assigned, like 6–31/1 ed., to the year 213.

The next work to be considered is the *disputationes*.[33] Here the

[25] e.g. D. 48.18.1.15 (8 *off. proc.*).
[26] D. 47.9.12 pr. (8 *off. proc.*).
[27] D. 1.16.4.5 (1 *off. proc.*).
[28] D. 28.1.5 (6 *Sab.*).
[29] Above, pp. 149–50.
[30] *Pal.* 1.639[1]; Kunkel (1967) 258.
[31] C. Cordi (16 Nov. 534) 3.
[32] The text reads perfectly well without the phrase *ut . . . rescripsit*.
[33] *Pal.* 2.387–421; Schulz (1946) 240, (1961) 305–7; *RE* 5.1446; Fitting (1908) 118 (omitting a text); Krueger (1912) 247 [196]; Solazzi (1946) 3. Genuineness denied by Beseler (1910) I 313; *Contra RE* 9 A1 (1961) 568 (Mayer-Maly).

indications drawn from citations of emperors, which run from book 3 to book 9, point to the Caracalla B period:

3 *disp.*	*D.* 13.7.26 pr.	imperator noster cum patre saepissime rescripsit
4 *disp.*	*D.* 28.3.12 pr.	et divus Hadrianus et imperator noster rescripserunt
4 *disp.*	*D.* 30.74	licet imperator noster cum patre rescripserit
6 *disp.*	*D.* 3.5.43	secundum divi Severi constitutionem
6 *disp.*	*D.* 40.5.46.3	a divo Severo rescriptum est
8 *disp.*	*D.* 41.1.5.1	est enim constitutum ab imperatore nostro et divo patre eius
8 *disp.*	*D.* 48.5.2.6	nam Claudius Gorgus damnatus est a divo Severo
8 *disp.*	*D.* 49.14.29.2	imperator noster cum patre rescripsit

The work belongs to Caracalla B, except possibly for the first two and last two books, which might belong to Caracalla A and Macrinus respectively. Since, however, there are no positive indications to this effect, the whole work should provisionally be assigned to Caracalla B. The year might be 214, 215, or 216.

De omnibus tribunalibus,[34] also in ten books, presents a similar picture. There are four citations of Caracalla and his father

1 *omn. trib.*	*D.* 26.10.7.2	ex epistula imperatoris nostri et divi Severi
8 *omn. trib.*	*D.* 50.13.1.10	ita enim rescripto imperatoris nostri et patris eius continetur
8 *omn. trib.*	*D.* 50.13.1.12	ita est rescriptum ab imperatore nostro et divo patre eius
8 *omn. trib.*	*D.* 50.13.1.13	divus Severus . . . prohibuit

Books 1 to 8 therefore fall into the Caracalla B period. In the absence of contrary indications, it seems best provisionally to assume that the last two books also belong to this period. In that case, consistently with the modular hypothesis, *de omnibus tribunalibus* may have been composed in 214, 215, or 216.

The references from *ad legem Iuliam et Papiam*,[35] in twenty books, are more helpful. There are just five:

3 *leg Iul. Pap.*	*D.* 23.2.45 pr.	ut rescripto imperatoris nostri et divi patris eius continetur

[34] *Pal.* 2. 992–1001; Schulz (1946) 256, (1961) 329; *RE* 5.1454; Fitting (1908) 119; Krueger (1912) 246[185]; Pernice (1893) 135; Wlaassak (1919) 69, showing that *omn. trib.* complements the *officia*; Kubler (1925) 280.

[35] *Pal.* 2.939–50; Schulz (1946) 188, (1961) 231; *RE* 5.1445; Fitting (1908) 117–18; Krueger (1912) 246[185]; Ferrini (1929a) II 236.

3 *leg Iul. Pap.*	D. 24.2.11.2	imperator noster cum divo patre suo rescripsit
4 *leg. Iul. Pap.*	D. 49.15.9	post rescriptum imperatoris Antonini et divi patris eius
18 *leg. Iul. Pap.*	D. 31.61.1	sed post rescriptum Severi
19 *leg. Iul. Pap.*	D. 4.4.2	divus Severus ait

Since ten books is the module for medium-scale works, the first ten books *ad legem Iuliam et Papiam* must be considered separately from the last ten. So far as the first ten are concerned, the evidence, such as it is, points once again to Caracalla B and the years 214, 215, or 216. It is inconclusive, since it comes from books 3 and 4 alone. If, however, we assume that the first two and last five books of this module belong to the same period, then the first ten books *ad legem Iuliam et Papiam* must, again, have been composed in those years. In that case, the medium-scale works of these three years were *disputationes, de omnibus tribunalibus* and these early books *ad legem Iuliam et Papiam*. We do not, however, know what year to assign to each of them.

This provisional conclusion fits in with the fact that no references pointing to the reign of Caracalla are found in the last ten books *ad legem Iuliam et Papiam*. These last ten books might, therefore, belong to 217, in which Caracalla was emperor for only the first three months. A positive indication that this is correct, albeit a slight one, is the fact that the text in 18 *leg. Iul. Pap.*[36] cites Severus without title. This mode of citation may be parallel to that which we struck in books 61, 64, and 71 *ed.*,[37] and which were interpreted as belonging to the reign of Macrinus,[38] and to the year 217.

What emerges is that, if the hypothesis that Ulpian composed the middle-range treatises in the five year period 213−17 is adopted, 213 must be the year of *off. proc.* and 217 that of books 11−20 *leg. Iul. Pap.* In that case it would be natural, though by no means compelling, to assign the first ten books *leg. Iul. Pap.* to 216, on the assumption that the two halves of it were completed in successive years. That would leave it open whether *disp.* or *omn. trib.* was composed in 214. The detailed placings cannot be decided without further evidence, which will be adduced in the next chapter. At this stage, the following allocation seems reasonable:

213	6−31/1 *ed.*, 1−10 *off. proc.*	Caracalla A and B
214	1−26/1 *Sab.*, 1−10 *disp.* or *omn. trib.*	Caracalla B
215	31/2−56/1 *ed.*, 1−10 *disp.* or *omn. trib.*	Caracalla B
216	26/2−51 *Sab.*, 1−10 *leg. Iul. Pap.*	Caracalla B
217	56/2−81 *ed.*, 11−20 *leg. Iul. Pap.*	Caracalla B and Macrinus

---

[36] D. 31.61.1 (18 *leg. Iul. Pap.*).
[37] D. 26. 5.18 (61 *ed.*), 42.6.1.3 (64 *ed.*), 43, 30.1.3 (71 *ed.*).
[38] Ch. 5 p. 142.

The minor works: Ulpian's calendar

Since our hypothesis has so far been attended with success, at least in the sense that it yields plausible results both for the major and medium-scale treatises, it is worth asking whether Ulpian's minor works can be fitted in the same chronological scheme. The urge to do this stems partly from the fact that, at first glance, some of the minor works such as *de censibus*, seem, to judge from references to the emperors, to belong to Caracalla A, a larger number, like *de fideicommissis*, to Caracalla B, and one or two, like *de adulteriis*, perhaps to Macrinus. At first sight, therefore, the pattern looks rather similar to that for the major and middle-range series of works. But could Ulpian have written these works at the same time as the others? Did he have enough time?

The number of works attributed to Ulpian which are clearly genuine, or at least not shown to be spurious, amounts, apart from the major and medium-scale treatises, to forty or forty-one. These comprise:

> de censibus 6
> de fideicommissis 6
> ad legem Iuliam de adulteriis 5
> de appellationibus 4
> ad legem Aeliam Sentiam 4
> de officio consulis 3
> ad edictum aedilium curulium 2
> institutionum 2
> de officio quaestoris 2 (or 1)
> de officio consularium 1
> de officio curatoris rei publicae 1
> de officio praefecti urbi 1
> de officio praefecti vigilum 1
> de officio praetoris tutelaris 1
> de sponsalibus 1
> ad orationem divi Antonini et Commodi 1

We cannot count in *de excusationibus 1*. This appears to have been written before the death of Severus,[39] and so is outside the quinquennium. The first five books of edictal commentary have also to be excluded, since they too must have been composed before 213−17.[40]

If forty or forty-one books are distributed over five years, they average eight or just over eight per year, supposing, in accordance with the modular hypothesis, the rate of work to have been constant or nearly so. In fact a module of $8\frac{1}{2}$ books a year would fit pretty well the number of books to be assigned. At the same time it dovetails with the $25\frac{1}{2}$ book module for major commentaries. To explain how this is so we must glance at the Roman calendar.

---

[39] *Pal.* 2.899¹; Mommsen (1908) II 169⁵⁵; Schulz (1946) 249−50, (1961) 318−20 argues that *excus.* is a post-classical compilation. At any rate, it does not count here.   [40] Above pp. 146, 153.

The official and legal year, including from 153 BC the consular year, began on 1 January.[41] The traditional Roman year, however, originally ran from 1 March, as is shown by the names of the months, such as September, October and, in the republic, Quintilis and Sextilis (=July and August). The gap between the two new years, from 1 January to 1 March, amounts to $8\frac{1}{2}$ weeks. At a rate of composition of a book a week, therefore, this period could notionally be assigned to the minor works. Three times $8\frac{1}{2}$ weeks is $25\frac{1}{2}$ weeks. Supposing, then, that the major commentaries stand to the minor works in the ratio of 3 to 1, they should be assigned three times as long a part of the year. Beginning on 1 March, $25\frac{1}{2}$ weeks takes us to 25 August. Let us assume that the composition of major commentaries is notionally assigned to this portion of the year. The end date is not arbitrary. The time of harvest was a judicial holiday. As the emperor Marcus prescribed, and Ulpian notes,[42] those engaged in agriculture at this time (*occupati circa rem rusticam*) should not be compelled to attend court unless the matter is really urgent. Hence in the harvest period, *tempus messium vindemiarumque*, comprising both grain and grapes, normal activities were interrupted. Landowners went to their estates to collect their rents and fix them for the next year.[43] A landowner taking a holiday from work would plausibly make it fit this practice. I take the holiday period to have run, in Ulpian's plan, for an eight-week period between 26 August and 21 October.[44] Then follows a ten-week period, to the end of the official Roman year, which, in the scheme suggested, is devoted to medium-scale works, again at the rate of a book a week. According to this suggestion, then, Ulpian's calendar in 213–17 was as follows:

1 January to 28 February	$8\frac{1}{2}$ weeks	minor works
1 March to 25 August	$25\frac{1}{2}$ weeks	major commentaries
26 August to 21 October	8 weeks	harvest holiday
22 October to 31 December	10 weeks	medium-scale works

The yearly total of 44 books would take 44 weeks to compose, on the assumption that, apart from the holiday period, Ulpian averaged one book a week. Over the five-year period a synopsis of Roman law in 220 books was planned. Of these 217 or 218 can plausibly be identified. Was the undertaking impossible? It required a methodical man, secretarial help, a good library, and a ready pile of notes on various topics. Why should not Ulpian have had all these? He needed to work hard, of course. The task

---

[41] *RE* 9.1.609–10.

[42] *D.* 2.12.1 pr. (4 *omn. trib.*).

[43] *D.* 7.8.10.4, 12 pr. (Ulp. 17 *Sab.*, Gai. 2 *rer. cott.*).

[44] The suggested period is more suitable to the vintage of grapes than to the harvest of cereals. See C. D. Smith (1979) 24, which gives harvest periods of June–July and mid-September–mid-October respectively for a Sicilian village in 1929; cf. D. Sperber (1974). Presumably Ulpian's practice was related to his own interests as a landowner, whatever these may have been.

called for the sort of assiduity which in our own day Max Kaser displays. In the ancient world distractions were fewer. If anyone sceptically argues that 44 books a year is too much, how does he explain the incontestable facts? A large part of Ulpian's 217 or 218 books were *certainly* composed under Caracalla, in a reign of six years. We know that Ulpian was prolific. What I am suggesting is that he was also, like many Romans, methodical and pertinacious.

The scheme outlined is meant to be taken with two qualifications, one minor, the other important. The minor point concerns the application of the module to the year 215. The suggested division between $25\frac{1}{2}$ books of major commentary and $8\frac{1}{2}$ books devoted to minor works applies to 213, 214, 216 and 217. In 215, however, the number of books of edictal commentary was 25 instead of $25\frac{1}{2}$. Hence, to make up the lost half book, 9 books of minor works were needed. With these 9 books the total of minor works for the 5 years 213–17 comes to 43. To fill these slots we find only 40 or 41 books available. Two or three books have escaped detection. Perhaps they were not available to Justinian's commissioners. They may have gone missing in the intervening centuries. It would be no surprise if this had been the fate, for example, of some monographs on obsolete legislation. In any event, the discrepancy is not such as to upset the hypothesis, or even cause serious qualms.

The second qualification is more significant. It is not really suggested that the order of composition each year was (i) minor works in January and February (ii) major commentaries from March to August and (iii) middle-range works from the end of October to the end of December. The purpose of the schedule was to fix the list of works to be completed in a given year at an average rate of composition of a book a week. In practice, however, Ulpian probably followed the schedule only approximately. He composed the minor, major and middle-range treatises to some extent concurrently. We have already met an example of this. In 213 the period Caracalla A runs, in the edictal commentary, from book 6 to book 19, and Caracalla B begins at book 22.[45] In *de officio proconsulis* Caracalla A runs from book 1 to book 3 and Caracalla B begins at book 4.[46] So, during the period in which Ulpian composed fourteen (or possibly sixteen) books *ad edictum*, he also concurrently composed three books *de officio proconsulis*. Strictly according to schedule, he should have finished all $25\frac{1}{2}$ books *ad edictum* before beginning the treatise on the provincial governor. The latter should, indeed, only have been started after the holiday period. But Ulpian was not so rigid. While writing mainly on the praetor's edict he took an occasional week off to switch to the proconsul. This relieved the tedium

---

[45] Ch. 5 pp. 132–141.
[46] Above, pp. 154–6.

which a continuous $25\frac{1}{2}$ weeks on the same project would have inflicted. Breaks were needed if the programme was to continue, week in and week out, for five years.

The schedule set out is designed, then, to show how, at the beginning of each year, the literary tasks for the year were planned. Execution followed approximately, but not exactly, the lines laid down. No doubt the minor works came mainly near the beginning of the year's programme, and the medium ones nearer the end. But we cannot point to a given week and say 'that is when book 22 on the edict was written'. What we can hope to discover is, in broad terms, what was composed in a given year, and approximately at what season.

In the next chapter I go on to consider the detailed assignment of the minor works to their respective years.

CHAPTER 7

Details of Ulpian's Suggested Programme

The minor works can be fitted with reasonable plausibility into the scheme set out in the last two chapters, but often only approximately. It will be convenient to deal in turn with the works which seem to belong to 213– 14, 215, and 216–17. They will be called early, middle and late works.

I. THE EARLY WORKS

For the early works the initial assumption is that 6–31/1 *ed.* together with 1–10 *off. proc.* were composed in 213, and that 1–26/1 *Sab.* and ten books either of *disputationes* or *de omnibus tribunalibus* were written in 214. However, this starting-point is provisional, and it may be as well to begin by strengthening it. A number of expressions occur exclusively in 6–31/1 *ed.* and *off. proc.* This suggests that they were composed about the same time. Thus, there are four texts in Ulpian with *destricte* ('indiscriminately'):

8 *ed.*	D. 3.3.13	sed haec neque passim admittenda sunt neque destricte deneganda
11 *ed.*	D. 4.4.7.8	et destricte probandum est
13 *ed.*	D. 4.8.15	Licet autem praetor destricte edicat
8 *off. proc.*	D. 48.18.1.26	hoc cavetur, ut neque destricte non habeatur, neque . . .

Discutere, in the sense of *diiudicare*, 'investigate or decide as a judge', is found in three texts:

13 *ed.*	D. 4.8.13.2	an consilio suo et auctoritate discuti litem paterentur
13 *ed.*	D. 4.8.25.1	et ideo cetera quoque discutere . . . et sententiam ferre debebit
2 *off. proc.*	D. 48.2.6	Levia crimina audire et discutere de plano proconsulem oportet

Commendatio, 'recommendation', comes twice:

11 *ed.*	D. 4.1.1	Utilitas huius tituli non eget commendatione

1 *off. proc.*   D. 1.16.4.3   edictum debet mittere continens com-
                                      mendationem aliquam sui

The same is true of *improbitas*, 'want of scruple':

14 *ed.*   D. 4.9.3.1   reprimendae improbitatis hoc genus
                                     hominum
2 *off. proc.*   D. 1.16.9.4   ne forte, dum improbitati ceditur,
                                     mediocres . . .

Periculosus, 'dangerous' in a legal, not a physical sense, is found in a quartet
of texts:

1 *ed.*   D. 39.2.1   Cum . . . periculosa   dilatio   praetori
                                     videtur
6 *ed.*   D. 3.1.1.3   qui   exaudire   non
                                     poterat . . . quod . . . ipsi erat pericu-
                                     losum futurum
26 *ed.*   D. 5.1.61 pr.   sed Celsus ait periculose esse . . . hoc
                                     metiri
8 *off. proc.*   D. 48.18.1.23   etenim res [quaestio] est fragilis et peri-
                                     culosa et quae veritatem fallat

These parallels tend to confirm that, if 6– 31/1 ed. was composed in 213,
so was *de officio proconsulis*. Assuming that this is the case, what other works
belong to this year? One sign of such a work will be that it was wholly or
partly composed in Caracalla A (before about the middle of 213). If, in a
joint citation, Severus precedes Antoninus, this is some evidence that the
work from which it comes belongs to 213.[1] If, later in the same work,
Caracalla precedes Severus, the evidence is strengthened. On the other
hand, a text in which Severus precedes Caracalla, and Caracalla is given no
title, may be from 217.[2] Again, such a text may simply be one of the rare
exceptions to the general practice in the Caracalla B period.[3] Additional
clues are required, and these will often consist in affinities, such as those set
out above, showing a relation between two or more works such that
certain expressions are exclusively or predominantly found only in them
and not in other works. These affinities provide evidence that the
works between which they exist were composed at or about the same time.

De Censibus 6

The first minor work to be discussed is *de censibus*, of which Lenel prints
ninety-six lines.[4] This contains the following references to contemporary

---

[1] Ch. 5 pp. 132–4, 153–6.   [2] Ch. 5 pp. 141–3.
[3] D. 26.10.3.13 (35 *ed.*), 26.8.5.3 (40 *Sab.*), 27.3.17 (3 *off. cons.*), perhaps 32.1.4 (1 *fid.*),
1.15.4 (1 *off. pr. urb.*), 27.1.9 (1 *off. pr. tut.*).
[4] *Pal.* 2.384–6; *Ind. Flor.* XXIV 16; Schulz (1946) 139[6], (1961) 330; *RE* 5.1.452; Fitting (1908)
118.

or recently dead emperors:

1 *cens.*	D. 50.15.1 pr.	huic enim divus Severus et imperator noster ius Italicum dedit
1 *cens.*	D. 50.15.1.2	quae a divo Severo Italicae coloniae rem publicam accepit
1 *cens.*	D. 50.15.1.3	cui divus Severus ius Italicum concessit
1 *cens.*	D. 50.15.1.4	imperator noster ius coloniae dedit
1 *cens.*	D. 50.15.1.7	divus quoque Severus coloniam deduxit
1 *cens.*	D. 50.15.1.9	a divo Severo ius coloniae impetravit
2 *cens.*	D. 1.9.12. pr.	ut scio Antoninum Augustum Iuliae Mammaeae consobrinae suae indulsisse
2 *cens.*	D. 50.15.3	rescripto imperatoris nostri ad Peligianum recte expressum est

The first text[5] shows that Severus is dead and Caracalla sole ruler. The order of mention of the emperors points to Caracalla A, and so to AD 213. The inference is probable, but not certain: it can be argued that *de fideicommissis 6*, rather than *de censibus*, is the main minor work of 213.

There are a few texts in which Ulpian condescendingly remarks of a rescript that it is 'correct' or 'quite right': *imperator recte/rectissime rescripsit*:

29 *ed.*	D. 17.1.6.7	sed rectissime divi fratres rescripserunt (213)
9 *off. proc.*	D. 48.19.8.12	imperator Antoninus rectissime rescripsit (213)
2 *cens.*	D. 50.15.3.1	rescripto imperatoris nostri recte expressum est

The argument from affinity would tend to show that *cens.* should be alloted to 213. Some other passages display an attitude towards emperors, including Caracalla, which could be termed condescending:

2 *Sab.*	D. 29.1.3	nam secundum nostram sententiam etiam divus Marcus rescripsit (214)
3 *off. proc.*	D. 50.2.3.1	imperator enim Antoninus edicto proposito statuit . . . et hoc recte
6 *Sab.*	D. 28.6.2.4	quae sententia rescripto imperatoris nostri . . . comprobata est, et merito (214)

This belongs to the early part of 214, and, though it confirms that *cens.* is early, does not enable us to decide between the two earliest years. The text about the indulgence shown to Julia Mamaea is of interest from the point of view of Ulpian's political career, and also because of the use of *scio*. This word (like *invenio*) is found in *de excusationibus*, which is generally taken to

<hr />

[5] D. 50.15.1 pr. (1 *cens.*).

have been composed during Severus' lifetime.[6] These and other epistemological words, as they may be termed, are mainly early.[7] Ulpian uses them to record his own experiences or the fruits of his reading. Virtually absent from the texts of 215 and 216, this personal testimony reappears a few times in 217.

The texts with *Scio* are:

4 *ed.*	D. 2.14.7.5	idem responsum scio a Papiniano
11 *ed.*	D. 4.2.9.3	sed ex facto scio . . . rescriptum esse (213)
11 *ed.*	D. 4.4.3.2	scio etiam illud aliquando incidisse
28 *ed.*	D. 14.1.7.12	et plerosque mandare scio (213)
68 *ed.*	D. 43.13.1.7	plerosque scio prorsus flumina avertisse (217)
68 *ed.*	D. 43.8.2.33	scio tractatum, an permittendum sit . . . (217)
14 *Sab.*	D. 48.19.3	ego quidem et ne quaestio de ea habeatur, scio observari (214)
20 *Sab.*	D. 34.2.19.8	ut in iunctura argentea scio me dixisse (214)
21 *Sab.*	D. 30.39.6	Scio ex facto tractatum (214)
7 *off. proc.*	D. 48.13.7	et scio multos et ad bestias damnasse (213)
10 *off. proc.*	D. 48.22.7.9	scio praesides solitos relegare (213)
1 *cens.*	D. 1.9.12. pr.	ut scio Antoninum Augustum . . . indulsisse
4 *disp.*	D. 28.5.35.1	unde scio quaesitum
1 *excus* (= 1 *off. pr. tut.*)	D. 27.1.15.16 FV 189	scio dubitatum . . . invenio tamen rescriptum
1 *off. pr. tut.*	FV 242	Scio tamen quosdam . . . haud impetrasse
1 *appell.*	D. 49.2.1.4	ut scio saepissime a divo Marco iudices datos
1 *appell.*	D. 49.1.3. pr.	Scio quaesitum . . .

Nescio is found only once:

8 *ed.*	FV 321	quod nescio ubi [Papinianus] legerit (213)

In 6 ed. there is a list of types of discharge from the army introduced by sentences beginning with *est*:

6 ed.	D. 3.2.2.2	est honesta . . . est causaria . . . est ignominiosa . . . est et quartum genus missionis (213)

---

[6] *Pal.* 2.899[1]; *RE* 5.1.1451.
[7] Below, p. 170.

The only real parallel in Ulpian's works comes in 1 *cens.*, where there is a list of places which have received grants of *ius Italicum*:

1 *cens.*	*D.* 50.15.1. 2, 3, 5, 10, 11	Est et Heliupolitana. . . . Est et Laodicena. . . . Est et Palmyrena Civitas. Est et in Bithynia Apamena. . . . Est et in Cilicia Selenus

De censibus is certainly early, and on the whole 213 is a slightly more probable date for it than 214.

Disputationum 10; de fideicommisis 6

In the last chapter the *disputationes*, discussions of points of law of the sort often called *quaestiones*, were assigned to 214 or 215.[8] As we shall see, there are strong affinities between this work and *de fideicommisis*.[9] It seems best, therefore, to discuss the date of these works together. They are, even on a first reading, very alike: full of vivacity and self-confidence, carried along in buoyant debate between the author and himself, or other lawyers.

The *disputationes*, we saw,[10] belong at least from book 3 to Caracalla B. To place them more precisely, we must take account of affinities with the major commentaries. One such emerges from the use of *probamus*, 'we approve', a plural of authority:

5 *Sab.*	*D.* 28.5.9.5	quam sententiam et ipse [Marcellus] et nos probamus (214)
20 *Sab.*	*D.* 36.2.5.1	hanc enim sententiam probamus (214)
32 *ed.*	*D.* 19.1.11.3	et Labeo et Sabinus putant et nos probamus (215)
33 *ed.*	*D.* 24.3.22.6	Nec non illud quoque probamus quod Labeo probat (215)
8 *disp.*	*D.* 35.2.82	Neratius ait, quod et nos probamus

At first sight these texts are neutral, so far as *disp.* is concerned, between 214 and 215. But if it belongs to 214, book 8 must come somewhere near the end of the year, and books 32 and 33 *ed.* near the beginning of 215. Hence, if *disp.* goes in 214, the texts bunch better than if it goes in 215, in which case 8 *disp.* would come near the end of 215, and create a larger gap between it and the previous text (33 *ed.*).

Much the same picture is presented by the texts with *dicet quis*, 'someone will argue':

13 *Sab.*	*D.* 38.17.2.41	etiam hos quis reiectos recte dicet (214)
25 *Sab.*	*D.* 32.55.7 (= 50.16.167)	et fortassis quis dicet (214)

---

[8] Ch. 6 p. 157.
[9] *Pal.* 2.903–26; *Ind. Flor.* xxiv 9; Schulz (1946) 255, (1961) 328; *RE* 5.1451; Fitting (1908) 117.
[10] Ch. 6 p. 157.

| 35 *ed.* | D. 27.9.7 pr. | multo magis quis impeditam alienationem dicet (215) |
| 4 *disp.* | D. 41.1.33.1 | Eadem distinctione quis utetur . . . aut cessare dicet |

If *disp.* belongs to 214, 4 *disp.* fits conveniently between the *Sab.* texts. Only two texts are found with *intellegendum erit*, 'it will have to be understood':

| 21 *Sab.* | D. 30.39.1 | hoc et . . . intellegendum erit (214) |
| 4 *disp.* | D. 28.5.35.3 | verumtamen hoc intellegendum erit |

This, again, supports the assignment of *disp.* to 214. The next phrase to be considered, *pari ratione*, 'for the same reason', brings in texts which show an affinity, not merely between *disp.* and the *Sab.* texts of 214, but between these and *fid.*

29 *ed.*	D. 15 1.11.9	nam qua ratione . . . pari ratione (213)
17 *Sab.*	D. 7.1.12.3	nam qua ratione . . . pari ratione (214)
26/1 *Sab.*	D. 23.2.12.4	pari ratione . . . possum ducere (214)
7 *disp.*	D. 17.1.29 pr.	pari ratione et si aliqua exceptio
8 *disp.*	D. 28.7.10 pr	pari ratione dicendum erit
4 *fid.*	D. 36.1.17.6	qua ratione . . . pari ratione etiam

Since the edictal text must belong to near the end of 213, and the second Sabinian text to almost the end of 214, the natural inference is that *disp.* belongs to 214, and that the same applies to 4 *fid.*

On the basis of these affinities I think that one can infer that *disp.* probably belongs to 214. What are the implications of this for *fid.*?

A point which demonstrates the close connection between *disp.* and *fid.* is the fact that in these works alone does Ulpian use *dixi* and *dicebam*, words appropriate to a record of what he has argued in oral debate.[11] There are five texts with *dixi* (from 2, 4, 5 *disp.*, 5, 6 *fid.*) and eleven with *dicebam* (from 3, 3, 4, 4, 4, 4, 5, 5, 7, 8 *disp.*, 2 *fid.*). These expressions are to be expected in *disp.*, since this work is a collection of records of oral debate. But there is no special reason to expect them in *fid.*, a treatise about the Roman law of trusts. The most reasonable explanation of their occurence in *fid.* is that Ulpian was concurrently working on *disp.*, and so had in mind certain oral discussions, in which he had taken part, which bore on the law of trusts.

The same is true of *referebam* 'I adduced the argument that', which also referes to oral discussion. There are three texts:

| 4 *disp.* | D. 29.1.19 pr. | secundum haec in proposito referebam |
| 4 *disp.* | D. 49.17.9 | idem referebam et si rem peculiarem filii pater legaverit |

[11] Ch. 4 nn. 113–14.

| 5 *fid.* | *D.* 35.1.92 | Papinianum quoque libro nono respon- |
| | | sorum scribere referebam |

Another expression which points to a link between *disp.* and *fid.* is *benignum est*, 'it is compassionate', which occurs twice:

| 8 *disp.* | *D.* 21.1.49 | et benignum est dicere |
| 1 *fid.* | *D.* 32.5.1 | hoc valere benignum est |

So far, then, the evidence rather favours the idea that *fid.* was composed in 214. But we must look at the direct evidence, beginning with the references in *fid.* to the emperors:

1 *fid.*	*D.* 32.1.4	epistula divi Severi et imperatoris nostri ius deportandi datum est
1 *fid.*	*D.* 32.1.9	et ita imperator noster rescripsit
2 *fid.*	*D.* 32.11.19	imperator noster rescripsit
2 *fid.*	*D.* 35.1.14	imperator noster rescripsit
3 *fid.*	*D.* 36.1.1.13	et est decretum a divo Severo
3 *fid.*	*D.* 36.1.3.4	imperator noster rescripsit
4 *fid.*	*D.* 36.1.15.4	et ita invenio ab imperatore nostro et divo patre eius rescriptum
5 *fid.*	*D.* 40.5.24.5	et est receptum ab imperatore nostro
5 *fid.*	*D.* 40.5.24.9	et imperator noster cum patre rescripsit
5 *fid.*	*D.* 40.5.26.1	decretum et a divo Severo constitutum est
5 *fid.*	*D.* 40.5.26.2	imperator noster cum patre rescripsit
5 *fid.*	*D.* 40.5.26.3	Idem imperator noster cum patre rescripsit
5 *fid.*	*D.* 40.5.26.8	et ita imperator noster cum patre suo rescripsit
5 *fid.*	*D.* 40.5.30 pr.	imperator noster rescripsit
5 *fid.*	*D.* 40.5.30.15	Imperator noster Antoninus rescripsit
5 *fid.*	*D.* 40.5.30.17	rescriptum imperatoris nostri et divi patris eius declarat
5 *fid.*	*D.* 35.1.92	quod divus Severus rescripsit . . . ex auctoritate divi Severi
6 *fid.*	*D.* 49.14.43	Imperator noster rescripsit

The *imperator noster* who is mentioned jointly with Severus in the first text must be Caracalla, and he is still sole emperor in book 6. Of the seven mentions of joint constitutions, six put Caracalla first. These lie between book 4 and 6. The first,[12] however, from book 1, makes Severus senior. It might therefore be the case that the first books of *de fideicommissis* belong to Caracalla A and the last three or more to Caracalla B. From this evidence *fid.* might belong to 213, or the early part might belong to 213 and the remainder to 214. Again, the text from book 1 might simply be an exception to the general practice in Caracalla B, perhaps explicable by the

12 *D.* 32.1.4 (1 *fid.*).

fact that the constitution referred to was an *epistula* rather than a rescript to
a private person.[13] To decide between these possibilities, let us examine the
affinities between *fid.* and the major commentaries. Several of the
epistemological words occur in *fid*: *memini*, *invenio* and variants, *retineo, nec
ignoro*:

17 *Sab.*	D. 7.8.2.1	apud Labeonem memini tractatum (214)
4 *fid.*	D. 36.1.18.5	ex facto tractatum memini
1 *off. pr. tut.*	FV 220	memini itaque me suadente ... p[raetorem] ...
6 *ed.*	Spicil. Solesm. ed. Pitra 1.282[14]	invenimus apud veteres (213)
53 *ed.*	D. 39.3.1.20	Apud Labeonem invenio relatum (215)
13 *Sab.*	D. 38.17.2.47	et invenimus rescriptum (214)
4 *fid.*	D. 36.1.15.4	et ita invenio . . . rescriptum
1 *off. pr. tut*	FV 177	inveni rescriptum
1 *excus.* (= 1 *off. pr. tut.*)	D. 27.1.15.16	scio dubitatum . . . invenio tamen. . . .
5 *fid.*	D. 35.1.92	et retineo me dixisse
4 *fid.*	D. 36.1.17 pr.	nec ignoro . . . Maecianum dubitare

The texts with *tractatum* (*est/esse* etc.) point rather towards 214:

14 *Sab.*	D. 38. 16.3.10	Est autem tractatum . . . (214)
17 *Sab.*	D. 7.4.3 pr.	unde tractatum est (214)
17 *Sab.*	D. 7.8.2.1	apud Labeonem memini tractatum (214)
21 *Sab.*	D. 30.39.6	scio ex facto tractatum (214)
23 *Sab.*	D. 34.3.7 pr.	ut est apud Iulianum tractatum (214)
28 *Sab.*	D. 40.7.9.2	Illud tractatum est . . . (216)
29 *ed.*	D. 15.1.3.5	tractatum est, an . . . (213)
31/2 *ed.*	D. 17.2.58 pr.	tractatum ita est apud Celsum . . . (215)
68 *ed.*	D. 43.8.2.33	scio tractatum an . . . (217)
2 *fid.*	D. 36.1.18 pr.	ex facto tractatum est, an . . .
2 *fid.*	D. 36.1.18.5	ex facto tractatum memini
4 *fid.*	D. 36.1.6.1	ideoque tractatum est apud Iulianum
6 *Sab.*	D. 5.1.50.1	tractatum est de aere alieno

There are just two Ulpianic texts with *inefficax*:

13 *ed.*	D. 4.8.11.5	ne sit inefficax [sententia] deficiente con- dicione (213)
5 *fid.*	D. 40.5.24.2	potest tractari, an non sit inefficax [libertas]

There are also just two texts in which Ulpian rejects in advance the

---

[13] Cf. D. 1.15.4 (1 *off. pr. urb.*), below, pp. 180–1.
[14] Pal. 2.440.

imputation to himself of certain conceivable views:

| 16 *ed.* | *D.* 6.2.7.17 | nec quisquam putet hoc nos existimare sufficere initio traditionis ignorasse alienam (214) |
| 1 *fid.* | *D.* 32.1.1 | haec utique nemo credet in testamentis nos esse probaturos |

On balance *fid.*, like *disp.*, appears to have been composed in 214. It may be, however, that this was not true of book 1. Though from the point of view of neat planning one might expect that *cens.* 6 and *fid.* 6, both of which are clearly early, were composed one in 213 and one in 214, another configuration is possible. Some books of each may have been written in 213, and others, including most of *fid.*, in 214. If that were so, and if *disp.* belongs to 214, the affinity between *fid.* and *disp.* would be explained, also the priority of Severus over Caracalla in book 1 of both *cens.* and *fid.* But certainly is beyond reach.

Institutionum 2

The two books of *institutiones*[15] run to 120 lines in the *Palingenesia*. One text refers to a reigning emperor:

| 2 *inst.* | *Coll.* 16.9 | Sed imperator noster . . . eas solas personas voluit admitti, quibus decimae immunitatem ipse tribuit |

The text is concerned, it seems, with Caracalla's legislation, restricting to a narrow circle of close relatives the right of intestate succession to freedmen. Arguments from affinity of style suggest that *Inst.* is an early work. Ulpian has two texts with *aequissimum putavit*, 'he thought it the fairest solution':

| 7 *ed.* | *D.* 2.10.1. pr. | aequissimum putavit praetor (213) |
| 2 *inst.* | *Coll.* 16.7 | nam aequissimum putavit (praetor) |

There are also two with *aequitate motus* 'moved by considerations of fairness':

| 26 *ed.* | *D.* 12.4.3.7 | sed ipse Celsus naturali aequitate motus (213) |
| 2 *inst.* | *Coll.* 16.9 | praetor aequitate motus |

A triad contain the word *libuerit*, as in *si libuerit*, 'if he pleases':

15 *Sab.*	*D.* 50.16.164.1	prout libuerit (214)
6 *disp.*	*D.* 40.5.46.3	si ei libuerit (214)
1 *inst.*	*D.* 43.26.1.2	cum sibi libuerit

---

[15] *Pal.* 2.926–30; *Ind. Flor.* XXIV 14; Schulz (1946) 171–2, (1961) 207–8; *RE* 5.1447; Fitting (1908) 117.

Utpote, 'namely', occurs in five Ulpianic texts, including two from *inst.*:

7 *Sab.*	D. 28.5.17.5	nec Aristo nec Aulus utpote probabile notant (214)
24 *Sab.*	D. 34.4.3.2	utpote re ipsa mora subsecuta (214)
47 *Sab.*	D. 46.1.8.8	utpote cum futurum sit [citing an opinion of Julian, 216]
1 *inst.*	D. 1.1.4	utpote cum iure naturali omnes liberi nascerentur
1 *inst.*	D. 1.4.1 pr.	utpote cum lege regia . . . populus conferat

There is perhaps also an affinity between the following passages, in which 'we' represent the legal system:

9 *ed.*	D. 3.3.33 pr.	in servo subsistimus . . . et hoc casu procuratorem eius esse admittimus . . . actionem autem intendere vetamus . . . eum vero qui de statu suo litigat procuratorem habere posse non dubitamus (213)
1 *inst.*	D. 1.1.6 pr.	cum aliquid addimus vel detrahimus iuri communi, ius proprium, id est civile efficimus

There is little doubt that *inst.* is early, but it is difficult to decide between 213 and 214.

Ad edictum aedilium curulium 2

There are no references to emperors in the surviving fragments of this commentary. But it has affinities with the major and medium treatises of the reign of Caracalla which suggest that it, too, belongs to that reign.[16] Thus, Ulpian has four texts with *accipias*, 'take it that . . .':

29 *ed.*	D. 15.1.3.7	idem accipias et in servi fideiussore (213)
1 *Sab.*	D. 28.1.20.3	Quae autem diximus . . . in omnibus testimoniis accipias (214)
8 *Sab.*	D. 29.2.30.1	et in eo ventre idem accipias (214)
1 *ed. cur.*	D. 21.1.19.4	ut neque consummatae scientiae accipias, neque . . .

There is also one text with *accipies*, 'you will take it that . . .':

15 *ed.*	D. 5.3.25.8	accipies, sive dolo desierit possidere, sive (213)

---

[16] *Pal.* 2.884–98; *Ind. Flor.* XXIV 1; Schulz (1946) 198, (1961) 244; *RE* 5.1439; (all wrongly treating this work as an appendix to *ad edictum*).

Four sentences begin with *Illud plane*, 'The following of course':

6 *ed.*	D. 3.2.6.6	Illud plane addendum est (213)
15 *ed.*	D. 5.3.31.4	Illud plane . . . imputari non potest (213)
29 *ed.*	D. 15.3.7.3	Illud plane verum est (213)
1 *ed. cur.*	D. 21.1.31.18	Illud plane haec actio exigit

Three analogous expressions are:

10 *ed.*	D. 3.6.3.3	Illud erit notandum (213)
12 *ed.*	D. 4.6.21.1	et erit notandum (213)
1 *ed. cur.*	D. 21.1.4.5	Illud erit adnotandum

There are four texts with *in causae cognitione versabitur*, . . . 'will be an issue at the trial':

9 *ed.*	D. 3.3.27 pr.
11 *ed.*	D. 4.4.13 pr.
11 *ed.*	D. 4.4.16 pr.
1 *ed. cur.*	D. 21.1.31.23

Mediocris, 'unimportant,' appears in three texts:

17 *Sab.*	D. 7.8.4 pr.	si . . . usus sit relictus homini mediocri (214)
1 *off. proc.*	D. 1.16.9.4	ne forte . . . mediocres desideria sua non proferant (213)
1 *ed. cur.*	D. 21.1.4.6	levis dolor aut mediocre ulcus

The work is clearly early, and perhaps has more affinities with 213 than 214. In that case *inst.* must belong to 214. In addition, from the point of view of subject-matter, *ed. cur.* fits better with the segment of commentary on the praetor's edict composed in 213, and *inst.*, a work largely about the *ius civile*, with the commentary on Sabinus, itself a work about the *ius civile*.

De officio praetoris tutelaris 1 [17]

This work appears to be early, but is in some respects puzzling. Some texts in it are identical with texts from *de excusationibus*,[18] which is generally held to have been composed before the death of Severus.[19] *Off. pr. tut.* is therefore thought, following Mommsen, to be a second edition or amplification of *excus.*[20] It certainly belongs to the reign of Caracalla, as the

---

[17] *Pal.* 2.960–6; *Ind. Flor.* XXIV 22; Schulz (1946) 249, (1961) 318; *RE* 5.1452; Fitting (1908) 118–19.

[18] D. 27.1.7 (1 *excus.*) = *FV* 240 (1 *off. pr. tut.*); *FV* 145 (1 *excus.*) = *FV* 222 (1 *off. pr. tut.*); D. 27.1.15–16 (Mod. 6 *excus.* -Ulp. 1 *excus.*) = *FV* 189 (1 *off. pr. tut.*).

[19] *FV* 125, 147, 159 (all 1 *excus.*); Fitting (1908) 115; but Ebrard (1917) 144; H. Krüger (1930) 303.

[20] Above, n. 17.

following references to emperors show:

I *off. pr. tut.*	D. 27.1.9	beneficio divi Severi et imperatoris nostri
I *off. pr. tut.*	FV 176	et ita imperator noster . . .
I *off. pr. tut.*	FV 177a	[imperatores] . . . riae Sabinae rescripser[unt]
I *off. pr. tut.*	FV 191	idque imperator noster et divus Severus Claudio Herodiano rescripserunt
I *off. pr. tut.*	FV 200	imperator noster cum patre Polo Terentiano rescripsit
I *off. pr. tut.*	FV 201	divus Severus Flavio Severiano rescripsit
I *off. pr. tut.*	FV 204	et ita . . . imperator Antoninus Augustus Cereali a censibus et aliis [rescripsit]
I *off. pr. tut.*	FV 210	idque im[perator noster rescripsit]
I *off. pr. tut.*	FV 211	[ut imperator noster Dio]doto praetori rescripsit
I *off. pr. tut.*	FV 212	ut divus Severus constituit
I *off. pr. tut.*	FV 232	ut imperator noster rescripsit
I *off. pr. tut.*	FV 234	ut Phi[lu]meniano imperator noster cum patre rescripsit
I *off. pr. tut.*	FV 235	quam epistulam quodam rescripto ad Vernam et Montanam pistores imperator noster cum patre interpretatus est . . . plus etiam imperator noster indulsit
I *off. pr. tut.*	FV 236	ut imperator noster et divus Severus Man[ilio] Cereali rescripserunt
I *off. pr. tut.*	D. 27.1.10.8	ut imperator noster cum patre rescripsit
I *off. pr. tut.*	FV 238–9	Por[c]a[ti]o Faustino rescripsit imperator noster cum patre. Item Furio Epaphrae . . . rescripsit

Of the eight texts in which Severus and Antoninus appear jointly, Caracalla precedes his father in seven. In the first,[21] however, Severus has priority. The pattern is therefore in its own way rather similar to that which appeared in *cens.* and *fid.* It is possible that *off. pr. tut.* may have been begun in Caracalla A and finished in Caracalla B, since if the module of minor books was $8\frac{1}{2}$ books a year, some book must have been left half finished at the end of a year. *Off. pr. tut.* may have been the choice for 213.

It looks early, but appearances may deceive. We have already come across two texts in it with *scio*,[22] and one each with *invenio*,[23] *inveni*[24] and *memini*[25]. It is therefore strong on epistemological words. How far this is

---

[21] D. 27.1.9 (I *off. pr. tut.*).
[22] FV 189, 242; above, p. 166.
[23] FV 189; above, p. 170.
[24] FV 177; above, p. 170.   [25] FV 220; above, p. 170.

due to the fact that it is a second edition or revision of *excus.* is uncertain. The case for saying that it was written in 213 or 214, or half in each, is one which rests on no more than a balance of probabilities.

Taken as a whole, the writings of these first two years are self-confident, even exuberant. Ulpian writes in a relaxed way, talks informally to the reader,[26] draws on personal experience,[27] feels free to compliment Caracalla on his rescripts[28] and Marcus on having the foresight to anticipate the author's own opinion.[29] It is a powerful start to an ambitious undertaking. The detailed programme for 213 and 214 may have read something like this:

213.	6–31/1	ad edictum
	1–10	de officio proconsulis
	1–6	de censibus
	1–2	ad edictum aedilium curulium
	½	de officio praetoris tutelaris
214.	1–26/1	ad Sabinum
	1–10	disputationum
	1–6	de fideicommissis
	1–2	institutionum
	½	de officio praetoris tutelaris

With the exception of *off. pr. tut.*, it is pretty certain that all these works are early: they fall into one or other of the years 213 and 214. But one cannot in some cases be sure which. *Cens.* and *fid.* might belong to either year, or be distributed between them.[30] The same is true of *ed. cur.* and *inst.*[31] Nor is it clear that *off. pr. tut.* belongs here at all.[32] Nevertheless, the proposed scheme is probably not far off the mark.

II. THE MIDDLE WORKS

The middle year of Ulpian's five-year plan was 215. We assumed that he was then writing a middle segment of edictal commentary, from book 31/2 to book 56/1.[33] The middle-range work for the year was thought to be either the *disputationes* or *de omnibus tribunalibus*.[34] If the arguments for holding *disp.* to have been written in 214[35] are accepted, it would follow

---

26 *Accipias, accipies*: above, p. 172; *dicet quis*: above, pp. 167–8.
27 *Scio, invenio, memini, retineo, dixi, dicebam, non ignoro*: above, pp. 166, 170.
28 D. 48.19.8.12 (9 *off. proc.*).
29 D. 29.1.3 (2 *Sab.*).
30 Above, pp. 164–71.
31 Above, pp. 171–3.
32 Above, pp. 173–4.
33 Ch. 5 pp. 144, 152–3.
34 Ch. 6 pp. 157–8.
35 Above, pp. 167–9.

by elimination that *omn. trib.* was composed in 215. But there are also positive indications that this is the case. There are affinities between *omn. trib.* and the thirties and forties of the edictal commentary.

Ulpian often uses *non tantum . . . verum etiam*, 'not only but also'. One variant of this, *nec tantum verum etiam*, occurs in five texts, all from the middle segment of edictal commentary:

37 *ed.*	D. 9.4.42.2 (215)
44 *ed.*	D. 38.2.16.5 (215)
46 *ed.*	D. 38.7.2.1 (215)
46 *ed.*	D. 38.7.2.2 (215)
49 *ed.*	D. 38.15.2.4 (215)

Another variant, this time a pleonastic one, is *non tantum, verum etiam quoque*, 'not only, but, in addition, also'. This is found in four texts:

36 *ed.*	D. 27.4.1.5 (215)
39 *ed.*	D. 37.4.3.pr. (215)
1 *omn. trib.*	D. 26.5.7
2 *off. cons.*	D. 25.3.5.12

Ulpian soon eliminated this unsatisfactory expression. But the distribution of these four texts suggests that the early part of the middle section *ad edictum* and the early books *de omnibus tribunalibus* were being composed at much the same time. This in turn is most easily explained if Ulpian had selected *omn. trib.* as his medium-scale work for 215 and was writing it in parallel with the edictal commentary—a pattern which he seems to have followed in 213 when the medium-scale work was *off. proc.* At the same time, if the evidence of these texts can be trusted, the minor work which occupied his attention was the three-book work on the duties of the consul.

This picture is confirmed by the study of another set of words, the diminutives of *minutus* viz. *minutulus*, 'tiny', and *minutatim*, 'piecemeal'. These rather precious expressions seem to have enjoyed Ulpian's favour for only a short time:

25 *Sab.*	D. 32.55.2	nisi quae (arbores) minutatim coincidun- tur (214)
37 *ed.*	D. 50.16.192	ut taxatio haec . . . ad minutulam summam referatur (215)
5 *omn. trib.*	D. 2.15.8.9	si . . . minutatim singulos convenire dif- ficile ei sit
2 *off. cons.*	D. 34.1.3	ne a singulis heredibus minutatim alim- enta petentes distringantur

Since the Sabinian commentary for 214 ended at book 26/1, the Sabinian text must belong to the last months of that year, the edictal text to the early months of 215. On this evidence *omn. trib.* and *off. cons.* were composed at much the same time, presumably 215.

Ulpian's use of certain long, impressive-sounding words falls in the same period and affords evidence that other treatises on the duties of public officials, besides the consul, were composed at much the same time. One such type of word is the adverb in four or more syllables which begins with the prefix *in-* and ends in *-ter*:

35 *ed.*	D. 26.10.3.17	inconsideranter
41 *ed.*	D. 37.11.2.7	indubitanter
2 *off. cons.*	D. 40.2.30	incunctanter
1 *off. quaest.*	D. 1.13.1.3	indifferenter

Not far removed from these is:

35 *ed.*	D. 26.10.3.16	pervicaciter

It looks from these texts as if the treatise on the office of quaestor and that on the consul belong together. The next group of words brings in two more treatises on public offices. This comprises adjectives or adverbs in *-osus* or *ose* which have at least five syllables. The list which follows contains all the words of this sort in Ulpian except for *iniuriosus* and *iniuriose*. These are omitted because they are technical terms which have necessarily to be used in the context of the delict of *iniuria*. The others are:

29 *ed.*	D. 14.6.3.3	pecuniae datio perniciosa . . . visum est (213)
33 *ed.*	D. 24.3.22.7	si tantus furor est, ita ferox, ita perniciosus (215)
35 *ed.*	D. 26.10.3.5	si . . . sordide egit vel perniciose pupillo
37 *ed.*	D. 47.2.50.4	non debet impunitus esse lusus tam perniciosus (215)
1 *off. quaest.*	D. 2.1.3	ad animadvertendum [in] facinorosos homines
1 *off. pr. urb.*	D. 1.12.1.10	Cum patronus . . . contumeliosum sibi libertum queratur
1 *off. cur. reip.*	D. 22.1.33 pr.	nam inter insolentiam incuriosam et diligentiam non ambitiosam multum interest
1 *off. cur. reip.*	D. 50.9.4. pr.	Ambitiosa decreta decurionum rescindi debent

From the occurence of these rather pretentious words it looks as if Ulpian, for whatever reason, was guilty at this period of rhetorical excesses which are not typical of his writing in general. Here are two ambitious antitheses:

35 *ed.*	D. 26.7.7.1	debuit enim partibus suis fungi non quidem praecipiti festinatione, sed nec moratoria cunctatione (215)

| 1 *off. cur. reip.* | D. 22.1.33 pr. | dummodo non acerbum se exactorem nec contumeliosum praebeat sed moderatum et cum efficacia benignum et cum instantia humanum |

Here is a rather overdrawn account of the sort of complaint brought by a slave against his owner which the urban prefect should listen to:

| 1 *off. pr. urb.* | D. 1.12.1.8 | non accusantes dominos . . . sed si verecunde expostulent, si saevitiam, si duritiam, si famem, qua eos premant, si obscaenitatem, in qua eos compulerint vel compellant, apud praefectum urbi exponant |

The texts set out have brought into play two further treatises on the duties of public officials, the urban praetor[36] and the curator of the republic.[37] Here are some further illustrations of the affinity between the middle segment of *ed.*, *omn. trib.*, and the *officia*. Twice Ulpian tells us that something 'ought rarely to be done', *raro/perraro faciendum est*:

| 1 *omn. trib.* | D. 26.10.7.3 | quod et perraro . . . faciendum est |
| 1 *off. cons.* | D. 5.1.82 | quod raro . . . faciendum est |

Liberalis, 'liberal' in the context of liberal arts or studies, also comes in twice:

| 8 *omn. trib* | D. 50.13.1 pr. | praeceptoribus tantum studiorum liberalium (215) |
| 1 *off. cur. reip.* | D. 50.9.4.2 | si ob liberalem artem fuerit constitutum |

Licentiam habet, 'he is allowed', occurs in two texts only:

| 33 *ed.* | D. 24.33.22.8 | tunc licentiam habet . . . adire iudicem (215) |
| 1 *off. pr. urb.* | D. 1.12.1.3 | Relegandi et deportandi . . . licentiam habet |

Closely related is *licentia erit*, 'it will be permissible':

| 33 *ed.* | D. 24.3.22.7 | licentia erit . . . nuntium mittere (215) |
| 35 *ed.* | D. 26.7.1.3 | licentia erit . . . in iudicium vocare (215) |

One of Ulpian's many expressions with *accipere* is *accipere nos oportet*, 'we must take it that', which is found in a quintet of texts:

18 *ed.*	D. 9.2.5.1 (213)
35 *ed.*	D. 26.2.3.1 (215)
44 *ed.*	D. 38.5.1.4 (215)
46 *ed.*	D. 38.8.1.6 (215)
1 *off. cons.*	D. 50.16.99.1

[36] D. 1.12.1.10 (above, p. 177), 1.12.1.8 (above).
[37] D. 22.1.33 pr. (above) 50.9.4 pr. (above, p. 177).

Finally, there may be a connection between *acerbum*, 'harsh', and *acriter*, 'harshly'. Each of these occurs only once:

3 *omn. trib.*	*D.* 47.10.35	praetor acriter exequii hanc rem debet (215)
1 *off. cur. reip.*	*D.* 22.1.33 pr.	dummodo non acerbum se exactorem praebeat

In summary, four works on the duties of public officials[37a]—the consul,[38] urban prefect,[39] quaestor,[40] and curator of the republic[41]—all seems to have affinities with the middle segment of edictal commentary, and also with *de omnibus tribunalibus*. This raises the question whether the entire programme of minor works for 215 consisted of monographs on the duties of public officers.

The modular scheme calls for nine books of minor works in this year, half a book more than usual, in view of the fact that only 25 books of edictal commentary, not $25\frac{1}{2}$, fall between 31/2 and 56/1 *ed.*[42] There are in fact enough books of this sort attributed to Ulpian to fill the programme, even if *off. pr. tut.*, which appears to be early, is left on one side:

> de officio consulis 3
> de officio quaestoris 2 (or 1)
> de officio consularium 1
> de officio curatoris reipublicae 1
> de officio praefecti urbi 1
> de officio praefecti vigilum 1

If the work on the quaestor is counted as two books, there are nine such books in all. If not, only eight. From two of these works, on the duties of the *consulares* (circuit judges in Italy) and the prefect of the watch, we have only three lines and one line respectively. It is not possible to show linguistically that they are akin to the other works of 215. But it seems a plausible assumption that, if four of these treatises belong to a given year, so do the other two, especially as, from a numerical point of view, they fit in neatly.

Notes on individual works follow.

De officio consularium 1[43]

The only sentence which survives from this work is not original Ulpian but comes from a constitution of Marcus. It contains nothing, therefore, to indicate the period in which the work was composed.

[37a] On works *de officio* see dell'Oro (1960).
[38] *D.* 25.3.5.12, 34.1.3, 40.2.20 pr., 5.1.82, 50.16.99.1 (above, pp. 176–8).
[39] Above, n. 36 and *D.* 1.12.1.3 (above, p. 178).
[40] *D.* 1.13.1.3, 2.1.3 (above, p. 177).
[41] Above, n. 37 and above, p. 179.   [42] Ch. 5 pp. 144–5.
[43] *Pal.* 2.950; Schulz (1946) 247, (1961) 315; *RE* 5.1452, 4.1140; not in *Ind. Flor.*

De officio consulis 2[44]

There are five passages which refer to contemporary emperors:

3 off. cons.	D. 27.3.17	Imperatores Severus et Antoninus rescripserunt in haec verba:
3 off. cons.	D. 42.1.15.1	imperator noster cum patre rescripsit
3 off. cons.	D. 42.1.15.3	rescriptum est ab imperatore nostro et divo patre eius
3 off. cons.	D. 42.1.15.4	constitutum est ab imperatore nostro
3 off. cons.	D. 42.1.15.8	imperator noster rescripsit

The reigning emperor is clearly Caracalla, in view of the references to joint constitutions of himself and his father. In two of these he precedes Severus, in the third Severus comes first. It is not therefore clear at first sight whether the work belongs to Caracalla A or B. It is more probable, however, that texts in which Severus precedes Caracalla will be found in period B than the other way around. This is especially true if the exact words of the constitutions are given, as in the first text listed here.[45] There is therefore no reason why *de officio consulis* should not have been composed in 215, which falls within Caracalla B.

De officio curatoris reipublicae 1[46]

There are three references to contemporary emperors:

1 off. cur. reip.	D. 50.12.1 pr.	ut imperator noster cum divo patre suo rescripsit
1 off. cur. reip.	D. 50.12.1.5	imperator noster cum divo patre suo ita rescripsit
1 off. cur. reip.	D. 50.12.1.6	imperator noster rescripsit

From the mention of joint constitutions of the reigning emperor and his father, Caracalla must be sole emperor at the time of composition. From the affinities noted earlier with expressions in 33–9 *ed.*, *off. quaest.* and *off. pr. urb.*, this monograph could also have been written in 215.

De officio praefecti urbi 1[47]

There are four references to present or recent emperors in this work:

1 off. pr. urb.	D. 1.12.1 pr.	epistula divi Severi ad Fabium Cilonem missa

---

[44] *Pal.* 2.951–8; *Ind. Flor.* xxiv 13; Schulz (1946) 243, (1961) 314; *RE* 5.1452; Solazzi (1922); Fitting (1908) 119.
[45] D. 27.3.17 (3 off. cons.).
[46] *Pal.* 2.958–9; *Ind. Flor.* xxiv 13; Schulz (1946) 243, (1961); Mommsen (1887–8) ii 1082; Kuebler (1925) 221; Liebenam (1897) 290; *RE* 5.1454; Fitting (1908) 119; Cassarino (1946–7) 299.
[47] *Pal.* 2, nn. 959–60; *Ind. Flor.* xxiv 19; Schulz (1946) 246, (1961) 313; *RE* 5.1454; Vigneux (1896); Fitting (1908) 120; Chastagnol (1960).

1 *off. pr. urb.*	*D.* 1.12.1.8	officium praefecto urbi a divo Severo datum est
1 *off. pr. urb.*	*D.* 1.12.1.14	Divus Severus rescripsit
1 *off. pr. urb.*	*D.* 1.15.4	Imperatores Severus et Antoninus Iunio Rufino praefecto vigilum ita rescripserunt . . .

Severus, *divus* in three references, is dead. It is not clear who is the current emperor. Caracalla is not ruled out. In the last text, however, where the two emperors are mentioned jointly, Severus comes first. So, if Caracalla is ruling, this looks like Caracalla A. The title *imperatores* rules out the reign of Macrinus. Caracalla B, however, cannot be ruled out since the text in which Severus comes first is an *epistula* in which the exact words of the constitution are given.[48] As in the instance from *off. cons.* noted above,[49] this is the type of case in which occasionally we find an exception to the general practice under Caracalla B. In all there are five or six such exceptions[50] to set against seventy-one texts which follow the standard pattern, and, at this period, put Caracalla first. It is possible that *off. pr. urb.* was composed in 213. On the other hand, given the affinities of its style, it may be significant that 215 is not ruled out.

De officio praefecti vigilum 1[51]

There are only five words from this work. They contain no clue to its date.

De officio quaestoris 2 (1)[52]

The twenty-nine lines from this work contain no references to contemporary emperors, but, as noted above,[53] by affinity of style it could belong to the year 215. If, contrary to most scholarly opinion,[54] the inscription to *D.* 2.1.3, ULPIANUS *libro secundo de officio quaestoris,* is accepted, we get a total of nine books of minor works for 215, as the modular scheme requires. Despite the Florentine Index, the inscription may indeed be right.

Though the evidence is not compelling, the affinities of style between the edictal commentary for 215, *omn. trib.* and four monographs on the duties of public officials incline me to think that in this year Ulpian's minor work programme concentrated on public offices.[54a]. In that case he may have

---

[48] Cf. *D.* 32.1.4 (1 *fid.*), 27.3.17 (3 *off. cons.*).

[49] *D.* 27.3.17 (3 *off. cons.*), above, p. 180.   [50] Above, n. 3.

[51] *Pal.* 2.960; *Ind. Flor.* XXIV 20; Schulz (1946) 246, (1961) 314; *RE* 5.1454; Baillie Reynolds (1926).

[52] *Pal.* 2.992; *Ind. Flor.* XXIV 23; Schulz (1946) 246, (1961) 314; Lydus, *De Mag.* 1.24.28; *RE* 5.1454.

[53] Above, n. 40.

[54] Karlowa I (1885) 742². But *D.* 2.1.3 is not likely to come from *off. proc.*, as he thinks, in view of *facinorosos* (above, p. 77), nor, for the same reason, is it likely to be post-classical (Schulz, 1946, 246⁸).

[54a] See on these generally dell' Oro (1960).

composed in this year:

> 31/2−56/1 ad edictum
> 1−10 de omnibus tribunalibus
> 1−3 de officio consulis
> 1−2 de officio quaestoris
> 1 de officio consularium
> 1 de officio curatoris reipublicae
> 1 de officio praefecti urbi
> 1 de officio praefecti vigilum

There is no positive evidence, however, as regards the books on the prefect of the watch and the consulars. The existence of the second book on the quaestor is speculative. The monograph on the urban prefect may belong to 213. Nevertheless, Ulpian's programme for this middle year was probably on the general lines set out.

III. THE LATE WORKS

In fixing the detailed programme for 216 and 217 we can begin by eliminating the minor works already assigned to the first three years of the quinquennium. This leaves:

ad legem Iuliam de adulteriis	5
ad legem Aeliam Sentiam	4
de appellationibus	4
de sponsalibus	1
ad orationem divi Antonini et Commodi	1

There are two missing books, since the modular scheme requires a total of seventeen books of minor works rather than fifteen. According to the previous chapter, the segment of major commentary for 216 was books 26/2 to 51 *ad Sabinum*, and for 217 books 56/2 to 81 *ad edictum*. The middle-range treatise for both years was *ad legem Iuliam et Papiam* in twenty books, the first ten in 216 and the last ten in 217.

If this outline is correct, a pattern emerges. Ulpian's commentaries on statutes, *leges*, belong to the last two years of the quinquennium. No work of this sort seems to have been composed in the first three years. Counting twenty books *ad legem Iuliam et Papiam*, we have to accommodate at least thirty books on statutes in the last two years. Indeed the true number may be higher, since the missing two books may have consisted of monographs concerning statutes which by the time of Justinian had become obsolete, such as the *lex Cornelia de adpromissoribus*. Somewhat as in the *digesta* of Celsus, Julian, and Marcellus,[55] the analysis of statutes formed an appendix to the discussion of other branches of the law.

---

[55] *Pal.* 1.163−9 (Cels. 28−39 *dig.*), 1.464−84 (Iul. 59−90 *dig.*), 1.627−32 (Marc. 21−31 *dig.*).

The various minor works are now dealt with in turn.

De appellationibus[56]

Ulpian often uses *et magis est*,[57] 'the better view is'. One variant of this, *magisque est*, occurs only in the following concentration of texts:

10 *leg. Iul. Pap.*	D. 37.14.16.1	
48 *Sab.*	D. 45.3.7. pr.	(216)
59 *ed.*	D. 42.4.3.3	(217)
60 *ed.*	D. 40.5.4.15	(217)
60 *ed.*	D. 40.5.4.16	(217)
60 *ed.*	D. 40.5.4.22	(217)
61 *ed.*	D. 28.8.8	(217)
61 *ed.*	D. 29.2.71.1	(217)
61 *ed.*	D. 29.2.71.9	(217)
75 *ed.*	D. 44.2.7.3	(217)
77 *ed.*	D. 46.7.3.3	(217)
77 *ed.*	D. 46.7.3.8	(217)
1 *appell.*	D. 49.4.1.9	

The first point to note is that this distribution of texts confirms our provisional conclusion[58] that the last books of Sabinian commentary (end of 216) were composed just before the last segment of edictal commentary, from book 56/2 , which belongs to 217. It also confirms the idea that the first ten books *ad legem Iuliam et Papiam* were composed in 216,[59] since, on that view, the tenth book of that work also belongs to the end of 216.

How does *appell.*, from which there is one text with *magisque est*, fit this scheme? Since the citation is from the first book, it is more likely to have been composed in 217 than 216. The first book of this work, if composed in 216, would be rather too distant from the rest of the texts.

Support for this comes from a study of another construction, *palam est*. In the earlier years Ulpian uses this at the end of a clause. *Palam est* follows the object or accusative and infinitive which it governs, as in *ex conducto actionem transire palam est*.[60] In the following texts, however, it is the other way round. *Palam est* precedes the object or accusative and infinitive which it governs:

46 *Sab.*	D. 19.1.10	palam est duas evictiones eum praestare debere (216)
49 *Sab.*	D. 18.4.2.3	palam est ad eum pretia rerum pervenisse (216)

---

[56] *Pal.* 2.379–84; *Ind. Flor.* XXIV 12; Schulz (1946) 256, (1961) 329; *RE* 5.1452; Fitting (1908) 120.
[57] Eighty-eight texts: *CDJ* 56, 63 ET MAGIS EST
[58] Ch. 6 p. 153.
[59] Ch. 6 pp. 157–8.
[60] D. 19.2.19.8 (Ulp. 32 *ed.*).

49 *Sab.*	D. 45.1.38.3	palam est committi stipulationem (216)
66 *ed.*	D. 42.8.3 pr.	palam est edictum locum habere (217)
69 *ed.*	D. 43.16.1.24	palam est eum vi deiectum videri (217)
70 *ed.*	D. 43.21.1.7	palam est et ad eum pertinere, qui. . . .(217)
76 *ed.*	D. 44.4.2 pr.	palam est autem hanc exceptionem ex eadem causa propositam (217)
77 *ed.*	D. 46.7.5.3	palam est recte rem defendi (217)
1 *appell.*	D. 49.4.1.11	et palam est eam esse propriam causam

The distribution indicates, once more, an association between the last books of Sabinian commentary and the last segment of edictal commentary. If the former belongs to the end of 216 and the latter to 217, it looks as if *appell.*, book 1 of which yields a text, presumably of the same period, must have been composed in 217.

It is worth drawing attention here to another expression whose distribution shows, like the preceding two, that the last segment of Sabinian commentary can properly be regarded as coming just before the last segment of edictal commentary. *Praeterea sciendum est*, 'furthermore', occurs in the following seven texts:

47 *Sab.*	D. 46.1.8.1	Praeterea sciendum est fideiussorem adhiberi (216)
64 *ed.*	D. 42.6.1.12	Praeterea sciendum est . . . non posse impetrari (217)
66 *ed.*	D. 42.8.6.9	Praeterea illud sciendum est eum . . . non videri (217)
70 *ed.*	D. 43.20.1.23	Praeterea illud sciendum est . . . (217)
70 *ed.*	D. 43.19.1.10	Praeterea sciendum est . . . aequissimum esse (217)
73 *ed.*	D. 42.8.10.6	Praeterea sciendum est posse quaeri . . . (217)
76 *ed.*	D. 44.4.4.10	Praeterea sciendum est . . . eum repelli solere (217)

It seems justifiable to adopt as a firm conclusion that the end of *Sab.* belongs to 216 and the last segment of *ed.* to 217. Can *appell.* have been composed in 217? One text from it refers to a reigning emperor:

| 4 *appell.* | D. 49.5.5.3 | idque rescriptis imperatoris nostri Antonini declaratur |

'Antoninus' might be Caracalla or Elagabal.[61] Since Caracalla was still emperor up to 8 April 217, the work could have been composed in that

---

[61] *Pal.* 2.379[1].

year. But in that case it must have been completed by 8 April, or rather by the time that the news of Caracalla's death reached Ulpian. This does not seem implausible.

Ad legem Iuliam de adulteriis[62]

A number of phrases from this work suggest that it, too, should be placed in 217. Another variant on *magis est* is *magis putamus*, 'we rather think', which comes twice:

47 Sab.	D. 46.1.8.5	magis putamus teneri fideiussorem (216)
2 adult.	D. 48.5.18.2	magis putamus mulierem . . . posse accusari

Praeripere, 'snatch away', is also found twice:

66 ed.	D. 42.8.6.7	neque enim debuit praeripere ceteris . . . bona (217)
2 adult.	D. 48.5.16 pr.	ne praeripiatur marito ius . . .

There are three texts with *nec/non ab re est*, 'it is not out of place':

60 ed.	D. 40.5.4.5	nec erit ab re existimare . . . (217)
77 ed.	D. 42.1.26	non ab re erit . . . sententiam proferre (217)
2 adult.	D. 48.5.18.6	sed non ab re est hoc probare

Nec/non mediocriter, 'to no small extent', is found twice:

57 ed.	D. 47.10.7.2	si vulneraverit non mediocriter, aequissimum erit . . . (217)
4 adult.	D. 48.5.30.3	nec enim mediocriter deliquit, qui . . .

In the last segment of edictal commentary Ulpian twice uses *perquam iniquum*, 'very unjust':

59 ed.	D. 42.4.3. pr.	Marcellus autem notat perquam iniquum esse . . . (217)
79 ed.	D. 36.3.14.1	Divus quoque Pius rescripsit . . . perquam iniquum ese . . . (217)

With this one can compare another way of saying the same thing:

2 adult.	D. 48.5.14.5	periniquum enim videtur esse, ut . . .

In the first text Ulpian is citing Marcellus, and plausibly so, since Marcellus in another text uses *periniquum*.[63] The argument from affinity here takes the form that it was this citation from Marcellus which suggested to Ulpian that he should use a word which was not normally part of his vocabulary.

---

[62] *Pal.* 2.931–9; *Ind. Flor.* XXIV 11; Schulz (1946) 188, (1961) 232; *RE* 5.1446; Fitting (1908) 120.
[63] D. 26.7.29 (Marc. 8 *dig.*).

A similar analogy is provided by *perquam durum* and *durissimum*, 'very hard':

60 *ed.*	D. 5.1.19.2	durissimum est . . . se defendi (217)
4 *adult.*	D. 40.9.12.1	quod quidem perquam durum est, sed ita lex scripta est

There are clearly strong arguments in favour of the view that *adult.* like *appell.* was composed in 217. Two difficulties, however, present themselves.

One is trivial. If both works belong to 217, we have nine books of minor works for that year, whereas the modular scheme requires only $8\frac{1}{2}$. This awkwardness would disappear if half a book *de appellationibus* was written in the previous year. It need not therefore detain us further. The other is more serious. A text in 2 *adult.* contains two references to recent emperors:

2 *adult.*	D. 48.5.14.3	Divi　　　Severus　　　et　　　Antoninus rescripserunt . . .
2 *adult.*	D. 48.5.14.8	poterit accusari ex rescripto divi Severi, quod supra relatum est.

Severus is patently dead. But what of Caracalla? One could, with Lenel and Fitting, take these texts as proof that *adult.* was composed after Caracalla's death. If, however, this inference rests on the use of the phrase *divi Severus et Antoninus*, it is not compelling. The second reference is to the same rescript as the first: in other words, the rescript, though technically a joint one, was in substance the work of Severus. This in itself sugests that Ulpian is here writing after Caracalla's death, when it was no longer necessary to treat him as the real author of joint constitutions. There is the further point that it is easier to insert *divus* or *divi* retrospectively into a text than to eliminate it.[64] If the first reference originally read *Severus et Antoninus rescripserunt*, without *divus*, the mode of citation would be entirely appropriate to the reign of Macrinus, and could belong to the year 217. In my opinion this is the correct interpretation. The five books on the *lex Iulia de adulteriis* were written in 217, but later than *de appellationibus*, which fell in the last months of Caracalla. Greater precision is not attainable.

Ad legem Aeliam Sentiam 4[65]

By a process of elimination this work must have been written in 216. The subject-matter is a statute of AD 4 relating to manumission. There is no reference, in the thirty-seven lines which have been preserved, to an emperor. A slender argument from affinity can, however, be extracted

---

[64] Mommsen (1905) II 169.
[65] *Pal.* 2.930—1; Schulz (1946) 189, (1961) 232; *RE* 5.1446. Not in *Ind. Flor.*

from these few lines:

| 42 *Sab.* | *D.* 50.17.31 | Verum est neque pacta neque stipulationes factum posse tollere (216) |
| 1 *Ael. Sent.* | *D.* 50.16.216 | Verum est eum qui in carcere clusus est non videri neque vinctum neque in vinculis esse |

De sponsalibus 1[66]

The two excerpts from this contain only seven lines as printed in the Palingenesia. They do not exclude the year 216, but neither do they point positively to it.

Ad orationem divi Antonini et Commodi 1

As we saw, though this work is not in the Florentine Index and is not confirmed by any inscription, it must have existed.[67] The quotation from it in Paul's monograph[68] contains the phrase *quaestio in eo est*, 'the point at issue is'. This is found otherwise only in the following texts of Ulpian:

40 *ed.*	*D.* 37.6.1.21	quaestio in eo est, an . . . an non (215)
41 *Sab.*	*D.* 47.2.43.11	quaestio in eo est, an (216)
43 *Sab.*	*D.* 41.1.23.1	quaestio in eo est, utrum (216)
71 *ed.*	*D.* 43.26.6.4	quaestio in eo est, ut (217)
cf. 1 *or. Ant. Comm.*	*D.* 23.2.60.4	quaestio in eo est, an

From the point of view of affinity, therefore, 216 is a possible year, as the modular scheme would require.

This brings us to the end of the discussion of the chronology of Ulpian's minor works. The plan which I attribute to Ulpian is seen more clearly if the results, tentative as they are in many instances, are set out in the form of a table, the major, middle-range and minor works being kept separate:

	Major	*Middle-range*	*Minor*	
213	6−31/1 *ed.*	1−10 *off. proc.*	1−6 *cens.* 1−2 *ed. aed. cur.* ½ *off. pr. tut.*	8½
214	1−26/1 *Sab.*	1−10 *disp.*	1−6 *fid.* 1−2 *inst.* ½ *off. pr. tut.*	8½

---

[66] *Pal.* 2.1198; *Ind. Flor.* XXIV 18; Schulz (1946) 253, (1961) 325; *RE* 5.1451.
[67] Ch. 3 p. 104.
[68] *D.* 23.2.60.4 (Paul 1 *or. d. Ant. et Comm.*).

215	31/2—56/1 ed.	1—10 omn. trib.	1—3 off. cons.	
			1—2 off. quaest	
			1 off. consular.	
			1. off. cur. reip	9
			1 off. pr. urb.	
			1 off. pr. vig.	
216	26/2—51 Sab.	1—10 leg. Iul. Pap.	1—4 leg. Ael. Sent.	
			1 spons.	6½
			1 or. d. Ant. et Comm.	(8½)
			½ appell.	
217	56/2—81 ed.	11—20 leg. Iul. Pap.	½—4 appell.	8½
			1—5 leg. Iul. adult.	

What is claimed for this scheme is not perfect accuracy—that would be a lucky chance—but that it is consistent with the historical record and the language of the works. It is supported by strong and detailed arguments. If it is to be refuted, positive counter arguments are called for, not mere scepticism.

As a check on the viability of the scheme, a statistical investigation may now be in point. Ulpian's preference for the future tense is a notable feature of his style. It varies, however, at different stages of his career. If the edictal commentary is divided into the four segments already discerned, Ulpian's use of the future is seen to vary in the following way:

Books	Lines	Instance of future	Mean per 100 lines
1—5 ed.	1024	88	8.6
6—31/1 ed.	10753	1019	9.5
31/2—56/1 ed.	8287	850	10.3
56/2—81 ed.	6934	593	8.6

Although the author's use of the future never falls below a rather high level, it rises to a peak in the middle segment of the edictal commentary and falls thereafter. Can this be used as a criterion to test the correctness of our hypothesis? The figures for the use of the future in the Sabinian commentary are:

Books	Lines	Instance of future	Mean per 100 lines
1—26/1 Sab.	5114	549	10.7
26/2—51 Sab.	5017	449	8.8

If we fit the segments of *Sab.* between those of *ed.* in the way suggested we get the following sequence:

pre-213	8.6
213	9.5
214	10.7
215	10.3
216	8.8
217	8.6

The suggested chronology therefore produce a plausible curve which rises steadily to a peak and then falls. A more linear curve, but one which fits the dates, is arrived at from the figures for relative idiosyncrasy given in chapter 2:

Date	Footnote references	References per 100 lines
pre-213	55	5.4
213	672	6.1
214	355	6.7
215	530	6.5
216	335	6.7
217	482	7.2

Here the trend is a rising one. Do the medium-scale works fit into the schemes presented by these two tables?

The figures for them are as follows, in the order of suggested dates, beginning with instances of use of the future:

Books	Lines	Instances of future	Mean per 100 lines
(213) *off. proc.* 10	1211	67	5.5
(214) *disp.* 10	1928	223	11.6
(215) *omn. trib.* 10	506	71	14.0
(216) 1–10 *Iul. Pap.*	404	42	10.4
(217) 11–20 *Iul. Pap.*	168	15	8.9

The number of lines from the last ten books of *leg. Iul. Pap.* is only 168. But this is enough to provide a reliable figure. Observed frequencies of word-use are regarded as reliable when the expected total for the text under consideration is not less than 10.[69] For the whole of Ulpian the mean number of uses of the future is 9.45 per 100 lines (43,135 lines, 4,362 uses of the future). Hence in any 100 lines of Ulpian one would expect, on the average, nearly ten uses of the future. The last ten books of *leg. Iul. Pap.* provide more than this.

The medium-range works, then, yield a curve for the use of the future which runs parallel to that for the major commentaries. It rises and falls rather more steeply, but the shape is the same. It looks, therefore, as if the

[69] Ellegard (1962) 14.

hypothesis advanced is a viable one. It is further strengthened if we go by the criterion of relative idiosyncrasy of style. This can be roughly assessed from the proportion of footnotes in chapter two referring to a given work in relation to the volume of excerpts derived from that work.

Work	Lines	References per 100 lines
(213) *off. proc.* 10	1211	6.3
(214) *disp.* 10	1928	6.6
(215) *omn. trib.* 10	506	7.9
(216–7) *Iul. Pap.* 20	572	9.6

The underlying idea, which was seen to be true in regard to the commentary *ad edictum*, is that an author's style becomes more idiosyncratic as he continues writing, so that his later works have more elements peculiar to himself than his earlier.

Only five[70] of the minor works yield enough material for the purpose of estimating the rate of use of the future tense. These are:

Books	Lines	Instances of future	Mean per 100 lines
(213) *ed. cur.* 2	853	72	8.4
(214) *fid.* 6	1403	107	7.6
(215) *off. cons.* 3	409	49	12.0
(217) *appell.* 4	276	32	11.6
(217) *adult.* 5	471	47	10.0

The works have been arranged in the suggested chronological sequence. They do not fit quite as well as the major and medium-scale treatises, though they arrange themselves in a sequence which bears some resemblances to that of the others. A similar pattern emerges from the figures for relative idiosyncrasy:

Work	Lines	References per 100 lines
(213) *ed. cur.* 2	853	6.4
(214) *fid.* 6	1403	6.0
(215) *off. cons.* 3	409	6.8
(217) *appell.* 4	276	9.4
(217) *adult.* 5	471	8.1

But the dating of the minor works is less secure than that of the major and medium treatises, and, while the general picture is not in doubt, it may be that some works assigned to 213 should appear in 214 and vice versa. The same may be true of 216 and 217.

On the whole there is reason to suppose that the suggested scheme represents, in broad outline, the project which Ulpian devised and carried out in 213–217.

---

[70] The figures for minor works with between 50 and 150 lines (lines, instances of future, mean per 100 lines) are: *Inst.* 120, 1, 0.8; *cens.* 96, 3, 3.1; *off. pr. urb.* 72, 7, 9.7; *off. cur. reip.* 67, 9, 13.4.

CHAPTER 8

Secretary *a libellis*

The *Historia Augusta*, in one of its subsidiary lives, that of Pescennius Niger,[1] says that Niger, later to fight Severus for the empire, wrote to both Marcus and Commodus about the administration of the state. He suggested that, to prevent inexperienced men acceding to high civil office, the legal advisers in the various departments (*assessores*) should afterwards continue to serve in those departments. Severus and many later emperors adopted this policy. This is shown, according to the *HA*, by the prefectures of Paul and Ulpian, who, having been members of Papinian's council, later became heads of department, one the secretary of records (*a memoria*), the other secretary of private petitions (*a libellis*). They were then immediately made prefects.

The same history, in the life of Alexander,[2] records that Alexander held both Paul and Ulpian in high regard. Some say, the author reports, they were appointed prefects by Elagabal, others by Alexander himself. Ulpian is stated, the *HA* continues, to have been a councillor of Alexander and head of chancery (*magister scrinii*) and both are said to have been assessors to Papinian.

In all this chaff, does any wheat lie hidden? Neither Paul nor Ulpian can have been assessor to Papinian as praetorian prefect (205–11), if by *assessor*[3] is meant someone holding the junior salaried post of legal adviser to a magistrate. The case is improved if we take *assessor* to mean an informal legal councillor.[4] Paul was a paid legal councillor of Severus,[5] and may have informally assisted Papinian also when the latter tried cases as praetorian prefect. So might Ulpian.[6] But neither was made prefect immediately after Papinian's death, for Caracalla then appointed Macrinus,[7] his ultimate assassin. A gap of eleven years intervened before, in

---

[1] *HA* Niger 7.4.
[2] *HA* Alexander 26.5.
[3] *D*. 1.22; *CJ* 1.51; Hitzig (1893); *RE* 1.423 (Seeck).
[4] Unpaid, in accordance with republican practice: Schulz (1946) 117; *D*. 31.29 pr. (Cels. 36 *dig.*).
[5] *D*. 4.4.38 pr. (Paul 1 *decr.*), 14.5.8 (1 *decr.*), 32.27.1 (2 *decr.*), 36.1.76 (2 *decr*), 29.2.97 (3 *decr.*).
[6] *D*. 4.2.9.3 (11 *ed.*) shows Ulpian as assessor to a praetor, presumably early in his career.
[7] Perhaps after an intermediate holder of the office: Dio 79.11.3.

222, Ulpian acceded to that high office.[8] There is no reliable evidence that Paul ever did so.

If, then, we eliminate the praetorian prefecture, the text can be taken to be saying that Papinian held the *memoria* and then the *libelli*, with Paul and Ulpian respectively as legal councillors. There is the difficulty that the office of records seems to have been held under Severus by a freedman.[9] So let Paul and the post *a memoria* be eliminated also. We know almost nothing of Paul's career, though, in my opinion, his reports of cases tried before Severus—the only law reports in the ancient world—permit the inference that he held at least one post, that of secretary of imperial trials (*a cognitionibus*) during this reign.[10] He was alive under Alexander, but whether he had by then attained other and higher offices is uncertain. His comments on the imperial jurisdiction make him a legal conservative, in contrast with Papinian, whose views Severus generally adopted.[11] If Paul's career stopped short at the *cognitiones*, which is no more than a speculation, it was becuase he did not share the cosmopolitan outlook of the Severan dynasty. The joint prefectures of Paul and Ulpian described by the *HA*[12] are palpably imaginary. They are the product of an inventive desire to turn Paul and Ulpian into the *divi fratres* of the law.

But of Ulpian we know more. He was prefect of supply in March 222,[13] praetorian prefect in December of that year.[14] He could have held the *libelli* at an earlier stage of his career, since that post was junior to a prefecture. But if so, it can hardly have been under Alexander, even if, with Syme,[15] we take the heroic step of supposing that he processed petitions on behalf of the Caesar Alexander in the closing stages of the reign of Elagabal. Did his tenure of the *libelli*, then, come under Severus, Severus and Caracalla, Caracalla alone, or Elagabal? In 1962 I made a preliminary survey of the problem,[16] and came to the conclusion, having regard to the style of the imperial rescripts, that Ulpian held the office mainly under Severus and Caracalla, between 200 and 212. Was this wide of the mark? Was Kunkel[17] right to suggest that, if Ulpian really held the post, which, he argues, is not securely attested, it was probably under Caracalla? Fortunately, a clear answer is possible.

That Ulpian held the *libelli* does not rest wholly on the unreliable and often fantastic evidence of the *HA*. The epitomizing historians of the fourth

---

[8] *CJ* 4.65.4.1 (1 Dec. 222).
[9] Syme (1970) 314 citing Castor (Dio 76.14.2), Marcius Festus (Herodian 4.8.4; *CIL* 14.3638).
[10] Honoré (1981) 15–6.
[11] Honoré (1981) 15–21.
[12] *HA* Niger 7.4; Alexander 26.5.
[13] *CJ* 8.37.4 (31 March 222).
[14] Above, n. 8.
[15] Syme (1970) 321.
[16] Honoré (1962) 207–12.
[17] Kunkel (1967) 246.

century, Eutropius[18] and Festus,[19] mention Ulpian's tenure of an office under Alexander which could be construed as the *libelli*.[20] It is now generally thought that *HA* was composed or revised later than these,[21] perhaps towards the very end of the fourth century, and drew material from the epitomizers, or at least Victor. From where, then, did the epitomizers get the idea? Perhaps from a *Kaisergeschichte*[22] which ran up to the battle of the Milvian bridge under Constantine. But this only displaces the problem. If it existed, did the *Kaisergeschichte* accurately report Ulpian's career?

Fortunately, we need not speculate about the sources of the statements in Victor, Eutropius, Festus, and the *HA*. The matter can be directly tested. The language of Ulpian's unquestionably authentic writings can be confronted with that of the rescripts of the Severan age, in order to see which, if any, are written in a similar style. The main source is the *Codex Iustinianus* (AD 534), which contains some 711 private rescripts (*subscriptiones*), derived from the *Codex Gregorianus* (AD 291–2). With this material available we can decide for ourselves whether Ulpian held the *libelli* and whether, in that case, he succeeded Papinian. It is true that, as has been pointed out, he cannot have done so in the way supposed by the *HA*. But Roman emperors might have adopted the policy that in the principal offices of state the holder's main adviser should whenever possible succeed him. Was this the case with Severus and the office a *libellis*? Did Ulpian succeed Papinian in this department?

For there is no doubt that Papinian held the *libelli* under Severus. Tryphoninus, legal councillor of Severus, tells us so,[23] in a passage which leaves no doubt that the personality of the secretary a *libellis* influenced the content of rescripts. Speaking of the purchase of mortgaged property by the mortgagee, he records a rescript of Severus which lays down that such a purchase is valid, since the mortgagor remains owner during the mortgage. This, he says, was issued while Papinian held the *libelli* (*libellos agente Papiniano*). In any case, the affinity between the language of Papinian in his juristic writing and the rescripts of 194–202 is close.

Thus, putting together juristic texts from Justinian's Digest and elsewhere with rescripts up to Diocletian, *rationis est*, 'it stands to reason', occurs nine times:

Pap. 4 *resp.*	D. 23.2.34 pr.	non fieri nuptias rationis est . . .
Pap. 4 *resp.*	D. 23.3.69.1	eas dotis portionem esse rationis est

---

[18] *Brev.* 8.23 (*adsessor vel scrinii magister*).
[19] *Brev.* 22.1 (*scriniorum magister*).
[20] 'Head of Department' could refer to letters, private petitions, records or imperial trials.
[21] Syme (1968), (1971). If the date of composition was, as he thinks, about 395, it is worth noting that this decade was a time of revived interest in classical law.
[22] Put forward by Enmann (1884) 337.
[23] D. 20.5.12 pr. (Tryph. 8 *disp.*).

Pap. 6 *resp.*	D. 29.5.21.1	actionem adhuc durare rationis est
Pap. 17 *qu.*	D. 31.66.4	fideicommissum esse retinendum rationis est
Marci. 4 *inst.*	D. 28.5.49.2	servum non iure manumissum videri rationis est [divi Sev. et Ant.]
Macer 2 *pub. iud.*	D. 48.21.2 pr.	Impp. Severus et Antoninus. . . . Eos non relinquere defensionem here-dibus rationis est
21 March 197	CJ 8.16.1	Alumnos tuos in causam pignoris non fuisse rationis est
25 Feb. 198	CJ 4.28.2	non esse locum decreto rationis est
Gordian III	CJ 4.52.2	fidem infringi minime rationis est

If we leave on one side the last text, which is later than the others and idiomatically different, since it expresses a negative proposition, all the citations come from Papinian or from constitutions of Severus and Caracalla. The obvious inference is that all were composed by Papinian, either in his capacity as a private jurist or as secretary *a libellis* to Severus and, from 198, Severus and Caracalla.

Non enim aequitas patitur, 'for equity does not allow', occurs once:

| Pap. 20 *qu.* | D. 31.70.1 | non enim aequitas hoc probare patitur |

The only comparable expression in juristic or imperial texts is:

| 21 Apr. 200 | CJ 6.2.1 | neque enim aequitas patitur, ut . . . persequaris |

Faenebris pecunia, 'money lent at interest', is found in only two texts:

| Pap. 11 *resp.* | D. 22.1.9 pr. | Pecuniae faenebris dupli stipulatum re-spondi non tenere |
| 27 Sept. 200 | CJ 4.32.3 | Quamvis usurae faenebris pecuniae peti non possunt |

Numerationem implere, 'to fulfil payment', is an awkward expression found only in a text of Papinian:

| Pap. 8 *qu.* | D. 20.4.1 pr. | residuae quantitatis numeratio impleta est |

There is, however, one close parallel:

| 30 June 196 | CJ 4.19.1 | Ut creditor, qui pecuniam petit, nume-ratam implere cogitur . . . |

Ea res non excusat, 'that does not excuse', comes just once:

| Pap. 1 *resp.* | D. 50.7.8 | ea res filium, quo minus profiscatur, non excusat |

There is, once again, one very close parallel:

26 Sept. 194	CJ 2.23.1	sed ea res fideiussores excusare non potest

In 1891 Kalb pointed out[24] that, among the jurists, only Papinian used *vita decedere* for to die; it occurs twenty-nine times in his texts.[24a] There are three 'imperial' texts, from 1 November 197, 26 December 200, and 13 September 205.[24b] The explanation of the third text may be left for the moment. The first two fall within the period of office which may plausibly be assigned to Papinian.

Coniectura pietatis, 'on the supposition of a pious motive', is found twice:

Pap. 9 *resp.*	D. 35.1.102	condicionem coniectura pietatis respondi defecisse
24 June 197	CJ 3.28.3.1	iniquitas per coniecturam maternae pietatis emendanda est

This last text also has *vita cessisse*, a hapax, which reminds us of *vita decedere* in the text cited above.

Condicionis incertum, 'the uncertainty of the condition', also comes twice:

Pap. 13 *qu.*	D. 37.11.11 pr.	qui propter incertum condicionis posse peti respondit
25 Nov. 200	CJ 2.3.1	Condicionis incertum conventione finitum est

Non inutiliter with the future passive, 'it will not be pointless to . . .', is found in five texts:

Pap. 28 *qu.*	D. 21.2.66.2	non inutiliter agetur
Pap. 11 *resp.*	D. 22.1.9.1	non inutiliter opponetur
Pap. 11 *qu.*	D. 26.7.37.1	non inutiliter convenietur
Pap. 13 *resp.*	D. 39.6.42	non inutiliter opponetur
12 Feb. 202	CJ 2.3.2	non inutiliter defenderis

Almost, but not quite, on all fours are two other passages:

22 Oct. 194	CJ 8.15.1	non inutilis erit exceptio
27 Dec. 210	CJ 3.1.2	non inutiliter uteris

This last text, couched in the active, is no doubt an imitation. The others all appear to stem from Papinian.

The parallels to which attention has been drawn cannot be mere coincidence, especially as we know that Papinian held the *libelli* under Severus. What they show is that he was composing rescripts on the emperor's behalf between 26 September 194 and 12 February 202.

[24] Kalb (1891) 329.
[24a] *CDJ* 27 VITA.
[24b] *CJ* 2.50.1 (1 Nov. 197), 2.3.1 (26 Dec. 200), 7.21.2 (13 Sept. 205).

Without giving precise dates, Kalb underlined the benefits to be gained from a comparison of the styles of private juristic writers and the drafters of imperial constitutions. But this method of research has until recently been neglected, or even been declared impossible.

Did Ulpian succeed Papinian as secretary a *libellis*? In answering this question we must bear in mind that, if Ulpian held the office after Papinian, he did so a decade before he began the main body of work for which he is known. Thus, *animadvertimus*, 'we notice', is found only in five texts:

Ulp. 1 *excus.*	*FV* 156	Formam ita celebrari animadvertimus, ut . . .
18 July 204	*CJ* 6.53.2	Agrum pluribus relictum animadvertimus
10 May 205	*CJ* 3.33.2	usum fructum legatum tibi animadvertimus
20 Sept. 207	*CJ* 3.26.2	Non animadvertimus, cur advocare velis
5 Oct. 290	*CJ* 5.16.14.1	Cum igitur lecto testamento animadvertimus . . .

Ulpian does not use this word in the main body of his writings, but only in this text from *excus.*, which, as has been seen,[25] was probably composed under Severus. The rescripts of these years, following Papinian's tenure of the *libelli*, are in the manner of the *early* Ulpian.

There are six texts with *non dubitamus*:

Ulp. 9 *ed.*	*D.* 3.3.33.1	procuratorem habere posse non dubitamus
Ulp. 22 *ed.*	*D.* 11.1.11.8	succurri ei, qui respondit, non dubitamus
Ulp. 40 *ed.*	*D.* 37.5.5.8	id liberis profuturum non dubitamus
Ulp. 41 *ed.*	*D.* 37.9.1.15	subvenire praetorem debere non dubitamus
Ulp. 3 *Iul. Pap.*	*D.* 23.2.45.3	non dubitamus competere ei hoc ius
Ulp. 6 *Iul. Pap.*	*D.* 4.6.38.1	non dubitamus id tempus ei non proficere
27 June 207	*CJ* 8.16.2	non dubitamus eum de ipsis agris cogitasse

Not far removed are the two following texts:

Ulp. 17 *Sab.*	*D.* 7.8.10.2	non dubitaremus quin valeret
Ulp. 48 *Sab.*	*D.* 45.3.7 pr.	non dubitaremus pro dominicis eum portionibus adquirere

As with *animadvertimus*, it may be that Ulpian's use of the plural—the plural of authority as it may be called—is influenced by his having

---

[25] Ch. 7, p. 173.

composed rescripts for the joint emperors Severus and Caracalla. But this need not be the case. The plural of authority is used by writers such as Gaius[26] who held no official position and are thought to have had a lowly social status. It expresses an intellectual, not a civil, superiority. *Frustra timere*, 'to entertain vain fears', is found in five texts:

Ulp. 11 *ed.*	*D.* 4.2.7 pr.	si quis meticulosus rem nullam frustra timuerit
Ulp. 47 *Sab.*	*D.* 45.2.3 pr.	In duobus reis promittendi frustra timetur novatio
20 Sept. 206	*CJ* 5.37.1	Frustra times administrare res adulescentis
17 Oct. 293	*CJ* 5.37.17	De successione sua tutores frustra timent
8 Nov. 294	*CJ* 7.35.6	temporis adversarii possessionem frustra times

The two texts from Diocletian are too far removed from the others to be taken into account. Note that the rescript of 206 is expressed in a very forceful way. *Nec enim facile*, 'for it is not lightly . . .', is found in only two texts:

Ulp. 46 *ed.*	*D.* 38.8.1.2	nec enim facile ulla servilis videtur esse cognatio
20 Sept. 205	*CJ* 9.1.2.1	Nec enim facile tutores . . . sententia notantur

Taking jurists and emperors together, *suasor*, *suasus*, and *suasio* are all hapax:

Ulp. 11 *ed.*	*D.* 4.4.13 pr.	hic enim velut adfirmator fuit et suasor
Ulp. 18 *ed.*	*D.* 9.2.9.1	Si quis per vim vel suasum medicamentum infundit
1 May 204	*CJ* 5.62.1	Falsa suasione credis te immunitatem habere

Grave est/videtur, 'it is/seems a serious matter', occurs in three texts:

Ulp. 27 *ed.*	*D.* 13.5.1 pr.	quoniam grave est fidem fallere
Ulp. 36 *ed.*	*D.* 12.3.4 pr.	grave enim videbatur periurium anceps subire
12 Sept. 204	*CJ* 9.41.2	Insolitum est et grave exemplo audiri servos adversus tutores

There are twin texts with *durior sententia*, 'a harsh sentence'.

Ulp. 6 *ed.*	*D.* 3.2.13.7	dicendum erit duriori sententia cum eo transactum
20 Feb. 205	*D.* 2.11.8	non laesit existimationem tuam sententia durior

[26] E. g. *nos scriptum invenimus* (*Inst.* 4.60); Honoré (1962) 144, 147, 152.

These both concern the relation of a sentence for crime to the mark of *infamia*. There is only one instance of *in peius reformare:*

Ulp. 1 *appell.*	D. 49.1.1. pr.	licet nonnumquam bene latas sententias in peius reformet

But there is a close analogy in the following constitution:

25 March 202	CJ 2.3.3	in deterius autem reformare non potest obligationem

Cautior appears in only one text:

Ulp. 77 *ed.*	D. 46.5.1.4	ut quis cautior sit et securior interposita stipulatione

But there is a rescript of the period with *cautius:*

29 Nov. 204	CJ 6.2.2	curate igitur cautius negotiari

Ad praetorem evocare occurs twice:

Ulp. 34 ed.	D. 25.4.1.9	semper dicemus marito licere uxorem ad praetorem evocare
23 Aug. 204	CJ 2.12.3 pr.	Eum qui res agit heredum evoca ad praetorem

Servari oportet comes in three times:

Ulp. 3 *off. proc.*	D. 27.9.11	idem servari oportet et si . . .
26 Jan. 206	CJ 5.14.1	Legem quam dixisti servari oportet
Sev. et Ant. (?202)	CJ 7.33.1.2	Quod etiam in re publica servari oportet

A triad of passages have *ratio reddi non/nec potest*:

Iav. 10 *epist.*	D. 45.1.108 pr.	cur non idem respondeatur, ratio reddi non potest
Ulp. 3 *Sab.*	D. 28.3.3.2	nec ratio diversitatis reddi potest
Ulp. 67 *ed.*	D. 37.6.5 pr.	haec in patre adoptivo ratio reddi non potest

There is a close analogy in the following passage:

26 June 204	CJ 6.28.1.1	nulla ratio reddi potest, quare . . .

There are only two texts with *necesse erit,* 'it will be necessary':

Ulp. 10 *ed.*	D 3.5.7.3	necesse erit et eum pertingi qui vetuit
25 April 208	CJ 6.35.2.1	quam adimi pupillo necesse erit secundum iuris formam

Sometimes a term, though not expressed by its author, is implied in an act in the law, such as a contract or will. In that case the term is valid though the author does not add it, *etsi hoc non adiciat:*

Ulp. 50 *Sab.*   *D.* 45.1.45.4   Filius patri dari stipulari videtur, etsi
                                           hoc non adiciat . . .

There is a close parallel in a rescript of 208:

16 Aug. 208   *CJ* 8.40.3.2   nam et cum hoc non adiciatur, singuli
                                         tamen in solidum tenentur

There are three texts[27] in which *attamen* is found without a preceding
conjunction such as *licet, quamvis,* or *quamquam:*

Ulp. 31 *ed.*   *D.* 17.2.33   et ideo societate coita pupillus non
                                          tenetur, attamen communiter gesto
                                          tenetur

Ulp. 1 *ed. cur.*   *D.* 21.1.1.10   ideoque redhiberi non posse . . . : atta-
                                          men ex empto actionem admittit

1 May 205   *CJ* 8.13.3   vim quidem facere non videntur, atta-
                                         men possessionem adipisci debent

The imperial rescripts which contain these close parallels with the language
of Ulpian run from 25 March 202[28] to 16 August 208.[29]
At a minimum, he held the office *a libellis* over six years. Indeed, he
probably held it for nearly a year longer. A rescript of 1 May 209 runs:

CJ 7.74.1   Scire debes privilegium dotis, quo mulieres utuntur in actione de
              dote, ad heredes non transire.

The construction *scire debes,* followed by the accusative and infinitive, if not
actually distinctive, is consistent with Ulpian's style,[30] and the direct form
of address, in which the petitioner is bluntly told what he ought to know or
think, is characteristic of him.[31] The next rescript, of 15 July 209, may also
be by his hand. It ends:

CJ 8.18.1   frustra putas tibi auxilio opus esse constitutionis nostrae ad eam rem
              pertinent is

The inverted construction and direct form of address point to Ulpian, but
the termination in a rather pedantic participial phrase does not. This might

---

[27] Possibly also Coll. 14.3.3 (Ulp. 9 *proc.*).

[28] *CJ.* 2.3.3 above, p. 198.

[29] *CJ* 8.40.3.2 above.

[30] *D.* 26.2.1.1 (Gai. 12 *ed. prov: item scire debemus* acc. inf.), 48.15.6.pr. (Call. 6 *cogn.* citing Hadrian *scire debet* acc. inf.), 50.1.13 (Pap. 2 *qu: cum scire deberet* acc inf.), 26.7.5.10 (Ulp. 35 *ed.: scire debet* acc. inf.), 45.1.29 pr. (Ulp. 46 *Sab. scire debemus* acc. inf.), *CJ* 6.50.1 (13 May 197 *scire debes* acc. inf.), 5.69.1, 2 (12 Oct. 205 *scire igitur debes* acc. inf.), 7.74.1 (1 May 209 above), 3.44.4 pr. (2 Nov. 223 *scire debes* acc. inf.).

[31] *CJ* 6.3.1 (30 Dec. 204 *scis*), 8.15.2 (14 Oct. 205), 5.62.3 (15 March 206), 8.40.3.1 (18 Aug. 208 all *intellegis*), 5.15.1 (20 July 204 *non ignoras*), 4.2.1 (1 July 204 *nec ipse ignorare videris*). 5.37.1 (20 Sept. 206 *frustra times*), 5.62.1 (1 May 204 *falsa suasione credis*).

be a transitional constitution in mixed style. The next text, of 30 December 209, is clearly by a new hand:

> *CJ* 7.8.3 Ab eo, qui bona sua pignori obligavit, quae habet quaeque habiturus esset, posse servis libertatem dari certum est

This more orthodox word order continues in the rescripts of 210 and 211. The direct form of address occurs only once,[32] and then it follows the accusative and infinitive. It looks, therefore, as if a change of tenure, in which Ulpian gave way to a new secretary *a libellis*, a less vigorous writer, occurred either between 1 May and 15 July 209 or between the latter date and 30 December of that year.

It turns out, therefore, that the notice in *HA* Pescennius Niger,[33] mangled as it is, dimly reflects the truth. Ulpian directly succeeded Papinian in the office *a libellis*. Indeed it seems possible to put his accession to and departure from office in a historical context. He replaced Papinian in February–March 202 on the occasion of the return to Rome of Severus from the east. This took place in the early months of the year and Severus occupied himself in Rome with duties of civil administration.[33a] Ulpian's departure from office in the course of 209 should, I believe, be linked to two other events which can plausibly be dated to that year, the conferring on Geta of the title of Augustus and the decision of Severus to leave him in the settled part of Britain in charge of civil administration while he and Caracalla went ahead with the troops.

Though the matter is controversial, Geta is generally thought to have attained the rank of Augustus during the course of 209. Of the coins of that year most record him as Caesar, but a minority make him an Augustus like his brother and father. That suggests a change during the course of the year. An Athenian inscription, which seems to be datable to November or December 209, records his assumption to the full imperial office.[34] If that is right, Geta's appointment must have been at least some months earlier.

Herodian states that, when the preparations for the campaign in Britain (which in the context means Caledonia) were complete, Severus summoned Geta and left him to exercise jurisdiction in the settled part of the province and to carry on the civil administration of the empire.[35] Neither Herodian nor Dio gives a clear account of Severus' last years in Britain, but what they say is consistent with the view that Severus felt the need to

---

[32] *CJ* 8.53.1 (27 June 210 acc. inf. *intellegis*).

[33] *HA* Niger 7.4.

[33a] Herodian 3.10.2; Dio 76.1.1; *HA* Severus 16.8; *RE* 2.4.1973. Note that *CJ* 2.32.1 does *not* show Severus in Sirmium on 18 March 202: Whittaker (1969) 1.325[4].

[34] *RE* 2.4.1568, 1978; *IG* II.1077, III.10; Hammond *MAAR* 24 (1956) 116; Cohen IV[2] (1884) 275 no. 204, 276 no. 212; Mattingley–Sydenham 4.1 (1936) Geta nos. 145–52, 179–81; *Der kleine Pauly* 2 (1967) 786 Geta 3. The dates advocated run from December 208 to October 209.

[35] Herodian 3.14.9, 3.15.6.

provide for the continuity of civil administration while he and Caracalla
sallied forth into the Scottish highlands. It would be consistent with
Severus' character to be concerned that letters and petitions should be
answered in his absence. At the same time, the need for this provided an
excuse for belatedly raising Geta to a dignity which in the normal course of
events, being only a year junior to Caracalla, he might have expected ten
years previously. The question would then arise whether Ulpian should
remain with Geta or go on with Severus and Caracalla. Papinian, as the
praetorian prefect accompanying the imperial expedition, went on with
them.[36] Perhaps Ulpian did so too, and hence it was necessary to make a
new appointment to the office of secretary *a libellis*. That would fit the
probable dates and explain the change in the style of rescripts during the
course of 209. The new secretary survived until 28 December 211,[37] the
date of Geta's murder, or near to it. He then disappears from the record. No
doubt he fell with Geta. Ulpian, then, probably held the *libelli* for just over
seven years, a long tenure.[38] This makes him the presumptive author of
some 76 rescripts collected, not of course chronologically, in *CJ*. But there
is a mystery. Of the 23 rescripts of AD 205, five, mainly from the month of
April, are apparently in the style of Papinian, not Ulpian. The same is true
of one of the seven texts of 206. It is the word order that enables one to be
fairly sure. Papinian's word order is orthodox. Sentences regularly end
with the main verb, often preceded by an infinitive, or with *est*.[39] Ulpian,
even at this early stage of his career, was much less orthodox. He avoids
concentrations of verbs, especially at the end of a sentence.[40] Here are six
texts from the period of Ulpian's tenure of the *libelli* which I suspect of
being composed by Papinian:

(i)   3 April 205   *CJ* 4.15.2   . . . debitores ad solutionem aucto-
                                     ritate praesidis provinciae comp-
                                     elluntur.

The sentence ends in a passive main verb. One may compare:

       1 July 200   *CJ* 3.31.2   . . . fructus restituere coguntur.
(ii)   20 April 205   *CJ* 7.8.1   Licet dotale mancipium vir quo sol-
                                     vendo est possit manumittere,
                                     tamen si te quoque pignori datum
                                     mulieri apparuerit, invita ea non
                                     posse libertatem adsequi non
                                     ambigitur.

       CJ 8.25.1   et per hoc iure te manumissum
                                     nec . . . in servitutem peti posse
                                     certum est.

[36] Herodian 3.14.9; Dio 77 (76) 14.5.   [37] Honoré (1981) 64–5.
[38] Papinian held the office for at least seven years and four months: above, p. 195.
[39] Honoré (1981) 57.   [40] Ch. 2 pp. 50, 67–70.

This rescript, divided by the compilers, has in both its parts verb concentrations of the sort which Papinian admits but Ulpian avoids: first *est, possit, manumittere*; then, *posse, adsequi, ambigitur*; lastly, *peti, posse, est*. Compare with the second part of the rescript:

| | 1 Jan. 196 | *CJ* 9.41.1 | . . . interrogari posse manifestum est. |

and for Papinian's habit of crowding together verbs at the end of a clause or sentence[41]:

| | 21 Oct. 194 | *CJ* 8.15.1 | non inutilis erit exceptio dumtaxat quod numeratum est exsolvi desideranti |
| (iii) | 20 April 205 | *CJ* 9.32.1 | . . . induci non oportet. exhibitis enim quae desiderantur suis iudicibus directa quaestio derelinquenda est. |

For the termination in a gerundive with *est*,[42] a parallel is:

| | 15 March 198 | *CJ* 4.28.3 | origo enim potius obligationis quam titulus actionis considerandus est. |
| (iv) | 26 April 205 | *CJ* 6.3.2 | . . . neque impositas operas praestare cogitur. |

Four rescripts between 194 and 200 have sentences ending in passive forms of *cogere*.[43] One of them is:

| | 1 Oct. 196 | *CJ* 6.39.1 | . . . fideicommissa praestare cogitur. |
| (v) | 13 Sept. 205 | *CJ* 7.21.2 | Si . . . mater vita decessit |

Vita decedere, we saw,[43] is confined, among the jurists, to Papinian.

| (vi) | 10 Feb. 206 | *CJ* 2.3.4. | causam finitam instaurari posse nulla ratio permittit. |

The concentration of verbs at the end of this sentence—*finitam, instaurari, posse, permittit*—is too dense for Ulpian, but not out of place for Papinian. One could compare:

| | 19 Feb. 197 | *CJ* 7.4.1 | nullo iure praestari eam ab eo qui rogatus non est desideras. |
| and | 9 May 197 | *CJ* 3.26.1 | . . . causam agendam esse ratio permittit.[44] |

---

[41] Cf. *CJ* 9.41.1 (1 Jan. 196 *interrogari posse manifestum est*), 6.39.1 (1 Oct. 196 *participatum est competit*), 3.15.1 (4 Oct. 196 *perfici debere satis notum est*), 4.28.3 (15 March 198 *prohibitum est nemini dubium est*), 6.54.3 (21 Nov. 196 *habuisti manifestum est*), 5.47.1 (*convictus fuerit non suffragabitur*), 5.54.1 (10 March 197 *comparari possit condemnari non oportet*), 2.30.1 (30 June 197 *non paruisse conqueteris manumissus non est*), 6.47.1 (31 July 199 *contestata est exigi posse manifestum est*), 6.25.1 (1 Oct. 199 *impeditum fuerit manifestum est*), 4.55.1 pr. (17 Sept. 200 *rumpatur accipere possunt*).

[42] Above, pp. 193–4.

[43] *CJ* 2.23.1. (26 Sept. 194), 4.19.1 (1 July 196), 6.39.1 (1 Oct. 196), 4.26.1 (9 May 197), 3.31.2 (1 July 200).　　　[44] *Ratio iuris permittit* D. 45.3.18.3 (Pap. 27 qu.)

Papinian became praetorian prefect on the fall of Plautianus in January 205,[45] so that he had no business, in theory, to be composing rescripts in 205–6. Yet he stood in for Ulpian on these occasions. Ulpian may have been ill or absent on business, presumably in or just before April 205. The two isolated rescripts of September 205 and February 206 could be accounted for by delay on the emperor's part in reaching a decision. If, for example, Severus wanted to take further advice before coming to a conclusion, or if there was some other cause of procrastination, the rescript ultimately issued would be based on a draft made some time, even several months, before-hand.[46] Hence the texts of September 205 and February 206 may have been substantially composed as early as April 205. On the other hand, Papinian may have stood in for Ulpian for more than one short period.

Leaving these few anomalous rescripts aside, the contrast between the imperial compositions of 194–202 and 202–9 is so striking that it is a surprise that it should for so long have escaped notice. The senior of these two lawyers, each of whom attained the praetorian prefecture, writes in a restrained, technical, impersonal and syntactically orthodox manner. He says nothing of himself, seldom addresses the petitioner directly and hardly ever resorts to imperatives. The law is stated, or understated, rather bleakly. One can hardly put the existence of a defence in law in a more subdued way than by saying to the defendant *non inutiliter defenderis*,[47] 'it will not be pointless for you to plead a defence'. How far from the badgering embodied in the following rescript of Ulpian, to the accompaniment of a volley of imperatives:

> Frustra times administrare res adulscentis, cuius curator es, ne hoc aliquis existiment commune periculum prioris temporis te recepisse. Sed ea quae agenda putas age et, quod magis interest omnium partium, insta ut iudex inter te et tutores datus quam primum partibus suis fungetur

Although the private writings of the Tyrian are forceful and egocentric, so that one can sense his vigorous directness,[48] nothing in them equals this. *Insta*, 'press on', surely affords a glimpse of Ulpian's own restless, energetic personality. His was not simply the story of a scholar who 'abandons erudition for administration, exploits court favour to satisfy an alert ambition, and is brought to ruin',[49] but that of a man of affairs who, after a solid period of public office under Severus, was nimble enough to negotiate the shoals of Caracalla's reign by devoting himself to scholarly writings of unimpugnable value to the emperor and the republic.

---

[45] Dio 76.10.7, 76.14.6; Victor *Caes.* 20.34; Zos. 1.9; *CIL* VI 228 (28 May 205).
[46] Honoré (1981) 47–9.
[47] *CJ* 2.3.2 (12 Feb. 202).
[48] Ch. 2 pp. 60–3.
[49] Syme (1971) 322.

CHAPTER 9

Ulpian as a Writer

I. INTRODUCTION

How good a scholar, lawyer, and writer was Ulpian? Is his reputation for lucid and careful exposition simply based on the accident that more of his work has survived than of that of other ancient lawyers? Divergent views have been held.

In 1885 Pernice wrote a critical article entitled 'Ulpian as a writer'.[1] Ulpian's works, in particular the edictal commentary, were, Pernice argued, unoriginal. They were also unsystematic. Each portion of the commentary was written in isolation from the rest, so that, in the course of the whole, the same subject recurred two or three times. The author used arguments of policy and convenience to support solutions which were doctrinally incorrect. His work was pitched at a low level. It was aimed at judges with little legal expertise. He frequently cited the views of earlier lawyers from secondary sources, mainly the works of later lawyers, without disclosing that he was doing so.

Concluding his investigation into Ulpian's faults, Pernice summed up:[2] 'The aim of this contribution will be achieved if it succeeds in putting people on their guard against Ulpian's writings from various points of view. When he speaks in his own name he may have copied from others. When he cites others he does not usually go back to the original source. When he asserts positive, historical facts without authority his statements must be taken with the greatest reserve. When he attempts to develop the law on his own initiative, he lacks for the most part incisiveness and creative power.'

In 1905 Ulpian found at least a partial defender in the person of Jörs. In his article for Pauly – Wissowa[3] Jörs came to the jurist's rescue so far as the use of sources was concerned. Ulpian had used a wider range of original legal writings than Pernice allowed for. When he used secondary sources he was following current practice. But Ulpian's defender was not whole-hearted. He did not think that the Tyrian had composed the bulk of his

---

[1] Pernice (1885) 443.
[2] Pernice (1885) 484.
[3] Jörs (1905) 1435, 1455 f.

works for the first time in the reign of Caracalla. That would have been impossible in the time. In particular, Jörs, adapting an argument first advanced by Mommsen, argued that the edictal commentary up to book 52 had been first drafted in the reign of Severus and only revised under Caracalla, when the last books were added. If Ulpian's repute as a scholar rose from the ashes, his claim to speed of composition sank.

The views of Pernice and Jörs were of course influenced by notions drawn from modern scholarship and, to some degree, from the intellectual climate of the late nineteenth century and the early twentieth. Pernice did not see that to cite from secondary sources was, in the ancient world, often a necessity. The author has read the original and made notes on it, but does not have it available at the time of writing. If he does, it is time-consuming to consult it. Generally a papyrus roll must be unrolled to find the relevant passage and then rolled up again. To locate a text in a roll is therefore a serious interruption in the flow of composition. Hence an author who wants to compose with reasonable speed is forced to take as the basis of his text a small number of sources which he has open before him at the time of writing. He can supplement these with notes taken from previous reading. Even when he has a well-stocked library, this is the best way to write a large-scale work.

From the reader's point of view it was equally difficult, in the ancient world, to consult references. In particular, in a voluminous work like the edictal commentary, it was awkward for him to look up passages earlier or later than the one he was perusing. Consideration for his readers, not scholarly incompetence, led Ulpian to compose each section of edictal commentary as if it were a self-contained unit. Certainly this method involved some repetition, and some danger of inconsistency. The examples, cited by Pernice, of internal inconsistencies in the jurist's work are in fact quite minor,[4] and at times simply reflect the fact that different definitions and interpretations are appropriate to different legal contexts.[5] But it is true that Ulpian lacks a systematic conceptual framework, such as that of nineteenth-century pandectism. He does not link together the different branches of the law by general notions, or try to deduce particular solutions from these notions. He attempts rather to find solutions which are appropriate to the context: just (*aequum*) or beneficial (*utile*), or which rest on the authority of the emperor or of some jurist whom he respects.

Ulpian is therefore (though Pernice failed to see this) catering for two types of reader. The busy judge or practitioner will want to find out as quickly as he can the state of the law of, let us say, deposit. This he can find in book 30 *ad edictum*, in a commentary which includes the explanations

---

[4] Pernice (1885) 451 f; Jörs (1905) 1458.
[5] e.g. the different definitions of *credere/creditor* in D. 12.1.1 pr. (26 *ed.*) and 50.16.12 (6 *ed.*) and of *bona* in D. 37.1.3 pr. (39 *ed.*), 36.4.5.6 (52 *ed.*), 50.16.49 (59 *ed.*).

about fault (*dolus*, *culpa*, etc.), which are relevant to deposits. These notions have to be explained again, however, in the context of other contracts. On the other hand, the more scholarly reader is given copious references to the earlier literature and to imperial constitutions. These include, as we shall see, references by work and book to the main sources which Ulpian consults as he writes.

Pernice's views are partly based, then, on a misunderstanding of the scholarly methods which were appropriate to the time of writing and to the needs of Ulpian's readers. Jörs, on the other hand, underestimated the capacity for work of scholars in the ancient world and their relative freedom from distraction. Nowadays it takes weeks to write a chapter or an article. The ancient world was simpler. Post arrived sporadically, not every day, as now. Methodical men, like Ulpian and Tribonian, helped by secretaries and slaves, could attend to their task of composition day after day, week after week. Not only could they be regular and assiduous; it was expected of them. In seeking, then, to assess Jörs's opinion that Ulpian could not have written for the first time what he appears to have written under Caracalla, one must not imagine oneself in the office of a modern law faculty or government ministry. If Ulpian's career has been correctly set out and dated in the earlier chapters,[6] he held the office *a libellis* from 202 and began his major writing only from 213. There were at least ten years for him to read and make notes. During this period he had the best possible access to past imperial rescripts and a good opportunity for keeping abreast of recent constitutions. There was nothing to prevent him making excerpts from or references to the materials he read under title headings, according to the scheme of the praetor's edict and the *digesta* of well-known authors such as Celsus, Julian and Marcellus. When the time came to launch the ambitious programme of 213–17 Ulpian had no need to do original research. It was enough to return to the main sources and to supplement these from notes, weaving the whole together in a way which was coherent from the point of view of topic rather than of conceptual interdependence. There was nothing to stop him dictating the text to a secretary.[6a]

II. THE MAIN SOURCES

There is substantial agreement on what these main sources were, at least for the major commentaries on the edict and Sabinus. Ulpian used the *quaestiones* and *responsa* of Papinian, the *digesta* of Celsus, Julian, and Marcellus, the edictal and Sabinian commentaries of Pomponius.

Pernice listed, in addition, among the main sources the *quaestiones* and

[6] Above, ch. 8; Pernice (1885) 456.
[6a] Hagendahl (1971), Schlumberger (1976).

responsa of Scaevola.[7] There is no evidence, however, that Ulpian used the *responsa*, and references to the *quaestiones* are sporadic.

Pernice was right, however, to stress that in the major commentaries Ulpian often took one of these sources as the main basis of his commentary on a particular topic. Thus in *quod falso tutore auctore gestum esse dicatur* (E 43) Ulpian relies mainly on Pomponius. For *de bonorum possessione contra tabulas* (E 142) he follows Marcellus. In *ad legem Aquiliam* Celsus is the leading source. In *de usufructu et usu legato* Julian is the model, with supplements from Celsus and Marcellus. *Depositi vel contra* draws on Pomponius, Julian and Marcellus. One has the impression in many titles *ad edictum* and *ad Sabinum* that the author is using all or a selection of these leading sources, and passing from one to the other as occasion prompts.

Is this impression correct? One way of testing it is to analyse the passages in which Ulpian cites a jurist by book or by work and book, e.g. *Iulianus libro septimo digestorum* or Pomponius *libro vicensimo quarto*. It seems a reasonable hypothesis that when the reference is in this form the author claims to have read the original text and is prepared to incur the reader's wrath if the latter cannot find the passage cited. Certainly there are exceptions.[8]

But if it is in general right to assume that the citations by book and/or work (henceforth called citations by book) point to a source read in the original, the works most often cited in this way are likely to have been the sources most often directly consulted during the process of composition.

References of this sort are very unevenly distributed among the *Digest* jurists. The following table gives the number of such references for each author who makes one, together with the percentage which his work forms of the whole *Digest*.[9] From this the frequency of such references, on the average, can be derived:

Digest jurists: citations by book

Jurist	Number of references by book	Percentage of Digest	References per 1 per cent of Digest
Labeo	4	1.08	
Iavolenus	2	1.01	
Celsus	1	0.91	
Pomponius	3	4.41	1.1
Africanus	2	1.74	
Scaevola	2	4.92	
Callistratus	3	1.12	
Papinian	2	5.69	0.4
Paul	32	16.74	1.9
Ulpian	520	41.56	12.5
Marcianus	28	2.43	11.5

[*See next page for n. 7, 8, and 9*]

Some prominent authors, such as Julian and Marcellus, make no such reference. In general, before Ulpian, citations by book are rare. Authors have one or two such citations for each percentage of *Digest* material. Ulpian has a dozen or so per percentage point, and, following him, so has Marcianus.

Ulpian, then, gives book references at about five or six times the rate of his predecessors. He purports to be more scholarly than they. Which authors does he cite? Five stand out. Without distinguishing at this stage between different works of the various authors, we find the following number of references by book to the juristic sources:

Juristic sources cited by Ulpian by book

Julian	172	Ofilius	6
Pomponius	84	Sabinus	5
Papinian	65	Mucius	3
Marcellus	63	Maecianus	3
Celsus	62	Africanus	1
Neratius	17	Arrianus	1
Labeo	11	Puteolanus	1
Pedius	9	Servius	1
Scaevola	7	Saturninus	1
Cassius	7	Tertullian	1

The references to Julian, Pomponius, Papinian, Marcellus, and Celsus are by far the most numerous. Why did Ulpian select them?

The list is at first sight straightforward. Papinian is the only contemporary to appear in it. Clearly Ulpian had some close relationship with the senior Severan jurist. It is indeed arguable that Papinian was Ulpian's teacher. Papinian is the only lawyer of the right generation whom Ulpian cites in the imperfect—a reminiscence of oral discussion.[10] It is true that this citation need not have been taken from a teaching context. But one other piece of evidence, though not conclusive, is worth noticing. Ulpian is reticent about his teachers. He uses *noster* of no one except the emperor, *meus* only of a fellow citizen of Tyre.[11] In book 69 *ed.*, however, he lets slip what may be a clue. He is discussing the common view (*quod volgo dicitur*) that we can keep possession of winter and summer pastures during the intervening months by intention alone (*animo*), despite physical absence.

---

[7] Pernice (1885) 459. He accuses Ulpian of using the *quaestiones* of Scaevola without acknowledgement. But Ulpian generalizes what in Scaevola is presented as the solution to a problem presented by a particular set of facts (e.g. *D.* 45.1.131.1; Scae. 13 *qu.* and 46.3.27; Ulp. 28 *ed.*).

[8] *D.* 33.9.3.2 (Ulp. 22 *Sab.*, citing Aristo, who cites Labeo *libro nono posteriorum*).

[9] *CDJ* intro. para. 4., for the percentages, and fiches 1, 5, 6, 11, 15, 19, 25, 34, 41, 45, and 62 for the *libro/libris* references.

[10] *D.* 24.1.23 (Ulp. 6 *Sab.*).

[11] *D.* 45.1.70 (Ulp. 11 *ed.*: *populari meo Glabrioni Isidoro*).

Ulpian remarks that Proculus, who is said to have propounded the view that we can, meant this as an example of a general principle—so he was taught: *id exempli causa didici Proculum dicere*.[12] One retains possession of any land which one leaves without intending to relinquish possession, not only of pastures.

From whom did Ulpian learn this? A difficult and convoluted passage of Papinian,[13] which has been complicated by compilatorial intervention, certainly appears to treat the temporary abandonment of winter and summer pastures as an example of a general principle that possession of land left unoccupied, but with no intention of giving it up permanently, may be retained by intention alone (*animo solo*). Was it, then, from Papinian that Ulpian learned to interpret the remark of Proculus in this way?

Despite his admiration for Papinian, whose *responsa* he annotated, Ulpian does not use the whole of his work as a source. From the thirty-seven books of *quaestiones* he cites by book up to book 19.[14] It is perhaps only the action of Justinian's edictal committee that has struck out references by book up to book 25.[15] So far as the nineteen books of *responsa* are concerned we have citations by book up to book 11.[16] None expressly refers or can plausibly be assigned to any later book. Why is this? The explanation is perhaps that the *responsa* were composed, at least from book 14 onwards,[17] after the death of Severus. The later books may have been available too late for Ulpian to digest before, in 213, he launched his five-year programme of writing. After that there was not time to keep abreast of new material other than imperial constitutions. The earlier books of *responsa* must however have been available earlier. An indication of this, apart from Ulpian's citation of them, is a passage in *de fideicommissis* in which he mentions an oral discussion. In the course of it Ulpian cited the 9th book of Papinian's *responsa* (*Papinianum quoque libro nono responsorum scribere referebam*).[18] The context is probably a disputation: the citation seems inappropriate to debate in the imperial council or advice given to a magistrate. After 213 Ulpian can hardly have had time for disputations. This is an indication that the first nine books of the *responsa* were available earlier. Perhaps they were published *seriatim*, in two or more sections: and the same cannot be ruled out for the *quaestiones*. Ulpian annotated the *responsa*, and would certainly have used the later books had they been available. But, again, it is not certain that his annotations stretched beyond book 9.[19]

---

[12] D. 43.16.1.25 (Ulp. 69 *ed.*), cf. 41.2.27 (Proc. 5 *epist.*).
[13] D. 41.2.44.2, 46 (Pap. 23 *qu.* and 2 *diff.*). Ulpian as a student in Rome? D. 47.10.5.5 (56 *ed.*: *ponamus enim studiorum causa Romae agere*).
[14] D. 7.8.4.1 (Ulp. 17 *Sab.*).   [15] D. 29.2.20.3, 4 (Ulp. 61 *ed.*).
[16] D. 30.41.5 (Ulp. 21 *Sab.*).
[17] D. 34.9.18 (Pap. 14 resp: *divus Severus*).
[18] D. 35.1.92 (Ulp. 5 *fid.*).   [19] *Pal.* 1.926, citing Paris; ZRG xviii 171, 177.

The four other principal sources—Celsus, Julian, Pomponius, and Marcellus—all belong to the first two-thirds of the second century. The most recent of them, Marcellus, was an author whose *digesta*, in thirty-one books[20], Ulpian annotated and whose views he often adopted. Marcellus was a pupil of Julian, whose work dominated the jurisprudence of the second century. This is reflected in the number of times he is cited by book—twice as often as the next most cited author, Pomponius. All but one of the citations of Julian probably refer to the ninety books of his *digesta*.[21] The remaining one is to his edition of the works of Minicius.[22] Ulpian probably had a substantial collection of Julian's writings, including unpublished manuscripts, for he says of Julian on six occasions *saepissime scripsit* or *scribit*,[23] a phrase which he uses otherwise only once, of a collection of materials by Vivianus which Ulpian used as a source.

Although the references to Pomponius are less than half those to his contemporary Julian, there is little doubt that for long stretches of his edictal and Sabinian commentary Ulpian followed the corresponding works of Pomponius, his *ad edictum* in more than eighty-three books,[24] and his thirty-six books *ad Sabinum*.[25] There are also references to Pomponius *epistulae*,[26] to his *lectiones*[27] and his work on stipulations,[28] the latter not available to Justinian's compilers. There is no reason to doubt that Ulpian read these lesser works, but he used them only marginally. Against 51 citations from Pomponius *ad edictum* and 24 *ad Sabinum* we have only 9 from other works. Pernice pointed out that Ulpian used Pomponius in fits and starts. Some titles seem to be derived almost exclusively from him; in others he is altogether absent. The reason for this probably lies in the scale on which Pomponius wrote. His work on the edict, for example, outran other edictal commentaries. Hence for many topics Ulpian, who was working to a plan which confined his edictal commentary to a fixed number of books, could not afford to reproduce Pomponius in detail. In others, where Pomponius was relatively economical, he could.

The last major source is Celsus. Ulpian cites by book and work his *digesta*, in 39 books,[29] his *epistolae*[30] and his *quaestiones*.[31] Only the first of these was available to Tribonian, and all but three of Ulpian's citations appear to come from it.

---

[20] *Pal.* 1.590–632.   [21] *Pal.* 1.318–484.

[22] *Pal.* 1.484–90.

[23] Honoré (1964) 13; *CDJ* 71.

[24] *Pal.* 2.15–44; *D.* 38.5.1.14, 27 (Ulp. 44 *ed.*).

[25] *Pal.* 2.86–148.

[26] *Pal.* 2.52–3.

[27] *Pal* 2.53–8.

[28] *Pal.* 2.151; *D.* 7.5.5.2 (Ulp. 18 *Sab.*).

[29] *Pal.* 1.127–69.

[30] *Pal.* 1.169; *D.* 4.4.3.1 (Ulp. 11 *ed.*).

[31] *Pal.* 1.169: *D.* 12.1.1.1 (Ulp. 26 *ed.*), 28.5.9.2 (Ulp. 5 *Sab.*), 34.2.19.3 (Ulp. 20 *Sab.*).

The sources on which Ulpian principally relied in his major commentaries were therefore seven;

Julian's *digesta*	(90 books):	171 citations by book
Marcellus' *digesta*	(31 books):	63 citations by book
Celsus' *digesta*	(39 books):	59 citations by book
Pomponius *ad edictum*	(83 books or more):	51 citations by book
Papinian's *quaestiones*	(37 books):	36 citations by book
Papinian's *responsa*	(19 books):	28 citations by book
Pomponius *ad Sabinum*	(36 books):	24 citations by book

Relatively speaking, therefore, the *responsa* of Papinian (if we assume that Ulpian had only the first eleven books available), the *digesta* of Marcellus and the *digesta* of Julian were the sources most thoroughly excerpted. Taken together the seven sources provided appropriate material for almost every title of the major commentaries but not for some of the more specialised works. But is the list of major sources complete? Ought the names of Labeo and Paul, in particular, to feature in it?

(i) *Labeo*

The *Digest* contains only eleven references by Ulpian to Labeo by book. Three are to his commentary on the urban edict,[32] one to his work on the edict of the peregrine praetor,[33] six to his *posteriora*,[34] one to his *pithana*.[35] One would expect more. The total number of Ulpian's references to Labeo by name is 350, which puts Labeo second to Julian (601) among Ulpian's named sources.[36] Is the reason for the small number of citations by book that Ulpian nearly always cited Labeo at second hand? Certainty is not possible, but there is evidence to suggest that Labeo may be under-represented as regards citations by book. This evidence is derived from the uneven distribution in the *Digest* of Ulpian's references by book.

Ulpian cites earlier jurists by book throughout the Sabinian commentary and sporadically in certain other works: *de fideicommissis*, the *disputationes*, *de officio proconsulis*, *de officio quaestoris*, *de omnibus tribunalibus*, *de appellationibus*. In his edictal commentary, however, such citations, though numerous, continue only until the end of book 52.[37] Why is this? Is it because, as Jörs thought,[38] they were put in during Ulpian's supposed first draft, made in the reign of Severus, which stopped at book 52? Or is

---

[32] *D.* 50.16.19 (Ulp. 11 *ed.*), 11.4.1.5 (1 *ed.*), 4.8.7 pr. (13 *ed.*)

[33] *D.* 4.3.9. 4a (Ulp. 11 *ed.*).

[34] *D.* 28.5.13.5, 6 (Ulp. 7 *Sab.*), 28.5.17.5 (ibid.).

[35] *D.* 46.4.8.2 (Ulp. 48 *Sab.*).

[36] Leading sources by number of citations: Julian 601, Labeo 350, Pomponius 313, Marcellus 219, Celsus 173, Papinian 116.

[37] *D.* 39.1.1.10 (52 *ed.*, citing Cels. 10 *dig.*), 39.1.5 pr. (52 *ed.*, citing Iul. 12 *dig.*), 39.1.5.16 (52 *ed.*, citing Iul. 49 *dig.*).

[38] Jörs (1905) 1439–40.

this feature due to the compilers, who stopped excerpting the references to individual books at this point?

According to the time schedule set out in chapters 6 to 7, Ulpian reached the middle of book 56 *ad edictum* by the end of 215. He continued with books 26/2 to 51 *ad Sabinum* in the year 216. Hence, even if Ulpian changed his mode of reference at the end of 216 one might expect such references in books 53, 54, 55, and the first half of 56 *ad edictum*. We do not find them. This might perhaps be an accident of excerpting. The compilers did not happen to want the passage in these books which contained the references to the sources by book. Pertinent, but still not conclusive, is the fact that *de appellationibus*, probably to be assigned to 217,[39] does contain a reference by book, viz. to Julian 45 *dig.*[40] The work on appeals may, however, belong to 216 rather than 217. More telling is the fact that, as will be explained, passages in which Ulpian cites his source with *inquit* (introducing an exact citation) in general run parallel to those in which he cites by book. These *inquit* passages *are* found in the later books of edictal commentary, viz. in books 57, 68, 69, 70, 71, and 81.[41] Since the purpose of the two devices is similar—to give the reader the exact words of the source or to guide him towards them—Ulpian is unlikely to have retained *inquit* but abandoned citation by book in the last twenty-nine books *ad edictum*. It is rather that the compilers struck out the book references but retained *inquit*. The first they could do without disturbing the sense of the text they were excerpting. The second had to be retained in order to give the correct sense.

To be precise, it was the edictal committee which did this. As we have shown in another study,[42] the edictal committee progressively reduced the amount of material it excerpted. Thus, the committee took less per book from the later than the earlier books of edictal commentary. The committee's second stint of edictal commentary began, according to Bluhme and the study referred to, in the middle of book 52. Suppose that, in reality, the break between the stint of the Sabinian and the edictal committee came half a book later, at the beginning of book 53.[43] It would then be explicable that, in pursuit of its policy of economy of excerpts, the edictal committee, from book 53 onwards, decided to omit references by book but to retain the brief and explicit *inquit*. This would explain the

---

[39] Above, pp. 183–5, 188.

[40] *D.* 49.4.1.14 (Ulp. 1 *appell.*, citing Iul. 40 *dig.* amended by Lenel to 45 *dig.*).

[41] *D.* 47.10.13.4 (57 *ed.*), 43.8.2.40 (68 *ed.*), 43.16.1.35 (69 *ed.*), 43.17.3.4 (69 *ed.*), 41.2.6 pr. (70 *ed.*), 43.19.1.11 (70 *ed.*), 43.30.3.4 (71 *ed.*), 43.24.7.3 (71 *ed.*), 43.23.1.8 (71 *ed.*), 39.1.21.7 (81 *ed.*), cf. 21.1.17.4, 21.1.23 pr. (1 *ed. cur.*).

[42] Honoré–Rodger (1970) 246, 296–306.

[43] *Op. cit.* 277–9. The transfer of these books from the Sabinian to the edictal committee raises many problems. I am inclined to think that books 54 and the first part of 55 were transferred first, thereafter the second part of book 52 and book 53.

absence of precise references from this book onwards better than a supposed change of style on the part of Ulpian himself. One may note that the other committees excerpting for the *Digest* did not follow suit. Thus, references by book are to be found in the *disputationes*[44] and *de appellationibus*,[45] excerpted by the Sabinian committee, and in *de fideicommissis*,[46] excerpted by the Papinian committee, though the excerpting of these works took place later in the commission's work than that of the later books of edictal commentary by the edictal committee.[47]

There is every reason, then, *pace* Jörs, to suppose that Ulpian continued throughout the edictal commentary to cite sources by book when he thought it helpful to do so and when he had the original to hand. This point has a bearing on the paucity of citations of Labeo by book. In the last segment of his edictal commentary Ulpian made particularly free use of Labeo. Labeo is mentioned by name 105 times in these books, and from this point of view outstrips all other sources, including Julian. Presumably, then, the compilers' policy of striking out book references has obscured the extent to which Ulpian cited Labeo in this way.

Another approach to the problem is to analyse Ulpian's use of *inquit*. This expression, like a book reference, prima facie indicates that the writer claims to have consulted the original source. The jurists cited by book and those cited with *inquit* ought therefore to be much the same, and to be cited a proportionate number of times or nearly so. The following list shows that in general this is the case. Ulpian uses *inquit*[48] in the *Digest* of the following writers:

Julian	57 times	Scaevola	2 times
Pomponius	20	Africanus	2
Celsus	16	Aristo	2
Labeo	13	Cassius	1
Marcellus	12	Maecianus	1
Papinian	12	Nerva	1
Pedius	7	Octavenus	1
Vivianus	5	Vitellius	1
Masurius Sabinus	3	Fulcinius	1
Neratius	3	Q. Mucius	1
Caelius Sabinus	3	Ofilius	1

[44] D. 29.2.40, 29.2.42 pr. (4 *disp*.), 41.1.33 pr. (4 *disp*.), 30.75.4 (5 *disp*.), 33.4.2 pr. (5 *disp*.), 36.1.23.3 (5 *disp*.).

[45] D. 49.4.1.14 (1 *appell*.).

[46] D. 36.1.18.1, 4, 6 (2. *fid*.), 36.1.15.3 (4 *fid*.), 36.1.17.6, 13 (4 *fid*.), 35.1.92 pr. (5 *fid*.), 40.5.24.8, 9 (5 *fid*.).

[47] According to Honoré (1978) 257 f, the edictal committee began excerpting the later books of edictal commentary on 20 February 531 and finished about 15 May 531. *Disputationes* was excerpted between 14 June and 6 July 531, *de appellationibus* between 20 May and 29 May 532, *de fideicommissis* between 21 June and 15 August 531.

[48] *CDJ* 61.

The total of Ulpian's references in the *Digest* to named jurists with *inquit* is 165. All other jurists together provide 30 (Labeo 4, Celsus 1, Gaius 3, Pomponius 1, Africanus 3, Paul 14, Marcianus 4). Ulpian therefore purports to give an exact citation of an earlier jurist far more frequently than his predecessors. The jurists whom he cites in this way largely correspond with those in the list, set out earlier, of book references. The difference, so far as major sources is concerned, is that Labeo's exact words are cited with *inquit* about the same number of times as those of Papinian, Celsus, and Marcellus. From the distribution of texts with *inquit*, therefore, Labeo would count as a main original source like the others. It is hardly possible to argue that the verbatim citations of Labeo are taken from Celsus or Pomponius, since these jurists hardly ever cite with *inquit*, just as they hardly ever cite by book. It is therefore not plausible to assert that the citations by Ulpian in either of these forms derive, except in rare instances, from secondary sources.

Ulpian cites Labeo with *inquit* in books 31, 53, 57, 62, 68, 71, 76, and 81 *ad edictum* and 17 and 49 *ad Sabinum*.[49] More than half the *inquit* references, therefore, come from the last segment of Ulpian's edictal commentary. This confirms our impression that the policy of Justinian's edictal committee of striking book references from the excerpts they made from this segment has resulted in a serious underestimate of the extent to which Ulpian used Labeo as an original source. Jörs saw more clearly than Pernice[50] that, while many citations of Labeo are taken from secondary sources, a large number are not.

(ii) *Paul*

The list of sources referred to by book or with *inquit* excites curiosity because, of contemporary authors, only Papinian is thus cited. Why? In particular why does Ulpian not cite either directly or from a secondary source his coeval Iulius Paulus, a major jurist who had published works on the edict and on Sabinus shortly before Ulpian, and who had written on a number of specialized topics which were to concern Ulpian too? Why, again, does Ulpian not cite Tryphoninus, another eminent contemporary, or Callistratus, an expert on public law? At least in the case of Paul it is impossible to suppose that he was ignorant of their published works. Yet he appears to overlook them.

Was Ulpian motivated by person rivalry or contempt? It has often been suggested that Paul and Ulpian were rivals.[51] The suggestion has some

---

[49] D. 17.1.10.8 (31 *ed.*), 39.2.15.33 (53 *ed.*), 39.3.4 pr. (53 *ed.*), 47.10.7.1 (57 *ed.*), 47.10.13.4 (57 *ed.*), 42.5.15.1 (62 *ed.*), 43.8.2.40 (68 *ed.*), 43.24.5.12 (71 *ed.*), 43.24.7.3 (71 *ed.*), 43.23.1.8 (71 *ed.*), 44.4.4.15 (76 *ed.*), 39.1.12 pr. (81 *ed.*) 7.1.12 pr. (17 *Sab.*), 18.4.2.17 (49 *Sab.*).

[50] Jörs (1905) 1477 f. noting D. 39.3.1.20 (53 *ed.*: *apud Labeonem autem invenio relatum*), 7.8.2 (17 *Sab.*: *apud Labeonem memini tractatum*) against Pernice (1885) 476 f.

[51] e.g. Krueger (1912) 298

merit. Ulpian wrote on many of the same topics that Paul had covered not long since. He adopts somewhat different methods. For instance he cites by book or with *inquit* far more often than Paul.[52] He seems to be aiming at a more scholarly audience. He is more concerned than Paul to justify the provisions of, for example, the praetor's edict.[53] But these features of Ulpian's work can be explained by the audience which Ulpian had in mind—the enlarged citizenship, now, since the issue of the *constitutio Antoniniana*, subject to Roman law. No doubt he took the view that Paul's works were inadequate in the new dispensation. This does not imply that he had a low opinion of Paul as a lawyer.

There is some reason to think that Ulpian, in composing his major commentaries, made use of Paul's work. It would, in the first place, have been strange not to read and profit from recent publications by a jurist of standing and a member of the imperial council. Secondly, as I argued in an earlier study,[54] it is easier to explain the textual chains in the *Digest* if we suppose that, for long stretches, the main commentaries used by the compilers ran parallel. This made possible a technique of excerpting by which, for example, Ulpian, Paul and Gaius *ad edictum* could be read together.[55] Ulpian was taken as the main text and was supplemented by short excerpts from the others when they diverged. This parallelism was only possible, if, to take the same example, Ulpian used Paul *ad edictum* and Paul used Gaius *ad edictum provinciale*. The argument is statistically coherent, but it is suggestive rather than compelling. Conversely there are a few passages in which it seems likely that Paul used Ulpian as a source,[56] again without naming him.

A further argument in favour of Ulpian's use of Paul can be derived from the resemblance of their styles. This can be tested statistically in the following way. Fifty common Latin words are selected (e.g. *si, non, est, et*) and the frequency with which the various jurists represented in the *Digest* use them is ascertained with the help of the *Concordance to the Digest Jurists*. There are thirteen jurists from whom we have enough material in the *Digest* to make reliable estimates of the frequency with which they use these words. For each of the fifty words the jurists can be ranged in order according to the relative frequency with which they use the word. For each pair of jurists we can measure whether one member of the pair tends to come close to or far from the other member of the pair in these fifty lists. This can be measured by what is called a Spearman non-parametric correlation. This gives an estimate of the probability that the resemblances

---

[52] Above, p. 207.
[53] Above, ch. 1 pp. 28–9.
[54] Honoré (1963) 362.
[55] Honoré–Rodger (1970) 250 f.
[56] *D.* 23.2.60.4 (1 *or. d. Ant et Comm.*), above ch. 3 p. 104; perhaps 27.9.13.1 (1 *or. d. Severi*).

between the members of each pair are not due to chance. A very high probability of this, close to unity, is therefore an indication of a likely close resemblance in point of style, and a lower correlation points to the lesser probability of a close resemblance in that respect.

So far as Ulpian is concerned, he correlates with each of the other twelve jurists on the basis of the fifty common words and expressions as follows:

Ulpian	1.0000	Marcellus	0.9343
Marcianus	0.9780	Modestinus	0.8939
Paul	0.9774	Callistratus	0.8768
Pomponius	0.9545	Africanus	0.8646
Gaius	0.9491	Papinian	0.8569
Tryphoninus	0.9401	Scaevola	0.7700
Julian	0.9390		

To my mind the table is persuasive and enhances one's confidence in the value of such calculations.[57] Marcianus, for whom the probability of stylistic affinity with Ulpian is very high, indeed close to unity, copied Ulpian in many respects. One of them, as we saw, is the habit of frequently giving book references when earlier jurists are cited. Marcianus' main sources are the same as Ulpian's. He cites Papinian 14 times. Marcellus 10, Pomponius 8, Julian 7, Celsus and Scaevola 4 each.[58] Eight references to Papinian,[59] 7 to Marcellus,[60] 5 to Pomponius,[61] 3 to Julian,[62] 2 to Celsus[63] and 1 each to Labeo,[64] Scaevola,[65] and Chrysippus[66] are by book. The resemblance to Ulpian is so close as to make one ask whether Marcianus was using the senior lawyer's library. Indeed, on the statistical test explained above, no two jurists among the thirteen stand closer than Ulpian and Marcianus. Marcianus was a teacher, as his sixteen books of *institutiones* show. But he cites such a wealth of imperial rescripts[67] that one might guess that, though he never held the *libelli*, he assisted Ulpian in that office.

The affinity between Ulpian and Paul, viewed statistically, is hardly less striking than that between Ulpian and Marcianus. How is it to be

[57] The jurists with whom there is a low correlation—the last five—are all writers, with the exception of Papinian, of whom Ulpian makes little use, for one reason or another. Papinian is one of his main sources, but his style is so markedly different from Ulpian's that the dissimilarity is to be expected.

[58] *CDJ* 19, 20.

[59] D. 20.4.12.5, 6, 9 (Marci 1 *hyp.*), 20.1.11.2 (1 *hyp.*), 48.21.3 (1 *del.*), 49.14.18.10 (1 *del.*), 48.17.1.4 (2 *pub. iud.*), 30.113.5 (7 *inst.*).

[60] D. 12.4.13 (3 *reg.*), 40.5.55.1 (4 *reg.*), 34.9.3 (5 *reg.*), 40.15.1.4 (1 *del.*), 49.14.18.10 (1 *del.*), 30.114.3 (8 *inst.*), 25.7.3.1 (12 *inst.*).

[61] D. 20.2.2, 20.2.5 pr. (1 *hyp.*), 20.1.13.2 (1 *hyp.*), 41.2.43.1 (3 *reg.*), 22.1.32 pr. (4 *reg.*).

[62] D. 20.5.7 (1 *hyp.*), 38.2.22 (1 *inst.*), 36.2.20 (6 *inst.*).

[63] D. 28.5.52.1 (3 *reg.*), 36.1.34 (8 *inst.*).

[64] D. 18.1.45 (4 *reg.*).

[65] D. 20.3.1.2 (1 *hyp.*).

[66] D. 1.3.2 (1 *inst.*).

[67] Below, p. 236.

explained? Not simply by the spirit of the age or the fact both jurists were members of the imperial council. So was Papinian, and perhaps Tryphoninus. Callistratus was also a contemporary. None of these stands as high in the list of correlations as does Paul. The easiest explanation is that Ulpian copied from Paul.

It may be useful at this point to say something of the next two jurists on the list of correlations, Pomponius and Gaius. That for long stretches Ulpian pretty well copies out Pomponius was rightly noted by Pernice.[68] That would account for a certain stylistic affinity. Is the same true of Gaius? Did Ulpian make use of Gaius' works on the urban and provincial edict? This is much less certain. That Paul used Gaius is clear enough. For example, the phrase *ex diverso*, which comes in 12 texts of Gaius' *Institutes*,[69] is also found in eleven texts of Paul[70] and otherwise only once each in Papinian[71] and Ulpian.[72] The passage in Ulpian may have been taken from Paul. Direct use of Gaius need not be postulated. Hence the relatively high correlation between Ulpian and Gaius (0.9491) may simply reflect the very high correlations between Ulpian and Paul (0.9774) and between Paul and Gaius (0.9723) respectively. The correct interpretation of the figures may be that Ulpian used Paul and Paul Gaius, without Ulpian's making direct use of Gaius. This is not to say that such use is ruled out, only that the evidence does not require it.

If I am right in thinking that, for Ulpian, Paul formed a major source, it remains to be shown why he did not cite him by name. There is an explanation of this at first sight surprising phenomenon which is consistent with the two jurists having been on good terms and having respected each other's work. This is the fact, that, unless I am mistaken, the Severan jurists never cite the work of a living author by name. Is there any example to the contrary? Papinian cites no one more recent than Africanus.[73] Callistratus stops at Julian[74] and Papirius Fronto.[75] Tryphoninus, composing under Severus or Caracalla, mentions Papinian, but only as secretary *a libellis*.[76] His most recent juristic citation is of Scaevola.[77] Ulpian cites the *quaestiones* and *responsa* of Papinian, but only when the latter is dead.[78] In the first five

---

[68] Pernice (1885) 459, 463, 473.

[69] Gaius *Inst.* 1.39, 78, 133; 2.64, 137, 245; 3.84, 126, 201; 4.3, 77, 109.

[70] *D.* 6.1.35 pr. (21 *ed.*), 47.10.6 (55 *ed.*), 10.2.41 (1 *decr.*), 26.7.53 (2 *decr.*), 32.97 (2 *decr.*), 8.4.18 (1 *man.*), 24.3.17 (7 *Sab.*), 27.1.31.4 (6 *qu.*), 46.1.56.1 (15 *qu.*), 18.1.57.2 (4 *Plaut.*), 44.7.47 (14 *Plaut.*).

[71] *D.* 22.3.26 (Pap. 20 *qu.*).

[72] *D.* 21.1.17.14 (Ulp. 1 *ed. cur.*).

[73] *D.* 35.1.71 pr. (Pap. 17 *qu.*).

[74] *D.* 5.1.36.1 (Call. 1 *cogn*), 49.14.3 pr. (Call. 3 *iur. fisc.*).

[75] *D.* 50.16.220.1 (Call 2 *qu.*), 14.2.4.2 (ibid.).

[76] *D.* 20.5.12 pr. (8 *disp.*).

[77] *D.* 20.5.12.1 (8 *disp.*), 49.17.19 pr. (18 *disp.*).

[78] Ulpian cites Papinian 116 times, always in *ed. Sab.*, *disp.*, *omn. trib*, or *fid.* The earliest references in *ed.* come in *D.* 4.4.7.10, 4.4.9.4, and 4.4.20 pr. (all 11 *ed.*). The edictal commentary from book 6 was begun in 213 (above, ch. 5). Papinian had been killed in late 212: Kunkel (1967) 224.

books of edictal commentary, written when Papinian was alive,[79] he refers to him only once: *responsum scio a Papiniano*[80]—which is a reminiscence, not a citation from a published work. It is true that in book 6 *ad Sabinum* Ulpian appears to cite Marcianus[81] (*iam enim complesse videtur annum quartum decimum, ut Marciano videtur*). But we know that Ulpian's Sabinian commentary went through a second edition,[82] and this wholly isolated reference to Marcianus has the air of a later addition to the text. There is no parallel elsewhere in Ulpian to a sentence ending '*ut . . . videtur*'[83] an uncharacteristically weak ending. This phrase therefore, may belong to a period after the death of Marcianus, the date of which we do not know. Marcianus himself, though writing after the death of Caracalla, cites no one later than Papinian,[84] not even Ulpian. This is the more remarkable given the extent of Ulpian's influence over him. Paul in one text[85] refers to a *responsum* of Ulpian which was cited to him by a client who consulted him. He disagreed with it. This, again, is not a citation from a published work. Paul also refers in five texts to Papinian. In one of these he speaks of Papinian's hearing a case as praetorian prefect.[86] In two others he mentions views expressed by Papinian as a member of the judicial council of Severus.[87] The remaining two passages cite opinions from the fifth book of Papinian's *responsa*.[88] One of these, from the monograph *ad orationem divi Severi*, was composed under Caracalla.[89] The other, from *ad orationem divi Antonini et Commodi* cannot be dated. There is reason to suppose, however, as argued earlier,[90] that the passage in question is copied from a work of Ulpian. There is nothing, therefore, to show that Paul, any more than the other Severans, cited living authors.

Given this, the problem is not to explain, by reference to rivalry or contempt, why Paul and Ulpian do not overtly cite one another but rather why the Severans, unlike their predecessors, avoid referring to contemporaries while they are alive. They may have been sensitive to the danger of giving or receiving offence, of *iniuria*. It is easier and safer to express one's real opinion of a dead author. Until recently English judges had a convention that the works of living authors should not be cited in court.[91] No doubt the point was to save both judge and author

[79] Probably in early 211: above pp. 25, 146–8. [80] *D.* 2.14.7.5 (Ulp. 4 *ed.*).
[81] *D.* 28.1.5 (6 *Sab.*).
[82] *C. Cordi* (16 Nov. 534) 3.
[83] *CDJ* fiche 74.
[84] Fourteen times, e.g. *D.* 48.16.14.5, 10, 13 (1 *SC Turpillianum*).
[85] *D.* 19.1.43 (5 *qu.*).
[86] *D.* 12.1.40 (3 *qu.*).
[87] *D.* 49.14.50 (3 *decr.*), 29.2.97 (3 *decr.*).
[88] *D.* 27.9.13.1 (Paul 1 *or. d. Sev.*), 23.2.60.4 (Paul 1 *or. d. Ant. et Comm.*).
[89] *D.* 27.9.13 pr. (Paul 1 *or. Sev.*: *imperator Antoninus et divus pater eius*).
[90] Above, ch. 3 p. 104.
[91] *Nicholls v. Ely Beet Sugar Factory Ltd.* [1936] Ch. 343, 349; R. E. Megarry, *Miscellany-at-Law* (1955) 328.

embarrassment. Perhaps the Severan jurists possessed a comparable sensibility.

III. OTHER DIRECT SOURCES

The list of authors cited by book etc. or with *inquit* affords evidence of the other first-hand sources used by Ulpian.

(a) *Neratius Priscus*, a leading jurist of the reign of Trajan,[92] is cited seventeen times by book[93] and three times with *inquit*.[94] The citations show that Ulpian used Neratius' *membrana*,[95] his *responsa*,[96] his *epistulae*,[97] and his edition of Plautius,[98] of which only the first two reached Justinian's compilers. The citations run from book 7 to book 36 *ad edictum* and from books 17 to 20 *ad Sabinum*. There is also a reference to Neratius' *responsa* in Ulpian's *disputationes*. (In general, the sources used by Ulpian in his major commentaries are also used for the *disputationes* and for *de fideicommissis*.)

In all Ulpian names Neratius as a source seventy-six times.[99] A good many of these citations are probably first hand. They include references in Ulpian 56, 57, 59, 71, 73, 75, 76 *ed.* and 1 *ed. aed. cur.*,[100] books from which the edictal committee struck out book and work references.

(b) *Sex. Pedius*, a jurist of the second half of the first century AD,[101] is cited nine times by book or work and seven times with *inquit*.[102] Ulpian mentions him forty times in all.[103] None of his works were available to Tribonian, but he composed a commentary on the praetor's edict in at least twenty-five books. This Ulpian cites by book, nine times, in the part of his own edictal commentary which lies between books 10 and 29.[104] The citations in the later books of Ulpian *ad edictum*, which lack a book reference, are either direct or come from Paul, who also used Pedius.[105] Pedius also wrote on the edict of the curule aediles.[106] This work was used

[92] *Pal.* 1.783–88.
[93] *D.* 5.3.13.3 (Ulp. 15 *ed.*), 8.3.5 pr., 2, 3 bis (17 *ed.*), 8.3.5.1 (17 *ed.*), 12.4.3.5 (26 *ed.*), 14.6.7 pr. (29 *ed.* bis), 15.1.9.1 (29 *ed.*), 19.1.11.12 (32 *ed.*), 13.1.12.2 (38 *ed.*), 7.1.7.3 (17 *Sab.*), 7.2.3 pr. (17 *Sab.*), 33.7.12.35, 43 (20 *Sab.*), 36.1.23.3 (1 *disp.*).
[94] *D.* 10.4.9.8 (24 *ed.*), 33.7.12.43 (20 *Sab.* bis).
[95] *D.* 8.3.3 pr., 2 (2 *membr.*), 8.3.3.3 bis (3 *membr.*), 7.1.7.3 (4 *membr.*), 5.3.13.3 (6 *membr.*), 12.4.3.5, 13.1.12.2. (*membr.*).
[96] *D.* 7.2.3 pr. (1 *resp.*), 36.1.23.3 (1 *resp.*), 14.6.7 pr. (1 and 2 *resp.*), 15.1.9.1 (2 *resp.*), 19.1.11.12 (2 *resp.*).
[97] *D.* 33.7.12.35, 43 (4 *epist.*).   [98] *D.* 8.3.5.1 (*Plaut.*).   [99] *CDJ* 64.
[100] *D.* 47.10.1.8.9 (56 *ed.*), 47.10.7.5 (57 *ed.*), 42.4.7.16 (59 *ed.*), 43.24.7.1 (71 *ed.*), 20.2.3 (73 *ed.*), 44.2.9.1, 11 (75 *ed.*), 44.4.4.18 (76 *ed.*), 21.1.25.3 (1 *ed. aed. cur.*).
[101] *Pal.* 2.1–10.
[102] *D.* 3.5.5.11 (10 *ed.*), 4.2.14.5 (11 *ed.*), 4.2.7 pr. (11 *ed.*), 4.3.1.4 (11 *ed.*), 4.7.4.2 (13 *ed.*), 4.8.7 pr. (13 *ed.*), 4.8.13.2 (13 *ed.*), 14.4.1.1 (29 *ed.*), 15.1.7.3 (29 *ed.*).
[103] *D.* 3.5.5.11, 13 (10 *ed.*), 4.7.4.2 (13 *ed.*), 4.8.13.2 (13 *ed.*), 15.1.7.3 (29 *ed.*), 21.1.23.9 (1 *ed. cur.*).
[104] *D.* 3.5.5.11 (10 *ed.*), 4.2.7 pr. (11 *ed.*), 4.2.14.5 (11 *ed.*), 4.3.1.4 (11 *ed.*), 4.7.4.2 (13 *ed.*), 4.8.7 pr. (13 *ed.*), 4.8.13.2 (13 *ed.*), 14.4.1.1 (29 *ed.*) 15.1.7.3 (29 *ed.*).
[105] *D.* 12.1.6 (Paul 28 *ed.*), 37.1.6.2 (Paul 41 *ed.*).
[106] *Pal.* 2.6–7.

by Ulpian, probably directly, though the edictal committee has excised all references to book from Ulpian *ed. aed. cur.*[107]

Their policy has also eliminated references by book etc. to Vivianus,[108] a late-first-century or early-second-century[109] jurist, who is cited five times with *inquit* but never by book. Four of the *inquits* come in Ulpian's first book on the curule aediles, one from book 69 on the edict.[110] These are all contexts from which book references have been struck out. So there is reason to think that Ulpian used Vivianus directly. Vivianus made a collection of material drawn inter alia from Labeo,[111] Proculus,[112] Sabinus[113] and Cassius,[114] perhaps at the end of the first century AD. Scaevola[115] and Ulpian used his material,[116] and refer to it with phrases such as *apud Vivianum relatum est*[117] or *quantum repeto apud Vivianum.*[118] In all Ulpian cites him by name nineteen times, always in his work on the praetor's edict or that of curule aediles. Vivianus' collection of material was not available to Justinian's compilers.

Caelius Sabinus,[119] consul in AD 69 and head of the Sabinian school in succession to Cassius, is cited three times with *inquit*[120] but never by book etc. The reason is the same. The *inquit* comes from Ulpian on the edict of the curule aediles, on which Caeliús wrote. Ulpian mentions him thirteen times in this commentary, fourteen if a text with 'Caecilius' is corrected.[121] He no doubt used Caelius directly, indeed as a main source, for this work, but not otherwise.

(*c*) *Cervidius Scaevola*[122] cannot be accounted a major source but Ulpian cites him seven times with a book reference[123] and twice with *inquit.*[124] He names him thirty-one times in all.[125] All the explicit references are to Scaevola's *quaestiones*. It is not clear that Ulpian used any other work of the

---

[107] *Ed. aed. cur.* was excerpted after book 81 *ed.*, but composed in 213 or 214 before Ulpian had progressed beyond book 31 *ed.*; above, pp. 172–3.

[108] *Pal.* 2.1225–8.

[109] D. 43.16.1.47 (69 *ed.*), 21.1.1.9 (1 *ed. cur. ter.*), 21.1.17.4 (1 *ed. cur.*).

[110] Above, n. 109.

[111] D. 43.24.13.5 (Ulp. 71 *ed.*).

[112] D. 29.7.14 pr. (Scae. 8 *qu.*).

[113] Ibid.

[114] Ibid.

[115] Ibid.

[116] CDJ 75.

[117] D. 21.1.17.3 (Ulp. 1 *ed. cur.*), Coll. 12.7.8 (Ulp. 18 *ed.*: *ex Viviano relatum est*).

[118] D. 29.7.14 pr. (Scae 18 *qu.*).

[119] *Pal.* 1.78–82.

[120] D. 21.1.17.1, 16 (1 *ed. cur.*), 21.1.38.11 (2 *ed. cur.*).

[121] CDJ 51 and D. 21.1.14.10 (Ulp. 1 *ed. cur.* where the context makes Caelius for Caecilius nearly certain).

[122] *Pal.* 2.215–322.

[123] D. 4.4.11.1 (11 *ed.*), 41.3.10.2 (16 *ed.*), 50.16.26 (16 *ed.*), 13.4.2.3 (27 *ed.*), 28.6.10.6 (1 *Sab.*), 7.1.25.6 (18 *Sab.*), 41.1.23.3 (43 *Sab.*).

[124] D. 13.4.2.3 (27 *ed.*), 41.3.10.2 (16 *Sab.*).

[125] CDJ 71.

Antonine jurist who taught Paul and Tryphoninus. Ulpian refers to him both in his major commentaries and four times in his *disputationes* (which correspond to *quaestiones*).[126] There is also a single reference in *de adulteriis*,[127] which may be taken from Paul *de adulteriis*.[128]

(d) *Volusius Maecianus*,[129] who was a member of Marcus' judicial council and prefect of Egypt, is cited thrice by book[130] and once with *inquit*.[131] All four passages come from Maecianus' sixteen books on *fideicommissa*. Ulpian mentions Maecianus sixteen times in all, ten in *de fideicommissis*[132] and thrice in the Sabinian commentary,[133] one reference in the latter being to Maecianus on *fideicommissa*.[134] Ulpian clearly used this work directly. In his work on the office of proconsul Ulpian refers to Maecianus when dealing with the *lex Pompeia de parricidiis*.[135] The reference is probably to Maecianus' fourteen book work on *iudicia publica*.[136] Ulpian may have had this work to hand, since it is not clear from what intermediate source he could have cited it.

(e) Ulpian cites *Masurius Sabinus*[137] five times by book etc.[138] and three times with *inquit*.[139] The book citations refer not to the *ius civile* of Sabinus, which formed the text on which *ad Sabinum* was a commentary, but to Sabinus' *libri ad Vitellium*. One of the *inquit* passages on the other hand no doubt refers to the *ius civile*.[140] The *libri ad Vitellium* are mentioned only in books 20 and 22 *ad Sabinum*.[141] Vitellius was a jurist of the time of Augustus, whose works Paul edited and annotated.[142] Hence either Vitellius, or Sabinus' reworking of him, must have been available in the Severan age. Ulpian could have used it as a direct source. In all Ulpian refers to Sabinus 119 times,[143] but many of these citations appear to be taken from later writers such as Pomponius, Celsus and Julian.

(f) *C. Cassius Longinus*,[144] co-founder of the Sabinian school and

126 D. 12.1.7 (Ulp. 1 *disp*.), 23.3.43 pr. (Ulp. 3 *disp*.), 36.1.23 pr. (Ulp. 5 *disp*.), 35.2.35 (Ulp. 6 *disp*.).
127 D. 23.5.13.4 (Ulp. 5 *adult*.).
128 Since Paul was a pupil of Scaevola, e.g. D. 2.14.27.2 (Paul 3 *ed*.).
129 *Pal.* 1.575−88.
130 D. 36.1.17.6, 13 (Ulp. 4 *fid*.), 7.1.72 (Ulp. 17 *Sab*.).
131 D. 36.1.17.6 (4 *fid*.).
132 D. 32.11.1 (2 *fid*.), 32.11.15 (2 *fid*.), 36.1.1.8 (3 *fid*.), 36.1.17 pr., 3.6.8.9 bis, 13 (4 *fid*.).
133 D. 7.4.3 pr. (7 *Sab*.), 7.1.72 (17 *Sab*. bis).
134 D. 7.1.72 (17 *Sab*.).
135 D. 48.9.6 (8 *off. proc*.).
136 Read by the compilers: *Pal.* 1.587−8.
137 *Pal.* 2.187−216.
138 D. 33.7.8 pr. (Ulp. 20 *Sab*.), 33.7.12.27 (20 *Sab*.), 34.2.19.17 (20 *Sab*.), 32.45 (22 *Sab*.), 33.9.3 pr. (22 *Sab*.).
139 D. 33.9.3 pr. (22 *Sab*.), 18.2.11 pr. (28 *Sab*.).
140 D. 18.2.11 pr. (28 *Sab*.).
141 Above, n. 138.
142 Available to the compilers: *Pal.* 1.1301−8.
143 *CDJ* 71.
144 *Pal.* 1.110−26.

restored from exile by Vespasian, is cited seven times by book,[145] once with *inquit*.[146] No work of Cassius was available to Tribonian. Ulpian cites from his *libri iuris civilis*, up to book 10.[147] All the citations come in Ulpian's *ad Sabinum*, and presumably Cassius' work was based on Sabinus' *ius civile*. The *inquit* passage, on the other hand, refers to a note of Cassius on Vitellius.[148] It looks as if Ulpian consulted these, and Cassius' *libri iuris civilis* at first hand. He mentions Cassius eighty-five times in all.[149] As with Sabinus, many of these texts must have been taken at second hand from Ulpian's main sources, such as Celsus, Pomponius and Julian.

(g) *Sex. Caecilius Africanus*,[150] who was active under Marcus, is cited once by book [151] and twice with *inquit*.[152] There is no evidence that Ulpian used the nine books of his *quaestiones*, which were available to Justinian's compilers. The work Ulpian refers to in his Sabinian commentary is the otherwise unknown *epistolae*,[153] in at least twenty books. The text says '*Africanus libro vicensimo epistularum apud Iulianum quaerit . . .*'. Perhaps the work consisted of Africanus' correspondence with Julian, which Ulpian acquired with Julian's other papers. The *inquit* passages come in Ulpian *de adulteriis*,[154] and perhaps indicate that Sex. Caecilius wrote a monograph on this topic. In all Ulpian cites Africanus only eight times.[155] His relative neglect of a well-known, though derivative, jurist may show that he preferred to consult the original text of Julian and had no very high opinion of Africanus' comments on him.

(h) Of the republican jurists *Ofilius*[156] is cited six times by book[157] and once with *inquit*,[158] while Q. *Mucius* is cited thrice by book[159] and once with *inquit*.[160] Pernice denied that any republican texts were available to Ulpian.[161] Jörs argued that these two at least were read by the Tyrian.[162] My view is that Ulpian excerpted these works from Vitellius' collection of republican texts.[163] The citations from Ofilius *libri actionum* and *libri iuris*

---

145 D. 29.2.25.4 (8 *Sab.*), 7.1.7.3 (17 *Sab.*), 7.1.9.5 (17 *Sab.*), 7.1.23.1 (17 *Sab.*), 7.1.70 pr., 2 (17 *Sab.*), 26.1.3.2 (37 *Sab.*).
146 D 33.7.12.27 (20 *Sab.*).
147 D. 7.1.70 pr. (Ulp. 17 *Sab.*).
148 D. 33.7.12.27 (20 *Sab.*).
149 *CDJ* 51.
150 *Pal.* 1.1–36.
151 D. 30.39 pr. (Ulp. 21 *Sab.*).
152 D. 48.5.14.1 (Ulp. 2 *adult.*) 40.9.12.6 (Ulp. 4 *adult.*).
153 *Pal.* 1.1.
154 Above, n. 152.
155 *CDJ* 50 (Africanus) and 51 (Caecilius).
156 *Pal.* 1.795–804.
157 D 33.9.3.5, 8 (Ulp. 22 *Sab.*), 32.55.1, 2, 4, 7 (Ulp. 25 *Sab.*).
158 D. 33.9.3.9 (Ulp. 23 *Sab.*).
159 D. 33.9.3 pr. (Ulp. 22 *Sab.*), 32.55 pr. (Ulp. 25 *Sab.*), 33.2.27 (Ulp. 44 *Sab.*).
160 D. 33.9.3.9 (Ulp. 23 *Sab.*).
161 Pernice (1885) 475 f.
162 Jörs (1905) 1785–6.   163 Above. n. 141. f.

partiti come from Ulpian 22 and 25 *ad Sabinum*.[164] Those from Q. Mucius *de iure civili* come in Ulpian 22, 25, and 44 *Sab*.[165] But the text in 44 *Sab*. is out of place, as Lenel remarks,[166] and we should no doubt read 24 for 44 *Sab*. The text is not concerned with the edict of the curule aediles, the topic of 44 *Sab*, but with a legacy of silverware. Finally, the *libri* of Sabinus *ad Vitellium* are mentioned only in 20 and 22 *Sab*.[167] Books 20 to 25 of Ulpian *ad Sabinum* are concerned with legacies.[168] Vitellius, I suggest, made a collection of texts on this subject. This included excerpts from Q. Mucius and Ofilius, on which Ulpian drew. It is interesting that the '*inquit*' text is unique—a text in the plural with *inquiunt* instead of *inquit*: '*Quintus Mucius et Ofilius inquiunt*'.[169] A joint citation of this sort is more natural if the source is a collection of readings. In all Ulpian cites Ofilius 32 times and Q. Mucius 21, but many of these citations are likely to be second hand, and to come from Labeo's *posteriora*, Celsus or Pomponius.

So far all the jurists listed have been cited both by book and with *inquit*, so that we can be fairly sure that Ulpian was using an original source or collection of material. The remaining jurists are cited in only one of the two modes, and for the most part once only. So the citation is more likely to have been taken from a secondary source than those considered so far. By book Ulpian cites Arrianus, *de interdictis*,[170] Puteolanus, *adsessoriorum libri*,[171] Servius, *libri ad Brutum*,[172] Q. Saturninus, *libri ad edictum*,[173] and Tertullianus, *libri quaestionum*.[174] Tertullian was a jurist intermediate between Pomponius and Ulpian.[175] His eight books of *quaestiones* were perused by Justinian's commission. There is no reason why Ulpian should not have read them too. He cites Tertullian thrice in all,[176] always in his Sabinian commentary. *Arrianus*,[177] also apparently a jurist later than Pomponius, is cited four times in all by Ulpian, twice by Paul. Again Ulpian could well have read his work on interdicts, while the other passages are either the fruit of his own reading or taken from Paul. *Puteolanus*[178] is a mystery, as are *adsessoria* (perhaps matters relevant to the office of assessor). His period is unknown. Only Ulpian mentions him. *Servius*[179] is the famous republican

---

[164] Above, n. 157.   [165] Above, n. 159.
[166] *Pal.* 2.1179¹.
[167] Above, n. 138.
[168] *Pal.* 2.1079—1109.
[169] *D.* 33.9.3.9 (Ulp. 23 *Sab.*).
[170] *D.* 5.3.11 (Ulp. 15 *ed.*).
[171] *D.* 2.14.12 (Ulp. 4 *ed.*).
[172] *D.* 14.3.5.1 (Ulp. 28 *ed.*).
[173] *D.* 34.2.19.7 (Ulp. 20 *Sab.*).
[174] *D.* 29.2.30.6 (Ulp. 8 *Sab.*).
[175] *Pal.* 2.341—4.
[176] *D.* 28.5.3.2 (Ulp. 3 *Sab.*), 29.2.30.6 (Ulp. 8 *Sab.*), 38.17.2.44 (Ulp. 13 *Sab.*).
[177] *Pal.* 1.69—70.
[178] *Pal.* 2.186.
[179] *Pal.* 2.322—44.

jurist Ser. Sulpicius Rufus who was consul in BC 51. His work on Brutus, in two books, is mentioned by Pomponius.[180] Did Ulpian read it? One cannot be sure. He mentions Servius 38 times in all.[181] Most of these citations surely come from secondary sources, Labeo's *posteriora* or someone later than he. Q. *Saturninus*[182] is another mysterious figure. Is he the same as Venuleius Saturninus,[183] who lived later than Hadrian, or Claudius Saturninus,[184] who wrote *de poenis paganorum*? Perhaps neither. Ulpian cites him in book 20 *ad Sabinum*. The text concerns the meaning of *aurum* (gold), just as the displaced text of Q. Mucius[185] was concerned with silver. Q. Saturninus, if he is not simply Q. Mucius in disguise, looks to me like another author from whose work excerpts about wills and legacies were collected by Vitellius.[186] Ulpian's text describes him as writing *ad edictum*, an unlikely context in which to discuss the definition of gold. Perhaps two citations have become conflated.

One last jurist whom Ulpian cites by book, though in a *Collatio* not a *Digest* text, is *Urseius*.[187] He was a jurist of the first century AD, whose work Julian edited.[188] Ulpian cites him four times in the *Digest*, always for his reports of the opinions of Sabinus,[189] Cassius,[190] or Proculus.[191] An opinion of Cassius is also cited *apud Urseium*.[192] Ulpian used his work, it seems, directly, not for his own views but as a source of the opinions of more eminent writers.

A number of jurists appear only in one or two *inquit* texts and are not cited by book. Ulpian twice uses *inquit* of *Aristo*,[193] a jurist of the late first century AD. In one text he cites from a note of Aristo,[194] probably on Sabinus' *libri ad Vitellium*.[195] The other text, truncated by Lenel, comes in Ulpian 71 *ed*.[196] Here the edictal committee may have eliminated a book reference after '*Aristo autem scribit*'. But Pomponius used Aristo as a source and many of Ulpian's forty-five references[197] to him seem to be taken

180 *D*. 1.2.2.44 (Pomp. 1 *enchir*.).
181 *CDJ* 71.
182 *Pal*. 2.1209.
183 Kunkel (1967) 181.
184 Kunkel (1967) 184.
185 *D*. 34.2.27 (Ulp. 44 *Sab*.).
186 Above, n. 163.
187 *Pal*. 2.1202.
188 *Pal*. 1.490–96.
189 *Collatio* 12.7.9 (Ulp. 18 *ed*.).
190 *D*. 44.5.1.10 (Ulp. 76 *ed*.).
191 *D*. 9.2.27.1 (Ulp. 18 *ed*.), cf. 39.3.11.2 (Paul 49 *ed*.).
192 *D*. 7.4.10.5 (Ulp. 17 *Sab*.).
193 *Pal*. 59–70.
194 *D*. 33.9.3.2 (Ulp. 22 *Sab*.).
195 These are mentioned in *D*. 33.9.3 pr.
196 *D*. 43.24.11.11 (Ulp. 71 *ed*.).
197 *CDJ* 50.

from Pomponius, Paul or Neratius. *Octavenus*,[198] another lawyer of that period, is cited with *inquit* once.[199] His work was not available to Tribonian and I doubt if Ulpian read it.[200] Pomponius and Paul both cite Octavenus. Pomponius no doubt used him directly. Ulpian mentions him eight times,[201] once *ut apud Pomponium scriptum est*,[202] which shows that in that text he took Octavenus' opinion from Pomponius. Nor is this the only instance of such dependence. In other texts Ulpian cites Octavenus in the imperfect, which again indicates dependence on Pomponius.[203] Ulpian also cites *Nerva*[204] with *inquit* in a text from book 71 *ad edictum*.[205] Here the edictal committee may have eliminated a book reference. The jurist in question is Tiberius' friend M. Cocceius Nerva, consul suffect in AD 22. None of his writing survived to the age of Justinian. It is doubtful if Ulpian read it in the original, though the text cited may have formed part of a collection of opinions by Atilicinus[206] or Vivianus[207] which Ulpian read. Finally there is one *inquit* text for *Fulcinius Priscus*,[208] a jurist of the first century AD whom Pomponius and Paul also cite, Paul twice in the imperfect.[209] Ulpian's *inquit*, which is his only reference to Fulcinius, may be derived from Pomponius or Paul.

In sum, the evidence shows that Ulpian had read widely in the juristic literature. He must have had a good library. His first-hand sources were probably more extensive than appears from the *Digest*. Thus *Vatican Fragments* 59–64, 70–1, 74–89, which contain excerpts concerning usufruct from Ulpian 17 *Sab.*, have a considerably wider range of citations and more book references than the corresponding passages as they appear in the *Digest*.[210] Of course Ulpian is not the only jurist who has suffered at the hands of Justinian's compilers in this way. But since he is peculiarly concerned to give references to original sources, we can be sure that in what has been lost there were relatively more such references than in the lost parts of texts by other jurists. Furthermore, there were jurists whose work Ulpian probably knew but did not choose to cite, or only infrequently.

[198] *Pal.* 2.794–6.
[199] *D.* 9.2.27.25 (Ulp. 18 *ed.*).
[200] In the text cited the mention of Octavenus follows immediately on one of Vivianus, on whom see above nn. 108f.
[201] *CDJ* 65.
[202] *D.* 5.3.16 pr. (Ulp. 15 *ed.*).
[203] Honoré (1962) Tabula laudatoria XI.
[204] *Pal.* 1.787–90.
[205] *D.* 43.24.3.4 (Ulp. 71 *ed.*).
[206] Below, n. 230.
[207] Above, nn. 108 f.
[208] *Pal.* 1.179–80; *D.* 25.1.1.3 (Ulp. 36 *Sab.*). The *inquit here* may not introduce a direct quotation; *proinde Fulcinius inquit. . . .*
[209] *D.* 31.49.2 (Paul 5 *Iul. Pap.*), 43.16.8 (Paul 54 *ed.*). It is possible that Paul (and ? Ulpian) used a collection of materials by Fulcinius which included opinions of Labeo and Mela. Below, nn. 269–70.
[210] See *Pal.* 2.1056–65.

Africanus may be an example,[211] along with Iavolenus[212] and Plautius.[213]

That is not to say that Ulpian eschews citation at second hand. On the contrary, he frequently resorts to it, as do other Roman lawyers. To these citations we now turn.

IV. COLLECTIONS OF JURISTIC OPINIONS

The discussion of first-hand sources revealed two collections of material which Ulpian probably used; one by Vitellius,[214] concerned with legacies and dating from the time of Augustus, and a second by Vivianus[215] compiled about the end of the first century AD. A third author, Urseius,[216] seems to have been used largely as a source of other jurists' opinions.

What are the signs that a collection of material is being used as a source? One is the running together of two or more opinions: for example, *Nerva Atilicinus responderunt*. Another is the use of the expression *extat*, as in *extat sententia*. A third is the use of *apud*, as in *apud Trebatium relatum est*. When the opinions of different jurists are run together this is an indication, not of course conclusive, that they have been found in a single source. *Exstat* or *extat* implies that the opinion exists, in the sense that a text of it is currently available in some source other than its author's own publication. *Apud* points to an edition, collection or, at the minimum, citation of someone else's work.

Let us begin with Ulpian's citations of republican jurists, which are often put together in a string, as the following examples show:

> Gallus Aquilius Ofilius Trebatius responderunt[217]
> Cascellius et Trebatius putant[218]
> Labeo et Cascellius aiunt[219]
> Quintus Mucius et Ofilius negaverunt[220]
> Ofilius et Trebatius responderunt[221]
> scribit enim Labeo et Trebatius[222]

What is the source of these citations? In the *posteriora Labeonis*, edited by

---

[211] Above, nn. 150−5.
[212] Below, n. 318.
[213] Below, n. 271.
[214] Above, nn. 140−2, 148, 163, 167.
[215] Above, nn. 108−18.
[216] Above, nn. 187 f.
[217] D. 30.30.7 (Ulp. 19 *Sab.*).
[218] D. 43.24.1.7 (Ulp. 71 *ed.*).
[219] D. 39.3.1.17 (Ulp. 53 *ed.*).
[220] D. 33.9.3.9 (Ulp. 22 *Sab.*).
[221] D. 4.8.21.1 (Ulp. 13 *ed.*).
[222] D. 19.1.13.22 (Ulp. 32 *ed.*). The singular verb is itself a sign of indirect citation of the second jurist listed.

Iavolenus, the jurists are always cited in a definite order, as follows:[223]

Q. Mucius
Gallus Aquilius
Servius
Ofilius
Cascellius
Trebatius and Tubero

The opinion of Labeo himself, as befits the work, is generally put first.[224] Now Ulpian's citations clearly conform to the same order, with the minor variation he sometimes follows chronological order and so puts Labeo after Trebatius, as in:

Trebatius autem et Labeo quamquam putant[225]
Trebatius et Labeo . . . dantem eum pervenire[226]

There is nothing to stand in the way of the conclusion that Ulpian derived these citations from Labeo's *posteriora*, which he cites by name six times.[227] A text in which Iavolenus' opinion is given immediately after that of Labeo[228] suggests that Ulpian knew Iavolenus' edition. However, he makes no other use of it. No doubt he preferred to consult the original, though this did not survive in the age of Justinian. Whether Labeo made the collection of republican opinions which form the basis of the strings of citation himself, or used a collection by another, is unclear. Certainly his collection was quite distinct from that of Vitellius,[229] which was confined to legacies.

Atilicinus[230] is a jurist whose name often appears as a member of a string, for example

Proculus Atilicinus[231]
Nerva Atilicinus[232]
Sabinus Atilicinus[233]

[223] *D.* 28.6.39 pr. (I *Iav. post. Lab: Labeonis Ofilii Cascellii Trebatii*) 28.6.39.2 (*Ofilius Cascellius*), 32.29 pr. (*Lab. 2 post. Iav. epit.: Cascellius Trebatius*), 32.29.1 (*id.: Quintus Mucius et Gallus*), 32.100.1 (*Iav. 2 post. Lab.: Ofilius Trebatius*), 32.100.4 (*id.: Labeo Trebatius*), 33.4.6.1 (*Lab. 2 post. Iav. epit.: Ofilius Cascellius*), 33.6.7 pr. (*Iav. 2 post. Lab.: Ofilius Cascellius Tubero*), 33.7.4 (*Iav. 2 post. Lab.: Labeo Trebatius*), 33.7.25.1 (*Iav. 2 post. Lab.: Labeo Trebatius*), 34.2.39 pr. (*Iav. 2 post. Lab.: Ofilius Labeo*), 35.1.40.4 (*Iav. 2 post. Lab.: Labeo Ofilius Trebatius*), 33.10.10 (*Iav. 3 post. Lab.: Labeo Ofilius Cascellius*), 40.7.39 pr. (*Iav. 4 post. Lab.: Quintus Mucius Gallus et ipse Labeo . . . Servius Ofilius*), 40.7.39.1 (*id.: Labeo Ofilius*), 40.7.39.4 (*id.: Labeo Ofilius . . . Labeonis et Ofilii*), 18.1.79 (*Iav. 5 post. Lab.: Labeo et Trebatius*), 33.7.26.1 (*Iav. 5 post. Lab.: Labeo Cascellius Trebatius*), 24.3.66.1 (*Iav. 6 post. Lab.: Labeoni Trebatio*), 24.3.66.2 (*id.: Labeo Trebatius*), 49.15.27 (*Iav. 9 post. Lab.: Labeo Ofilius Trebatius*), 33.10.11 (*Iav. 10 post. Lab.: Labeo Trebatius*).
[224] The only exception is *D.* 34.2.39 pr. (*Iav. 3 post. Lab.*).
[225] *D.* 10.3.6.6 (Ulp. 19 *ed.*).   [226] *D.* 40.7.3.11 (Ulp. 27 *Sab.*).
[227] *D.* 4.3.9.3 (11 *ed.*), 28.5.13.5,6 (7 *Sab.*), 28.5.17.5 (7 *Sab.*), 7.8.2.1 (17 *Sab.*), 33.9.3.2 (22 *Sab.*).
[228] *D.* 18.4.2.17 (Ulp. 49 *Sab.*).   [229] Above, nn. 140–2, 148, 163, 167, 214.
[230] *Pal.* 1.71–4.   [231] *D.* 4.8.21.9 (Ulp. 13 *ed.*), 8.3.5.1 (Ulp. 17 *ed.*), 15.1.17 (29 *ed.*).
[232] *D.* 44.4.4.8 (Ulp. 76 *ed.*), cf. 34.3.16 (Paul 9 *Plaut.*).   [233] *D.* 10.3.6.4 (Ulp. 19 *ed.*).

Sometimes the order is reversed, as in:

Atilicinus Sabinus Cassius[234]
Atilicinus Nerva Sabinus[235]

Ulpian sometimes inserts *et* between the names.[236] Julian[237] and Paul[238] do not. But clearly all three are directly or indirectly using the same collective source. That the source is a collection made by Atilicinus himself is likely. Atilicinus was a contemporary of Proculus.[239] So he was either junior to or coeval with the other jurists listed. His name however appears either first of last in the lists. When it comes last it is in the natural chronological position of the editor of a collection of opinions by others. When it comes first this is a sign that a later author is consulting the edited work (and so names the editor first) and then reverts to chronological order when he comes to name the jurists cited by the editor. This is why, in the lists Atilicinus Sabinus Cassius[240] and Atilicinus Nerva Sabinus,[241] the latest jurist is named first and the earliest second. If, on the other hand we find Atilicinus in the middle, as in:

Neratius Atilicinus Proculus[242]

then the source is not the collection of juristic opinion by Atilicinus but some work of Neratius or (at two removes) Pomponius in which use was made of Atilicinus' collection. Ulpian cites Atilicinus eleven times, but probably did not use his collection directly. Though he does say of one opinion of Atilicinus that it exists, he does not claim to find any information *apud Atilicinum*. His source will have been Neratius, Pomponius, Julian or Paul, all of whom he used directly.

Atilicinus, then, probably collected opinions of Nerva, Proculus, Sabinus, Cassius and perhaps Fulcinius[243] and added his own. Ulpian cited him at second hand. The form of citation tends to depend on the intermediate source. Thus, Neratius (see above) and Pomponius usually mention the source, though chronologically later, first. For example, Pomponius cites Neratius before Aristo, though Aristo was senior[244] and though Neratius is citing Aristo rather than the other way around. Thus

---

[234] D. 17.2.52.18 (Ulp. 31. *ed.*), cf. 45.2.17 (Paul 8 *Plaut.*).
[235] D. 35.2.49 pr. (Paul 12 *Plaut.*).
[236] Texts in nn. 231–3 above.
[237] D. 12.4.7 pr. (Iul. 16 *dig.*: *Nerva Atilicinus*).
[238] Texts in nn. 232, 234, 234 above and 2.14.27 pr. (Paul 3 *ed.*: Neratius Atilicinus Proculus).
[239] D. 23.4.17 (Proc. 11 *epist.*: Atilicinus Proculo suo salutem).
[240] D. 17.2.52.18 (Ulp. 31 *ed*), 45.2.17 (Paul 8 *Plaut.*).
[241] D. 35.2.49 pr. (Paul 12 *Plaut.*).
[242] D. 2.14.27 pr. (Paul 3 *ed.*).
[243] D. 25.2.6 pr. (Paul 7 *Sab.*). Alternatively Fulcinius may have collected opinions which included those of Atilicinus. Below, n. 268.
[244] D. 40.4.46. (Pomp. 7 *var. lect*: *Aristo Neratio Appiano* [*Prisco* scr. Mommsen] *rescripsit*).

Pomponius says:

> Neratio et Aristoni placebat[245]
> Neratius et Aristo recte putant[246]
> Neratius et Aristo et Ofilius probant[247]

Pomponius has taken Aristo's opinion from a work of Neratius, and, in the last text, that of Ofilius from Aristo. So when we find Ulpian mentioning Atilicinus first in a list, his source is probably Neratius or Pomponius rather than Celsus or Julian, who prefer to follow the chronological order.

Aristo seems also to have made a collection of juristic material, or at any rate to have annotated Labeo,[248] Sabinus,[249] and Cassius.[250] Ulpian cites his notes on the latter two.[251] Indeed he cites him forty-five times in all.[252] But he did not use Aristo's collection, if, as Lenel thinks,[253] it existed, directly. He does not claim to find texts *apud Aristonem*. His source is rather Neratius, Pomponius, or Paul. Pomponius in particular made free use of Aristo's work, which he seems to have edited, if we go by Paul's text which says: *est relatum apud Sextum Pomponium digestorum ab Aristone libro quinto*.[254]

Of the collections of material which we can discern, then, Ulpian seems to have used those of Vitellius, Labeo, Urseius and Vivianus directly but those of Atilicinus and (if he made one) Aristo only indirectly. The question remains whether this conclusion adequately accounts for the use of *exstat/extat* and *apud* in Ulpian's texts. *Exstat* is used of the opinions of Ofilius,[255] Servius,[256] Sabinus,[257] Cassius,[258] Nerva,[259] Atilicinus,[260] and Neratius.[261] All these might be found in the works of Vitellius, Labeo, Urseius, Vivianus, Neratius, or Pomponius, if we assume that the opinion of Nerva and Atilicinus was reproduced by Neratius (or Pomponius). The list of authors *apud* whom Ulpian finds information is longer. They comprise Mucius, Servius, *Servii auditores*, Ofilius, Trebatius, Labeo, Mela, Vitellius, *veteres*, Sabinus, Cassius, Minicius, Pedius, Plautius, Urseius,

[245] *D.* 17.2.62 (Pomp. 13 *Sab.*).
[246] *D.* 40.7.5 pr. (Pomp. 8 *Sab.*).
[247] *D.* 30.45 pr. (*Pomp.* 6 *Sab.*).
[248] *D.* 28.5.17.5 (Ulp. 7 *Sab.*), 43.24.5 pr. (Ulp 71 *ed.*).
[249] *FV* 88 (Ulp. 18 *Sab.*), 7.8.6 (Ulp. 17 *Sab.*), 33.9.3.1 (Ulp. 22 *Sab.*).
[250] *D.* 7.1.7.3 (Ulp. 17 *Sab.*), 7.1.17.1 (Ulp. 18 *Sab.*), 39.2.28 (Ulp. 81 *ed.*).
[251] Above, nn. 248–9.
[252] *CDJ* fiche 50.
[253] *Pal.* 1.61¹.
[254] *D.* 24.3.44 pr. (Paul 5 *qu.*).
[255] *D.* 43.20.1.17 (70 *ed.*).
[256] *D.* 27.7.4 pr. (Ulp. 36 *ed.*).
[257] *D.* 39.2.15.12 (Ulp. 53 *ed.*).
[258] *D.* 43.21.11.1 (Ulp. 71 *ed.*).
[259] *D.* 44.4.4.8 (Ulp. 76 *ed.*).
[260] *D.* 44.4.4.8 (Ulp. 76 *ed.*).
[261] *D.* 42.4.7.16 (Ulp. 59 *ed.*).

Celsus, Vivianus, Pomponius, Julian, Marcellus, Scaevola, and Tertullian.[262] Most of these are authors whom Ulpian consulted at first hand or whose works were excerpted or edited by others whom he consulted at first hand. This does not, however, account for the mention of Mela and Plautius.

Mela[263] was a jurist intermediate in period between Servius Sulpicius and Proculus, perhaps a lawyer of the early empire. Ulpian cites him thirty times,[264] and also cites opinions of Aquilius Gallus and Servius *apud Melam*.[265] Another Ulpianic text couples the opinion of Labeo and Mela.[266] Paul couples Mela and Fulcinius.[267] Africanus cites the tenth book of some work of Mela.[268] It is not easy to see from what secondary source Ulpian derived his numerous citations of Mela. One possibility is a collection of material by Fulcinius Priscus.[269] Certain texts of Paul lead one to think that he used such a collection, which included opinions of Labeo and Mela.[270] Ulpain might have had access to the same source. On the other hand it is not impossible that he read Mela directly.

Ulpian cites *Plautius*,[271] a jurist of the Flavian dynasty whose work was edited by Iavolenus, Neratius, Pomponius and Paul, only once. Even then he cites it not for Plautius' opinion but for that of his editors (*omnes auctores apud Plautium*).[272] Presumably Ulpain knew his work but did not think highly of his talent.

V. SOURCES CITED PURELY AT SECOND HAND

When Ulpian cites from collections of juristic opinions he cites at second hand, but generally the editor will have purported to give the exact text of the original author. In the instances now to be considered this is often not the case. Ulpian simply takes from his primary sources, especially his main sources (Papinian, Celsus, Julian, Pomponius, Marcellus) opinions of others which he finds mentioned in them, not necessarily verbatim. That he often did this is obvious. Indeed Ulpian makes no attempt to hide it:

---

[262] Texts in *CDJ* 50.
[263] *Pal* 1.691−6.
[264] *CDJ* 63.
[265] D. 19.1.17.6 (Ulp. 32 ed. *Gallus Aquilius*), 33.9.3.10 (Ulp. 22 *Sab.*: *Servius*), 19.5.20.1 (Ulp. 32 ed.: *apud Melam quaeritur*).
[266] D. 19.2.13.8 (Ulp. 32 *ed.*).
[267] D. 25.2.3.4 (Paul 7 *Sab.*).
[268] D. 50.16.207 (Afr. 3 *qu.*).
[269] Above, n. 209.
[270] D. 31.49.2 (Paul 5 *Iul. Pap.*), 25.2.3.4 (Paul 7 *Sab.*).
[271] Lenel (1889) 2.13−14.
[272] D. 7.2.1.3 (Ulp. 17 *Sab.*).

> Catonem quoque scribere lego[273]
> Mauricianus dicitur existimasse[274]
> Tubero definit, ut Celsus refert[275]

That he cited at second or third hand was one of the principal reproaches which Pernice levelled against the Tyrian jurist.[276] He was particularly critical not so much of these overt instances but of Ulpian's habit of citing at second hand without saying so. That Ulpian did this is, again, quite clear. Thus, discussing the vesting of annuities, he favours vesting at the beginning of the year:[277]

> et Labeo Sabinus et Celsus et Cassius et Iulianus . . . hoc probaverunt

The *digesta* of Celsus and Julian are among Ulpian's main direct sources. For Celsus, in turn, Labeo and Sabinus are important sources.[278] Julian often cites Cassius.[279] On the other hand Celsus cites Cassius only once[280] and Julian cites Labeo only twice.[281] We can safely conclude that in Ulpian's text the citations of Labeo and Sabinus are taken from Celsus, that of Cassius from Julian. Hence the text, if expanded, would read 'Celsus argues for the vesting of an annuity at the beginning of the year and cites in support Labeo and Sabinus. Julian also favours the beginning of the year and cites in support Cassius'. There are a number of parallels, in which the indirect source precedes the main source, as in:

> et ita Sabinus et Celsus scribunt[282]
> Labeo et Marcellus scribunt[283]

The citation of Sabinus is taken from Celsus, and that of Labeo from Marcellus. Another way of dealing with an indirect citation may be illustrated by:[284]

> (Celsus) scripsit, quam sententiam et Tubero probat

This looks as if the late republican Tubero is expressing approval of an opinion of Celsus, consul for the second time under Hadrian. But Ulpian is simply following the text of Celsus, in which he finds the opinion of

---

[273] *D.* 21.1.10.1 (Ulp. 1 *ed. cur.*).
[274] *D.* 41.10.1.1 (Ulp. 15 *ed.*).
[275] *D.* 15.1.5.4 (Ulp. 29 *ed.*).
[276] Pernice (1885) 473 f.
[277] *D.* 36.2.12.1 (Ulp. 23 *Sab.*).
[278] Honoré (1962) tab. laud. II.
[279] Honoré (1962) tab. laud. VII.
[280] *D.* 33.7.12.20 (Ulp. 20 *Sab.*).
[281] *D.* 13.4.2.8 (Ulp. 27 *ed.*), 44.4.4.1 (Ulp. 76 *ed.*).
[282] *D.* 43.26.8.1 (Ulp. 71 *ed.*).
[283] *D.* 12.5.4.3 (Ulp. 26 *ed.*).
[284] *D.* 7.8.2.1 (Ulp. 17 *Sab.*).

Tubero. We can be sure of this because Celsus cites Tubero as often as he cites any jurist except Proculus.[285]

When Ulpian uses a primary source A, who cites his own primary source(B) first, then a second source (C) cited by B, Ulpian generally follows the order BCA. Thus:[286]

> et ita Neratio et Aristoni videtur et Pomponius probat

Here Ulpian is using Pomponius (A), Pomponius Neratius (B), who in turn cites Aristo (C). As noted above,[287] Pomponius in such a case tends to invert the chronological sequence of authorities, as here. Ulpian does so too. So when we find a sequence which, from a chronological point of view, runs 1, 3, 2, as in:[288]

> Labeo Neratius et Aristo opinantur

the likelihood is that Ulpian has taken the citations from Pomponius, who in turn has used two sources, Labeo and Neratius, and derived the citation of Aristo from the latter. On the other hand when Ulpian puts Aristo in the right chronological position, as in:[289]

> et ita Aristoni et Neratio et Iuliano visum est

the likelihood is that he is using Julian alone as a primary source, since Julian does not normally invert the chronological order.[290] In other instances it is difficult to detect the primary source:

> et Labeo et Sabinus putant et nos probamus[291]
> et Labeo et Cassius scribunt[292]

It is not likely, given the conjunction, that Ulpian was here using Labeo in the original. The source might be Celsus, Julian, Neratius, Pomponius, or the collections of material by Urseius, Vivianus, or Fulcinius. The possibilities are too many to settle on a firm choice.

To proceed further along these lines would be to undertake an analysis of the use of sources by Ulpian's own main sources. This lies outside the scope of the present book. There remain some jurists cited by our author who have not yet been mentioned. Nothing is known of *Aufidius Chius*[293] as a

---

[285] Honoré (1962) tab. laud. II (eleven mentions of Proculus, ten each of Labeo and Tubero). It says something for Ulpian's integrity that in three of the five texts in which he cites Tubero he makes it clear that Celsus is the source of the citation. Can one argue from this in favour of a direct use of, for example, Mela?

[286] D. 7.2.3.2 (Ulp. 17 *Sab.*).

[287] Above nn. 244 f.

[288] D. 28.5.9.14 (Ulp. 5 *Sab.*).

[289] D. 35.1.7 pr. (Ulp. 18 *Sab.*).

[290] D. 40.12.20 (Iul. 4 *Minic.*), 19.1.24.1 (Iul. 15 *dig.*), 12.4.7 pr. (Iul. 16 *dig.*).

[291] D. 19.1.11.3. (Ulp. 32 *ed.*).

[292] D. 28.2.6 pr. (Ulp. 3 *Sab.*).

[293] Apparently a freedman: Martial 5.61.10; Kunkel (1967) 135.

lawyer. Ulpian cites him for an opinion of Atilicinus.[294] The same is ture of *Cartilius*,[295] *Paconius*,[296] and *Publicius*,[297] each of whom are once cited by the Tyrian. There are also a number of prominent members of the Labeonic or Proculian school whom Ulpian cites but does not seem to have known at first hand. In chronological order, the first is *M. Cocceius Nerva* the elder,[298] friend of Tiberius and grandfather of the emperor. Ulpian cites him sixteen times,[299] once in the interesting combination (Alfenus) Varus et Nerva[300]—perhaps derived from Paul. The famous *Proculus*,[301] who was active under Nero, is cited forty-five times[302] but never by book or with *inquit*. Ulpian does not seem, therefore, to have known his *epistulae*, though these were available to Tribonian. Ulpian cites a note by Proculus on Labeo. Celsus is his source for this.[303] Notes by Proculus on Labeo's *posteriora* may have come to Ulpian via Iavolenus.[304] Virtually all Ulpian's main sources cite Proculus. Hence there is no need to suppose that Ulpian read him in the original. *Nerva the younger*,[305] a contemporary of Proculus, is the next jurist of this school whom Ulpian does not appear to have known at first hand. He cites him five times, once with Pegasus (*Pegasus et Nerva filius responderunt*).[306] The chronological order is inverted, and so this citation may come via Pomponius. The next head of the Proculian school is *Pegasus*,[307] urban prefect under Vespasian. Ulpian cites him twenty-three times.[308] There is evidence that Pomponius[309] and Julian[310] were intermediate sources for his views. Ulpian often cites him in combination: Trebatius et Pegasus,[311] Labeo et Pegasus,[312] Sabinus et Pegasus,[313] Proculus et Pegasus,[314] Cassius et Pegasus.[315] Perhaps Pegasus made a collection of previous opinions to which he added his own comments. This could have served as a source book. But if such a

---

[294] *FV* 77 (Ulp. 17 *Sab.*).
[295] *Pal.* 1.106; *D.* 13.6.5.13 (Ulp. 28 *ed.*).
[296] *Pal.* 1.804; *D.* 13.6.1.1 (Ulp. 28 *ed.*).
[297] *Pal.* 2.186; *D.* 38.17.2.8 (Ulp. 13 *Sab.*: *Africanus et Publicius temptant dicere*).
[298] *Pal.* 1.787–790; above nn. 204 f.
[299] *CDJ* 64.
[300] *D.* 6.1.5.3 (Ulp. 16 *ed.*).
[301] *Pal.* 2.159–84.
[302] *CDJ* 67.
[303] *D.* 3.5.9.1 (Ulp. 10 *ed.*).
[304] *D.* 7.8.1.4 (Ulp. 17 *Sab.*).
[305] *Pal.* 1.791–2.
[306] *D.* 3.2.2.5 (Ulp. 6 *ed.*).
[307] *Pal.* 2.9–12.
[308] *CDJ* fiche 66.
[309] *D.* 7.1.12.2 (Ulp. 17 *Sab.*).
[310] *D.* 7.1.25.7 (Ulp. 18 *Sab.*).
[311] *D.* 41.1.41 (Ulp. 9 *ed.*).
[312] *D.* 33.7.12.3 (Ulp. 20 *Sab.*).
[313] *D.* 12.5.4. pr. (Ulp. 26 *ed.*).
[314] *D.* 15.1.30 pr. (Ulp. 29 *ed.*).
[315] *D.* 7.1.12.2 (Ulp. 17 *Sab.*).

Ulpian as a Writer

compilation existed, it was not available either to Ulpian or the compilers of the sixth century.

The last head of the Proculian school to be mentioned is *Iuventius Celsus the elder*,[316] father of the author of *digesta*. Ulpian's one reference to him[317] comes from his son's work.

This analysis of Proculian sources confirms the impression that Ulpian in general preferred the jurists of the Sabinian school, with whom he was better acquainted at first hand. But even with them he remained selective. Thus *Iavolenus Priscus*,[318] the first-century jurist who was Julian's teacher, though head of the Sabinian school, is cited only three times. One of these texts suggests that Ulpian knew Iavolenus' fifteen *libri ex Cassio*,[319] a second that he knew his ten books *ex posterioribus Labeonis*.[320] Internal evidence points to his having annotated Iavolenus' *epistulae*.[321] Why, then, does he refer to him so little? Only, perhaps, because Ulpian did not esteem him as a lawyer.

There are four more writers whom Ulpian cites. *Alfenus Varus*,[322] a pupil of Servius, is mentioned seven times.[323] The texts could come from Labeo's *posteriora*,[324] Pomponius,[325] or Paul[326]. *Aufidius Namusa*,[327] another auditor of Servius, is cited twice. The same intermediate sources spring to mind.[328] Vindius,[329] consul in AD,138 is mentioned thrice. One text suggests derivation from Julian,[330] one from Pomponius.[331] Mauricianus,[332] active under Pius, comes in twice, once with *Mauricianus dicitur existimasse*,[333] which does not purport to be a direct citation. He may come to Ulpian through Paul, who cites him.[334]

In sum, Ulpian's use of juristic sources is extensive and scholarly, though, as Pernice correctly discerned, he did not disdain the use of secondary

---

[316] *Pal.* 1.127–8.

[317] *D.* 12.4.3.7 (Ulp. 26 *ed.*).

[318] *Pal.* 1.278–316.

[319] *D.* 28.2.6 pr. (Ulp. 3 *Sab.*).

[320] *D.* 18.4.2.17 (Ulp. 49 *Sab.*), and perhaps *D.* 28.5.17.5 (Ulp. 7 *Sab.*).

[321] *D.* 38.5.12 (Iav. 3 *epist.*) contains what looks like a note of Ulpian: '*quid enim dicemus . . . agi non possit*'.

[322] *Pal.* 1.38–54.

[323] *CDJ* 50 (Alfenus), 75 (Varus).

[324] *D.* 32.29.2 (*Lab.* 2 *post. Iav epit*).

[325] *D.* 50.16.239.6 (Pomp. 1 *enchir.*), 18.1.18.1 (Pomp. 9 *Sab.*).

[326] *D.* 17.2.65.8 (Paul 32 *ed.*), 39.3.2.5 (Paul 49 *ed.*), 50.16.77 (Paul 49 *ed.*) and, for Paul's epitome of the *digesta* of Alfenus, *Pal.* 1.45–53.

[327] *Pal.* 1.75–6.

[328] *D.* 35.1.40.3 (*Iav.* 2 *post. Lab.*), 33.5.20 (*Lab.* 2 *post. Iav. epit.*), 33.4.6.1 (*Lab.* 2 *post. Iav. epit.*), 39.3.2.6 (Paul 49 *ed.*).

[329] *Pal.* 2.1223–4.

[330] *FV* 77 (Ulp. 17 *Sab.*: *Vindius tamen, dum consulit Iulianum*).

[331] *D.* 5.1.5 (Ulp. 5 *ed.*: *Pomponius et Vindius scripserunt*) cf. 2.9.2.1 (Paul 6 *ed.*).

[332] *Pal.* 1.690–2.

[333] *D.* 41.10.1.1 (Ulp. 15 *ed.*).

[334] *D.* 6.1.35.1 (Paul 21 *ed.*).

material. He used the available sources selectively, preferring the original minds and relegating the more derivative authors to a secondary role. The charge that he passed over his great contemporary Paul out of rivalry is not made out. Ulpian was entitled to think, with pride, that he had transmitted to posterity a good selection of what was best in Roman jurisprudence.

VI. IMPERIAL SOURCES

Private jurisprudence was not the whole story, nor even, in Ulpian's age, the central theme. That role was reserved for imperial constitutions. These were still primarily rescripts, documents addressed to private individuals or officials setting out the law relevant to their circumstances. An increasing role, however, was coming to be played by imperial legislation in the form of edicts, such as the *constitutio Antoniniana*, or *senatusconsulta* passed at the instance of the emperor. For these the imperial address (*oratio*) was now the authoritative text. Thus were political realities symbolised. But, even if the will and form were the emperor's, the voice remained that of the jurist, who still composed those texts which required a knowledge of the law.[335]

It is necessary, then, to be alive to a certain irony. When Ulpian cites with approval a constitution of Severus or Caracalla, he is as often as not citing a text in the preparation of which he or Papinian or Menander or some other professional colleague has played a leading role. His situation is not so different from that of Tribonian, praising himself in texts issued by Justinian but composed by his quaestor.[336]

The table that follows[337] attempts to present a picture of the gradually changing weight of imperial constitutions in relation to private jurisprudence. In order to ensure that frequency of citation is likely to be a reliable index of the author's practice, the jurists listed are confined to those for whom there are at least 3,000 words in the *Digest*.[338]

So far as the citation of jurists is concerned, this table shows great individual variation. Those most inclined to document their texts in this way, Labeo, Pomponius, and Ulpian, come from three different centuries. What they have in common is that they are as much interested in scholarship as in practice. Those jurists who are oriented mainly towards practice, on the other hand, like Scaevola and Papinian, are sparing in their citations. So, for a different reason, is Callistratus, who is mainly concerned with criminal and public law, the domain of imperial constitutions. Yet when all necessary reservations have been made, Ulpian stands out in his own age for his concern with the juristic literature—a concern stronger than Paul's and

[335] Honoré (1981) 41–53.
[336] Honoré (1978) 204.
[337] Source *CDJ*, relevant fiches, and intro. §4.
[338] *CDJ* intro. §4.

Jurist	Percentage of Digest	Citations of named jurists	Citations per 1 %	Citations of emperors	Citations per 1 %
Labeo	1.08	101	93.5	0	0
Iavolenus	1.01	11	10.9	0	0
Iulianus	4.40	51	11.6	2	0.5
Pomponius	4.41	361	81.9	30	6.8
Gaius	3.95	87	22.0	12	3.0
Africanus	1.74	14	8.0	8	4.6
Scaevola	4.92	27	5.5	16	3.3
Callistratus	1.12	9	8.0	89	79.5
Papinianus	5.69	48	8.4	72	12.7
Paulus	16.74	694	41.5	116	6.9
Ulpianus	41.56	2577	62.0	461	11.1
Tryphoninus	1.28	15	11.7	18	14.1
Marcianus	2.43	62	25.5	148	60.9
Modestinus	2.44	27	11.1	110	45.1

much stronger than that of Marcianus, to take two contemporaries who for the most part expound private law.

The extent to which the various authors refer to imperial constitutions also depends on the subject-matter, but, in contrast with the citation of jurists, there is a clear temporal progression. In the first century imperial law is a negligible element in legal writing. In the second its weight relative to juristic opinion grows. Callistratus writes in the reign of Severus but cites him with or without Caracalla only four times in eighty-nine references. His centre of gravity lies in the late Antonine age. Even before Severus, therefore, the emperor's rescripts had become a dominant force in criminal and public law. Papinian reflects a further development. His practice was wide and general, yet he too cites emperors more often than jurists—though it must be confessed that he is sparing in mentions of either. In Paul and Ulpian, on the other hand, the balance is different. There are five or six references to jurists for each one to an imperial constitution. The reason is, in large measure, that in their major commentaries they summarize the whole of the relevant law rather than concentrating on points of growth. Marcianus, who follows Ulpian in so much, tilts the balance the other way: more than two constitutions to each juristic reference. Modestinus has four times as many. It is this predominance of imperial sources that heralds the decline of private legal writing, the so-called 'end of the classical age'.

Ulpian's policy in choosing between juristic and imperial sources is governed by the context. In private law he cites rather few constitutions; in public law, in which he made an original and creative contribution, many. Thus, he cites the text, or part of the text, of 69 constitutions in the

Digest.[339] Of these 29 come from areas of public law, 13 from the work on the office of the proconsul,[340] 8 from that on the consul,[341] 2 relate to the curator of the republic,[342] 2 to the urban prefect,[343] two are drawn from *de omnibus tribunalibus*,[344] 2 from the treatise on appeals.[345]

Constitutions in any number are cited by Ulpian only from Trajan onwards. The following table gives the number of times each emperor is cited:[346]

Caesar	I	Pius	113
Augustus	5	Marcus and Verus	43
Claudius	2	Marcus	65
Nero	2	Marcus and Commodus	2
Titus	I	Severus	46
Domitian	I	Severus and Antoninus	61
Nerva	I	Antoninus (Caracalla)	46
Trajan	14	imperator	I
Hadrian	48	princeps/principes	9

The list suggests that Ulpian's reading went back to Trajan and Hadrian.[347] As with jurists, so with emperors, Ulpian is selective. He certainly knew the rescripts of Commodus and Pertinax, but he does not cite any, despite the fact that Callistratus,[348] Papinian,[349] Marcianus,[350] and Modestinus[351] cite Commodus, while Callistratus[352] and Modestinus[353] cite Pertinax. A certain fastidiousness or caution is at work here. Paul shares it.

It can be assumed that when Ulpian cites the text of a constitution, and often when he does not (or when Justinian's commission makes it appear that he does not) he has consulted the original text, a copy in the *liber*

---

[339] Source: Gualandi (1963) I 17–229.

[340] D. 1.16.6.3 (1 *off. proc.*: Sev. and Ant.), 26.5.12.2 (3 *off. proc.*: Pius), 50.4.6 pr (4 *off. proc.*: Marcus and Verus), 50.7.7 (id.: Sev. and Ant.), 48.8.4.2 (7 *off. proc.*: Hadrian), 48.6.6 (id.: Pius), 48.18.1.1 (8 *off. proc.*: Hadrian), 48.18.1.16 (id.: Sev.), 48.18.1.22 (id.: Hadrian), 48.18.1.27 (id.: Marcus and Verus), 1.6.2 (id.: Pius), 47.14.1 pr. (id.: Hadrian), 48.20.6 (10 *off. proc.*: Hadrian).

[341] D. 35.1.50 (1 *off. cons.*: Pius), 40.12.27 pr. (id.: Marcus and Verus), 25.3.5.7 (2 *off. cons.*: Pius), 25.3.5.14 (id.: Marcus), 34.1.3 (id.: unidentified, Pius), 1.7.39 (3 *off. cons.*: Marcus), 27.3.17 (id.: Sev. and Ant.), 50.12.8 (id.: Marcus and Verus).

[342] D. 50.10.5 pr. (1 *off. cur. reip.*: Pius), 50.12.1.5 (id.: Sev and Ant.).

[343] D. 1.12.1.4 (1 *off. pr. urb.*: Sev.), 1.15.4 (id.: Sev. and Ant.).

[344] D. 50.13.1.10, 12 (8 *omn. trib.*: Sev and Ant.).

[345] D. 49.1.1.1 (1 *appell.*: Pius), 49.9.1 (4 *appell.*: Marcus and Verus).

[346] Source: CDJ, relevant fiches.

[347] First constitutions cited verbatim: D. 29.1.1 pr. (Ulp. 45 ed.: Trajan's *mandata*), 29.5.1.28 (Ulp. 50 ed.: rescript of Hadrian), 37.10.3.5 (Ulp. 41 ed.: same), and texts cited n. 340 above.

[348] D. 12.3.10 (Call 1 *qu.*), 35.3.6 (Call 4 *cogn.*).

[349] D. 22.3.26 (Pap. 20 *qu.*).

[350] D. 40.10.3 (Marci. 1 *inst.*), 49.14.31 (Marci. 4 *inst.*).

[351] D. 25.3.6.1 (Mod. 1 *manu.*), 27.1.6.8 (Mod. 2 *excus.*).

[352] D. 50.6.6.2, 13 (Call 1 *cogn.*).

[353] D. 40.5.12.2 (Mod. 1 *manu.*).

libellorum rescriptorum,[354] or a collection which reproduced the text of the constitution. One such collection, which gave, at least occasionally, the text of rescripts of Marcus and Verus or Marcus alone, is that of Papirius Iustus,[355] whose twenty books of *constitutiones* Justinian's compilers excerpted. Pernice[356] thought that Ulpian did not use this, but the texts which he cites do not point to Ulpian's ignorance of Papirius, because they are not on the same point. It is true, however, that Ulpian does not explicitly mention Papirius at all. He does cite one rescript from the *semenstria*,[357] a source which Tryphonius also uses.[358] The term seems to mean a 'six-monthly record'[359] but whether it contained the text of imperial constitutions or only a summary is unclear, since none of the surviving references reproduces the text. That Ulpian consulted some collection or collections of imperial texts seems likely from his use of expressions such as:

> exstat divi Pii rescriptum[360]
> rescriptum exstat divi Severi[361]
> exstat quidem senatusconsultum Vitrasianum[362]
> extat divi Marci rescriptum[363]
> extat epistula divorum fratrum[364]
> extat rescriptum divorum Marci et Veri[365]

Whether these expressions refer to the *semenstria*, and, if so, what exactly it contained, must be left open. In general, the bulk of the constitutions cited by Ulpian will have come from his own reading of the *liber libellorum rescriptorum*. Any secretary *a libellis* will have needed to consult this source in order to discover what precedents there were on the points on which the petitioners wished to consult the emperor. He will in any case have wanted to read past rescripts in order to get in idea of the appropriate style in which to compose them. Whether, as Pernice asserts,[366] Ulpian's reading was unsystematic and he read only rescripts bearing on the particular topic on which he had to advise the emperor, is uncertain. Even if Pernice is right, a

---

354 Honoré (1981) 26—7.

355 *Pal.* 1.947—52.

356 Pernice (1885) 456, citing *D.* 4.4.9.5 (Ulp. 11 *ed.*) and 39.4.7.1 (2 *const.*), the latter concerning a *pupillus*, not a minor, and amounting simply to a particular indulgence—exactly the sort of material which Ulpian, with his gaze fixed on the general rule (cf. *D.* 1.4.1.2), would not use.

357 *D.* 29.2.12 (Ulp. 11 *ed.*: *et est in semenstribus Vibiis Soteri et Victorino rescriptum*).

358 *D.* 2.14.46 (Tryph. 2 *disp.*: Marcus), 18.7.10 (Scae. 7 *dig.*: note of Claudius viz. Tryph.: Marcus).

359 Heumann—Seckel (1907) 532 confine them to Marcus' reign.

360 *D.* 27.8.6 (Ulp. 1 *ed.*), cf. 27.10.1.1 (Ulp. 1 *Sab.*), 36.3.1.11 (Ulp. 79 *ed.*), 49.1.1.1 (Ulp. 1 *appell.*).

361 *D.* 26.10.1.7 (Ulp. 35 *ed.*).

362 *D.* 40.5.30.6 (Ulp. 5 *fid.*).

363 *D.* 27.8.1.2 (Ulp. 36 *ed.*).

364 *D.* 48.18.1.27 (Ulp. 8 *off. proc.*).

365 *D.* 40.5.30.13 (Ulp. 5 *fid.*).

366 Pernice (1885) 457.

secretary who held office for over seven years would in that time deal with every branch of the law on which rescripts might be sought, especially under an energetic emperor such as Severus, who attached importance to providing a proper legal advice service.

Pernice accuses Ulpian of passing off as his own statements of the law which from other sources we know to have come from an imperial constitution.[367] In the case he refers to Ulpian in his edictal commentary reproduces[368] what we know from a text of Paul[369] to have been the words of a constitution of Marcus and Verus. But for all we know Ulpian did make it clear that he was citing an imperial constitution, and Justinian's compilers, in the interests of brevity, struck out the introductory words. Since Ulpian's works are in general well documented, and since he likes to cite the original text when he can, and to attribute it to its author, he should not be convicted of fraudulently presenting imperial law as his own invention merely on the strength of this coincidence.

Given that Ulpian aims at a balance between juristic and imperial sources, and is ready to cite either or both when they seem appropriate, how does he perceive their relation to one another? Does imperial law prevail over juristic law, or are they on a level?

At first sight he seems to put them on a level, as in:

> scripsit Iulianus et est rescriptum[370]
> ut Papinianus respondit et est rescriptum[371]
> hoc enim et relatum est et rescriptum[372]
> ut inde sit et dictum et rescriptum[373]
> et hoc et rescriptum et responsum est[374]
> ut et constitutum est et responsum[375]

No particular order is followed. Sometimes the jurist is mentioned first; in the last two examples the rescript or constitution comes first. So far as juristic opinion is concerned, no special priority is accorded to *responsa*. Other expressions (*dicta, relata*) are treated as equivalent. This accords with what we know from elsewhere of Ulpian's attitude to *responsa*. He does not specially esteem them. He cites none of his own. Nor does he cite those of Marcellus, a main source,[376] or of Scaevola.[377] Only Papinian's[378] are

---

[367] Pernice (1885) 455.
[368] D. 27.8.1.10 (Ulp. 36 ed.).
[369] D. 26.5.24 (Paul 9 resp.: *divi Marcus et Verus Cornelio Proculo*).
[370] D. 13.7.13 pr. (Ulp. 28 ed.).
[371] D. 48.18.4 (Ulp. 3 disp.).
[372] D. 50.1.2.5 (Ulp. 1 disp.).
[373] D. 2.15.7.2 (Ulp. 7 disp.).
[374] D. 4.4.7.9 (Ulp. 11 ed.).
[375] D. 3.2.13.7 (Ulp. 6 ed.).
[376] Above, n. 20.
[377] Above, n. 122 f.
[378] Above, nn. 10 f.

treated with particular respect. This may reflect a preference for those
sources which set out a general rule rather than a decision on particular facts
which is sometimes (often, in the case of Scaevola) not explained or
motivated.

Though juristic opinion is plainly treated as a source of law, Ulpian does
not speak as if it were binding on himself. Like other Roman jurists, he feels
free to dissent from even the unanimous opinion of his fellows. The notion
that juristic opinion is binding law, given certain conditions, is, as Gaius
clearly implies,[379] a precept addressed to judges, not jurists.

Imperial constitutions are different. Ulpian can praise them,[380] and
occasionally criticize them,[381] but they bind him and, from the jurist's
point of view, settle the law. Thus, Ulpian thinks, if a *peculium* is bequethed
to a slave by way of legacy, it should include a debt owing to the slave from
his master.[382] Yet he concedes that this is contrary to a rescript of Severus
and Antoninus, of which he gives the text. He then goes on: 'But what if it
was the testator's intention (that the slave should be able to claim what the
owner owes)? Certainly he should be allowed to set-off his expenditure
against what he owed his master. Again, if the owner records (in the will)
what he owes the slave, does the debt form part of the legacy?' There is then
a discussion of the opinions of three jurists, Pegasus, Nerva, and Atilicinus.
The latter held that the debt was not part of the legacy. Ulpian concludes
that his opinion is right, *because it is consistent with the rescript:* 'quod verum
est, quia consonat rescripto'.

Ulpian is no theorist, but the view underlying this sentence is perhaps
that the rescript is declaratory of the true state of the law. It is this way of
looking at legal problems that makes it possible, for example, for the
Tyrian to say of a rescript of Marcus that it conforms to his own
opinion.[383] Thus, on a point in the law of *postliminium* 'there is no doubt
after the rescript of the emperor Antoninus and his deified father'.[384] But at
other times Ulpian speaks in a way which implies that a rescript has
changed the law. Thus a rescript of Marcus allowed a slave owner to accuse
his slave of adultery. 'After this rescript, therefore', says Ulpian, 'the owner
has a duty (in an appropriate case) to accuse his own slave.'[385] A boy under
age (*pupillus*) who has concerned himself with the affairs of another can

---

[379] *Inst.* 1.7.

[380] D. 17.1.6.7 (29 *ed.*), 48.19.8.12 (9 *off. proc.*), 50.15.3.1 (2 *cens.*), 50.2.3.1 (3 *off. proc.*), 28.6.2.4 (6
Sab.).

[381] D. 42.1.15.9 (Ulp. 3 *off. cons.*), 33.8.6.4 (25 *Sab.*).

[382] D. 33.8.6.4 (25 *Sab.*).

[383] D. 29.1.3 (Ulp. 2 *Sab.*), cf. 36.1.19.1 (15 *Sab.*: *ut est et rescriptum*), 26.8.5.3 (Ulp.: *et ita est
rescriptum*), 49.1.1.2 (*Ulp. 1 appell.*: *huic consequenter videtur rescriptum*), 38.17.2.47 (Ulp. 13 *Sab.*: *et
invenimus rescriptum*).

[384] D. 49.15.9 (Ulp. 4 *Iul. Pap.*).

[385] D. 48.2.5 (Ulp. 3 *adult.*), cf. 31.61.1 (Ulp. 18 *Iul. Pap.*: *Iulianus quidem ait . . .sed post rescriptum
Severi*).

'after the rescript of the deified Pius' be sued to the extent of his enrichment.[386] On whatever theory, then, even a single rescript is conclusive. Yet, if we read between the lines, Ulpian can be critical of rescripts. Caracalla gave a ruling that debts could be taken in execution, if necessary. This applies, on the better view (*magis est*) only to debts admitted to be due, says Ulpian. Yet one might argue that the judge should decide whether they are due, as in the case of tangible property. 'But the contrary has been laid down by rescript' (*sed contra rescriptum est*).[387] The implication is that the rescript, though open to criticism, must be followed. Nevertheless, while rescripts bind jurists, they do not bind emperors. An emperor may depart from his own prior view of the law or that of his predecessors.[388] A jurist, if advising an emperor as secretary *a libellis* or imperial councillor, may urge him to take a different view from that presented by a previous rescript or even line of rescripts. The rules about the sources of law establish a hierarchy. Emperors bind jurists, jurists bind judges. Emperors do not bind themselves, and jurists do not bind themselves or one another either. *Quod principi placuit legis habet vigorem,*[389] says Ulpian with characteristic decisiveness. But it is law only until the emperor can be induced to take a different view. Besides, it is effectively law only if publicized. There are rescripts, like those of Commodus, which Ulpian omits to cite.[390] He had reservations, we may deduce, about some decisions of the imperial court. 'Everyone knows how often it is necessary to resort to an appeal in order to correct the injustice or incompetence of a judge. But appeals sometimes change a decision for the worse, and the judge who gives judgment last does not necessarily give it best.'[391] Given the importance of appeals to the emperor, this is rather strong language. Indeed, Ulpian, though he admits the legal force of imperial judicial decisions (*decreta*), speaks of them as if they were not true constitutions:

> et est decretum ab imperatore Severo et constitutum[392]
> decretum et a divo Severo constitutum est[393]

A rescript can also be distinguished from a 'real' constitution, with general force, such as an edict:[394]

> saepius rescriptum et constitutum est

These expressions can hardly be intended simply as hendiadys. Like a *responsum*, a rescript or decree can be confined to the particular case for

---

[386] D. 3.5.3.4 (Ulp. 10 *ed.*).
[387] D. 42.1.15.9 (Ulp. 3 *off. cons.*).
[388] D. 37.14.17 pr. (Ulp. 11 *Iul. Pap.*), 49.14.6 pr. (Ulp. 63 *ed.: varie rescriptum est: puto tamen* . . .).
[389] D. 1.4.1 pr. (Ulp. 1 *inst.*).
[390] Above, nn. 348 f.
[391] D. 49.1.1 pr. (Ulp. 1 *appell.*).
[392] D. 49.5.26.1 (Ulp. 5 *fid.*).
[393] D. 49.14.25 (Ulp. 19 *Sab.*).
[394] D. 29.7.1 (Ulp. 4 *disp.*).

which it is given. It is only when it expresses a general principle that it makes law. Of this the issue of an edict or other general form of constitution is the best evidence.

VII. ULPIAN AS A LAWYER

The assessment of Ulpian's contributions to particular branches of the law is a matter for specialists in those branches. This section is concerned rather with Ulpian's general quality as a lawyer and his approach to the solution of legal problems. Pernice complained that he tended to arrive at solutions not on strictly legal grounds but for reasons of convenience or policy.[395] This complaint, even if factually correct, as indeed it is, is less compelling now than it was in the late nineteenth century. No one now thinks of law as a purely deductive discipline. It is rather accounted a merit in a lawyer to want to fit the law to the society in which it is to operate and to be eager to fill gaps and carve out exceptions to settled rules, when this can be done with due regard to reasonable expectations and to the structure of the system as a whole.

Pernice also objected that Ulpian was, for the most part, unoriginal, indeed monotonous. It seems to me that he was not mistaken. He rightly complains of the flatness of many of Ulpian's comments. 'This is true'. 'This rescript covers many points'.[396] 'But I think so-and-so'. 'We accept this as the law'. The impression conveyed to the reader is one of calm, orderly, progression from one topic to the next; of security and wise disposition. Intellectual excitement is missing. The fire of Celsus, the subtlety of Papinian, the ingenuity of Julian lie beyond Ulpian's smooth, gubernatorial spirit.

Does it follow that, apart from lucidity and scholarly care, Ulpian has little merit as a writer? That would be an unfair conclusion. Though not inventive, he had the qualities of a good judge or legislator: a sense of proportion, of moderation, and a sure instinct for the just solution.

The first of these runs through every aspect of Ulpian's work. His prose is well proportioned. No sentence or clause is too long. He expounds the law point by point. He keeps a balance between juristic and imperial sources. Within the former, the more recent are taken into account but not permitted to predominate. The same is true of the emperors whose rescripts are used. Important as are Severus and Caracalla, they are not allowed to upstage Hadrian, Pius and Marcus.

When applied to human conduct, sense of proportion becomes the virtue of moderation. That Ulpian set great store by this can be seen from

---

[395] Pernice (1885) 443; Wieacker (1961) 154.
[396] D. 29.5.1.29 (Ulp. 50 *ed.*).

his language. Usually so controlled and unadorned, when he speaks of the conduct of officials strong feelings obtrude. Administration must be conducted without laxity, but also without pressing harshly on the citizen. As regards delation, a path is to be trodden between supine blindness to the facts and over-scrupulous inquisition: [397]

> ut neque neglegentia crassa aut nimia securitas expedita sit neque delatoria curiositas exigatur

Suppose that in administering his office a tutor fails to sell perishable goods belonging to his ward in due time, so that the ward suffers a loss. Is it an excuse that the tutor was waiting for his co-tutors to agree to the sale, or that they wished to put the matter off? He will not easily be excused. His duty is to carry out his duties without precipitation but also without undue delay: [398]

> non quidem praecipiti festinatione sed nec moratoria cunctatione

The praetor by his edict promised to compel an attorney (*cognitor*) to defend an action in certain events. Julian listed some exceptions, for example, if the *cognitor* was away on the business of the local authority (*res publica*). These excuses, says Ulpian, should not be automatically accepted, neither should they be systematically denied. Each case deserves to be examined on its merits: [399]

> Sed haec neque passim admittenda sunt neque districte deneganda, sed a praetore cause cognita temperanda

Provincial governors are not allowed to convert the personal effects of condemned persons whose property is forfeit to their own use. In practice most of them collect any forfeited coins and send them to the treasury. This is over-scrupulous (*perquam nimiae diligentiac est*). [400] The governor could use the money for official purposes. In an action for the recovery of an inheritance fruits must be accounted for, including rents of urban property. What about brothels? The income from a brothel should be included, says Ulpian. Many respectable men own property on which there are brothels. [401] Suppose that the provincial governor finds that the funds of a local authority are invested in a way which does not yield interest. What should he do? He must consider the interests of the local authority, but without being harsh or insulting (e.g. if the investment is in some project to which the local community attaches great importance). He should seek to combine efficiency with moderation and persistence with humanity: [402]

---

[397] D. 22.6.6 (Ulp. 18 *ed.*).   [398] D. 26.7.7 (Ulp. 35 *ed.*).
[399] D. 3.3.13 (Ulp. 8 *ed.*).
[400] D. 48.20.6 (Ulp. 10 *off. proc.*).
[401] D. 5.3.27.1 (Ulp. 15 *ed.*).
[402] D. 22.1.33 pr. (Ulp. 1 *off. cur. reip.*).

dummodo non acerbum se exactorem nec contumeliosum praebeat, sed moderatum et cum efficacia benignum et cum instantia humanum: nam inter insolentiam incuriosam et diligentiam non ambitiosam multum interest

No doubt this outlook on government and office holding owes much to Severus. Ulpian praises for its elegance the letter of Severus and Antoninus in which they explain to provincial governors how to steer a middle course between a total refusal to take gifts, which is inhuman, and greedy acceptance of everything offered, which is contemptible:[403]

nam valde inhumanum est a nemine accipere, sed passim vilissimum est et omnia avarissimum

Provincial governors are sometimes faced with the problem of a man who, to avoid condemnation, alleges that he has information bearing on the emperor's safety—for example, of a plot against him. Some governors refuse to listen to such allegations, others do, others again inquire what it is that the condemned man wants to tell the emperor and in the light of that decides either to execute the sentence or not. This seems to be the middle way:[404]

quod videtur habere mediam rationem

Ulpian adds this in his opinion (*ut mea fert opinio*) such talk should not be given a hearing after sentence has been passed, since the motive at that stage is undoubtedly to escape execution of the sentence. The condemned man should rather be punished for keeping silent for so long about a matter of grave importance.

Ulpian has a traditional conception of virtue as moderation (*media ratio*). This is unexciting, but it is a merit of his writing, especially in matters of public administration, that he clings steadily to the middle ground.

Sense of proportion is also needed in keeping a balance between adherence to settled rules and departure from them in the interests of justice in the individual case. Ulpian respects received doctrine and procedures, and tries to satisfy the claims of justice by filling gaps in the law or carving out exceptions in a way which does not disturb the main structure. Thus, fruits from your tree fall on my land. I send my cattle to eat them. In common sense, you should have some remedy. But Aristo, who thinks of three possible statutory actions, concludes that none of them will, for technical reasons, fit the facts. Well, says Ulpian, a supplementary action must be made available:[405]

in factum itaque erit agendum

---

[403] D. 1.16.6.3 (Ulp. 1 *off. proc.*).
[404] D. 48.19.6 pr. (Ulp. 9 *off. proc.*).
[405] D. 19.5.14.3 (Ulp. 41 *Sab.*).

The grammatical form of this remark, with its inversion of the future gerund, guarantees its genuineness. The same is true in the following case. One man pushes another who in turn pushes a slave and kills him. Can the first man be sued for killing a slave? Proculus said not. The first man did not kill the slave. What of the second? He killed the slave, but was not at fault. So he cannot be sued either. Proculus seems to imply that the slave's owner has no remedy. Accordingly, says Ulpian, a supplementary action must be given against the first man:[406]

> secundum quod in factum actio erit danda adversus eum qui impulit.

A slave is instituted heir by will, but is only entitled to take in default of a child of the testator, whose wife is pregnant at his death. If approached by a free heir, the praetor would order certain measures for the custody of the offspring, to ensure that some other child was not covertly introduced as the testator's. Aristo, a jurist whose outlook resembled Ulpian's, held that the slave should be protected in this case. 'I think this is correct', says Ulpian.[407] 'It is in the public interest that offspring should not be covertly substituted, and that the dignity of the orders and of families should in that way be preserved. Hence the slave, whoever he may be, as he has an expectation of succeeding, should be heard on his own behalf and on that of the state.'

A father could make his son heir and provide by a special instrument, kept secret until the son came of age, who should be substituted for him as heir, should he die under age. In the case considered by Ulpian the father died, then the son died under age. His mother claimed the son's inheritance on the ground that the father's will, which (she believed) provided for a substitute for the son, had been revoked. It was held that it had not. Then the mother discovered that the father had not in fact made a substitution. So she was, after all, entitled to the son's inheritance. But could she now sue, or was she barred by the plea of *res judicata*? Neratius held that she was. Ulpian agrees that the case is one of *res judicata*, but, in the circumstances, he says, the mother must be given a remedy, since in the first action only the point about the revocation of the will was in issue:[408]

> ego exceptionem obesse ei rei iudicatae non dubito: sed ex causa succurrendum erit ei, quae unam tantum causam egit rupti testamenti

I give you some money. I intend it as a gift, but you think it is a loan. You spend the money. Can I sue (by *condictio*) to recover the amount? Julian held

---

[406] *D.* 9.2.7.3 (Ulp. 18 *ed.*).
[407] *D.* 25.4.1.13 (Ulp 34 *ed.*). Ulpian considers that slaves have, if not rights, at least interests. Thus, a slave's *peculium* is not reduced merely because he deliberately injures himself. A slave is entitled to do this: *licet enim etiam servis naturaliter in suum corpus saevire.*
[408] *D.* 44.2.11 pr. (Ulp. 75 *ed.*).

that there was no gift, and possibly no loan. Ulpian is clear that in the absence of agreement there is no contract. So the property in the coins did not pass to you and in principle I can sue you by *condictio*. But this would not be just, since you spent the money, as I intended you to. Hence it is dishonest of me to reclaim the money, and you should have the defence of dishonesty (*exceptio doli*).[409]

> quare si eos consumpserit, licet condictione teneatur, tamen doli exceptione uti poterit, quia secundum voluntatem dantis nummi sunt consumpti

Quite apart from the linguistic marks of genuineness—the future tense *poterit*, the inversion of *sunt consumpti*—the use of *quare* clearly shows Ulpian's train of thought. *Because* technical rules seem to give me a right to recover, a way must be found to protect you.

Enough has been said to give the reader an idea, of course fragmentary, of Ulpian's approach to the pressure points at which the interests of justice seem to require settled rules to be bent or stretched.

Ulpian's view of the way to resolve the conflict between settled rules and the interests of justice seems, again, to owe something to that of Severus. Suppose the testator leaves someone a legacy and asks him to emancipate his own children. Can the children claim their emancipation by way of trust (*fideicommissum*)? Ulpian says that they cannot, because the praetor in charge of trusts does not intervene in the case of children as he does when the trust is one of freedom for a slave. Ulpian reports Papinian's view that the legatee should not be compelled to emancipate his son in such a case. His own opinion, however, is different. Though the children cannot claim under a trust, the legatee, who has received the legacy in contemplation of the emancipation, should be compelled outside the ordinary system of procedure (*extra ordinem*) to do so, just as if the legacy were conditional on the emancipation. Otherwise the testator's will is circumvented.[410] Consistently with this view (*cui rei consequens est*), Severus took action in a case in which a mother made her son and his sons joint heirs and asked him to emancipate them, but did not create a trust of the inheritance in favour of her grandchildren. Severus ordered the son to emancipate the grandchildren and hand over the inheritance to them.

> ex auctoritate divi Severi emancipare eos compulsus est hisque restituere hereditatem

Severus acts outside the ordinary course of law. Ulpian speaks as if Severus were adopting the jurist's point of view. But this is probably just his unhistorical way of writing. Rather, the Severan administration—the

[409] *D.* 12.1.18 pr. (Ulp. 7 *disp.*).
[410] *D.* 35.1.92 (Ulp. 5 *fid.*).

emperor himself, Papinian, and no doubt others—was imbued with a sense of purpose, which infected the Tyrian too. The legal system must be made to work, to provide adequate remedies. The watchword was *utilitas*, giving effect to both public and private interests. This is what, according to Ulpian, the law aims at, or is about. The study of law has two aspects, public and private. Public law concerns the Roman state; private, the interests of individuals. For there are both public and private interests:[411]

> Huius studii duae sunt positiones, publicum et privatum. Publicum ius est quod ad statum rei Romanae spectat, privatum quod ad singulorum utilitatem: sunt enim quaedam publice utilia, quaedam privatim.

With its emphasis on utility, and the mention of public interests before private, this is as good a statement as we shall find of the Severan philosophy of government.

Utilis, utilitas and their inflections, together with *inutilis* and *inutilitas*, when used in this sense, are markedly more popular in the Severan age than in the early empire or under the Antonines:[412]

	Percentage of Digest	Uses of utilis etc.	Number per 1 percent of Digest
Jurists up to Julian	9.14	11	1.20
Pomponius to Scaevola	17.80	27	1.52
The Severans	72.36	180	2.49

Within the last group the figures for Papinian, Paul, and Ulpian reach the level of significance:

Papinian	5.69	20	3.51
Paul	16.74	42	2.51
Ulpian	41.56	107	2.57

The strongest influence among the jurists of the age, on this point also, was probably Papinian. Ulpian follows suit, and fills in the details.

What sort of lawyer was he? Not a man of keen analytical power, certainly no genius. His importance lies in the part he played in the transmission of the Roman legal heritage. From this point of view, he is Tribonian's real forerunner. Indeed his work amounts to a precodification. But he was not just a compiler. His Latin prose is cool and lucid. If readers of the *Digest* have the impression that the texts are composed in the language of the late republic or early empire, this is in large measure because so much of it is excerpted from Ulpian. Nor was he simply a clear

---

[411] *D.* 1.1.1.2 (Ulp. 1 *inst.*).
[412] Source: *CDJ* relevant fiches.

expositor. He had a good feeling for the just solution, and the energy to argue for it. As we look back on the history of legal culture we can think of him, though politically a failure, as the right man in the right place at the right time.

TABLE I

List of words and phrases referred to in the text and footnotes

References in the form 5[107] are to chapters and footnotes.
References in the form 185 are to pages.

Table I 251

Table I 253

Table I 255

Table I 257

TABLE II

References to legal texts

References in the form 2^{370} are to chapters and footnotes.
References in the form 81 are to pages

1. *Digesta Iustiniani* (D.)

I.I.I.I $1^{220, 224, 338}$, $2^{109, 200, 521}$
I.I.I.2 9^{411}
I.I.I.3 $1^{205, 232}$, 2^{248}
I.I.4 2^{377}; 172
I.I.6 pr. $2^{223, 235, 238}$; 172
I.I.10 pr. 4^{66}
I.I.10.1 4^{79}
I.2.2 pr. 2^{203}
I.2.2.44 9^{180}
I.3.2 9^{66}
I.4.1 pr. 9^{389}; 172
I.4.1.2 9^{356}
I.5.1.8 5^{15}
I.5.8 5^{10}
I.5.10 $2^{14, 228}$
I.5.17 $1^{198}, 4^{23}, 6^{16}$; 134
I.6.2 $2^{751}, 9^{340}$
I.6.6 $2^{159, 411}$
I.7.15.2 $2^{115, 468}$
I.7.17.4 2^{567}
I.7.32.1 5^{10}
I.7.39 9^{341}
I.9.1 pr. 1^{327}
I.9.1.1 2^{742}
I.9.8 2^{467}
I.9.10 2^{107}
I.9.12 pr. 1^{238}; 165–6
I.10.1.2 2^{142}

I.12.1 pr. 180
I.12.1.3 7^{39}; 178
I.12.1.4 9^{343}
I.12.1.5 $2^{325}, 3^{15}$
I.12.1.8 $2^{291, 547, 743}, 3^{14}, 7^{36}$; 178, 181
I.12.1.10 $2^{599}, 7^{36}$; 177
I.12.1.14 181
I.13.1 pr. $2^{659}, 3^{18}$
I.13.1.3 $2^{730}, 3^{16}, 7^{40}$; 177
I.14.3 2^{17}
I.15.2 $2^{433}, 3^{23}$
I.15.4 $7^{3, 13}, 9^{343}$; 181
I.16.4 pr. 6^{24}; 154
I.16.4.2 2^{87}
I.16.4.3 2^{506}; 164
I.16.4.5 $1^{152}, 6^{27}$; 154
I.16.6.3 $2^{715}, 6^{19}, 9^{340, 403}$; 154
I.16.7 pr. 2^{697}
I.16.9.2 2^{597}
I.16.9.3 2^{632}
I.16.9.4 164, 173
I.16.9.5 2^{726}
I.16.10 pr. 2^{135}
I.17.1 $5^{13}, 6^{23}$
I.18.6 pr. 4^{171}

I.18.6.2 4^{209}
I.18.6.4 4^{173}
I.18.6.6 $4^{203, 204}$
I.18.6.7 4^{205}
I.18.7 4^{226}
I.18.13 pr. 2^{696}
I.18.13.1 2^{428}
I.19.1.2 2^{380}
I.22 8^{3}
I.22.5 1^{114}
I.22.6 1^{114}

2.1.1 4^{81}
2.1.3 $2^{606}, 7^{40, 54}$; 177
2.1.7 pr. 147
2.1.7.2 2^{289}
2.1.15 2^{170}
2.1.17 4^{150}
2.1.19 pr. 4^{114}
2.2.1 pr. $1^{208}, 2^{165}$
2.2.1.2 $5^{104, 105}$
2.2.3.1 2^{401}
2.2.3.3 146
2.2.3.4 2^{15}
2.2.4 2^{714}
2.4.4.2 2^{385}
2.4.8.1 2^{81}
2.4.10.2 5^{104}
2.4.10.5 5^{102}
2.4.10.9 5^{104}
2.7.1 pr. 1^{208}

Table II 261

D
4.8.24.4 2^{166}
4.8.25.1 2^{425}; 163
4.8.28 2^{396}, 4^{44}
4.8.31 $2^{679, 683}$
4.8.32.16 2^{18}
4.9.1.1 1^{208}
4.9.1.5 1^{291}
4.9.3.1 2^{132}; 164
4.9.3.3 2^{328}
4.9.7.3 2^{305}

5.1.2 pr. 146
5.1.2.3 2^{564}
5.1.2.4 2^{420}
5.1.2.5 2^{127}
5.1.5 2^{478}, 9^{330}
5.1.18.1 $2^{31, 488}$
5.1.19.2 $2^{166, 477,}$ 487, 661; 186
5.1.36.1 9^{74}
5.1.45 pr. 2^{396}, 4^{43}
5.1.50.1 2^{661}; 170
5.1.52.2 2^{149}
5.1.52.4 2^{15}
5.1.61 pr. 2^{245a}; 164
5.1.81 $4^{224, 227}$
5.1.82 7^{38}; 178
5.2.8.2 2^{712}
5.2.8.6 2^{736}
5.2.8.9 2^{292}
5.2.8.11 2^{147}
5.2.8.14 2^{135}
5.2.23 pr. 2^{117}
5.2.27.3 4^{182}
5.3.3.6 2^{220}
5.3.9 2^{735}
5.3.11 2^{97}, 9^{170}
5.3.13.1 2^{159}
5.3.13.3 $9^{93, 95}$
5.3.13.4 2^{401}
5.3.13.8 2^{160}
5.3.13.9 2^{305}
5.3.16 pr. 9^{202}
5.3.18 pr. 2^{159}
5.3.20.12 2^{25}; 132
5.3.20.15 2^{291}

5.3.25.5 $2^{398, 683}$
5.3.25.6 2^{15}
5.3.25.8 $2^{198, 387}$; 172
5.3.25.9 $2^{26, 276}$
5.3.25.11 2^{424}
5.3.25.15 2^{398}
5.3.27.1 9^{401}
5.3.31 pr. $2^{39, 126}$
5.3.31.2 2^{144}
5.3.31.4 173
5.3.37 2^{305}
5.3.43 5^{15}
5.4.1.4 2^{293}
5.4.6 pr. 4^{182}

6.1.1.2 2^{132}
6.1.1.3 2^{97}
6.1.5.1 2^{274}
6.1.5.3 9^{300}
6.1.9 $2^{100, 300}$
6.1.13 2^{126}
6.1.15.1 2^{311}
6.1.15.3 2^{155}
6.1.35 pr. 9^{70}
6.1.35.1 9^{334}
6.1.37 2^{400}
6.1.78 2^{388}
6.2.7.12 3^{12}
6.2.7.13 $2^{97, 367}$
6.2.7.17 2^{267}; 171
6.2.9.1 2^{290}
6.2.11 pr. 5^{25}; 133
6.2.11.3 $2^{122, 123}$

7.1.3.1 2^{106}
7.1.7.1 $2^{160, 548}$
7.1.7.3 $9^{93, 95, 145,}$ 250
7.1.9.2 2^{160}
7.1.9.4 2^{167}
7.1.9.5 9^{145}
7.1.12 pr. 2^{160}, 9^{49}
7.1.12.2 $9^{309, 315}$
7.1.12.3 168
7.1.12.4 $2^{166, 317b}$

7.1.12.5 2^{401}
7.1.13.3 $2^{16, 160}$
7.1.13.4 2^{634}, 4^{39}
7.1.13.5 $2^{16, 376b}$
7.1.13.7 2^{471}
7.1.13.8 $2^{385, 628}$
7.1.15.2 2^{738}
7.1.17 pr. 2^{126}
7.1.17.1 9^{250}
7.1.22 2^{236}
7.1.23.1 9^{145}
7.1.25.1 $2^{122, 217}$
7.1.25.3 2^{127}
7.1.25.5 $2^{67, 132, 735}$
7.1.25.6 2^{217}, 9^{123}
7.1.25.7 9^{300}
7.1.27.1 2^{681}
7.1.43 2^{704}
7.1.60 pr. 2^{104}
7.1.70 pr. $9^{145, 147}$
7.1.70.4 2^{400}
7.1.72 $9^{130, 133, 134}$
7.2.1.1 2^{401}
7.2.1.3 2^{122}, 9^{272}
7.2.3 pr. $9^{93, 96}$
7.2.3.2 9^{286}
7.2.4 2^{118}
7.2.8 2^{81}
7.4.1 pr. 2^{35}
7.4.1.2 2^{677}
7.4.3 pr. 9^{133}; 170
7.4.3.2 $2^{166, 317b}$
7.4.5 pr. 2^{86}
7.4.10.1 $2^{106, 274}$
7.4.10.5 2^{160}, 9^{192}
7.4.10.7 $2^{125, 161}$
7.4.10.11 2^{201}
7.4.29.2 2^{155}
7.5.5.1 $2^{490, 491, 617}$
7.5.3 2^{155}
7.5.5.2 $2^{490, 491}$, 9^{28}
7.5.10.1 2^{340}
7.5.11 2^{333}
7.6.1.3 $2^{68, 114, 402}$
7.6.5.1 2^{116}
7.6.5.6 2^{300}
7.8.1.4 9^{304}

Table II   263

D

7.8.2.1 2[110, 127, 191]; 9[50, 227, 284]; 170
7.8.4 pr. 2[343, 639]; 173
7.8.4.1 2[56], 9[14]
7.8.6 2[33, 323], 9[249]
7.8.10.2 2[114, 117]; 196
7.8.10.3 2[116]
7.8.10.4 6[43]
7.8.12 pr. 6[43]
7.8.12.1 2[162, 490, 491]
7.9.1.2 2[154]
7.9.1.7 2[121]
7.9.3.1 2[291]
7.9.3.4 2[65]
7.9.7 pr. 2[166, 317b]
7.9.9. pr. 2[49]
7.9.9.1 2[154]

8.1.20 2[180]
8.2.3 2[379]
8.2.17.1 2[81]
8.3.1.1 2[497]
8.3.3 pr. 9[93, 95]
8.3.3.2 9[93, 95]
8.3.3.3 9[93, 95]
8.3.5.1 2[497], 9[93, 98], 231
8.3.35 2[72]
8.4.2 133
8.4.6.2 2[94]
8.4.13.1 4[139, 210]
8.4.18 9[70]
8.5.4.2 2[59]
8.5.8.5 2[81]
8.5.10.1 2[106]
8.5.15 4[199]

9.1.1.4 2[409, 591]
9.1.1.6 2[540]
9.1.1.7 1[233], 2[308]
9.1.1.15 2[121]
9.2.5.1 2[291]; 178
9.2.5.2 2[242]
9.2.7.3 2[330], 9[406]

9.2.7.4 2[308]
9.2.7.8 2[725]
9.2.9.1 2[8, 573]; 197
9.2.11.8 2[330]
9.2.11.10 2[16]
9.2.21.1 2[260]
9.2.21.2 2[226]
9.2.22 pr. 2[76, 79]
9.2.23.4 2[756]
9.2.25.2 2[137]
9.2.27.1 9[191]
9.2.27.9 2[267]
9.2.27.11 2[166, 317b]
9.2.27.17 2[291, 324, 578]
9.2.27.25 9[199]
9.2.27.28 2[324]
9.2.27.30 2[626, 627]
9.2.27.31 2[412]
9.2.29.1 5[25]; 133
9.2.29.7 2[750]
9.2.41 pr. 2[88], 3[29]
9.2.45 pr. 2[393]
9.2.49.1 2[290]
9.2.51.2 2[205]
9.3.1.1 1[208]
9.3.1.2 2[468]
9.3.5.2 2[122, 123]
9.3.5.5 2[87]
9.3.5.11 2[220]
9.4.2.1 2[166, 256, 317b]
9.4.2.8 2[66]
9.4.3 2[394]
9.4.5.1 2[110]
9.4.8 2[170]
9.4.31 2[396]
9.4.35 2[96]
9.4.38.3 2[104]
9.4.42.2 176

10.1.4.1 2[375]
10.1.4.8 2[396], 4[44]
10.1.8.1 4[213]
10.2.4.3 2[590]
10.2.8 pr. 2[590]
10.2.18.1 2[69, 754]

10.2.18.3 5[23, 25, 74]; 133
10.2.20.1 133
10.2.20.3 2[129]
10.2.29 2[375]
10.2.54 2[116]
10.3.4.4 2[83]
10.3.6.4 9[233]
10.3.6.6 9[225]
10.3.6.9 2[300]
10.3.7.8 2[166]
10.3.7.13 2[96, 104, 115]
10.3.12 2[324]
10.3.14.1 4[46]
10.3.21 2[672]
10.3.23 2[117]
10.4.1.1 1[208]
10.4.3.2 2[137]
10.4.3.9 2[110]
10.4.3.14 2[470]
10.4.7.4 2[149]
10.4.9 pr. 2[412]
10.4.9.2 2[683]
10.4.9.8 9[94]
10.4.11 pr. 2[670]
10.4.11.1 2[122, 181, 504, 582]
10.4.19.1 2[159]
10.4.20 4[76]

11.1.2 1[208]
11.1.4.1 2[394]
11.1.9.4 2[113, 296, 701]
11.1.11.3 2[122]
11.1.11.4 2[477]
11.1.11.7 2[543]
11.1.11.8 2[139, 633, 670]; 196
11.1.16 pr. 2[90]
11.1.16.1 2[90]
11.3.1.1 2[216]
11.3.1.4 2[59]
11.3.3 pr. 2[505, 582]
11.3.5 pr. 2[427]
11.3.9 pr. 2[499]
11.3.9.1 2[510]
11.3.9.3 2[127, 511]

D

11.3.11 pr. 2[160]
11.3.11.1 2[511]
11.3.14.9 2[122]
11.4.1.2 2[418]
11.4.1.5 9[32, 385]
11.5.1.2 2[137, 390]
11.5.1.3 2[43]
11.6.1 pr. 1[208]
11.6.1.1 2[104, 725]
11.6.3 pr. 2[683]
11.6.5 pr. 2[331]
11.6.7.3 5[60]; 134
11.7.2.1 2[156]
11.7.2.8 2[166]
11.7.4 2[126, 267]
11.7.4.3 2[396]
11.7.6 pr. 2[409, 712]
11.7.8 pr. 2[127]
11.7.8.2 2[350]
11.7.12 pr. 5[30, 48, 58]; 134
11.7.12.3 1[208]
11.7.14.2 2[158]
11.7.14.3 2[518]
11.7.14.7 2[731], 5[29]; 134
11.7.14.11 2[398, 731]
11.7.14.14 2[747]
11.7.31 pr. 2[84]
11.7.43 2[43]
11.8.1.3 2[285]
11.8.1.6 2[434]
11.8.1.8 2[110]

12.1.1 pr. 9[5]
12.1.1.1 9[31]
12.1.6 9[105]
12.1.7 9[126]
12.1.9.3 2[317b]
12.1.9.8 2[713]
12.1.11 pr. 2[127, 515]
12.1.12 pr. 2[104]
12.1.18 pr. 9[409]
12.1.24 4[2, 133]
12.1.26 4[182]
12.1.40 9[86]

12.2.3 pr. 2[663]
12.2.5 pr. 2[356]
12.2.7 2[290]
12.2.9.4 2[592], 5[58]
12.2.9.6 2[166, 317b]
12.2.11.1 2[295]
12.2.11.2 2[490, 491]
12.2.11.3 2[310]
12.2.13.2 4[135]
12.2.13.6 5[27, 47, 58]; 134
12.2.16 146
12.2.30.2 2[375]
12.2.34.7 2[170]
12.3.1 2[216]
12.3.4 pr. 2[169, 712], 5[29, 51, 58]; 135, 197
12.3.4.1 5[29, 51]; 135
12.3.4.2 2[192]
12.3.10 9[348]
12.4.3 pr. 2[56]
12.4.3.1 5[58]
12.4.3.5 9[93, 95]
12.4.3.7 2[34], 9[317]; 171
12.4.3.8 2[733, 748]
12.4.5.4 2[149]
12.4.7 pr. 9[237, 290]
12.4.13 9[60]
12.5.2.2 5[29]; 134
12.5.4 pr. 9[313]
12.5.4.3 2[705], 9[283]
12.6.3 5[10]
12.6.9 2[477]
12.6.15 pr. 2[396], 4[44]
12.6.23.1 6[4]; 150
12.6.25 4[98]
12.6.26 pr. 5[60]; 134
12.6.26.12 2[123]
12.6.26.13 2[401]
12.6.31 2[396]
12.6.59 3[12]
12.7.1 pr. 2[379]

13.1.10.2 2[309, 739]
13.1.12.2 9[93, 95]
13.1.17 2[174]

13.3.1 pr. 2[175]
13.3.3 2[358, 367]
13.4.2.3 2[231, 499], 9[123, 124]
13.4.2.8 9[281]
13.4.4.1 2[438]
13.5.1 pr. 1[208], 2[169]; 197
13.5.1.1 2[394]
13.5.3.1 2[56]
13.5.14.1 2[445]
13.5.16.4 2[247]
13.6.1.1 2[137], 9[296]
13.6.3.4 2[324]
13.6.3.6 2[551]
13.6.5.2 2[376a]
13.6.5.8 2[110]
13.6.5.11 2[42]
13.6.5.13 9[295]
13.6.7.1 2[670]
13.6.7.8 2[166]
13.6.12.1 2[408]
13.6.13.2 2[275]
13.6.18 pr. 2[291]
13.6.18.1 2[118]
13.7.4 2[107]
13.7.8 pr. 2[126]
13.7.9.1 2[105]
13.7.9.3 2[175, 278]
13.7.11.4 2[167]
13.7.11.5 2[527]
13.7.11.6 5[29]; 134
13.7.13 pr. 2[376c], 9[370]
13.7.16.1 2[76, 80]
13.7.24 pr. 2[272]
13.7.24.1 2[24, 638]
13.7.24.2 2[22]
13.7.26 pr. 2[712]; 157
13.7.27 4[200, 215]
13.7.36 pr. 2[268, 376c, 712, 756]; 147
13.7.36.1 2[592]

14.1.1. pr. 1[208]
14.1.1.5 2[63, 126, 225]
14.1.1.6 2[611]
14.1.1.8 2[160]

Table II   265

D

17.1.29.5 $2^{504, 582}$
17.1.29.6 2^{670}
17.1.49 2^{18}
17.1.58 2^{180}
17.1.60.2 2^{86}
17.2.5 pr. 4^{95}
17.2.29.2 2^{207}
17.2.33 2^{93}; 199
17.2.52.5 5^{59}; 134
17.2.52.10 2^{126}
17.2.52.16 4^{95}
17.2.52.17 4^{95}
17.2.52.18 2^{81}, 4^{95}, $9^{234, 240}$
17.2.55 2^{195}
17.2.58 pr. 2^{470}; 170
17.2.62 9^{245}
17.2.63 pr. 2^{91}
17.2.63.3 2^{132}
17.2.63.5 $2^{165, 317a}$
17.2.63.6 2^{220}
17.2.63.8 $2^{88, 240}$
17.2.65.3 2^{375}
17.2.65.8 9^{326}
17.2.73 $4^{94, 106}$

18.1.15.2 2^{275}
18.1.18.1 9^{325}
18.1.24 2^{704}
18.1.28 2^{142}
18.1.35.2 2^{162}
18.1.45 9^{64}
18.1.57.2 2^{470}, 9^{70}
18.1.58 2^{118}
18.1.79 9^{223}
18.2.2 pr. 2^{127}
18.2.4.5 2^{104}
18.2.4.6 2^{285}
18.2.9 $2^{172, 460}$
18.2.11 pr. 2^{703}, $9^{139, 140}$
18.2.16 2^{158}, 5^{59}; 134
18.3.4 pr. $5^{30, 49, 58}$; 134
18.3.4.1 2^{166}
18.3.4.4 2^{22}

18.4.2.3 $2^{16, 157}$; 183
18.4.2.4 2^{105}
18.4.2.6 2^{40}
18.4.2.7 $2^{45, 159}$
18.4.2.10 2^{13}
18.4.2.11 $2^{296, 309}$
18.4.2.16 2^{296}
18.4.2.17 2^{181}, $9^{49, 228, 320}$
18.5.3 2^{18}
18.6.1 pr. 2^{295}
18.6.2.1 $2^{18, 117}$
18.6.4 pr. $2^{32, 181, 633}$
18.6.4.2 $2^{59, 217, 290}$
18.6.18 2^{154}
18.7.1 2^{475}
18.7.10 9^{358}

19.1.4.1 2^{396}, 4^{44}
19.1.7 2^{479}
19.1.10 2^{157}; 183
19.1.11.3 2^{210}, 9^{291}; 167
19.1.11.5 2^{88}
19.1.11.6 2^{187}
19.1.11.12 $9^{93, 96}$
19.1.11.16 $2^{217, 668}$
19.1.11.18 $2^{22, 132}$
19.1.13 pr. 2^{351}
19.1.13.3 $2^{13, 538, 773}$
19.1.13.5 2^{81}
19.1.13.7 2^{241}
19.1.13.9 2^{14}
19.1.13.14 2^{159}
19.1.13.20 2^{670}
19.1.13.22 9^{222}
19.1.13.25 2^{81}
19.1.13.31 2^{245a}
19.1.17.6 2^{704}, 9^{265}
19.1.17.7 2^{88}
19.1.13.25 84
19.1.24.1 9^{290}
19.1.32 2^{166}
19.1.43 1^{59}, $4^{3, 123}$, 9^{85}

19.2.9.1 2^{670}, $5^{50, 58}$; 134
19.2.9.4 $5^{30, 48}$; 134
19.2.11 pr. 2^{117}
19.2.13.5 2^{404}
19.2.13.6 2^{463}
19.2.13.8 9^{266}
19.2.13.11 $2^{454, 575}$
19.2.15.2 $2^{524, 586}$
19.2.15.5 2^{522}; 134
19.2.15.6 5^{31}; 134
19.2.19 pr. 2^{404}
19.2.19.1 5^{30}
19.2.19.2 $2^{46, 394}$
19.2.19.4 2^{59}
19.2.19.6 2^{756}
19.2.19.8 7^{60}
19.2.19.9 $5^{30, 50, 58}$; 134
19.2.25.2 2^{562}
19.2.49 pr. 5^{15}
19.5.5.2 2^{396}
19.5.5.4 4^{55}
19.5.14.3 2^{324}, 9^{405}
19.5.20 pr. 2^{523}
19.5.20.1 $2^{400, 523}$, 9^{265}

20.1.11.2 9^{59}
20.1.13.2 9^{61}
20.1.15.1 2^{713}
20.1.16.6 2^{82}
20.1.16.8 2^{275}
20.1.21.1 2^{166}
20.1.27 $3^{30, 33, 39}$
20.2.1 5^{11}
20.2.2 9^{61}
20.2.3 9^{100}
20.2.5 9^{61}
20.3.1.2 9^{65}
20.4.1 pr. 194
20.4.9 pr. 2^{479}
20.4.12.5 9^{59}
20.4.12.9 9^{59}
20.5.7 9^{62}
20.5.12 pr. 8^{23}, 9^{76}
20.5.12.1 9^{77}

Table II 267

Table II 269

D

26.6.2 I^{58}
26.7.1.3 178
26.7.3.2 $2^{99, \ 217, \ 267}$
26.7.3.3 2^{90}
26.7.3.4 $5^{29, \ 47, \ 58}$; 135
26.7.3.5 2^{348}
26.7.3.6 2^{102}
26.7.3.8 2^{643}
26.7.5.2 2^{529}
26.7.5.3 2^{309}
26.7.5.5 2^{14}
26.7.5.8 2^{300}
26.7.5.10 8^{30}
26.7.7 pr. $2^{475, \ 560}$, 9^{398}
26.7.7.1 177
26.7.7.2 2^{737}
26.7.7.3 2^{576}
26.7.7.4 5^{60}; 135
26.7.7.7 2^{507}
26.7.7.12 2^{102}
26.7.9 pr. 2^{712}
26.7.9.1 2^{267}
26.7.9.6 $2^{85, \ 646}$, $5^{30, \ 48, \ 58}$; 135
26.7.9.7 $2^{105, \ 106}$
26.7.9.9 2^{81}
26.7.12.1 5^{13}
26.7.19 4^{108}
26.7.23 2^{529}
26.7.28.1 3^{30}
26.7.29 7^{63}
26.7.37.1 195
26.7.37.2 2^{82}
26.7.53 9^{70}
26.7.54 2^{35}
26.7.57.1 2^{479}
26.7.61 2^{714}
26.8.1.1 2^{570}
26.8.5 pr. 2^{107}
26.8.5.2 $2^{97, \ 306}$
26.8.5.3 $2^{376c, \ 477}$, 6^{4}, 7^{3}, 9^{383}; 150
26.8.5.4 $2^{94, \ 679}$
26.8.5.5 2^{104}

26.8.5.6 2^{94}
26.10.1 pr. I^{208}, 2^{713}
26.10.1.3 2^{231}
26.10.1.4 2^{296}, $5^{30, \ 50, \ 58}$; 135
26.10.1.5 2^{217}
26.10.1.7 5^{60}, 9^{361}; 135
26.10.3. pr. 5^{60}; 135
26.10.3.2 2^{105}
26.10.3.5 2^{737}; 177
26.10.3.6 2^{296}
26.10.3.7 $2^{305, \ 355}$
26.10.3.9 2^{529}
26.10.3.13 $5^{55, \ 58}$, 7^{3}; 135
26.10.3.16 177
26.10.3.17 2^{728}; 177
26.10.3.18 2^{478}
26.10.4.2 2^{559}
26.10.5 2^{170}
26.10.7.2 157
26.10.7.3 178

27.1.2.9 I^{58}
27.1.3 2^{394}
27.1.4 I^{58}
27.1.6.6 6^{21}; 154
27.1.6.8 $5^{13, \ 15}$, 9^{351}
27.1.6.17 5^{15}
27.1.7 3^{13}, 7^{18}
27.1.8.9 I^{58}
27.1.9 7^{21}; 174
27.1.10.8 I^{58}; 174
27.1.13.2 $I^{58, \ 59}$
27.1.13.6 5^{15}
27.1.13.7 5^{15}
27.1.15 pr. 5^{15}
27.1.15.6 3^{9}
27.1.15.16 2^{190}, 3^{13}, 7^{18}; $166, 170$
27.1.19 2^{667}
27.1.23 pr. 4^{110}
27.1.23.1 4^{111}
27.1.31.4 9^{70}
27.1.44 pr. 5^{56}
27.1.45.3 2^{388}

27.1.45.4 2^{375}
27.1.46.2 5^{56}
27.2.1.1 5^{59}; 135
27.2.1.2 $2^{90, \ 127}$
27.2.1.3 2^{217}, 5^{60}; 135
27.2.2.2 2^{88}
27.2.3.2 2^{438}
27.2.3.3 2^{722}
27.3.1.2 2^{81}, 5^{72}
27.3.1.3 5^{60}; 135
27.3.1.4 2^{155}
27.3.1.11 2^{305}
27.3.1.13 2^{529}, $5^{29, \ 51, \ 58}$; 135
27.3.1.15 $2^{290, \ 712}$, 5^{29}; 135
27.3.1.20 2^{22}
27.3.5 2^{166}
27.3.13 2^{56}
27.3.17 2^{166}, $7^{3, \ 45, \ 48, \ 49}$, 9^{341}; 180
27.3.19 4^{108}
27.4.1 pr. I^{208}
27.4.1.3 2^{309}
27.4.1.5 $2^{14, \ 106}$; 176
27.4.1.7 2^{186}
27.4.3 pr. 2^{394}
27.4.5 $4^{108, \ 109}$
27.5.1.2 $5^{60, \ 72}$; 135
27.5.1.3 2^{142}
27.5.1.5 $2^{104, \ 529}$
27.5.1.7 2^{59}
27.6.1 pr. I^{208}
27.6.5 2^{122}
27.6.6 2^{151}
27.7.4 pr. $2^{29, \ 133, \ 217}$, 9^{256}
27.7.4.3 2^{492}
27.8.1 pr. 2^{641}
27.8.1.2 2^{30}, 3^{38}, 9^{363}
27.8.1.10 9^{368}
27.8.1.17 2^{698}
27.8.2 4^{113}
27.8.4 2^{643}
27.8.6 9^{360}

D

27.9.1 pr. 4^{153}, 5^{59}; 135
27.9.1.2 4^{153}
27.9.3 pr. $5^{29,\ 51,\ 58}$; 135
27.9.3.5 2^{113}
27.9.5.3 2^{296}
27.9.5.4 2^{13}
27.9.5.9 $2^{548,\ 700}$
27.9.5.10 2^{745}
27.9.5.12 2^{13}
27.9.5.14 $2^{295,\ 700}$
27.9.7 pr. 2^{298}; 168
27.9.7.3 2^{189}
27.9.7.4 2^{87}
27.9.8 pr. 2^{142}
27.9.9 $4^{152,\ 208}$
27.9.10 $4^{152,\ 214}$
27.9.11 2^{150}; 198
27.9.13 pr. 5^{56}, 9^{89}
27.9.13.1 $9^{56,\ 88}$
27.10.1.1 9^{360}
27.10.5 2^{479}

28.1.5 2^{116}, 5^{9}, 6^{28}, 9^{81}
28.1.9 2^{622}
28.1.20.2 2^{81}
28.1.20.3 2^{386}; 172
28.1.20.9 2^{542}
28.1.21.2 2^{394}
28.1.21.3 2^{448}
28.1.22.4 2^{88}
28.1.22.5 2^{224}
28.1.22.6 2^{142}
28.2.1 2^{24}
28.2.2 4^{70}
28.2.3.4 2^{160}
28.2.6 pr. 2^{376b}, 9^{292}, 319
28.2.12 pr. 2^{385}
28.2.28.3 2^{66}
28.2.29.5 2^{217}
28.3.3.2 198
28.3.3.6 2^{123}
28.3.6.6 $2^{23,\ 158}$
28.3.6.8 $2^{376a,\ 712}$

28.3.6.9 $2^{376d,\ 459}$
28.3.6.10 2^{15}, 3^{736a}
28.3.7.6 2^{478}
28.3.12 pr. 2^{85}; 157
28.4.1.1 2^{688}
28.4.2 4^{113}
28.5.1.5 $2^{230,\ 711}$
28.5.2.1 2^{199}
28.5.3.2 9^{176}
28.5.3.4 $2^{245a,\ 500}$
28.5.4.2 $2^{216,\ 217}$
28.5.6.2 2^{245a}
28.5.6.4 $2^{166,\ 317b}$
28.5.9.2 9^{31}
28.5.9.4 2^{167}
28.5.9.5 2^{210}; 167
28.5.9.14 2^{162}, 9^{288}
28.5.9.20 2^{104}
28.5.13.5 $9^{34,\ 227}$
28.5.13.6 $9^{34,\ 227}$
28.5.17.1 2^{161}
28.5.17.4 2^{401}
28.5.17.5 $9^{34,\ 227,\ 248,\ 320}$; 172
28.5.30 134
28.5.35 pr. $2^{88,\ 292}$, 4^{113}
28.5.35.1 1^{241}, $2^{34,\ 295,\ 556}$, 4^{114}; 166
28.5.35.2 $2^{217,\ 530}$
28.5.35.3 1^{135}, $2^{10,\ 88,\ 95,\ 476}$; 168
28.5.35.5 4^{114}
28.5.48 pr. 2^{275}
28.5.49.2 194
28.5.51 pr. 4^{85}
28.5.51.2 9^{63}
28.5.85.1 2^{285}
28.6.2 pr. 2^{290}
28.6.2.4 1^{112}, 2^{99}, 9^{380}; 149, 165
28.6.10.5 2^{195}
28.6.10.6 $2^{166,\ 236,\ 317b}$, 9^{123}
28.6.16 pr. 2^{375}
28.6.23 2^{100}
28.6.38.1 2^{396}, 4^{44}

28.6.39 pr. 9^{223}
28.6.39.2 9^{223}
28.6.43.2 4^{122}
28.7.8 pr. 2^{752}
28.7.8.2 2^{83}
28.7.8.5 2^{155}
28.7.8.6 2^{171}
28.7.10 pr. 168
28.8.3 2^{154}
28.8.5.1 2^{644}
28.8.7.1 1^{208}
28.8.7.2 2^{106}
28.8.7.3 2^{620}
28.8.8 2^{152}; 183

29.1.1 pr. 5^{15}, 9^{347}
29.1.3 1^{113}, 2^{268}, 7^{29}, 9^{383}; 165
29.1.6 2^{158}
29.1.9.1 2^{376c}
29.1.11 pr. 2^{296}
29.1.13.2 2^{175}
29.1.13.3 2^{475}
29.1.13.4 $5^{29,\ 52,\ 58}$; 135
29.1.15.1 2^{306}
29.1.19 pr. $4^{113,\ 116}$; 168
29.1.19.1 2^{116}
29.1.19.2 2^{22}
29.1.28 2^{88}
29.1.41.5 2^{296}
29.2.6.2 2^{285}
29.2.6.3 149
29.2.12 9^{357}
29.2.13 pr. 2^{562}
29.2.13.1 2^{110}
29.2.17.1 2^{562}
29.2.20.1 $2^{477,\ 731,\ 733}$
29.2.20.2 2^{440}
29.2.20.3 9^{15}
29.2.20.4 9^{15}
29.2.21.1 2^{121}
29.2.21.3 2^{562}
29.2.24 2^{127}
29.2.25.2 2^{376c}

Table II 271

D

29.2.25.4 9^{145}	**29.5.15** pr. 2^{72}	**30.120.1** 4^{99}
29.2.30.1 $2^{385,\,386}$; 172	**29.5.21.1** 194	
29.3.30.3 $2^{394,\,427}$	**29.6.1.1** 2^{296}	**31.8.3** 2^{396}
29.2.30.5 2^{81}	**29.7.1** 2^{712}, 9^{394}	**31.29** pr. 8^{4}
29.2.30.6 $9^{174,\,176}$	**29.7.9** $3^{30,\,33}$	**31.43.1** 2^{375}
29.2.35 pr. 2^{496}	**29.7.14** pr. $9^{112,\,113,}$ $^{114,\,115,\,118}$	**31.49.2** $9^{209,\,270}$
29.2.40 9^{44}		**31.61.1** 6^{36}, 9^{385}; 158
29.2.42 pr. $2^{130,\,158,}$ ^{749}, 4^{115}, 9^{44}	**29.7.19** 3^{31}	**31.64** 5^{10}
29.2.62 2^{180}		**31.66.4** 194
29.2.67 4^{84}	**30.4.1** $1^{137,\,143}$	**31.67.10** 5^{10}
29.2.71.1 2^{152}; 183	**30.4.9.8** 2^{134}	**31.68** 4^{122}
29.2.71.9 2^{152}; 183	**30.37** pr. 149	**31.69.4** 2^{18}
29.2.86 pr. 5^{12}	**30.7.1.1** 2^{735}	**31.70.1** 194
29.2.97 1^{129}, 8^{5}, 9^{87}	**30.12.3** 2^{122}	**31.76** pr. 2^{375}
29.3.2.1 $2^{245a,\,672}$	**30.30.7** 9^{217}	**31.77.16** 2^{375}
29.3.2.7 2^{116}	**30.33.2** 2^{94}	**31.82** pr. 2^{275}
29.3.8 2^{91}	**30.34.4** $2^{158,\,290}$	**31.87.3** 1^{324}, 3^{28}
29.3.10.2 2^{633}	**30.37** pr. 6^{4}; 149	**31.87.4** 1^{324}, 3^{28}
29.3.12 2^{590}	**30.37.1** 2^{104}	
29.4.1 pr. $1^{208,\,504,}$ ^{582}	**30.39** pr. 2^{181}, 9^{151}	**32.1.1** 2^{266}; 171
29.4.1.1 $2^{38,\,477}$	**30.39.1** 2^{365}; 168	**32.1.4** $7^{3,12,\,48}$; 169
29.4.1.5 2^{15}	**30.39.6** 2^{470}; 166, 170	**32.5.1** 2^{164}; 169
29.4.1.12 2^{127}	**30.39.7** 2^{552}	**32.11** pr. $1^{18,\,134,\,141,}$ $^{149,\,206}$
29.4.2.1 2^{254}	**30.41.3** 6^{4}; 149	**32.11.1** 9^{132}
29.4.3 2^{18}	**30.41.4** 2^{151}	**32.11.2** 2^{446}
29.4.4.1 2^{68}	**30.41.5** 9^{16}; 149	**32.11.6** 2^{143}
29.4.6 pr. 2^{86}	**30.41.7** 2^{376c}	**32.11.8** 2^{407}
29.4.6.1 2^{365}	**30.41.13** 2^{403}	**32.11.13** 2^{731}
29.4.6.2 2^{253}	**30.43.1** 2^{149}	**32.11.15** 9^{132}
29.4.10 pr. 2^{754}	**30.44.2** 2^{160}	**32.11.19** 169
29.4.10.2 $2^{117,\,125,}$ $^{127,\,151,\,328}$	**30.45** pr. 9^{247}	**32.11.20** 2^{668}
	30.47.1 2^{351}	**32.11.21** $2^{23,\,158}$
29.5.1.3 2^{414}	**30.49.1** 2^{295}	**32.13** 2^{375}
29.5.1.7 2^{110}	**30.50.1** 2^{407}	**32.27.1** 8^{5}
29.5.1.13 2^{90}	**30.50.2** 2^{717}	**32.29** pr. 9^{223}
29.5.1.24 2^{154}	**30.53.8** 2^{305}	**32.29.1** 9^{223}
29.5.1.28 9^{347}	**30.71.1** 2^{67}	**32.29.2** 9^{324}
29.5.1.29 9^{396}	**30.71.4** 2^{218}	**32.38.7** 4^{47}
29.5.3.11 2^{141}	**30.71.5** 2^{90}	**32.45** 9^{138}
29.5.3.12 2^{478}	**30.74** 2^{290}; 157	**32.49** pr. 2^{434}
29.5.3.14 2^{116}	**30.75.4** 9^{44}	**32.49.4** 2^{102}
29.5.3.17 2^{670}	**30.113.5** 9^{59}	**32.50.4** 2^{317b}
29.5.5.1 2^{16}	**30.114.3** 2^{72}	**32.52.1** 2^{229}
	30.114.3 9^{60}	**32.52.5** 2^{15}
	30.115 2^{158}	**32.52.9** 2^{483}
	30.120 pr. 4^{99}	
	30.120 pr. 4^{101}	

D

32.55 pr. 9^{159}
32.55.1 9^{157}
32.55.2 2^{181}, 9^{157}; 176
32.55.4 9^{157}
32.55.5 1^{152}
32.55.7 $2^{64, 298, 311}$, 9^{157}; 167
32.52.7a 2^{195}
32.64 2^{14}
32.68 pr. $4^{99, 100, 107}$
32.70.9 2^{158}
32.70.10 2^{158}
32.70.12 $2^{22, 181}$
32.89 2^{127}
32.100.1 9^{223}
32.100.4 9^{223}

33.1.3.2 2^{616}
33.1.3.3 2^{263}
33.1.19.1 2^{88}
33.2.15.1 4^{138}
33.2.27 9^{159}
33.3.1.10 2^{81}
33.4.1.4 2^{359}
33.4.1.10 2^{88}
33.4.1.12 2^{187}
33.4.2 pr. $2^{149,738}$, 9^{44}
33.4.2.1 2^{476}, 4^{113}
33.4.6.1 $9^{223, 328}$
33.5.20 9^{328}
33.6.7 pr. 9^{223}
33.6.9.3 2^{721}
33.6.11 2^{292}
33.6.13 2^{159}
33.7.4 9^{223}
33.7.8 pr. 9^{138}
33.7.8.1 2^{655}
33.7.12.2 2^{99}
33.7.12.3 9^{312}
33.7.12.14 $2^{22, 181}$
33.7.12.19 2^{528}
33.7.12.20 9^{280}
33.7.12.27 $2^{248, 444, 450, 761}$, $9^{138, 146, 148}$

33.7.12.31 2^{647}
33.7.12.35 $9^{93, 96}$
33.7.12.43 $9^{93, 96}$
33.7.25.1 9^{223}
33.7.26.1 9^{223}
33.8.6.1 2^{317b}
33.8.6.2 2^{21}
33.8.6.4 $2^{81, 64}$, $9^{381, 382}$; 149
33.8.8.7 6^{4}; 149
33.8.8.8 $2^{116, 227, 235}$
33.9.1 $2^{398, 537}$
33.9.3 pr. $9^{138, 139, 159, 195}$
33.9.3.1 9^{249}
33.9.3.2 2^{129}, $9^{8, 194, 227}$
33.9.3.5 9^{157}
33.9.3.6 2^{290}
33.9.3.8 9^{157}
33.9.3.9 $9^{158, 160, 169, 220}$
33.9.3.10 2^{59}, 9^{265}
33.9.3.11 2^{554}
33.9.4.5 2^{275}
33.10.10 9^{223}
33.10.11 9^{223}

34.1.3 7^{38}, 9^{341}; 176
34.1.11 4^{122}
34.1.14 pr. 2^{739}
34.1.14.1 2^{148}, 5^{13}, 6^{23}
34.1.14.2 2^{274}
34.1.14.3 $1^{120, 152}$, 2^{497}, 4^{113}
34.2.9 2^{712}
34.2.19.2 2^{376b}
34.2.19.3 $2^{166, 317a, 435}$, 9^{31}, 173
34.2.19.8 1^{102}, 2^{270}; 166
34.2.19.10 2^{561}
34.2.19.13 2^{220}
34.2.19.17 9^{138}
34.2.19.20 2^{220}
34.2.23.2 $2^{480, 581, 595}$

34.2.25.10 $2^{410, 570}$
34.2.25.11 2^{605}
34.2.27 pr. 9^{185}
34.2.27.1 2^{16}
34.2.34.2 $2^{375, 756}$
34.2.39 pr. $9^{223, 224}$
34.3.3.4 $2^{18, 110}$
34.3.5. pr. 2^{245a}
34.3.5.2 $2^{35, 155}$
34.3.5.4 2^{344}
34.3.7 pr. $2^{376c, 470}$, 5^{85}; 170
34.3.9 2^{376c}
34.3.16 9^{232}
34.3.20.1 2^{97}
34.4.3.2 172
34.4.7 2^{701}
34.5.13.4 2^{76}
34.5.13.6 2^{121}
34.5.15 2^{275}
34.9.2.2 2^{81}
34.9.3 9^{60}
34.9.5.5 2^{18}
34.9.5.9 5^{15}
34.9.9.1 2^{625}
34.9.18 9^{17}
34.9.22 2^{149}

35.1.7 pr. 9^{289}
35.1.9 2^{245a}
35.1.10 pr. $2^{17, 97, 677}$
35.1.14 169
35.1.15 2^{508}
35.1.40.3 2^{180}, 9^{328}
35.1.40.4 9^{223}
35.1.50 2^{106}, 9^{341}
35.1.52 2^{82}
35.1.62.1 2^{756}
35.1.68 2^{375}
35.1.71 pr. 9^{73}
35.1.78.1 3^{12}
35.1.82 2^{117}
35.1.92 1^{121}; $2^{36, 84, 193, 271}$; 4^{116}; $9^{18, 46, 410}$; 169–70
35.1.102 195
35.2.11.2 5^{10}

Table II 273

D

37.6.1.2 2^{103}
37.6.1.11 $2^{340, 633}$
37.6.1.13 2^{117}
37.6.1.17 $2^{104, 337}$
37.6.1.19 2^{28}
37.6.1.21 2^{132}; 187
37.6.1.23 2^{394}
37.6.2.5 5^{88}
37.6.5 pr. $2^{274, 295}$; 198
37.6.9 3^{32}
37.7.9 2^{127}
37.8.1.1 $1^{208, 670}$
37.8.7 $2^{18, 113}$
37.9.1.5 $2^{106, 225}$
37.9.1.7 2^{81}
37.9.1.11 $2^{69, 756}$
37.9.1.14 2^{108}
37.9.1.15 $2^{106, 139}$; 196
37.9.7.1 $2^{97, 359, 700}$
37.9.7.2 2^{90}
37.10.1.3 2^{175}
37.10.1.5 $2^{106, 660}$
37.10.1.8 2^{132}
37.10.1.11 2^{422}
37.10.3.5 $2^{446, 753}$, 9^{347}
37.10.3.7 2^{85}
37.10.3.12 2^{353}
37.10.3.13 $2^{165, 166, 317a, 317b, 756}$
37.10.5.1 2^{85}
37.10.5.3 2^{311}
37.11.1.4 2^{257}
37.11.1.6 2^{292}
37.11.1.9 2^{175}
37.11.1.11 2^{463}
37.11.2 pr. 1^{208}
37.11.2.4 $2^{110, 225, 566}$
37.11.2.7 2^{686}; 177
37.11.5.1 2^{351}
37.11.6 2^{629}
37.11.11 pr. 195
37.12.1 pr. 1^{208}, 2^{477}

37.12.1.4 2^{379}
37.13.1.1 2^{142}
37.14.1 2^{507}
37.14.16 pr. $2^{88, 712}$
37.14.16.1 $2^{152, 245, 309}$; 183
37.14.17 pr. $9^{388, 470}$
37.15.1.2 4^{150}
37.15.5.1 2^{317b}
37.15.7.5 2^{545}

38.1.2 pr. 1^{208}
38.1.4 2^{160}
38.1.7.1 2^{182}
38.1.7.5 2^{503}
38.1.9.1 2^{102}
38.2.1 1^{208}, 2^{661}
38.2.2 9^{62}
38.2.3.20 $2^{220, 231}$
38.2.8 pr. 2^{670}
38.2.8.1 2^{369}
38.2.10.1 2^{109}
38.2.12.4 2^{22}
38.2.12.5 2^{473}
38.2.14.2 2^{677}
38.2.14.4 2^{88}
38.2.14.6 2^{461}
38.2.14.8 2^{677}
38.2.14.11 2^{360}
38.2.16.5 176
38.2.16.8 2^{106}
38.2.25 2^{479}
38.2.42.2 2^{275}
38.4.1.6 2^{733}
38.4.1.8 $2^{1.17}$
38.4.3.2 2^{225}
38.4.3.5 2^{13}
38.4.5.1 2^{401}
38.5.1.1 $2^{242, 244}$
38.5.1.4 2^{391}; 178
38.5.1.6 $2^{90, 116, 285}$
38.5.1.13 2^{261}, 4^{97}
38.5.1.14 2^{117}, 9^{24}
38.5.1.15 $2^{88, 325}$
38.5.1.17 2^{308}
38.5.1.20 2^{285}
38.5.1.21 2^{90}

38.5.1.22 2^{38}
38.5.1.27 2^{56}, 9^{24}
38.5.3 pr. 2^{85}
38.5.6 2^{375}
38.5.12 9^{321}
38.6.1.3 $2^{88, 562}$
38.6.1.4 2^{217}
38.6.1.5 1^{208}
38.6.1.6 2^{225}
38.7.2.1 2^{106}; 176
38.7.2.2 176
38.8.1.2 197
38.8.1.4 2^{291}
38.8.1.5 2^{292}
38.8.1.6 2^{391}; 178
38.8.1.8 $2^{290, 475}$
38.9.1.6 2^{100}
38.9.1.7 2^{562}
38.9.1.11 2^{562}
38.9.1.12 2^{405}
38.11.1.1 2^{88}
38.15.2.4 176
38.16.1 pr. 2^{706}
38.16.1.1 2^{376}; 149
38.16.1.7 2^{125}
38.16.1.10 2^{56}
38.16.1.11 2^{109}
38.16.2 pr. 2^{290}
38.16.2.5 2^{225}
38.16.2.7 2^{562}
38.16.3.9 2^{459}
38.16.3.10 170
38.17.1.2 2^{466}
38.17.1.3 6^{4}; 149
38.17.1.6 4^{72}
38.17.1.10 2^{25}
38.17.1.11 2^{116}
38.17.1.12 2^{392}
38.17.2.2 149
38.17.2.4 6^{4}
38.17.2.8 9^{297}
38.17.2.9 2^{280}
38.17.2.17 2^{225}
38.17.2.34 2^{241}
38.17.2.37 2^{400}
38.17.2.41 2^{298}; 167
38.17.2.43 2^{290}

Table II 275

D

38.17.2.44 $2^{345, 401}$, 9^{176}

38.17.2.47 2^{214}, 9^{383}; 149, 170

38.17.5 pr. 2^{671}

39.1.1.1 2^{370}

39.1.1.10 5^{90}, 9^{37}

39.1.5 pr. 5^{90}

39.1.3.2 2^{401}

39.1.5 pr. 9^{37}

39.1.5.2 2^{135}

39.1.5.4 2^{662}

39.1.5.6 2^{59}

39.1.5.10 $2^{135, 305}$

39.L.5.12 2^{140}

39.1.5.16 9^{37}

39.1.12 pr. 9^{49}

39.1.20.2 2^{309}

39.1.20.5 2^{477}

39.1.20.7 2^{309}

39.1.20.10 2^{513}

39.1.20.13 2^{309}

39.1.21 pr. 5^{2}

39.1.21.6 2^{326}

39.1.21.7 9^{41}

39.2.1 164

39.2.4 pr. 2^{300}

39.2.4.1 2^{385}

39.2.4.5 2^{743}, 5^{102}

39.2.4.6 2^{168}

39.2.4.8 5^{103}

39.2.13 pr. 2^{166}

39.2.13.1 $2^{116, 296}$

39.2.13.2 2^{117}

39.2.13.21 2^{441}

39.2.15 pr. 2^{326}

39.2.15.3 2^{137}

39.2.15.5 2^{385}

39.2.15.10 2^{756}

39.2.15.12 $2^{40, 130, 133}$, 9^{257}

39.2.15.13 $2^{151, 639}$

39.2.15.31 2^{326}

39.2.15.33 2^{309}, 9^{49}

39.2.15.34 $2^{160, 285}$

39.2.15.35 2^{290}

39.2.24 pr. $2^{140, 394}$, 5/2

39.2.24.9 2^{412}

39.2.26 5^{2}

39.2.28 5^{2}, 9^{250}

39.2.29 2^{275}

39.2.30 5^{2}

39.2.37 2^{694}

39.2.40.1 2^{756}

39.3.1.16 2^{444}

39.3.1.17 9^{219}

39.3.1.20 2^{190}, 9^{50}; 170

39.3.1.21 2^{81}

39.2.1.23 $2^{102, 245b, 252}$

39.3.2.5 9^{326}

39.3.2.6 9^{328}

39.3.4 pr. 2^{91}, 9^{49}

39.3.4.2 2^{85}

39.3.6.2 2^{13}

39.3.6.3 2^{744}

39.3.6.6 2^{300}

39.3.8 2^{106}

39.3.11.2 2^{10}

39.3.11.2 9^{191}

39.4.3.1 2^{394}

39.4.5.1 2^{204}

39.4.7.1 9^{356}

39.4.12 pr. 1^{208}, 2^{502}

39.4.12.2 2^{104}

39.4.13.2 2^{118}

39.4.14 2^{83}

39.4.16.4 2^{712}

39.5.7.2 2^{27}

39.5.7.3 2^{199}

39.5.7.4 2^{90}

39.5.7.5 $2^{97, 135}$

39.5.7.6 2^{476}

39.5.12 $2^{97, 334}$

39.5.16 4^{70}

39.5.19.3 2^{296}

39.6.2 2^{409}

39.6.5 2^{609}

39.6.31.3 2^{72}

39.6.35.3 4^{51}

39.6.37 pr. 2^{135}

39.6.37 pr. 2^{290}

39.6.42 195

40.1.4.1 2^{413}

40.1.4.12 2^{475}

40.1.14.1 5^{13}

40.2.5 1^{125}

40.2.8 $1^{124, 151}$

40.2.16 2^{134}, 3^{5}

40.2.20 pr. 2^{729}, 3^{17}, 7^{38}; 177

40.2.20.1 2^{708}

40.2.20.2 $2^{329, 467}$

40.4.12 2^{309}

40.4.13.2 $2^{69, 754}$

40.4.13.3 $2^{195, 290}$

40.4.46 9^{244}

40.4.50 3^{32}

40.4.55 pr. 2^{158}

40.4.56 5^{15}

40.5.4.1 2^{156}

40.5.4.2 2^{274}

40.5.4.3 $2^{103, 117}$

40.5.4.5 $2^{100, 285, 296}$; 185

40.5.4.11 2^{291}

40.5.4.14 2^{103}

40.5.4.15 2^{152}; 183

40.5.4.16 2^{152}; 183

40.5.4.17 2^{285}

40.5.4.22 183

40.5.12. pr. 5^{15}

40.5.12.2 9^{353}

40.5.24 pr. 2^{175}

40.5.24.2 2^{64}; 170

40.5.24.5 $2^{44, 376}$; 169

40.5.24.8 2^{731}, 9^{46}

40.5.24.9 9^{46}; 169

40.5.24.12 2^{327}

40.5.24.14 $2^{305, 407}$

40.5.24.16 2^{13}

40.5.24.17 $2^{13, 64}$

40.5.24.19 2^{20}

40.5.24.21 $2^{376a, 712}$

Table II 277

D

43.23.1.8 $2^{131, 389}$, $9^{41, 49}$
43.24.1.1 1^{208}, $2^{504, 582}$
43.24.1.2 2^{35}
43.24.1.3 2^{376b}
43.24.1.5 2^{38}
43.24.1.7 9^{218}
43.24.3.1 2^{154}
43.24.3.3 2^{105}
43.24.3.4 2^{285}, 9^{205}
43.24.5 pr. 9^{248}
43.24.5.1 2^{405}
43.24.5.12 9^{49}
43.24.7.1 9^{100}
43.24.7.3 $9^{41, 49}$
43.24.7.4 2^{379}
43.24.7.6 2^{246}
43.24.9 pr. 2^{225}
43.24.11.1 $2^{29, 133}$, 9^{258}
43.24.11.8 $2^{30, 133}$, 285
43.24.11.11 9^{196}
43.24.11.13 $2^{225, 285}$
43.23.13.4 2^{293}
43.24.13.5 $2^{43, 68}$, 407, 712, 9^{111}
43.24.13.7 2^{125}
43.24.9 2^{309}
43.24.15 pr. $2^{85, 626}$, 627
43.24.15.4 2^{758}
43.24.15.8 2^{106}
43.24.15.11 2^{285}
43.24.15.12 $2^{120, 296}$
43.24.21.1 2^{15}
43.26.1.2 1^{71}
43.26.1.3 2^{52}
43.26.2.2 1^{208}, 2^{165}
43.26.4.1 2^{134}
43.26.6.4 $2^{55, 128}$, 672, 713; 187
43.26.8.1 9^{282}
43.26.8.5 2^{181}
43.26.8.6 $2^{175, 279}$

43.26.15 pr. 2^{165}
43.26.20 4^{96}
43.29.3 pr. $2^{70, 744}$
43.29.3.1 2^{220}
43.29.3.3 2^{477}
43.29.3.5 $2^{465, 504}$, 582
43.29.3.7 2^{302}
43.29.3.12 2^{51}
43.29.3.13 $2^{157, 346}$
43.30.1.3 5^{81}, 6^{37}; 141
43.30.1.5 2^{675}
43.30.3.4 9^{41}
43.30.3.6 2^{385}
43.32.1.4 2^{296}
43.33.2 2^{333}

44.1.2.2 2^{604}
44.1.2.4 2^{245a}
44.2.7 pr. 2^{285}
44.2.7.1 2^{127}
44.2.7.2 2^{475}
44.2.7.3 $2^{152, 296}$; 183
44.2.7.5 2^{285}
44.2.9 pr. 2^{13}
44.2.9.1 9^{100}
44.2.9.11 9^{100}
44.2.11 pr. 9^{408}
44.2.11.10 2^{303}
44.3.2 3^{31}
44.3.5.1 2^{84}, 4^{113}
44.4.2 pr. 2^{157}; 184
44.4.2.5 2^{683}
44.4.4.1 2^{34}, 9^{281}
44.4.4.6 2^{160}
44.4.4.8 $2^{133, 155}$, $9^{232, 259, 260}$
44.4.4.10 2^{317b}; 184
44.4.4.15 9^{49}
44.4.4.16 $2^{334, 335}$
44.4.4.17 2^{125}
44.4.4.18 9^{100}
44.4.4.21 2^{285}
44.4.4.22 2^{400}
44.4.4.23 $2^{16, 98, 107}$, 195

44.4.4.24 2^{13}
44.4.4.26 $2^{145, 712}$
44.4.4.29 2^{16}
44.4.4.31 2^{264}
44.4.4.33 2^{88}
44.4.4.34 2^{154}
44.4.7 pr. 6^{10}
44.4.7.1 2^{317b}
44.5.1.6 $2^{285, 317b}$
44.5.1.10 2^{88}, 9^{190}
44.5.1.12 $2^{70, 744}$
44.6.1.1 $2^{13, 296}$
44.7.1.15 2^{204}
44.7.44.6 2^{117}
44.7.47 9^{70}

45.1.1.2 $2^{105, 477}$
45.1.1.3 $2^{70, 744}$
45.1.1.5 2^{629}
45.1.1.6 $1^{18, 19, 142,}$ 147, 149, 206, $2^{81, 718}$
45.1.3.1 2^{166}
45.1.26 2^{215}
45.1.29 pr. 8^{30}
45.1.29.1 2^{24}
45.1.38 pr. 2^{172}
45.1.38.3 2^{157}; 184
45.1.38.9 2^{245a}
45.1.38.12 2^{13}
45.1.38.22 $2^{304, 477,}$ 478
45.1.41 pr. $2^{104, 245b,}$ 249, 263
45.1.45.4 199
45.1.63 2^{97}
45.1.70 1^{71}, 9^{11}
45.1.72.2 2^{84}
45.1.91.1 2^{396}
45.1.91.6 2^{180}
45.1.99 pr. 2^{170}
45.1.108 pr. 198
45.1.131 9^{7}
45.2.3 pr. 2^{35}; 197
45.2.3.1 2^{141}
45.2.9 pr. 2^{396}, 4^{43}
45.2.12.1 2^{94}
45.2.17 $9^{234, 240}$

Table II 279

D
45.3.7 pr. 2^{152}; 183, 196
45.3.11 $2^{113, 214, 285}$
45.3.12 2^{214}

46.1.6.1 2^{35}
46.1.8.1 184
46.1.8.3 2^{113}
46.1.8.5 185
46.1.8.6 2^{143}
46.1.8.7 2^{292}
46.1.8.8 172
46.1.8.12 2^{141}
46.1.33 2^{125}
46.1.51.2 2^{375}
46.1.56.1 9^{70}
46.1.71 pr. 2^{18}
46.2.2 2^{87}
46.3.5.2 6^{4}; 150
46.3.7 2^{317b}
46.3.12.1 2^{122}
46.3.12.3 2^{195}
46.3.14.1 2^{529}
46.3.24 $2^{339, 457}$
46.3.27 9^{7}
46.3.43 4^{77}
46.3.73 2^{180}
46.3.78 $2^{626, 627}$
46.3.98.3 2^{388}
46.3.103 2^{714}
46.4.6 2^{87}
46.4.8 pr. $2^{140, 629}$
46.4.8.2 9^{35}
46.4.13.1 $2^{296, 306}$
46.5.1.4 2^{653}; 198
46.5.5 2^{479}
46.6.4.2 2^{154}
46.6.4.3 2^{97}
46.6.4.7 2^{296}
46.7.3.3 $2^{152, 326}$, 183
46.7.3.6 2^{291}
46.7.3.7 2^{296}
46.7.3.8 2^{152}; 183
46.7.5.3 $2^{157, 296}$; 184

46.7.5.4 2^{94}
46.7.5.5 2^{59}
46.7.5.6 2^{125}
46.7.5.7 2^{117}
46.7.5.8 2^{154}
46.7.13 pr. 4^{113}
46.8.12.2 2^{430}
46.8.12.2 2^{519}
46.8.15 2^{180}
46.8.20 2^{110}

47.1.1 pr. $2^{90, 92}$
47.1.2.5 2^{437}
47.2.1.1 2^{82}
47.2.3.1 2^{35}
47.2.4 2^{394}
47.2.7.1 2^{91}
47.2.12.2 $2^{231, 401, 712}$
47.2.14.17 2^{231}
47.2.17.1 2^{376b}
47.2.17.2 $2^{90, 478}$
47.2.18 4^{51}
47.2.21 pr. 2^{107}
47.2.21.8 $2^{76, 78}$
47.2.21.10 2^{90}
47.2.22.1 2^{396}
47.2.25.2 2^{142}
47.2.27 pr. $2^{107, 175}$
47.2.39 2^{15}, $4^{114, 120}$
47.2.41.3 2^{172}
47.2.43.5 2^{159}
47.2.43.8 2^{15}
47.2.43.11 2^{128}; 187
47.2.46 pr. $2^{91, 92, 473}$
47.2.46.5 2^{149}
47.2.46.8 $2^{81, 88}$
47.2.48.7 2^{143}
47.2.50.3 2^{494}
47.2.50.4 177
47.2.52.6 2^{13}
47.2.52.18 4^{95}
47.2.52.20 4^{112}
47.2.71 2^{85}
47.2.93 $2^{135, 719}$
47.3.2 2^{27}

47.4.1.1 1^{208}, $2^{165, 504, 582, 652}$
47.4.1.6 2^{175}
47.4.1.7 2^{712}, $5^{29, 47, 58}$; 135
47.4.1.11 2^{309}
47.4.1.14 2^{105}
47.5.1.2 2^{47}
47.6.1 pr. 1^{208}, 2^{672}
47.6.1.1 2^{317b}
47.6.1.2 2^{670}
47.8.2.1 1^{208}
47.8.2.8 2^{679}
47.8.2.10 2^{103}
47.8.2.11 2^{291}
47.8.2.22 2^{220}
47.8.2.23 $2^{175, 404}$
47.8.2.27 2^{16}
47.8.4.3 $2^{69, 225, 291, 754}$
47.9.1.1 1^{208}
47.9.1.2 $2^{245a, 292}$
47.9.3 pr. 2^{475}
47.9.3.3 $2^{97, 105}$
47.9.3.7 $2^{15, 268}$
47.9.10 4^{175}
47.9.12 pr. 6^{26}; 154
47.10.1 pr. 2^{245a}
47.10.1.8 9^{100}
47.10.1.9 9^{100}
47.10.3.1 2^{296}
47.10.3.4 2^{478}
47.10.5.3 2^{285}
47.10.5.5 9^{13}
47.10.5.8 2^{498}, 5^{86}
47.10.6 9^{70}
47.10.7.1 $2^{245a, 317b, 380, 702}$, 9^{49}
47.10.7.2 $2^{135, 305, 414, 699}$; 185
47.10.7.4 2^{499}
47.10.7.5 9^{100}
47.10.7.6 1^{253}; 135, 137
47.10.7.7 $2^{599, 654}$
47.10.7.8 2^{569}
47.10.9 pr. 2^{127}

Table II 281

D

50.12.6.2 6^{21}; 154	**50.16.19** 9^{32}	**2.3.3** $1^{154, 163}$, 8^{28}; 198
50.12.6.3 6^{21}; 154	**50.16.26** 9^{123}	**2.3.4** 202
50.12.8 9^{341}	**50.16.45** 2^{291}	**2.3.8** 1^{270}
50.13.1 pr. 178	**50.16.46** pr. 2^{245a}	**2.12.3** pr. 198
50.13.1.3 $1^{217, 227}$, $2^{311,532}$	**50.16.46.1** 2^{710}	**2.18.10** 4^{136}
50.13.1.4 1^{218}, 2^{13}	**50.16.49** 9^{5}	**2.23.1** 1^{150}, 8^{42}; 195
50.13.1.5 1^{219}, 2^{417}	**50.16.60.1** 2^{110}	**2.30.1** 8^{41}
50.13.1.6 2^{503}	**50.16.77** 9^{326}	**2.32.1** 8^{33a}
50.13.1.10 2^{86}, 9^{344}; 157	**50.16.99.1** 1^{136}, 2^{391}, 7^{38}; 178	**2.50.1** 8^{24b}
50.13.1.11 $2^{452, 635}$	**50.16.99.2** 2^{313}	
50.13.1.12 2^{376c}, 9^{344}; 157	**50.16.111** 2^{245a}	**3.1.2** 195
50.13.1.13 157	**50.16.130** 2^{706}	**3.15.1** 8^{41}
50.13.1.15 2^{13}	**50.16.131.1** 2^{107}	**3.26.1** 202
50.14.2 $2^{15, 504, 582}$	**50.16.141** 2^{458}	**3.26.2** 196
50.14.3 2^{484}	**50.16.164** pr. 2^{127}	**3.28.3.1** 195
50.15.1 1^{139}	**50.16.164.1** 171	**3.31.2** 8^{42}; 201
50.15.1 pr. $1^{66, 79}$, $2^{566,589,659}$, 3^{22}, 7^{5}; 165	**50.16.167** $2^{64, 298, 311}$; 167	**3.32.3** 4^{136}
50.15.1.1 5^{13}, 6^{23}	**50.16.178** pr. 2^{111}	**3.33.2** 196
50.15.1.2 2^{379}, 3^{19}; 165, 167	**50.16.178.2** 2^{245a}	**3.44.4** pr. 8^{30}
50.15.1.3 2^{379}, 3^{19}; 165, 167	**50.16.185** 2^{291}	
50.15.1.4 1^{256}; 165	**50.16.192** 176	**4.2.1** 8^{31}
50.15.1.5 2^{379}, 3^{19}; 167	**50.16.195.2** 2^{233}	**4.14.3** 4^{140}
50.15.1.7 165	**50.16.195.3** 2^{217}	**4.15.2** 201
50.15.1.9 165	**50.16.195.4** 2^{525}	**4.19.1** 8^{42}; 194
50.15.1.10 2^{379}, 3^{19}; 167	**50.16.199** 2^{234}	**4.26.1** 8^{42}
50.15.1.11 2^{379}, 3^{19}; 167	**50.16.207** 9^{268}	**4.28.2** 194
50.15.3.1 1^{112}, 2^{435}, 3^{20}, 9^{380}; 165	**50.16.213.2** 4^{67}	**4.28.3** 8^{41}; 202
50.15.4.10 2^{712}	**50.16.216** 187	**4.32.3** 194
50.15.8 1^{140}	**50.16.220.1** 9^{75}	**4.44.1** 1^{270}
50.15.8.6 1^{255}	**50.16.239.6** 9^{325}	**4.52.2** 194
50.16.3 pr. 2^{394}	**50.16.244** 2^{376a}	**4.55.1** pr. 8^{41}
50.16.6.1 2^{394}	**50.17.9** 2^{245b}	**4.55.4.1** 4^{176}
50.16.10 2^{559}	**50.17.23** 2^{172}	**4.65.4.1** $1^{41, 59, 278, 285, 289, 292}$, 8^{8}
50.16.12 9^{5}	**50.17.31** 187	
50.16.15 2^{673}	**50.17.34** $2^{245b, 296}$	**5.14.1** 198
	50.17.47 pr. $2^{504, 582}$	**5.15.1** 8^{31}
	50.17.157.2 2^{106}	**5.16.14.1** 196
	50.17.209 2^{228}	**5.37.1** 8^{31}; 197
		5.37.17 197
	2. *Codex Iustinianus* (CJ)	**5.47.1** 8^{41}
		5.54.1 8^{41}
	1.51 8^{3}	**5.62.1** 2^{9}, 8^{31}; 197
		5.69.1.2 8^{30}
	2.3.1 8^{24b}; 195	
	2.3.2 8^{47}; 195	**6.2.1** 194

Table II 283

CJ
6.2.2 198
6.3.1 8^{31}
6.3.2 202
6.25.1 8^{41}
6.28.1.1 198
6.35.2.1 198
6.39.1 $8^{41, 42}$; 202
6.44.1 1^{180}
6.47.1 8^{41}
6.50.1 8^{30}
6.53.2 196
6.54.3 8^{41}
6.54.5 4^{172}
6.54.6 5^{38}

7.3.1 1^{162}
7.4.1 202
7.8.1 201
7.8.3 1^{176}; 200
7.8.4 4^{136}
7.21.2 8^{24b}; 202
7.33.1.2 198
7.35.6 197
7.49.1 5^{77}
7.56.1 4^{136}
7.62.1 1^{174}
7.74.1 $1^{174}, 8^{30}$; 199

8.1.1 4^{180}
8.13.3 199
8.15.1 195, 202
8.15.2 8^{31}
8.16.1 194
8.16.2 196
8.18.1 1^{175}; 199
8.25.1 201
8.37.4 $1^{41, 59, 267, 276}, 4^{3, 125}, 8^{13}$
8.40.3.1 8^{31}
8.40.3.2 8^{29}; 199
8.52.1 4^{174}
8.53.1 8^{32}

9.1.2.1 197
9.1.3 $1^{269}, 4^{137}$
9.8.1 1^{333}

9.9.9 1^{335}
9.32.1 202
9.41.1 8^{41}; 202
9.41.2 197

10.4.1 pr. 4^{178}
10.40.7 pr. 1^{69}
10.42.8 4^{161}
10.44.1 4^{165}
10.44.2 4^{166}
10.52.5 4^{163}
10.52.6 pr. 4^{159}
10.64.1 4^{163}

3. Codex Theodosianus (CTh)

1.2.2 1^{158}
1.2.3 1^{158}
1.2.9 1^{158}
1.2.10 1^{57}
1.2.11 1^{158}
3.12.1 4^{13}
4.4.3.3 $1^{57, 265}$
8.16.1 4^{12}
12.1.19 4^{157}
12.17.1 pr. 4^{159}

4. Collatio legum Mosaicarum et Romanarum (Coll.)

1.6.1 6^{23}
5.3 4^{5}
6.2.1–4 4^{7}
7.4.1 2^{87}
8.3 6^{23}
11.7.5 2^{753}
12.5.2 $2^{618, 688}$
12.7.6 5^{24}; 133
12.7.8 2^{102}
12.7.9 9^{189}
14.3.2 $1^{10}, 2^{97}$
14.3.3 154
15.2.1 $2^{533, 534}$
15.2.2 2^{445}
15.2.5 2^{541}
15.3 4^{6}

16.4 4^{7}
16.7 171
16.9 171

5. Fragmenta Vaticana (FV)

44 4^{92}
71 2^{398}
75.5 2^{619}
77 $9^{294, 330}$
80 2^{129}
87 2^{130}
88 9^{249}
90 2^{82}
119 5^{15}; 154
123 2^{535}
125 7^{19}
145 $3^{13}, 7^{18}$
147 7^{19}
148 2^{580}
153 3^{10}
155 2^{406}
156 $2^{226a, 598}$, 196
159 7^{19}
161 3^{11}
176 174
177 $2^{396}, 7^{24}$; 170
177a 174
188 2^{291}
189 $3^{13}, 7^{18, 22, 23}$; 166
191 174
200 174
201 174
204 174
207 2^{170}
210 2^{175}; 174
211 174
212 174
220 $1^{122}, 2^{191}, 7^{25}$; 170
222 $3^{13}, 7^{18}$
224 5^{10}
232 174
234 174
235 6^{23}; 174
236 174

FV

238	I74
239	I74
240	3^{13}, 7^{18}
242	1^{243}, 7^{22}; 166
266	5^{29}, 134
269	$2^{296, \, 626, \, 627}$
287	4^{93}
321	2^{385}; 166

6. Gai Institutiones (G. Inst.)

1.32c	5^{13}
1.34	5^{13}
1.39	9^{69}
1.47	5^{13}
1.78	9^{69}
1.102	4^{33}
1.133	9^{69}
2.64	9^{69}
2.79	2^{76}
2.119	4^{33}
2.124	4^{33}
2.137	9^{69}
2.147	4^{33}
2.181	4^{54}
2.193	2^{104}
2.232	4^{33}
2.245	9^{69}

3.43	4^{33}
3.84	9^{69}
3.126	9^{69}
3.176	2^{123}
3.189	2^{116}
3.199	2^{121}
3.201	9^{69}
4.3	9^{69}
4.77	9^{69}
4.109	9^{69}
4.127	2^{121}
4.155	2^{122}

7. Pauli Sententiae (PS)

5.12.11	2^{590}

8. Tituli ex corpore Ulpiani (Ulp.)

2.4	4^{45}
5.6	$4^{9, \, 48}$
5.7	4^{9}
5.8	4^{24}
6.14	4^{38}
6.17	4^{38}
7.4	4^{24}
8.5	$4^{27, \, 33}$
10.3	4^{24}
11.3	$4^{58, \, 59, \, 60}$
11.5	$4^{58, \, 61}$

11.20	4^{56}
11.24	4^{56}
11.28	4^{50}
17.2	$4^{21, \, 29}$
19.4	4^{24}
19.8	4^{34}
19.16	4^{58}
20.6	4^{9}
20.14	4^{24}
22.6	4^{14}
22.17	4^{33}
22.20	4^{31}
22.22	4^{52}
23.6	4^{33}
24.1	$4^{62, \, 64}$
24.16	4^{33}
25.1	4^{63}
26.1	4^{9}
26.1a	4^{9}
26.7	4^{28}
28.6	4^{33}
29.2	4^{33}

9. Epitome C. Gregoriani et Hermogeniani Wisigothica (ECGHW)

14.1	1^{271}

Bibliography

ALBERTARIO, E. (1922). '*Tituli ex Corpore Ulpiani*': *BIDR* 32.73

ALFÖLDY, G. (1968). 'Septimius Severus und der Senat': *Bonner Jb.* 168.112.

—— (1972). 'Der Sturz des Kaisers Geta und die antike Geschichtsschreibung': Bonner HAC 1970: *Antiq.* 10.19.

ANRW (1972–). *Aufstieg und Niedergang der römischen Welt* (Berlin etc.), ed. Temporini, H.

ARANGIO – RUIZ, V. (1921). 'Sul *liber singularis regularum. Appunti Gaiani*': *BIDR* 30.178

—— (1946). *Rariora* (Rome, reprint 1970).

—— (1957). 'Frammenti di Ulpiano *libro 32 ed.* in una pergamena egiziana': *AG* 153.140.

—— (1960). 'Di nuovo sul frammento di Ulpiano in *PSI* 1449': *BIDR* 63. 281.

—— (1965). 'I passi di Ulpiano 18 *ad edictum* comuni alla *collatio* e al *digesto*': St. *Biondi* II (Milan).

BAILLIE REYNOLDS, P. K. (1926). *The vigiles of imperial Rome* (Oxford).

BALOG, E. (1913). 'Die Gleichzeitigkeit der Gardepräfektur des Iulius Paulus und Domitius Ulpianus': *Et. P.F. Girard* (Paris) 339.

BARNES, T. D. (1967). 'The family and career of Septimius Severus': *Historia* 16.87.

—— (1968). 'Legislation against Christians': *JRS* 88.32.

—— (1972). 'Ultimus Antoninorum': Bonner HAC 1970: *Antiq.*[4] 10.53.

BARNS, J. W. B. – PARSONS, P. – REA, J. – TURNER, E. G. (1966). *Oxyrhynchus Papyri* 31 (London).

BARBIERI, G. (1952). *L'albo senatorio da Settimio Severo a Carino* (Rome).

BEHRENDS, O. (1969). 'Der Assessor zur Zeit der klassichen Rechtswissenschaft': *ZS* 86.192.

BELL, H. I. (1947). 'The *constitutio Antoniniana* and the Egyptian poll-tax: *JRS* 37.17.

BENARIO, H. W. (1958a). 'Rome of the Severi': *Latomus* 17.712.

—— (1958b) 'Julia Domna *mater senatus et patriae*': *Phoenix* 12.67.

BERGER, A. (1953). *Encyclopedic dictionary of Roman law* (Philadephia).

BESELER, G. (1910–20). *Beiträge zur Kritik der römischen Rechtsquellen* (Tübingen).

—— (1925). 'Miscellanea': *ZS* 45. 188.

—— (1930). 'Romanistische Studien': *ZS* 50(1930) 18.

—— (1936). 'Römische Disziplin': *St. Riccobono* 1.313

BESNIER, M. (1937). *L'empire romain de l'avènement des Sévères au concile de Nicée* (Paris).

BIDEZ, J. (1939). 'Literature and philosophy in the eastern half of the empire': *CAH* 12.611.

BIRLEY, A. (1971). *Septimius Severus. The African emperor* (London).

BLUHME, F. (1820). 'Die Ordnung der Fragmente in den Pandektentiteln': *ZGR* 4. 257 = *Labeo* 6 (1960)50.

BONNEAU, D. (1969). 'Ulpien et l'irrigation en Egypte': *RHD* 47. 5.

BOWERSOCK, G. W. (1969). *Greek Sophists in the Roman Empire* (Oxford).

BRASSLOFF, S. (1933). 'Ulpianus de edendo': *Phil. Wochenschr.* 53.591.

BREMER, F. P. (1863). *De Domitii Ulpiani institutionibus* (Bonn).

—— (1868). *Die Rechtslehrer und Rechtsschulen im römischen Kaiserreich* (Berlin).

—— (1883). 'Ulpians Verhältnis zu Gallien': *ZS* 4.184.

BUCKLAND, W. W. (1922). 'Did Ulpian use Gaius?': *LQR* 38. 38.

—— (1926). 'Gaius and *liber singularis regularum*': *LQR* 40.185.

—— (1937). 'Gaius and the *liber singularis* again': *LQR* 53. 508.

—— (1963). *A textbook of Roman law from Augustus to Justinian*[3] (ed. Stein, P., Cambridge).

CAH (1939). *Cambridge Ancient History* (vol. 12 New York), ed. Cook, S. A., Adcock, P. E., Charlesworth, M. P., Baynes, N. H.

CALDER, W. M. (1923). 'Ulpian and a Galatian inscription': *Class. Rev.* 37. 8.

CANCELLI, F. (1973). 'Tituli ex corpore Ulpiani': *NDI* 19. 392.

CASSARINO, S. (1946–7). 'Note critiche sul *liber singularis de officio curatoris reipublicae* di Ulpiano': *Ann. sem. giur. Catania* NS 1. 299.

CDJ (1980). *Concordance to the Digest Jurists* (Oxford), ed. Honoré, T., Menner, J. References are to fiche numbers unless otherwise stated.

CERVENCA, G. (1966). 'Su due lacune nella Palingenesia di O. Lenel': *Iura* 17. 66.

DE CEULENEER, A. (1880). *Essai sur la vie et le règne de Septime-Sévère.*

CHAMPLIN, E. (1978). 'The life and times of Calpurnius Piso': *JRS* 68. 95.

CHASTAGNOL, A. (1960). *La préfecture urbaine à Rome sous le bas-empire* (Paris).

—— (1964). 'Le problème de l'histoire Auguste: Etat de la question': Bonner HAC 1963, *Antiq.*[4] 2. 43.

—— (1967). 'Emprunts de l'histoire Auguste aux *Caesares* d'Aurelius Victor': *Rev. Phil.* 41. 85.

—— (1970). Recherches sur l'histoire Auguste: *Antiq*[4]. 6.

CITATI, A. G. (1927). *Indice delle parole, frasi e costrutti ritenuti indizio di interpolazione nei testi giuridici romani* (Milan).

COHEN, H. (1884). *Description historique des monnaies frappées sous l'empire romain* (Paris).

COLLINET, P. (1912). 'Histoire de l'école de droit de Beyrouth': *Ed. hist. sur le droit de Justinien* II (Paris).

COSTA, E. (1894–9). *Papiniano* (4 vols., Bologna).

CRIFÒ, G. (1976). 'Ulpiano': *ANRW* ii. 15.708.

CROOK, J. A. (1955). *Consilium principis* (Cambridge), reprint New York 1975.

—— (1967). *Law and life of Rome* (London).

DESSAU, H. (1889). 'Ueber Zeit und Persönlichkeit der SHA': *Hermes* 24. 337.

DIERAUER, U. (1977). *Tier und Mensch im Denken der Antike* (Amsterdam).

DIOSDI, G. (1971). 'Das Gespenst der Prädigesten': *Labeo* 17. 187.
DIRKSEN, H. E. (1842). *Die SHA. Andeutungen zur Textes-Kritik und Auslegung derselben* (Leipzig).
DITTENBERGER, W. (1903). 'Athenaeus und sein Werk. Apophoreton': *47 Vers. deut. Phil. und Schul.* (Berlin) 21.
DOMASZEWSKI, A. v. (1908). *Die Rangordnung des römischen Heeres* (Bonn).
—— (1909). *Geschichte der römischen Kaiser* (Leipzig).
DOWNEY, G. (1961). *A history of Antioch in Syria* (Princeton NJ).
DURRY, M. (1938). *Les cohortes prétoriennes* (Paris).
DUSANIC, S (1964). 'Severus Alexander as Elagabal's associate': *Hist.* 13. 487.

EBRARD, F. (1917). *Die Digesterfragmente ad formulam hypothecariam und die Hypothecarrezeption* (Leipzig).
ECKHARDT, B. (1978). *Iavoleni epistulae* (Berlin).
ELLEGARD, A. (1962). *A statistical method for determining authorship* (Gothenburg).
ENMANN, A. (1884). 'Eine verlorene Geschichte der römischen Kaiser': *Phil. supp.* 4. 337.
ENSSLIN, W. (1954). *Praefectus praetorio: RE* 22. 2. 2391.

FELLETTI-MAJ, B. M. (1950). *Siria, Palestina, Arabia settentrionale nel periodo romano* (Rome).
FERRINI C. (1929a). 'I commentari di Ulpiano e di Paolo *ad legem Iuliam et Papiam*': *Opere* ii (Milan) 236.
—— (1929b). 'Postille esegetiche ai frammenti del commentario di Ulpiano alle formule edittale *ad legem Aquiliam*': *Opere* ii. 95.
FITTING, H. (1908). *Alter und Folge der Schriften römischer Juristen von Hadrian bis Alexander* (Halle).
—— (1912). 'Rechtsgeschichtliche Kleinigkeiten': *ZS* 29. 280.
FLEMING, W. B. (1915). *The history of Tyre* (New York).
FORTE, B. (1972). *Rome and the Romans as the Greeks saw them* (Rome).
DE FRANCISCI, P. (1938). *Storia del diritto romano*² ii. 1 (Milan).
FREZZA, P. (1968). 'La cultura di Ulpiano': *SDHI* 34. 363.
FUCHS, H. (1938). *Der geistige Widerstand gegen Rom in der antiken Welt* (Berlin).

GARNSEY, P. (1967). 'Adultery trials and the survival of the *quaestiones* in the Severan age': *JRS* 57. 56.
—— (1970). *Social status and legal privilege in the Roman empire* (Oxford).
GAUDEMET, J. (1954). 'L'empereur interprète du droit': *Fests. Rabel* ii (Tübingen) 169.
—— (1957). *La formation du droit séculier et du droit de l'église au IV et V siècles* (Paris).
—— (1967). *Institutions de l'antiquité* (Paris).
GIANELLI, C–MAZZARINO, S. (1956). *Trattato di storia romana* (Rome).
GILLIAM, F. (1965). 'Dura rosters and the *constitutio Antoniniana*': *Hist.* 14. 74.
GILLIAM, J. P. – MANN. J. C. (1976). 'The northern British frontier from Antoninus Pius to Caracalla': *Arch. Aeliana* 48. 1.
GILMORE WILLIAMS, M. (1902). 'Studies in the lives of the Roman emperors: Julia Domna': *Am. J. Arch.* 6. 259.

GIUFFRÈ, V. (1974). 'Arrio Menandro e la letteratura *de re militari*': *Labeo* 20. 362.
GRADENWITZ, O. (1887). *Interpolationen in den Pandekten* (Berlin).
GROSSO, F. (1968*a*). 'Ricerche su Plauziano e gli avvenimenti del suo tempo': *Att. Acad. Lincei. Rendi.* 23. 7.
—— (1968*b*). 'Il papiro Oxy. 2565 e gli avvenimenti del 222–224': *Att. Lincei Rendi.* 23. 205.
GRUPE, E: (1899). 'Gaius und Ulpian': *ZS* 20. 90.
GUALANDI, G. (1963). *Legislazione imperiale e giurisprudenza* (2 vols. Milan).
GUARINO, A. (1957). 'La méthode de compilation des *digesta Iustiniani*': *RIDA*³ 4. 268.
GULICH, C. B. (1969). *Athenaeus: the Deipnosphists* (Cambridge, Mass.).
GUNDEL, H. G. (1966). 'Papyrologisches zur *constitutio Antoniniana*': *Kurzb. an den Papyrussamml.* 22. 8.

HAGENDAHL, H. (1971). 'Die Bedeutung der Stenographie für die spätlateinische christliche Literatur': *Jb. AC* 14. 24.
HAMMOND, M. (1940). 'Septimius Severus, Roman bureaucrat': *Harv. Stud. Class. Phil.* 51. 137.
HANNESTAD, K. (1944). 'Septimius Severus in Egypt. A contribution to the chronology of the years 198–202': *Class. et mediaev.* 6. 194.
HARTKE, W. (1951). *Römische Kinderkaiser. Eine Strukturanalyse römischen Denkens und Daseins* (Berlin).
HASEBROEK, J. (1916). *Die Fälschung der Vita Nigri und Vita Albini in den SHA* (Heidelberg).
—— (1921). *Untersuchungen zur Geschichte des Kaisers Septimius Severus* (Heidelberg).
HAY, J. S. (1911). *The amazing emperor Heliogabalus* (London).
HERRMANN, P. (1972). 'Überlegungen zur Datierung der *constitutio Antoniniana*': *Chiron* 2. 519.
HERZIG, H. E. (1972). 'Die Laufbahn des L. Septimius Severus': *Chiron* 2. 393.
HEUMANN, H. – Seckel, E. (1907). *Handlexicon zu den Quellen des römischen Rechts*⁹ (Jena, reprint¹⁰ 1958).
HITZIG, H. F. (1893). *Die Assessoren der römischen Magistrate und Richter* (Munich).
HOHL, E. (1956). 'Herodian und der Sturz Plautians': *Akad. Wiss. Berlin Kl. Phil.* usw. 2. 3.
HONORÉ, A. M. (= T. 1962). 'The Severan lawyers. A preliminary survey: *SDHI* 28. 162.
—— – Rodger, A. F. 'How the Digest commissioners worked': *ZS* 87. 246.
HONORÉ, T. (1978). *Tribonian* (London).
—— (1981). *Emperors and lawyers* (London).
HOWE, L. L. (1942). *The praetorian prefect from Commodus to Diocletian AD* 180–305 (Chicago).
HUSCHKE, P. E. (1875). *Zur pandektenkritik* (Leipzig).

JARDÉ, A. (1925). *Études critiques sur la vie et le règne de Sévère Alexandre* (Paris).

JOLOWICZ, H. F. – NICHOLAS, B. (1972). *Historical introduction to the study of Roman law*³ (Cambridge).

JONES, A. H. M. (1968). 'The *dediticii* and the *constitutio Antoniniana*:' *Studies in Roman government and law* (Oxford) 129.

JÖRS, P. (1887). 'Domitius 88': *RE* V. 1435.

KAEMMERER, F. (1827). *Observationes iuris civilis* (Rostock).

KAIBEL, G. (1887). *Athenaei Dipnosophistorum libri 15* (3 vols., Leipzig).

KALB, W. (1888). *Das Juristenlatein* (Nuremberg).

—— (1890). *Roms Juristen nach ihrer Sprache dargestellt* (Leipzig).

KARLOWA, O. (1885, 1901). *Römische Rechtsgeschichte* (2 vols., Leipzig).

KASER, M. (1966). *Das römische Zivilprozeßrecht* (Munich).

—— (1971). *Das römische Privatrecht* I² (Munich).

—— – Schwartz, F (1956). *Die interpretatio zu den Paulussentenzen* (Cologne).

KIPP, T. (1909). *Geschichte der Quellen des römischen Rechts*³ (Leipzig).

KOLB, F. (1972). 'Litterarische Beziehungen zwischen Cassius Dio, Herodian und HA': *Antiq.*⁴ 9.

KOLENDO, J. (1965). 'Étude sur les inscriptions de Novae': *Arch.* (*Sofia*) 16. 124.

KOSCHAKER, P. (1907). Review of Schulz, F. (1906): *ZS* 28. 454.

KRALL, J. (1888). 'Studien zur Geschichte des alten Aegypten III: Tyros und Sidon: *Sitzb. d. phil. – hist. Class. d. Kais. Akad. Wiss.* 117 (Vienna) 631.

KRUEGER, P. (1912). *Geschichte der Quellen und Literatur des römischen Rechts* (Leipzig).

KÜBLER, B. (1925). *Geschichte des römischen Rechts* (Leipzig etc.).

KUNKEL, W. (1953). 'Der Prozess der Gohariener vor Caracalla:' *Fests. Lewald* (Basle) 81 = *Kleine Schriften* (Weimar 1974) 255.

—— (1967). *Herkunft und soziale Stellung der römischen Juristen* (Graz etc.).

—— (1974). *Consilium, consistorium: Kleine Schriften* (Weimar) 405.

LACHMANN, K. (1838). 'Kritischer Beitrag zu Ulpians Fragmenten': *ZGR* 9. 174.

LECLERE, H. (1952). Ulpien: *Dict. Arch. Chrét.* 15.2 (Paris) 2862.

LENEL, O. (1927) *Das Edictum Perpetuum*³ (Leipzig).

LEVY, E. (1954). *Pauli sententiae: a Palingenesia of the opening titles* (Ithaca NY).

LIEBENAM, W. (1900). *Die Städteverwaltung im römischen Kaiserreich* (Leipzig).

LIEBS, D. (1973). '*Ulpiani opinionum libri VI*': *TR* 41. 279.

V. LUBTOW, U. (1953). 'Ulpians Konstruktion des sogennanten Vereinbarungs-darlehen': *Synt. Arangio-Ruiz* (Naples) 1272.

LUZZATTO, (1951) 'Appunti sul *ius Italicum*': *RIDA* 5. 79.

MACMULLEN, R. (1967). *Enemies of the Roman order* (Cambridge, Mass.).

—— (1974). *Roman social relations* (New Haven, Conn.).

DE MARTINO, F. (1965). *Storia della constituzione romana* IV (Naples).

MATTINGLEY, H. (1975). *Coins of the Roman empire in the British Museum*² v (ed. Carson, R. A. G., Hill, P. V. Oxford).

MATTINGLY, H. – SYDENHAM, E. A. (1936–8). *The Roman imperial coinage* (5 vols., 1923–49 London).

MAYER-MALY, T. (1961). Ulpianus: *RE* 9 A 1. 567.

MENGIS, K. (1920). *Die schriftstellerische Technik im Sophistenmahl des Athenaios* (Paderborn)

MIHAILOV, G. (1963). 'Septimius Severus in Moesia inferior and Thrace': *Act. antiq. Philoppopolitana Stud. hist. phil.* 113.

MILLAR, F. (1962). 'The date of the *constitutio Antoniniana*': *J. Egypt. Arch.* 48. 124.

—— (1964). *A study of Cassius Dio* (Oxford).

—— (1968). 'Local cultures in the Roman Empire: Libyan, Punic and Latin in North Africa': *JRS* 58. 126.

—— (1977). *The emperor in the Roman world* (London).

MOMMSEN, Th. (1870). 'Die Kaiserbezeichnung bei den römischen Juristen': *ZRG* 9. 97 = *GS* II (1905–7) 155.

—— (1887–8). *Römisches Staatsrecht*³ (3 vols., Leipzig).

—— (1890). 'Zu Papinians Biographie': *ZS* 11. 30.

—— (1892). 'Gordians Dekret von Skaptoparene': *ZS* 12. 262 = *GS* II. 172.

—— (1905–17). *Gesammelte Schriften* (3 vols., Berlin, reprint 1965).

MODRZEJEWSKI, J. (1968). 'Les préfets d'Égypte au début du règne d'Alexandre Sévère': *Pap. Lugduno-Bat.* 17 (Lyons) 59.

MODRZEJEWSKI, J.–ZAWADSKI, T. (1967). 'La date de la mort d'Ulpien et la préfecture du prétoire au début du règne d'Alexandre Sévère': *RHD* 45. 565.

MULLER, L. (1969). 'Un' applicazione della tecnica elettronica alla critica delle fonti romanistiche': *Iura* 19. 197.

MUNDLE, I. (1961). '*Dea caelestis* in der Religions politik des Septimius Severus und der Julia Domna': *Hist.* 10. 228.

MURPHY, G. J. (1945). *The reign of the emperor L. Septimius Severus from the evidence of inscriptions* (Philadelphia).

NDI (1957–   ). *Novissimo Digesto Italiano* (20 vols., Turin).

NÖRR, D. (1965). *Origo: RE* Supp. X. 433 = *TR* (1963) 525.

—— (1969). '*Imperium* und *Polis* in der hohen Prinzipatzeit: *Münch. Beitr. Pap. u. ant. Rechtsgesch.* 50 (Munich).

—— (1972a). 'Ethik von Jurisprudenz in Sachen Schatzfund': *BIDR* 75. 11.

—— (1972b). 'Spruchregel und Generalisierung': *ZS* 89. 84.

—— (1973). '*Iurisperitus sacerdos*': *Fests. Zepos* (Athens etc.) 555.

—— (1979). 'Zur Herrschaftsruktur des römischen Reiches: Die Stadte des Osten und das *Imperium*': *ANRW* ii. 7. 1. 3.

ORESTANO, R. (1973). Ulpiano: *NDI* 19. 1106.

DELL ORO, A. (1960). *I libri de officio nella giurisprudenza romana* (Milan).

D'ORS, A. (1942–3). *Divus—Imperator*. Problemas de cronología y transmisión de las obras de los jurisconsultos romanos': *ADHE* 14. 33.

—— (1966). Una, nueva hipótesis sobre P. Giss. 40: *Kurzb. aus den Papyrussamm.* 22 (Giessen) 3.

Pal. Lenel, O., *Palingenesia Iuris Civilis* (2 vols., Graz 1889, reprint 1960).

PALANQUE, J. R. (1933). *Essai sur la préfecture du prétoire du bas-empire* (Paris).

PALM, J. (1959). *Rom, Römertum und imperium in der griechischen Literatur der Kaiserzeit* (Lund).

PASSERINI, A. (1939). *Le coorti pretorie* (Rome).

PERNICE, A. (1885). 'Ulpian als Schriftsteller': *Sitzb. Berlin Akad. Wiss. phil.-hist. Kl.* 444 (Berlin, reprint 8 *Labeo* (1962) 351).

—— (1893). 'Parerga: Das Tribunal und Ulpians Bücher *de omnibus tribunalibus*': *ZS* 14 (1893) 135.

PETERS, H. (1913). 'Die oströmischen Digestenkommentaren und die Entstehung der Digesten': *Berich. sachs. Gesell. Wiss. phil.-hist. Kl.* 65. 3 = *Labeo* 16 (1970) 183.

PFLAUM, H-G (1948). *Le marbre de Thorigny* (Paris).

—— (1960–1). *Les carrières procuratoriennes équestres sous le haut-empire romain* (4 vols., Paris).

—— (1978). 'Les amours des empereurs dans l' histoire auguste': Bonner HAC 1975–6: *Antiq.*[4] 13. 157.

PIGANIOL (1954). *Histoire de Rome*[4].

PIR ([1]1897–, [2]1933–). *Prosopographia imperii Romani Saec. I II III* (ed.[1] Dessau, H., ed.[2] Groag, E.–Stein, A., Berlin etc.).

PLATNAUER, M. (1918). *The life and reign of the emperor L. Septimius Severus* (Oxford, reprint 1965).

RADINGER, C. (1895). *Meleagros von Gadara* (Innsbruck).

REGGI, R. (1951). 'Note anonime ai *digesta* di Marcello': *St. Parm.* 4. 21.

REINMUTH, O. W. (1935). 'The prefect of Egypt from Augustus to Diocletian': *Klio* 34.

—— (1967). 'A working list of the prefects of Egypt 30 BC to 299 AD': *Bull. Am. Soc. Pap.* 4. 112.

REINTJES, A. (1961). *Untersuchungen zu den Beamten bei den SHA* (Dusseldorf).

REY-COQUAIS, J. P. (1978). 'Syrie romaine': *JRS* 68. 44.

ROBERTSON, A. S. (1977). *Roman Imperial Coins in the Hunter Coin Cabinet iii* (Oxford).

ROTONDI, G. (1922). 'I *libri opinionum*, di Ulpiano e le *sententiae* di Paolo': *Scr. Giur.* 1. (Rome) 453.

RUBENSOHN, M. (1890). 'Zu der Chronologie des Kaisers Severus Alexander': *Hermes* 25. 340.

SALMON, P. (1971). 'La préfecture du prétoire de Iulius Paulus': *Latomus* 30. 664.

SANTALUCIA, B. (1965). 'Le note pauline ed ulpianee alle *quaestiones* ed ai *responsa* di Papiniano': *BIDR* 68. 49.

—— (1971). *I libri opinionum di Ulpiano* (2 vols., Milan).

SASSE, C. (1958). *Die constitutio Antoniniana, eine Untersuchung über den Umfang der Bürgerrechtsverleihung auf Grund des Papyrus Giss. 40. 1* (Wiesbaden).

—— (1965). 'Literaturübersicht zur *constitutio Antoniniana*': *J.J. Pap.* 15. 329.

SAUMAGNE, C. (1966). 'Observations sur la *constitutio Antoniniana*': *Mél. Carcopino* (Paris) 849.

v. SAVIGNY, F. 'Neuentdeckte Fragmente des Ulpian': *ZGR* 9. 1.

SCHILLER, A. A. (1953). 'The jurists and the prefects of Rome': *BIDR* 57–8. 60.

SCHLEIERMACHER, W. (1961). 'Eine neue Benefiziarinschrift aus Großzkrotzenborg': *Germania* 39. 166.

SCHLUMBERGER, J. (1976). '*Non scribo sed dicto*': Bonner HAC 1972–4 *Antiq.*⁴ 12. 221.

SCHMIDLIN, B. (1970). *Die römischen Rechtsregeln* (Cologne etc.).

SCHÖNBAUER, E. (1956). '*Tituli ex corpore Ulpiani* in neuer Analyse': *St. de Francisci III* (Milan) 303. *Iura.* 16. 105.

—— (1961). 'Die Ergebnisse der Textstufenforschung und ihre Methode': *Iura* 12. 112.

—— (1965). 'Drei interessante Inschriften aus Ephesus': *Iura* 16. 105.

SCHULZ, F. (1906). *Sabinus-Fragmente in Ulpians Sabinus-Commentar* (Halle) = *Labeo* 10 (1964) 50. 234.

—— F. (1926). *Die Epitome Ulpiani der Cod. Vat. Reginae* 1128 (Bonn).

—— (1946). *History of Roman legal science* (Oxford).

—— (1951). 'Die Ulpianfragmente des P. Ryl. 474 und die Interpolationenforschung': *ZS* 68. 1.

—— (1961). *Geschichte der römischen Rechtswissenschaft* (Weimar).

SCHULZE, E. Th. (1891). 'Zum Sprachgebrauche der römischen Juristen': *ZS* 12. 100.

SCIASCIA, G. (1952). 'Prefazione e dizionario di Ulpiani regulae (S. Paolo)' = *Varietà giuridiche* (Milan 1956) 177.

SEGRÈ, A. (1966). '*La constitutio Antoniniana* e il diritto dei novi cives': *Iura* 17. 1.

SESTON, W. (1966). 'Marius Maximus et la date de la *constitutio Antoniniana*': *Mél. d'arch. et d'hist. Carcopino* 877.

SESTON, W. –EUZENNAT, M. (1971) 'Un dossier de la chancellerie romaine: la tabula Banasitana': *Comp. Rend. Acad. Inscr.* 468.

SHERWIN-WHITE, A. N. (1972). 'The Roman citizenship: a survey of its development into a world franchise': *ANRW* 1. 2. 23.

—— (1973). *The Roman citizenship* ²(Oxford).

SMITH, C. D. (1979). *Western Mediterranean Europe* (London).

SOLAZZI, S. (1920). 'Leggendo i libri *de officio consulis*': *Rend. Ist. Lomb.*² 5. 3. 121.

—— (1946). 'Per la storia della giurisprudenza romana': *AG* 133. 3.

SPERBER, D. (1974). *Roman Palestine 200–400. Money and prices* (Ramat-Gan).

STEIN, A. (1925). 'Stellvertreter der praefecti praetorio': *Hermes* 60.94.

—— (1927). *Der römische Ritterstand* (Munich).

STEIN, P. (1966). *Regulae iuris: From juristic rules to legal maxims* (Edinburgh).

STRACHAN-DAVIDSON, J. L. (1912). *Problems of the Roman criminal law* (2 vols., Oxford).

STRAUB, J. (1972). 'Cassius, Dio und die Historia Augusta': Bonner HAC 1970 *Antiq.*⁴ 10. 271.

—— (1978). 'Juristische Notizien in der Historia Augusta': Bonner HAC 1975/6 *Antiq.*⁴ 13. 195.

STROUX, J. (1950). 'Die neuen Ulpianfragmente und ihre Bedeutung fur die Interpolationenforschung': *Misc. Ac. Berol.* 1. 2 (Berlin) 1.

SYME, R. (1968). *Ammianus and the Historia Augusta* (Oxford).

—— (1970). 'Three jurists': Bonner HAC 1968–9: *Antiq.*⁴ 7. 309 = *Roman Papers* (Oxford 1978) 790.

—— (1971). *Emperors and biography* (Oxford).

—— (1972a). 'The composition of the *Historia Augusta*. Recent Theories': *JRS* 62. 123.

—— (1972b). 'Lawyers in Government: the case of Ulpian': *Proc. Am. Phil. Soc.* 115. 406.

TALAMANCA, M. (1971). 'Su alcuni passi di Menandro di Laodicea relativi agli effetti della *constitutio Antoniniana*': St. *Volterra* (Milan) v 433.

—— (1976). 'Gli ordinamenti provinciali nella prospettiva dei giuristi tardoclassici': *Circ. Tosc. dir. rom. e stor. dir.* 4. 95.

THALLER, E. (1875). *Étude critique sur les doctrines particulières au jurisconsulte Ulpien* (Th. Paris)

TIMPE, D. (1967). 'Ein Heiratsplan Kaiser Caracallas': *Hermes* 95. 470.

VIGENEUX, P. E. (1896). *Essai sur l'histoire de la praefectura urbis à Rome* (Paris).

VIR (1903–). *Vocabularium Iurisprudentiae Romanae* (Berlin).

DE VISSCHER, F. (1961). 'La *constitutio Antoniniana* et la dynastie africaine des Sévères': *RIDA* 8.229

VITTINGHOFF, (1951). 'Römische Stadtrechtsreform der Kaiserzeit': *ZS* 68. 435.

VOGT, J. (1969). 'Zu Pausanias und Caracalla': *Historia* 18. 299.

VOLTERRA, E. (1937). 'Antiche ricerche sul latino di Ulpiano': *SDHI* 3. 158.

—— (1951). 'Storia del diritto romano e storia del diritto orientale': *Riv. it. Sc. giur.* 88. 134.

WALSER, G. (1975). 'Die Severer in der Forschung 1960– 1972': *ANRW* ii. 2. 67.

WATSON, A. (1962). 'Two studies in textual history': *TR* 30. 209.

—— (1978). Review of Honoré (1978): *LQR* 94. 459.

WENGER, L. (1953). *Die Quellen des römischen Rechts* (Vienna).

WESTERMAN, W. L. –SCHILLER, A. A. (1954). *Apokrimata. Decisions of Septimius Severus on legal matters* (New York).

WHITTAKER, C. R. (1969– 70). *Herodian* (2 vols., Cambridge, Mass.)

WIEACKER, F. (1949). 'Dopplexemplare der Institutionen, Florentins, Marcians und Ulpians': *RIDA* 3. 577.

—— (1953). '*FV* 75 und 76. Über Ulpians Sabinuskommentar in der nachklassischen Zeit': St. *Arangio-Ruiz* 4. 241.

—— (1960). *Textstufen klassischer Juristen* (Göttingen).

—— (1961). *Vom römischen Recht*[2] (Stuttgart).

—— (1973). 'I *libri opinionum* (di Ulpiano?)': *Labeo* 9.196.

WIELING, H. J. (1974). '*Eine neuendeckte Inschrift Gordians III und ihre Bedeutung für das Verständnis der constitutio Antoniniana*': *ZS* 91. 364.

WIFSTRAND, S. A. (1926). *Studien zur griechischen Anthologie* (Lund).

WILLIAMS, W. (1974). 'The *libellus* procedure and the Severan papyri': *JRS* 64.86.

—— (1976). 'Individuality in the imperial constitutions. Hadrian and the Antonines': *JRS* 66.67.

WLASSAK, M. (1919). *Zum römischen Provinzialprozeß* (Vienna).

WOLFF, H. J. (1959). 'Zur Palingenesie und Textgeschichte von Ulpians *libri ad edictum*': *Iura* 10. 1.

—— (1949). 'Ulpian 18 ad *edictum* in *Collatio* and *Digest* and the problem of the post-classical editions of classical works': *Scr. Ferrini*[4] (Milan) 64.

—— (1976). 'Die *constitutio Antioniniana* und Pap. Giessensis 40' (Cologne).

YOUTIE, H. C.–SCHILLER, A. (1955). 'Second thoughts on the Columbia Apokrimata (P. Col 123)': *Chron d.'égyp.* 30. 321.

ZIEGLER, R. (1978). 'Antiocheia, Laodicea und Sidon in der Politik der Severer': *Chiron* 8. 493.

DE ZULUETA, F. (1939). 'P. Ryl. iii. 474: New fragments of Ulpian *ad edictum*': *St. Besta* (Milan) 137.

General Index

Scotland, 200–1, 215
scrinium, 19, 42
second editions, 34, 156, 218
secretary *a libellis, see a libellis*
segments of *ad edictum*, 140–4
Sejanus, 37
semenstria, 238
semitic languages, 15
senate, 4–5, 39–40, 44
senatusconsulta, 235; *Orphitianum* 111–12;
  Vitrasianum 238
Seneca, 17, 32
seniority, 44
Septimius Severus, *see* Severus
Servii auditores, 229, 234
Servius Sulpicius, 208, 223–4, 227, 229–
  30, 234
Severan age, 6, 21, 62, 122, 221, 247
Severus, 1–5, 10–11, 24–6, 45, 244; and
  Caracalla 1–2, 5, 7, 11, 23–4, 45, 197,
  237, 240, 242, priority over 33, 133, 138,
  141–2, 150–1, 157–8, 169, 174, 180–
  1, 186; and Geta 2, 5, 20, 24, 200–1; and
  lawyers 2–4, 246–7; and Papinian
  193–5; and Plautianus 5; and Ulpian
  200, 246–7; constitutions of 130, 132–
  5, 138–44, 149–50, 154–8, 165, 169,
  174, 180–1, 186, 194, 235–8, 241;
  council of 16, 19, 191, 193, 217; death of
  25; policy of 1–4, 247–8; return of to
  Rome 24, 200; reign of 15–25, 121,
  165–6, 211, 217, 236 *and see* Alexander
Sextus Caecilius, *see* Africanus
Sidon, 10, 12
Silvinus, 34
Soaemias, 4, 34
sources, 204, 206–42; juristic and imperial
  235–42
spurious works, 106–28
statistics, vii, 215–16
Stilicho, 42
Stoicism, 31
Straub, 8, 22
style, v–vii, 46–85; adverbs 79–81; adjectives 76–9; assonances 118, 125; asyn-
  deton 112; attitudinal phrases 58–65;
  change of 123–4, 128, 144–8; coherence 49; conjunctions 52–7; criteria 47–
  50; evanescent features 163–90, 196;
  expository phrases 57–8; future tenses
  65–7, 146, 188–90; inversion 67–70,

112–13; lucidity 50–1; nominal phrases
125–6; nouns 74–6; pervasive features
49, 92; plural 61–5, 196; subdued 25;
verbs 70–4; verb clusters 124–7; word
order 67–70, 112–13, 123–4
subscriptiones, 193
superprefect, 37–8
Syncellus, 7
Syria, 4, 10–1, 20, 29, 31; Coele 11;
  Phoenice 11

Tacitus, 23
Tarautas, 142
taxation, 11, 29
Tertullian, 30, 208, 223, 230
tetrarchs, 10, 42, 121–2
Thaumaturgus, 30
Theophilus, 83
Tiberius, 14, 17, 225, 233
titulature, 131
Titus, 237
toga virilis, 24
trading stations, 10
Trajan, 22–3, 51, 131, 219, 237
Trebatius, 226–7, 229, 233
trials, 2–3, 24, 44
Tribonian, 206, 210, 219, 222, 225–6, 233,
  235, 247
Tribonian, v
tributum, 11
Tryphoninus, 3, 52, 193, 216–17, 221,
  236, 238
Tubero, 227, 231–2
Tyana, 24, 30–1
tyranny, 26, 33
Tyre, 9–12, 14–15, 31, 33–4, 45, 208

Ulpian, and Alexander 34–8, 40, 42–3,
  118, Caracalla 25–6, 28, 33, 75, 118,
  Flavianus and Chrestus 37–9, 46, Gaius
  214, Julia Domna 30–1, 33, Mamaea 34,
  37, Marcus 64, 175, Modestinus 41, 116,
  Papinian 193, 196, 200–3, 208–9, Paul
  193, 196, 200–2, 208–9, 214–19, Severus 21, 33, 45; as administrator 123,
  assessor? 15–19, lawyer 82, 240–8, secretary *a libellis* 7–8, 16, 19, 22, 24, 196–
  203, 206, *praefectus annonae* 35–6, 45,
  praetorio 35–41, 44, 191–2, superprefect
  37–9, theorist 240–1; aversion to tric-
  kery 76, 105; background 1–8;